Inhalt

Preface / Vorwort 6

Tolkien Seminar 2013

Adaption –
schlechter Abklatsch oder kreative Interpretation? 10
Thomas Fornet-Ponse (Jerusalem)

Peter Jackson's Adaptation of *The Lord of the Rings*:
Cash or Kudos? 26
Annie Birks (Angers)

Splatter in Middle-earth? War and Violence between
Book and Screen—a Comparison 44
Tobias Hock (Aachen) & Frank Weinreich (Bochum)

Erzählstrukturen in J.R.R. Tolkiens *Der Herr der Ringe*
und in Peter Jacksons Filmadaption 62
Julian Tim Morton Eilmann (Aachen)

Angelsächsisches Rohan? Tolkiens anti-normannischer Reflex
unterstützt durch Peter Jacksons Filmadaption 76
Annika Röttinger (Hannover)

Music as a Narrative Element in
The Lord of the Rings Radio Plays 86
Heidi Steimel (Scharbeutz)

The Presence of Music in J.R.R. Tolkien's Middle-earth
and Songs & Poems of *The Lord of the Rings* set to Music 96
Tobias Escher (Bingen)

Leben in Mittelerde?
Tolkien-Adaptionen im Liverollenspiel 118
Stephanie Bauer (Augsburg)

Recreating *The Lord of the Rings:* from Roleplaying to
Board Games. A Narratological Analysis 134
Natalia González de la Llana (Aachen)

Bringing Tolkien to the Table:
Blending and Conceptual Metaphor in Board Game
Adaptations of *The Lord of the Rings* and *The Hobbit* 146
Timo Lothmann & Nicole Hützen (Aachen)

Mittelerde auf Spielbrettern – (k)ein Kinderspiel 160
Christian Weichmann (Braunschweig)

Das Mittelerde-Sammelkartenspiel. Eignung und
Besonderheiten 178
Thorsten Werner (Hamburg)

Fanfiction as Criticism 188
Renée Vink (Hilversum)

Additional Essay

A Vision of Middle-earth: Contemporary Views in
Peter Jackson's *The Lord of the Rings* Trilogy 204
David Goldie (Aix-Marseille)

Zusammenfassungen der englischen Beiträge 218

Summaries of the German Essays 225

Hither Shore

Interdisciplinary Journal
on Modern Fantasy Literature

Jahrbuch der
Deutschen Tolkien Gesellschaft e. V.

Tolkien Adaptations

Tolkien-Adaptionen

Interdisziplinäres Seminar der DTG
26. bis 28. April 2013, Aachen

Herausgegeben von:
Thomas Fornet-Ponse (Gesamtleitung),
Marcel Aubron-Bülles, Julian Eilmann,
Thomas Honegger, Rainer Nagel,
Alexandra Velten, Frank Weinreich

SCRIPTORIUM OXONIAE

Bibliografische Information der Deutschen Bibliothek

Die Deutsche Bibliothek verzeichnet diese Publikation in der Deutschen Nationalbibliografie; detaillierte bibliografische Daten sind im Internet über http://dnb.ddb.de abrufbar.

ISBN 978-3-9810612-8-4

Zweite Auflage: korrigierte Fassung vom 11. Juni 2014

Hither Shore, DTG-Jahrbuch 2013
veröffentlicht im Verlag »Scriptorium Oxoniae«

Deutsche Tolkien Gesellschaft e. V. (DTG)
E-Mail: info@tolkiengesellschaft.de

Scriptorium Oxoniae im atelier für TEXTaufgaben e. K.
Brehmstraße 50 · 40239 Düsseldorf · Germany
E-Mail: rayermann@scriptorium-oxoniae.de

Hither Shore, Gesamtleitung: Thomas Fornet-Ponse
E-Mail: hither-shore@tolkiengesellschaft.de

Vorschläge für Beiträge in deutscher oder englischer Sprache (inklusive Exposé von ca. 100 Wörtern) werden erbeten an o.g. E-Mail-Adresse.

Alle Rechte verbleiben beim Autor des jeweiligen Einzelbeitrags. Es gilt als vereinbart, dass ein Autor seinen Beitrag innerhalb der nächsten 18 Monate nach Erscheinen dieser *Hither-Shore*-Ausgabe nicht anderweitig veröffentlichen darf.

Abwicklung: Susanne A. Rayermann, Düsseldorf
Layout/Design: Kathrin Bondzio, Solingen
Umschlagillustration: Anke Eißmann, Herborn
Druck und Vertrieb: Books on Demand, Norderstedt

Alle Rechte vorbehalten.

Reviews / Rezensionen

Arnulf Krause: Die wirkliche Mittelerde. Tolkiens Mythologie
und ihre Wurzeln im Mittelalter 230

Tolkien Studies. An Annual Scholarly Review. Vol. IX (2012) 231

Fastitocalon. Vol. 3-1 & 2. Humour and the Fantastic 232

Barbara Kowalik (ed.): O What A Tangled Web: Tolkien and
Medieval Literature. A View from Poland 233

Julian Eilmann/Allan Turner: Tolkien's Poetry 236

Adam Roberts: The Riddles of the *Hobbit* 237

Christopher Scarf: The Ideal of Kingship in the Writings of
Charles Williams, C.S. Lewis and J.R.R. Tolkien. Divine Kingship
is Reflected in Middle-earth 240

Tolkien Studies. An Annual Scholarly Review. Vol. X (2013) 241

Unsere Autorinnen und Autoren /
Our Authors 246

Siglen-Liste 254

Index 256

Preface /

According to popular convention, the tenth edition of the German Tolkien Society's (DTG) yearbook is an ideal occasion to look back, benevolently or critically, to its development since the beginning. Concerning the three central elements of the spectrum covered in this publication, the envisaged bilingualism as well as the pervading interdisciplinary approach, all named in the first preface, this tenth edition can serve as a good example. While the latter two points are finding clear expression, the case stands quite differently for the inclusion of other authors. The practical examination of the different aspects of Tolkien's work over the past years has shown that many areas have not been adequately researched, some hardly at all – and the list of possible topics for upcoming conferences tends to get longer rather than shorter. In order to tackle these *desiderata*, the focus on Tolkien and his work was stronger than initially planned. This should not be seen as limitation or a neglect of other authors and their work but accommodates the statutory mandate of the DTG, which stipulates academic research into Tolkien's work in its diverse facets, the examination of research extant and opening up new fields of research.

The volume in hand succinctly expresses this concern, as only few other works have been adapted on a similar scope as *The Lord of the Rings*: There are not only the two widely-known movies by Ralph Bakshi and Peter Jackson as well as fan films, but also radio dramas, musicals, board games, roleplaying games, PC and online roleplaying games, art, music, parodies etc. As a thorough academic discussion – with the exception of Jackson's films – has not been carried out yet, this became the objective of the tenth Tolkien Seminar of the German Tolkien Society, which was held 26-28 April 2013 in Aachen. The basic questions about the manifold adaptations of *The Lord of the Rings* were which elements of the work were borrowed and which were transformed and thus interpreted, which additional interpretational options were opened up, deepened and utilised through other media and forms of expression, and also how the view on the adapted work changed after encountering the adaptation.

Collecting the contributions from the Seminar, presenting the whole scope of the existing adaptations of *The Lord of the Rings* and analysing them with different methodological approaches, this reading cannot only unlock many answers and further perspectives on these questions but also show the openness of the work that renders this abundance a possibility. The interdisciplinary approach also enables a comprehensive view of "adaptation" as a phenomenon and could be of interest for an overall adaptation theory. Apart from these contributions, this volume contains a thematically fitting article by David Goldie from the Seminar 2011 (Potsdam) as well as detailed reviews of topical research literature.

Finally, we would like to extend our thanks to Prof. Dr. Peter Wenzel and his team at the Rheinisch-Westfälische Technische Hochschule Aachen, Julian Eilmann and the Tolkien AG study group of the Inda-Gymnasium in Aachen as well as Walking Tree Publishers for their support and assistance. I would also like to thank all contributors, my co-editors, Marie-Noëlle Biemer for translations, Susanne A. Rayermann and Kathrin Bondzio at Scriptorium Oxoniae, all those who enabled the publication of the tenth volume of *Hither Shore*.

Thomas Fornet-Ponse

Vorwort

Die mittlerweile zehnte Ausgabe des Jahrbuchs der Deutschen Tolkien Gesellschaft kann entsprechend einer üblichen Gepflogenheit zum Anlass genommen werden, wohlwollend oder kritisch auf die Entwicklung seit den Anfängen zurückzuschauen. Mit Blick auf die im damaligen Vorwort genannten drei zentralen Elemente des abgedeckten Spektrums, der anvisierten Zweisprachigkeit sowie des sich durchziehenden interdisziplinären Ansatzes kann dieser zehnte Band als gutes Beispiel dienen – denn während die letzten beiden einen klaren Ausdruck finden, verhält es sich mit der Berücksichtigung anderer Autor_innen deutlich anders. Die konkrete Auseinandersetzung mit den unterschiedlichen Aspekten des Werkes Tolkiens in den letzten Jahren hat nämlich gezeigt, wie viele Bereiche noch nicht ausreichend oder fast gar nicht erforscht wurden – und die Liste der möglichen Themen für folgende Seminare wird eher länger als kürzer.

Um sich dieser Desiderata anzunehmen, fiel die Konzentration auf Tolkien und sein Werk stärker aus als ursprünglich geplant. Sie ist jedoch nicht als Einschränkung und Ausblendung anderer AutorenInnen und Werke zu verstehen, sondern trägt dem satzungsgemäßen Auftrag der DTG Rechnung, sich wissenschaftlich der Erforschung des Tolkien'schen Werkes in seinen unterschiedlichsten Facetten zu widmen, bekannte Forschungen zu überprüfen und neue Felder zu erschließen.

Der vorliegende Band drückt dieses Anliegen prägnant aus, da nicht viele andere Werke in einer ähnlichen Bandbreite wie *The Lord of the Rings* adaptiert worden sein dürften: Es gibt nicht nur die beiden bekannten Verfilmungen von Ralph Bakshi und Peter Jackson sowie Fan-Filme, sondern auch Hörspiele, Musicals, Brettspiele, Rollenspiele, Computer- bzw. Online-Rollenspiele, Kunstwerke, Musikstücke, Parodien etc. Da eine gründliche wissenschaftliche Auseinandersetzung – mit der Ausnahme der Filme Jacksons – bislang nicht stattfand, war diese das Ziel des zehnten Tolkien Seminars der DTG, das vom

26. bis 28. April 2013 in Aachen stattfand. Die grundlegende Fragestellung im Blick auf die sehr unterschiedlichen Adaptionen des *The Lord of the Rings* war, wie welche Elemente des Werkes aufgenommen bzw. transformiert und auf diese Weise interpretiert werden, welche zusätzlichen Interpretationsmöglichkeiten durch andere Medien und Ausdrucksformen eröffnet, vertieft und genutzt werden, aber auch, wie sich der Blick auf das adaptierte Werk nach der Begegnung mit der Adaption verändert.

Indem in den hier versammelten Seminarbeiträgen die ganze Bandbreite der existierenden Adaptionen zu *The Lord of the Rings* mit unterschiedlichen methodischen Ansätzen analysiert wird, kann ihre Lektüre nicht nur viele Antworten und weiterführende Perspektiven auf diese Fragen erschließen, sondern auch die Offenheit dieses Werkes vor Augen führen, die eine solche Fülle ermöglicht. Des Weiteren erlaubt die Interdisziplinarität einen umfassenden Blick auf das Phänomen der »Adaption« und könnte damit auch für die Frage einer übergreifenden Adaptionstheorie von Interesse sein. Neben diesen Beiträgen enthält Band 10 mit dem Aufsatz David Goldies einen thematisch gut passenden Beitrag des Seminars 2011 (Potsdam) sowie wie üblich ausführliche Rezensionen aktueller Forschungsliteratur.

Abschließend sei für den Erfolg des Seminars herzlich Prof. Dr. Peter Wenzel und seinem Team von der Rheinisch-Westfälischen Technischen Hochschule Aachen, Julian Eilmann und der Tolkien AG des Inda-Gymnasiums in Aachen sowie dem Verlag *Walking Tree Publishers* für die freundliche und tatkräftige Unterstützung gedankt. Ebenfalls danke ich sehr allen Beitragenden, den Mitgliedern des Board of Editors, Marie-Noëlle Biemer für die Übersetzungen sowie Susanne A. Rayermann und Kathrin Bondzio vom *Scriptorium Oxoniae*, die diesen zehnten Band von *Hither Shore* möglich gemacht haben.

Thomas Fornet-Ponse

Adaption – schlechter Abklatsch oder kreative Interpretation?

Thomas Fornet-Ponse (Jerusalem)

Auf den ersten Blick – z.B. in den Duden – ist die Sache klar: Eine Adaption (bzw. Adaptation) meint biologisch die Anpassung eines Organismus oder von Organen an Umweltbedingungen, soziologisch die Anpassung des Menschen an seine soziale Umwelt und drittens die Umarbeitung eines literarischen Werkes, um es an die Erfordernisse einer anderen literarischen Gattung oder eines anderen Kommunikationsmediums wie Film oder Fernsehen anzupassen (Duden, Eintrag »Adaptation«). In allen drei Fällen geht es darum, eine bestehende Entität an etwas anzupassen, d.h. sie so zu verändern, dass ihre Funktion(en) oder ihre Leistungsfähigkeit erhalten bleibt oder optimiert wird. Damit ist zugleich ein klares Kriterium für die Güte einer Adaption angegeben, nämlich der Grad, in dem diese Funktion(en) erfüllt bzw. ihre Leistungsfähigkeit erhalten oder verbessert werden bzw. wird.

Im für unsere Fragestellung relevanten dritten Fall der Anpassung eines literarischen Werkes an die Erfordernisse eines anderen Genres oder Mediums sprechen wir besser von Sinn als von Funktion oder Leistungsfähigkeit, womit das Kriterium der Güte einer Adaption in dem Grad bestünde, in dem der Sinn eines Werkes in dem anderen Genre oder Medium vermittelt würde. Dies entspricht der weit verbreiteten Intuition, Adaptionen zu beurteilen, indem von Werktreue und von Freiheiten, die sich z.B. ein Regisseur genommen habe, gesprochen wird. Adaptionen haben demnach einen abgeleiteten Status und werden nicht als eigenständiges Kunstwerk wahrgenommen, sondern vom Original aus beurteilt.

Wird dies aber der Eigenart einer Adaption wirklich gerecht – zumal, wenn jemand (wie viele, die über die Jackson-Adaption dazu kamen, *The Lord of the Rings* zu lesen) zunächst die Adaption und dann erst das adaptierte Werk kennen lernt? Eine Verteidigung der Intuition begegnet dem Problem, dass in anderen Kommunikationsmedien bestimmte Aussagemöglichkeiten des Ursprungsmediums nicht bestehen – dafür aber andere, die dem Ursprungsmedium nicht zur Verfügung stehen. Insofern liegt es nahe, die weit verbreitete Intuition grundlegend infrage zu stellen und zu überlegen, wie eine Adaptionstheorie aussehen kann, die den unterschiedlichen Ausdrucksmöglichkeiten des jeweiligen Mediums gerecht wird. Dabei wird auch deutlich, welche Probleme damit verbunden sind, eine Adaption in dem Maße als gelungen anzusehen, in dem sie als werktreu angesehen werden kann – ganz abgesehen von der Schwierigkeit, den Sinn eines literarischen Werkes zu bestimmen. Was also ist eine Adaption und was geschieht bei einer solchen?[1]

I. Was ist eine Adaption? Produkt und Prozess

Eine Definition von »Adaption« auf etymologischer Grundlage trifft auf die gerade genannten Probleme, da das mittellateinische Wort *adaptatio* mit »Anpassung« übersetzt werden kann. Deutlich wird immerhin die zweifache Bedeutung, da zum einen der Prozess und zum anderen das Produkt der Anpassung gemeint sein können. Es ist sehr weit verbreitet, Adaptionen als sekundär und daher von geringerem Wert anzusehen, da sie die Güte des »Originals« nie erreichen könnten. Dies drückt sich in der Wortwahl von »Original« und »Vorlage« aus, weswegen »adaptiertes Werk« vorzuziehen ist – und statt eine Adaption als Anpassung zu verstehen, bietet sich eher Transformation an, womit der Akzent deutlicher auf den Eigen- und Besonderheiten der jeweiligen Medien liegt.[2] Bei den adaptierten Werken handelt es sich keineswegs nur um literarische Texte, auch wenn diese immer noch im Zentrum der Aufmerksamkeit stehen (vgl. Leitch, *Crossroads* 63ff). Obwohl Adaptionen nicht als bloße Anpassung ohne (bzw. mit nur geringem) eigenen künstlerischen Wert verstanden werden sollten, untersucht man sie nicht in ihrem Charakter als Adaptionen, wenn man sie als autonome Werke analysiert. Vielmehr sind sie zu untersuchen »as deliberate, announced, and extended revisitations of prior works« (Hutcheon xiv, vgl. 6). Dies schließt kurze intertextuelle Bezüge aus, aber Parodien beispielsweise ein und lässt kaum eine genaue Abgrenzung zu. Hutcheon plädiert für ein Kontinuum, das auf der einen Seite mit Werken beginnt, die sich einem theoretischen Ideal der Treue verpflichtet sehen, beispielsweise Übersetzungen oder Transkriptionen von Orchestermusik für einzelne Instrumente, und über Kurzfassungen und Bereinigungen bzw. zensierte Versionen bis hin zu Spin-Offs, Vorläufern und Nachfolgern etc. reicht (kritisch dazu Leitch, *Crossroads* 74f).[3]

---

1 Die folgenden Überlegungen folgen im Wesentlichen den Überlegungen Linda Hutcheons. Vgl. Stam, *Introduction* 8-11 für zentrale Einflüsse auf die Adaptation Studies durch Poststrukturalismus, Erzählforschung und Rezeptionsästhetik etc. sowie Leitch, *Crossroads* zu einem Überblick über jüngere Entwicklungen in den Adaptatation Studies.
2 Wenn Kreuzer von einer »interpretierenden Transformation« spricht und dabei meint, zunächst müsse der Sinn des Werkganzen erfasst sein (28), stellt sich die Frage, ob ohne weiteres von *dem* Sinn des Werkganzen gesprochen werden kann.
3 Sanders unterscheidet zwischen Adaption und Appropriation, die sich zwar in bestimmten Bereichen überlappen, dennoch unterschieden werden können. Während eine Adaption die Beziehung zum adaptierten Werk eindeutig ausweist, bewegt sich eine Appropriation in der Regel stärker von diesem weg in Richtung eines neuen kulturellen Produktes. Da

Diese Bandbreite an möglichen Adaptionen macht deutlich, wie unterschiedlich die von einer Adaptionstheorie zu berücksichtigenden Aspekte sind. Dazu gehört auch die Spannung zwischen der weiten Verbreitung von Adaptionen und der in Wissenschaft und Journalismus gängigen Ansicht, zeitgenössische Adaptionen seien meist sekundär, abgeleitet und insofern weniger wert. Vor allem Filmadaptionen werden oft mit drastischen Worten wie Verletzung, Verrat, Untreue etc.[4] abgelehnt, was auf der (post-)romantischen Wertschätzung ursprünglicher Schöpfung und ursprünglicher Kreativität beruht. Dies widerspricht der Tradition auch in der Weltliteratur, Geschichten zu übernehmen und zu teilen.[5]

Für die große Zahl von Adaptionen trotz angeblicher Minderwertigkeit sprechen nach Hutcheon neben der Freude an der veränderten Wiederholung auch mögliche finanzielle Anreize. Letztere können für die konkrete Gestalt einer Adaption sehr bedeutsam sein, da sich in ihnen die Erwartungshaltung der Rezipienten niederschlagen und auf diese Weise den kreativen Prozess selbst beeinflussen kann – z.b. ist die Finanzierung aufwendiger Filmadaptionen oder Computerspiele oft nur mit begründeter Aussicht auf entsprechende Einnahmen möglich. Die Freude an der veränderten Wiederholung dürfte maßgeblich zur Beliebtheit von Adaptionen beitragen. Denn Adaptionen legen Wert darauf, nicht einfach als autonome Werke zu erscheinen, sondern sich als Werke zu präsentieren, die sich auf (mindestens) ein anderes Werk beziehen.

> It is not a copy in any mode of reproduction, mechanical or otherwise. It is repetition but without replication, bringing together the comfort of ritual and recognition with the delight of surprise and novelty. As *adaptation*, it involves both memory and change, persistence and variation. (173)

Mit vielen anderen (insbesondere Robert Stam) wendet sich Hutcheon dagegen, die Nähe oder Treue zum adaptierten Werk zum Maßstab der Beurteilung zu

---

der Bezug zum verarbeiteten Werk nicht so deutlich ist wie bei einer Adaption, stellt sich die Frage nach der Abgrenzung zu einem Plagiat. (Vgl. Sanders 15-41)

4 »Infidelity resonates with overtones of Victorian prudishness; betrayal evokes ethical perfidy; deformation implies aesthetic disgust; violation calls to mind sexual violence; vulgarization conjures up class degradation; and desecration intimates a kind of religious sacrilege toward the ›sacred word‹.« (Stam, dialogics 54, vgl. Stam, Introduction 3) Vgl. ausführlicher zur (Un-)Treue mit Blick auf die implizierte ethische Sprache Leitch, *Ethics* sowie unter anderer Perspektive Cobb.

5 »Romanticism – waning in England and waxing in North America – fostered dreams of individual originality reflective of national genius. Whereas the demand for originality was meant to elevate both the artist and the nation she or he might represent, openly acknowledged appropriation or adaptation was potentially read as evincing an author's lack of agency since the result was regarded as hybrid and thus unoriginal and uncreative.« (Balestrini 6)

erheben.[6] Dies basiere auf der fehlerhaften Annahme, Adaptierende wollten den adaptierten Text lediglich reproduzieren. Vielmehr sind sehr unterschiedliche Intentionen denkbar, eine Hommage genauso wie eine Kritik. Um zu einem geeigneten Maßstab zu gelangen, ist es wichtig, die unterschiedlichen Perspektiven des Phänomens »Adaption« im Blick zu behalten:

- An acknowledged transposition of a recognizable other work or works
- A creative *and* an interpretive act of appropriation/salvaging
- An extended intertextual engagement with the adapted work
Therefore, an adaptation is a derivation that is not derivative – a work that is second without being secondary. It is its own palimpsestic thing. (Hutcheon 8)

Adaption ist einerseits ein formal definierbares Produkt und andererseits ein kreativer und rezipierender Prozess. Die meisten Adaptionstheorien gehen davon aus, es sei die Geschichte, für deren Elemente wie Thema, Ereignisse, Charaktere, Symbole, Bilder etc. Äquivalente in den unterschiedlichen Zeichensystemen gesucht werden. Allerdings gibt es große Unterschiede: Themen oder Protagonisten können sehr einfach von einem Text in ein anderes Medium gebracht werden, wohingegen sich die einzelnen Teile einer Geschichte durch eine Adaption sehr stark verändern können (und teilweise müssen). Entscheidend ist nach Hutcheon besonders die grundsätzliche Art der Präsentation (erzählend, zeigend, interagierend), da mit jedem Modus unterschiedliche Dinge auf unterschiedliche Weise adaptiert werden. Videospiele können z.B. sehr gut die jeweilige physische Welt adaptieren, weniger aber die geistigen Gehalte.

Adaptionen als Produkt sind oft »re-mediations, that is, specifically translations in the form of intersemiotic transpositions from one sign system (for example, words) to another (for example, images)« (Hutcheon 16); wichtig ist der bewusste und ausgewiesene Bezug zum adaptierten Werk. Auch wegen dieser Veränderung des Zeichensystems ist der Maßstab der Treue fragwürdig, da sie bei einem Medienwechsel unmöglich ist und dieser automatische Unterschied auch bei sehr geradlinigen Adaptionen durch »realistische« Regisseure klar zu erkennen ist (vgl. Stam, *Introduction* 17). Daher plädieren Albrecht-Crane und Cutchins dafür, den Akzent der Forschung gegen das Paradigma der Werktreue auf die Unterschiede und nicht auf die gewöhnlich evozierte Ähnlichkeit zu legen. Denn eine Adaption, die eine reine »Transposition« in dem Sinne wäre,

---

6 Die Nähe einer Adaption zum adaptierten Werk gehört dementsprechend bei Leitch auch nicht zu den vier Charakteristika, aufgrund derer man von einem eigenen Genre der (Film-)Adaptionen sprechen könne (vgl. *Adaption* 114f). Stam betont, auch wenn man über die Treuediskussion hinausgehen müsse, stelle diese doch wichtige Fragen bezüglich der Wiederschöpfung von Plot, Charakteren, Themen etc. (*Introduction* 14).

dass sie sich nicht »wesentlich« vom adaptierten Werk unterscheidet, bräuchte nicht eigens untersucht zu werden. Eine solche Transposition ist aber nicht möglich. Adaptierende »must interpret, re-working the precursor text and choosing the various meanings and sensations they find most compelling (or most cost effective), then imagine scenes, characters, plot elements, etc., that match their interpretation« (Albrecht-Crane/Cutchins 16). Die von Verfechtern einer Werktreue geforderte Ähnlichkeit sehen sie schon allein aufgrund der fundamentalen Unterschiede zwischen Romanen und Filmen als unmöglich an, zumal die Differenz erst Kunst ermögliche und Adaptionen durch ihre Entfernung vom adaptierten Werk nicht beeinträchtigt würden. Insofern wollen sie mit Bakhtin (und Derrida) Adaptionen primär als Antworten auf andere Texte verstanden wissen und nicht als Übertragung eines Dings (das vorgestellte »Wesen« eines Romans) in einen anderen Kontext. »In this context ›adaptations‹ may be understood as ›readings‹, paths the filmmakers take through source text(s) that themselves are paths through other texts« (18).

Die damit angesprochene Intertextualität einer Adaption betrifft in ihrem Prozess nicht nur die kreative Interpretation bzw. interpretative Schöpfung des bzw. der Adaptierenden, sondern auch die »palimpsestöse« Intertextualität des Publikums.[7] Weil eine Adaption sich zunächst ein Werk aneignet, sind Adaptierende erst Interpreten und dann Schaffende, was mit der Wahl des Mediums sehr unterschiedliche Adaptionen des gleichen Werkes erklärt. In der Regel – und insbesondere bei langen Romanen – wird bei einer Adaption gekürzt oder zusammengefasst, wenngleich es auch Adaptionen von Kurzgeschichten o.ä. gibt. »Whatever the motive, from the adapter's perspective, adaptation is an act of appropriation or salvaging, and this is always a double process of interpreting and then creating something new« (Hutcheon 20). Sie betont die Nähe zur westlichen Tradition der *imitatio* oder *mimesis* und schlägt vor, der mangelnde Erfolg einer Adaption liege vielleicht weniger im Grad ihrer Treue zu einem früheren Text als vielmehr in mangelnder Kreativität. Indem Adaptionen als solche ausgewiesen werden, ist der intertextuelle Bezug zum adaptierten Werk offensichtlich und gegenüber allen anderen nichtausgewiesenen Bezügen zu anderen Werken hervorgehoben – selbst für jene, die dieses nicht kennen. Dies bestimmt die Rezeption der Adaption, da auch die Vertrautheit mit dem adaptierten Werk und unsere eigene Interpretation darüber entscheiden, ob wir eine Adaption als gelungen oder nicht gelungen ansehen. »But no matter what our response, our intertextual expectations about medium and genre, as

---

7 Vgl. Genette 7-14 für die unterschiedlichen Beziehungen zwischen Texten: Intertextualität, Paratextualität, Metatextualität, Hypertextualität und Architextualität. Auf Genette (und Bakhtin) stützt sich auch Stam stark (vgl. *Introduction* 26-31). Den Aspekt der Intertextualität betonen auch Albrecht-Crane und Cutchins.

well as about this specific work, are brought to the forefront of our attention« (Hutcheon 22).

Indem Adaption nicht nur als Produkt sondern auch als Prozess wahrgenommen wird, können die verschiedenen grundlegenden Arten der Präsentation und Wahrnehmung stärker in den Blick genommen werden – Geschichten werden erzählt oder gezeigt oder wir können mit ihnen interagieren. Alle beziehen uns in unterschiedlichem Grad und auf unterschiedliche Weise ein: Im erzählenden Modus werden wir durch unsere Vorstellung einbezogen, die zwar durch den Text kontrolliert, aber nicht durch andere Sinneswahrnehmungen eingeschränkt wird. Dies geschieht im zeigenden Modus, der uns durch die auditive und visuelle Wahrnehmung und in den Ablauf der Geschichte einbezieht, ohne dass wir etwas wiederlesen oder überspringen können. Jeder Modus »has at its disposal different means of expression – media and genres – and so can aim at and achieve certain things better than others« (24). Romane können sehr gut die Gedanken und Gefühle der Charaktere vermitteln, wohingegen Filme eine Welt nicht erst ausführlich beschreiben müssen und Computerspiele es uns erlauben, sie zu betreten und in ihr zu handeln. Über Medien und Genres hinaus ist der weitere Kontext für eine Adaptionstheorie von Bedeutung, da sie bewusst eingesetzt werden, um narrative Erwartungen zu kanalisieren und zu vermitteln.

> The contexts of creation and reception are material, public, and economic as much as they are cultural, personal, and aesthetic. This explains why, even in today's globalized world, major shifts in a story's context – that is, for example, in a national setting of time period – can change radically how the transposed story is interpreted, ideologically and literally. (28)

Gerade die unterschiedlichen Modi sprechen dagegen, Adaptionen primär als abgeleitet und hinsichtlich ihrer Treue oder Untreue zum so genannten »Quelltext« zu bewerten. Schließlich kann eine Adaption als eigenständiges Werk bewertet werden, wofür Treue eine wenig hilfreiche ästhetische Kategorie ist. Des Weiteren kann der Einfluss einer Adaption weit über das hinausgehen, was als Ähnlichkeit zum adaptierten Werk gemessen werden kann. Hutcheon und Bortolotti schlagen daher eine Homologie zur evolutionären Adaptation vor, d.h. eine auf einen gemeinsamen Ursprung weisende Strukturähnlichkeit, wonach Geschichten sich durch Adaption entwickeln und nicht unveränderlich sind sowie zuweilen auch eine Migration in andere Kulturen oder Medien stattfindet.[8] »Stories, in a manner parallel to gens, replicate; the adaptation of

---

8 Sie modifizieren Richard Dawkins Theorie des »Mems«, indem sie von Geschichten und nicht Ideen ausgehen. Vgl. auch Sanders.

both evolve with changing environments« (Bortolotti/Hutcheon 444). Dies soll dabei helfen, den Diskurs über »Treue« zu überwinden und den Erfolg einer Geschichte anders zu verstehen. Denn in der Biologie würde rein deskriptiv von Adaptationen als unterschiedliche Anpassungen an neue Bedingungen etc. gesprochen. Dementsprechend sei der Erfolg einer Geschichte vom Erfolg ihres Trägers, also der jeweiligen Adaption, zu unterscheiden; erstere würde an ihrer Fortdauer, Reichhaltigkeit und Diversität gemessen und letztere durch »its efficacy in propagating the narrative for which it is a vehicle« (452). Auf diese Weise wird einerseits der eigenständige Charakter einer Adaption nicht geleugnet und sie andererseits als Adaption in den Blick genommen. Darüber hinaus kann bei diesem Modell der beiderseitige Nutzen gesehen und die angenommene Rivalität zwischen Literatur und Film überwunden werden, die nach Stam zu den wichtigsten Gründen gehört, (filmische) Adaptionen abzulehnen (vgl. Stam, *Introduction* 4). Die Grenzen dieser Homologie liegen in der Zufälligkeit der Mutation und der Intentionalität der Veränderungen in einer Adaption. Wie Sanders ausführt, macht der Bezug zu Biologie oder Ökologie auch auf den Unterschied zu einer ideenarmen Kopie oder Imitation aufmerksam, da Adaption ein aktiver Seinsmodus sei und wie Appropriationen ihre eigenen Intertexte herstellen und somit mit anderen Adaptionen in Dialog stehen. »Perhaps it serves us better to think in terms of complex processes of filtration, and in terms of intertextual webs or signifying fields, rather than simplistic one-way lines of influence from source to adaptation« (Sanders 24).

II. Was geschieht bei einer Adaption?

Ein Verständnis von Adaption, das dieses Phänomen zum einen als Produkt und Prozess und zum anderen die unterschiedlichen Repräsentationsweisen – erzählend (Romane, Kurzgeschichten etc.), zeigend (Theater, Filme etc.) und interagierend (Videospiele, Themenparks etc.) – berücksichtigt, verlangt auch nach einer komplexeren Untersuchung der Frage, was bei einer Adaption geschieht. Diese strukturiert Hutcheon mithilfe der sechs Fragen: Was, wer, warum, wie, wann und wo; damit wendet sie sich den Vorzügen und Grenzen für unterschiedliche Formen der Adaptionen, dem Prozess und den Adaptierern, aber auch dem Publikum wie dem Kontext einer Adaption zu.

Was?

Bei dieser Frage geht es um die Form der Adaption und wie diese durch den Modus des adaptierten Werkes und denjenigen der Adaption beeinflusst wird. Da es uns hier um die Adaptionen von Tolkiens *The Lord of the Rings* geht,

beschränke ich mich auf die Bewegung vom erzählenden Modus zu den anderen Modi.
»[A] novel, in order to be dramatized, has to be distilled, reduced in size, and thus, inevitably, complexity« (36). Obwohl dies oft negativ als (nicht rein quantitativer, sondern qualitativer) Verlust wahrgenommen und kritisiert wird – wie zahlreiche Reaktionen auf die Jackson-Adaption deutlich zeigen – kann eine Konzentration des Plots zuweilen verstärkend wirken. Viele Informationen eines Romans können sehr gut in die Handlung auf einer Bühne oder Leinwand umgesetzt werden, wobei es unvermeidbar ist, im Prozess der Dramatisierung Themen, Charaktere und Stil neu zu akzentuieren und fokussieren. Dabei sind auditive Elemente genauso wichtig wie visuelle. Die Transkodierung eines gedruckten Textes ist wegen der unterschiedlichen Zeichensysteme für kein darstellendes Medium leicht (vgl. Giddings et al. 6). Neben dem Medium wird beim Wechsel von einem erzählenden zu einem zeigenden Modus des Öfteren auch das Genre gewechselt, was ebenfalls die Erwartungen des Publikums verändern kann.

Beim Wechsel in den interaktiven Modus fühlt man sich stärker einbezogen und das Gefühl für den Zusammenhang wird durch den Spieler in einem nicht bloß vorgestellten oder wahrgenommenen Raum erzeugt. O'Flynn weist auf eine Besonderheit des interagierenden Modus hin, da der Maßstab der Treue einer Adaption zum adaptierten Werk angezweifelt werde, aber »adaptation via interactive media often necessitates the identification of a core theme or experience associated with the original that then functions as the organizing principle for designing« the adaptation as an individual experience« (O'Flynn 84, vgl. 90). Auf diese Weise würden frühere Überzeugungen reanimiert und zudem die Parameter dessen erweitert, was als Adaption gelten könne. Aufgrund des interagierenden Charakters ist es auch unangemessen, von einem »Benutzer« zu sprechen, da dies einen einseitigen Konsum nahelegt, statt dessen aber ein teilnehmender Einbezug vorliegt, wodurch die Erfahrung und Entwicklung der Geschichte verändert werden kann.

Diese Unterschiede zwischen den Modi führen zu einer ganzen Reihe weit verbreiteter Annahmen, z.B. derjenigen, nur der erzählende Modus könne sowohl Intimität als auch Distanz in Erzählperspektiven umsetzen bzw. darüber hinaus lege der erzählende Modus den Akzent auf Interiorität, während Exteriorität am besten von den beiden anderen umgesetzt werde. Wie Hutcheon anhand diverser Beispiele zeigt, treffen solche Annahmen in dieser Pauschalität ebenso wenig zu wie diejenigen, nur der erzählende Modus könne Beziehungen zwischen Vergangenheit, Gegenwart und Zukunft herstellen, während den anderen nur die Gegenwart bleibe oder nur sprachlich könne Mehrdeutigkeit, Ironie, Symbolen, Metaphern, Schweigen, Abwesenheiten etc. Rechnung getragen werden (vgl. 52-77).

Wer und Warum?

Zwei weitere vor allem für den Prozess der Adaption wichtige Fragen sind, wer adaptiert und warum adaptiert wird. Die erste Frage ist komplizierter, als zunächst angenommen werden könnte, denn in der Regel sind mehrere Personen beteiligt, sodass »the move to a performance or interactive mode entails a shift from a solo model of creation to a collaborative one«« (80). Besonders kompliziert ist es bei Film und Fernsehen, denn hier kommen Drehbuchautoren, Komponisten, Schauspieler, Bühnenbildner, Regisseure etc. in Frage, wobei in der Regel letztere als primäre Adaptierer gelten. »But no matter how much he or she is the magus and controller, the director is also a manager, an organizer of other artists upon whom he or she must rely to produce that new work« (83).[9] Im Prozess vom Drehbuch über die Drehaufnahmen bis hin zur Endbearbeitung vergrößert sich die Distanz zum adaptierten Werk. Im Falle einer Bühnenaufführung entfällt die strukturierende Arbeit des Schnittmeisters und kommt dem Regisseur noch mehr Verantwortung zu. Der adaptierte Text wird weniger reproduziert als vielmehr interpretiert und neu geschaffen. Auch wenn der Regisseur in der Öffentlichkeit als für die Adaption als Adaption verantwortlich gilt, greift er in der Regel auf ein Drehbuch zurück, weswegen Drehbuchautor und Regisseur als die primären Adaptierer angesehen werden sollten, wohingegen die anderen Künstler weniger stark involviert sind.

Bezüglich ihrer Motive sind die wichtigen ökonomischen Aspekte zu nennen, da viele Adaptionen sich dem Wunsch verdanken, am Erfolg des adaptierten Werkes teilzuhaben oder mit Blick auf das prinzipiell beschränkte Budget von Filmen, Fernsehserien etc. kein Risiko hinsichtlich des zu erwartenden Publikums einzugehen. Die besonders auf bekannte Schauspieler und Regisseure ausgerichtete Ökonomie der Filmwelt führt auch zu einer geringeren Bedeutung des Drehbuchautors und sogar des (oft eher unbekannten) Autors des adaptierten Texts. Neben finanziellen Aspekten sind juristische relevant, da z.B. urheberrechtliche Fragen eine ursprünglich intendierte Adaption verhindern können. Andere Motive, mit denen viele frühe cineastische Adaptionen von Dante, Shakespeare und anderen Werken der Weltliteratur erklärt werden können, betreffen das eigene kulturelle Kapital, das mit solchen adaptierten Werken erhöht werden soll, oder das pädagogische Anliegen, solche Werke zu verbreiten bzw. Schülern und Studentinnen schmackhaft zu machen.

Neben diesen eher äußerlichen Gründen gibt es auch die persönlichen der Adaptierenden sowohl für die Entscheidung, ein Werk zu adaptieren, als auch

---

9   Westbrook weist zusätzlich auf die Zensur hin, die sich etwa im *Production Code* deutlich ausdrückt (vgl. 36). Dazu ausführlicher auch Berger, der zusätzlich die Wirkung der Adaption auf das adaptierte Werk in den Blick nimmt und meint, »that an adaptation of a controversial and contemporary novel can make that novel ›safe‹ and ›contained‹ within a sphere of influence that could include a whole range of texts« (155).

für die Wahl des Mediums. »They not only interpret that work but in so doing they also take a position on it« (92). Dies ist manchmal eine Hommage (je nach Rechtelage kann es sein, dass etwas anderes gar nicht erlaubt wird), zuweilen eine klare Kritik, aber auch ein Beitrag zu aktuellen gesellschaftlichen Debatten ist möglich – oder gerade die Vermeidung einer solchen.

Aufgrund dieser Vielzahl von Motiven und der Bedeutung der individuellen Fähigkeiten und Interessen der Adaptierenden für die Adaption plädiert Hutcheon dafür, die Intentionalität im kreativen Prozess (wieder) stärker zu berücksichtigen, ohne damit die Autorenintention zum alleinigen Kriterium der Bedeutung und des Werts eines Kunstwerks erheben zu wollen (ähnlich Albrecht-Crane/Hutchins 19). Denn die unterschiedlichen Intentionen könnten durchaus für die Interpretation relevant sein und hinterlassen oft Spuren im Werk. »When giving meaning and value to an adaptation *as an adaptation*, audiences operate in a context that includes their knowledge and their own interpretation of the adapted work. That context may also include information about the adapter, thanks to both journalistic curiosity and scholarly digging« (111).

Wie?

Der auf den ersten Blick verwunderliche Bezug der Frage nach dem Wie auf das Publikum erklärt sich dadurch, den gesamten Prozess einer Adaption und damit auch die möglichen Reaktionen des Zielpublikums zu berücksichtigen. Zur vermutlich reizvollen Mischung aus Wiederholung und Unterschied beim Erleben einer Adaption als Adaption kommt die palimpsestöse Natur einer Adaption, also der aus den intertextuellen Bezügen stammende Reiz, mehr als einen Text bewusst zu erfahren; zuweilen liegen auch Bezüge zu früheren Adaptionen vor. Ein deutliches Beispiel sind die diversen *Herr-der-Ringe*-Brettspiele, die schon durch ihr Aussehen eher auf die Jackson-Adaption verweisen denn auf das Buch – eine interessante Nebenerscheinung sind die an den Filmen orientierten Cover mancher Buchausgaben, wodurch der Paratext des Buches eine Adaption desselbigen zitiert.

Um eine Adaption als Adaption zu erfahren, ist es nötig, das adaptierte Werk zu kennen – kennen wir es nicht, wissen wir vielleicht, dass es eine Adaption ist, erfahren es aber wie jedes andere Werk. »[W]e need to recognize it as such and to know its adapted text, thus allowing the latter to oscillate in our memories with what we are experiencing« (120f). Lücken können mit Informationen aus dem adaptierten Text gefüllt werden, worauf Adaptierende besonders beim Wechseln von einem Repräsentationsmodus in einen anderen vertrauen (müssen). Indem sie ihren Charakter als Adaption ausweisen, schaffen sie bestimmte Erwartungen der Rezipienten, insofern zum »Erwartungshorizont« das adaptierte Werk gehört. Umgekehrt kann eine Adaption den Blick auf das adaptierte Werk verändern, wie viele Äußerungen nahelegen, nach denen die eigenen Vorstellungen verschiedener Charaktere durch die Jackson-Adaption nachhaltig eingeschränkt wurden. Für Personen, die das adaptierte Werk erst nach der Adaption kennenlernen, können sich aus hermeneutischer Perspektive sogar Vorrang und Originalität umkehren. Ein wissendes Publikum hat aber nicht nur Erwartungen, sondern stellt auch Ansprüche, insbesondere wenn es Fans des adaptierten Werkes sind.[10]

Zu diesem Wissen zählt das Wissen um die Möglichkeiten des Mediums, die wiederum die Erwartungen des Publikums beeinflussen. Computerspieler erwarten z.B., die narrative und visuelle Welt (meist eines Films) betreten und in ihr handeln zu können, wohingegen interagierende Elemente in einem Theaterstück das Publikum zuweilen eher verstören können. Andere Aspekte dieser Kenntnis sind die Kenntnis der Tradition und neuerer Entwicklungen des Genres, aber auch über den Regisseur und seine bisherigen Werke. Sind wir aber ein unwissendes Publikum, »we simply experience the work without the palimpsestic doubleness that comes with knowing. From one perspective, this is a loss. From another, it is simply experiencing the work for itself, and all agree that even adaptations must stand on their own« (127). Adaptierende müssen also den Erwartungen von sowohl einem wissenden als auch einem unwissenden Publikum entgegenkommen.[11]

Über diesen Unterschied hinaus sind die unterschiedlichen Repräsentationsmodi und deren Binnendifferenzierung sehr wichtig. Hat das adaptierte Werk ein relativ klar begrenztes Zielpublikum, wird man bei einer Adaption z.B. für das Fernsehen versuchen, dieses auszuweiten und dazu die Möglichkeiten des Mediums nutzen; ein Theaterstück fordert in der Regel die Vorstellung der Zuschauer stärker heraus als ein Film. Die unterschiedlichen Modi und Medien betreffen unser Bewusstsein unterschiedlich und benötigen unterschiedliche Dekodierungsprozesse: »Telling requires of its audience conceptual work; showing calls on its perceptual decoding abilities« (130). Bei der Reaktion des Publikums spielt es eine Rolle, ob wir wie bei der Lektüre eines Romans oder beim Computerspiel in der Regel allein sind oder wie bei den performativen Medien meistens in einer Gruppe im Dunkeln sitzen. In den unterschiedlichen Medien werden Zeit und Raum unterschiedlich wahrgenommen: Film und Fernsehen sind viel repräsentationalistischer und realistischer als ein Theaterstück; wenn wir zu Hause lesen oder einen Film sehen, können wir mehr als im Kino kontrollieren, wie viel und wann wir etwas erfahren (vgl. Gast 9); Filme müssen kürzer sein als Romane.

---

10 Dies verstärkt sich, wenn ein Buch sehr früh eine Filmadaption erfährt, da »the fan culture was arguably not expecting a reinterpretation of the story, but simply a retelling of it in a new medium« (Bortolotti/Hutcheon 449).
11 Wie O'Flynn ausführt, gibt es aber verschiedene Adaptionen für digitale Medien, die für unwissende Interaktanten kaum zugänglich bzw. verständlich sind (vgl. 90-95).

Unterschiedlich sind ferner die Grade bzw. unterschiedlichen Arten des Eintauchens durch die Vorstellung, die auditive und visuelle Wahrnehmung oder die Interaktion. Auch ein Leser nimmt nicht einfach nur den Text passiv auf, sondern trägt aktiv zum ästhetischen Prozess bei. »Knowing or unknowing, we experience adaptations across media differently than we do adaptations within the same medium. But even in the latter case, adaptation *as adaptation* involves, for its knowing audience, an interpretive doubling, a conceptual flipping back and forth between the work we know and the work we are experiencing« (139). Wie Leitch betont, erfolgt dies nicht nur bei Adaptionen, sondern bei jeder Lektüre oder jedem Sehen eines Theaterstücks, Bildes oder Films; bei Adaptionen sei dies aber stärker gefordert und unentbehrlich. »Comparisons that are discretionary in all texts, because they are all intertexts, become foundational to the extent that any audience experiences an adaptation as an adaptation« (*Adaptation* 117).

Wo und wann?

Schließlich ist noch der kulturelle, soziale und geschichtliche Kontext der Adaption zu bedenken, der sich zuweilen sehr kurzfristig gravierend verändern kann und somit die Neuakzentuierungen und vor allem Neuinterpretationen betrifft. Häufig wird die Zeit verändert, in der die Geschichte spielt; andere relevante Aspekte sind die Art des Druckes, die Größe des Bildschirms oder die Hardware. Ebenfalls zum Kontext rechnet Hutcheon Elemente der Repräsentation und Rezeption wie Werbung, Pressemeldungen und Berichte. »Whether an adapted story is told, shown, or interacted with, it always happens in a particular time and space in a society« (144). Während oft schon ein kurzer Zeitraum ausreicht, um den Kontext am selben Ort und in derselben Kultur deutlich zu verändern – wie die Rezeption von Tolkiens Werk in der Hippie-Kultur belegt, stehen transkulturelle Adaptionen vor bedeutenden Herausforderungen, die oft durch eine Verlegung in die eigene Kultur gelöst werden sollen. »Transcultural adaptations often mean changes in racial and gender politics« (147). Dabei ist nicht nur der Kontext der Schaffung einer Adaption wichtig, sondern ebenso der der Rezeption, wobei performative Medien eine kulturübergreifende Adaption am stärksten herausfordern, da es nicht damit getan ist, das adaptierte Werk zu übersetzen, sondern auch die visuellen und auditiven Elemente der neuen Umgebung entsprechen müssen. Indem durch solche Transformationen oder Transplantationen von lokalen Besonderheiten in einen anderen Kontext neue und hybride Ergebnisse entstehen, kann man in diesen Fällen von einer »Indigenisierung« sprechen. Hutcheon legt den Akzent auf die Aktivität seitens der Adaptierenden: »people pick and choose what they want to transplant to their own soil. Adapters of traveling stories exert power over what they adapt« (150). Wie Hutcheon am Beispiel von *Carmen* und den zahlreichen Adaptionen zeigt, gibt es sehr viele Möglichkeiten, eine Geschichte zu indigenisieren, z.b. historisierend oder enthistorisierend, rassifizierend oder entrassifizierend oder verkörpernd oder entkörpernd (vgl. 158-167; vgl. für *Romeo und Julia* als anderes Beispiel Levenson).

III. Adaption als Interpretation

Die unterschiedlichen Aspekte, die für die konkrete Form und Rezeption einer Adaption relevant sind, belegen die Notwendigkeit einer komplexen Adaptionstheorie, nach der eine Adaption nicht einfach als Anpassung eines Werkes bzw. seines »wesentlichen Gehaltes« an ein neues Genre, Medium o.ä. verstanden werden kann. Vielmehr ist es ein viel komplexeres Phänomen, das auch nicht erschöpfend dadurch erklärt wird, eine Adaption als Interpretation zu verstehen. Damit soll dieser Aspekt keineswegs verneint oder geringgeschätzt werden. Aber weil eine Adaption in der Regel keine diskursiv-theoretische Interpretation ist, sondern ein eigenes Kunstwerk, ist ihr eine Bedeutungsoffenheit zuzusprechen, die einer solchen Interpretation nicht zukommt und sich in Interpretationen ausdrückt, die von den Adaptierenden nicht anvisiert waren, sondern von den Rezipienten aufgedeckt werden (ein ähnliches Phänomen schildert Eco 11f).

Nichtsdestoweniger sind Adaptionen auch aus poststrukturalistischer Perspektive Interpretationen, da sie als Lektüren oder Pfade durch andere Texte verstanden werden können; Adaptionen seien immer Interpretationen und Interpretationen immer Adaptionen. »The story, so to speak, is never separate from the telling. There is no such thing as an abstractable (or extractable) ›essence‹ in a novel or film that can be adapted to a new medium so that one may say, ›It's the same story, it's just told in a different way‹« (18). Wegen des offenen Charakters eines Kunstwerks ist die Intertextualität des Publikums nicht zu unterschätzen, da die Interpretation durch die Adaptierenden und durch die Leser, Hörer oder Interakteure erfolgt. Deshalb können Adaptionen als Dialoge mit anderen Texten, inklusive der adaptierten Texte, gelten, die wiederum in Dialog mit den Adaptionen stehen.

Heutzutage kann wohl kaum jemand *The Lord of the Rings* lesen, ohne dabei die Adaption durch Peter Jackson und ihre Rezeption zu berücksichtigen. Adaptionen sind also viel eher Hommagen, Kritiken oder Parodien denn bloße Anpassungen.

Die Frage nach Originalität und ihrer Bedeutung für die künstlerische Einschätzung eines Werks ist somit von großer Bedeutung für eine Adaptionstheorie, da mit ihr entweder die abschätzige Einstellung gegenüber Adaptionen begründet oder eine solche kritisiert wird. »In American studies and adaptation studies, the growing awareness of long-standing interdependencies requires new ways of perceiving self and other – not as binaries but as reciprocally influential elements of a culture in flux« (Balestrini 8f). Hierarchien könnten durch eine laterale Sicht nebeneinander existierender und miteinander verwobener Phänomene ersetzt werden, womit Hybridität und Interdisziplinarität weniger auf Hierarchie und Machtverhältnisse und mehr auf kontextuelles Zusammenspiel und gegenseitiges Lernen ausgerichtet wären (vgl. 17f).[12]

Indem Adaptionen Geschichten wiedergeben, sie aber nicht bloß kopieren, können sich darin die beiden Möglichkeiten finden, eine Geschichte zu verstehen: »as a specific cultural representation of a ›basic ideology‹ and as a general human universal« (Hutcheon 176). Die adaptierten Werke werden durch die Adaptionen nicht vergessen, sondern vielmehr lebendig erhalten, was nach Hutcheon für die Analogie zur Evolution in der Biologie spricht, da Adaptionen die Weise seien, in der Geschichten sich entwickeln und sich durch kulturelle Selektion an neue Zeiten und andere Orte anpassen.

Ein zentraler Unterschied zur Biologie besteht wie erwähnt in der Intentionalität von Adaptionen innerhalb einer Kultur gegenüber zufälligen Mutationen in der Biologie, womit eine komplexe Kausalitätsstruktur vorliegt; »in a cultural context, adaptations influence culture and culture influences the nature of adaptations« (Bortolotti/Hutcheon 453). Geschichten würden immer und immer wieder erzählt und veränderten sich mit jeder Wiedergabe, seien aber als die gleiche erkennbar. Deswegen seien frühere Werke nicht wertvoller als spätere – unterlegene Geschichten hätten nicht überlebt. Es gebe aber nur sehr wenige Geschichten, die nicht aus anderen entstanden seien. »In the workings of the human imagination, adaptation is the norm, not the exception«[13] (Hutcheon 177).

In den meisten Fällen sind solche Geschichten aber nicht nur auf eine einzige frühere Geschichte zurückzuführen, sondern in sie sind viele verschiedene Elemente eingegangen. Diesen Umstand beschreibt Tolkien in seinem Bild des »Cauldron of Story« (OFS 44f), in dem die uns erzählte Geschichte brodelt und der schon immer auf dem Feuer gestanden habe, »and to it have continually been added new bits, dainty and undainty« (45).

---

12 Wie O'Flynn ausführt, vergrößern manche neuen Adaptionen im interagierenden Modus die Komplexität dieser Unterscheidung zwischen vertikaler und lateraler Ausrichtung, z.B. wenn Alternate Reality Games vor manchen Filmen oder Fernsehprojekten veröffentlicht werden und in diesen die Fans den Inhalt der Adaption selbst generieren (vgl. bes. 98; ferner Moore 191).
13 »But adaptations in a sense make manifest what is true of all works of art – that they are all on some level ›derivative‹« (Stam, *Introduction* 45).

Bibliographie

Albrecht-Crane, Christa and Dennis Cutchins. "Introduction: New Beginnings for Adaptation Studies". *Adaptation Studies. New Approaches.* Eds. Christa Albrecht Crane and Dennis Cutchins. Madison: Fairleigh Dickinson University Press, 2010, 11-22

Balestrini, Nassim Winnie. "Adaptation Studies and American Studies: Interfaces". *Adaptation and American Studies. Perspectives on Research and Teaching.* Ed. Nassim W. Balestrini. Heidelberg: Universitätsverlag Winter, 2011, 1-29

Berger, Richard. "Converting the Controversial: Regulation as 'Source Text' in Adaptation". *Adaptation Studies. New Approaches.* Eds. Christa Albrecht Crane and Dennis Cutchins. Madison: Fairleigh Dickinson University Press, 2010, 150-159

Bortolotti, Gary R. and Linda Hutcheon. "On the Origin of Adaptations: Rethinking Fidelity Discourse and 'Success'-biologically". *New Literary History* 38 (2007): 443-458

Cobb, Shelley. "Adaptation, Fidelity, and Gendered Discourses". *Adaptation* 4 (2011): 28-37

Duden. Deutsches Universalwörterbuch. ⁴2001

Eco, Umberto. *Nachschrift zum Namen der Rose.* München: DTV, ⁹2003

Gast, Wolfgang. »Lesen oder Zuschauen? Eine kleine Einführung in den Problemkreis ›Literaturverfilmung‹«. *Literaturverfilmung.* Hg. Wolfgang Gast. Bamberg: C.C.Buchners, 1993, 7-11

Genette, Gerard. *Palimpsestes. La literature au second degré.* Paris: Éditions du Seuil, 1982

Giddings, Robert et al. *Screening the novel: The theory and practice of literary dramatization.* London: MacMillan, 1990

Hutcheon, Linda. *A Theory of Adaptation.* New York: Routledge, 2006

Kreuzer, Helmut. »Arten der Literaturadaption«. *Literaturverfilmung.* Hg. Wolfgang Gast. Bamberg: C.C.Buchners, 1993, 27-31

Leitch, Thomas. "Adaptation Studies at a Crossroads". *Adaptation* 1 (2008): 63-77

---. "Adaptation, the Genre". *Adaptation* 1 (2008): 106-120

---. "The Ethics of Infidelity". *Adaptation Studies. New Approaches.* Eds. Christa Albrecht-Crane and Dennis Cutchins. Madison: Fairleigh Dickinson University Press, 2010, 61-77

Levenson, Jill L. "The Adaptations of Juliet and Her Romeo". *Adaptation and American Studies. Perspectives on Research and Teaching.* Ed. Nassim W. Balestrini. Heidelberg: Universitätsverlag Winter, 2011, 195-212

Moore, Michael Ryan. "Adaptation and New Media". *Adaptation* 3 (2010): 179-192

O'Flynn, Siobhan. "Designing for the Interactant: How Interactivity Impacts on Adaptation". *Adaptation and American Studies. Perspectives on Research and Teaching.* Ed. Nassim W. Balestrini. Heidelberg: Universitätsverlag Winter, 2011, 83-102

Sanders, Julie. *Adaptation and appropriation.* London: Routledge, 2006

Stam, Robert. "The dialogics of adaptation". *Film adaptation.* Ed. James Naremore. New Brunswick, NJ: Rutgers, 2000, 54-76

---. „Introduction: The theory and practice of adaptation". *Literature and film: A guide to the theory and practice of film adaptation.* Eds. Robert Stam and Alessandra Raengo. Oxford: Blaxwell, 2005, 1-52

Tolkien, John R.R. *On Fairy-stories. Expanded edition, with commentary and notes.* Eds.Verlyn Flieger and Douglas A. Anderson. London: HarperCollins, 2008

Westbrook, Brett. „Being Adaptation: The Resistance to Theory." *Adaptation Studies. New Approaches.* Ed. Christa Albrecht Crane and Dennis Cutchins. Madison: Fairleigh Dickinson University Press, 2010, 25-45

Peter Jackson's Adaptation of *The Lord of the Rings*: Cash or Kudos?

Annie Birks (Angers)

Preamble: The Movies and the Critics

On July 7, 2012, the French daily newspaper *Le Monde* published a four-page article on J.R.R. Tolkien including an interview with Christopher Tolkien who was invited to express his views on Peter Jackson's adaptation of *The Lord of the Rings*[1]. Christopher clearly bemoaned "the gap between the beauty, the *gravitas* of the [original] work and what it has become" and declared: "Such degree of commercialization reduces the aesthetic and philosophical impact of this creation to nothing" (my translation from the French). He regretted that the book had been "eviscerated" to give birth to "an action film for the 15 to 25 year olds". In other words, his father's heritage had become a source of "intellectual despair" and his father himself had turned into "a monster devoured by his popularity and absorbed by the absurdity of the time". Furthermore at the time the article was written, he expressed his fear for the adaptation of *The Hobbit* which was likely to be of the same ilk.

At the end of the 1950s, J.R.R. Tolkien was already wary of potential screen adaptations following the success of *The Lord of the Rings*, but he was probably a long way from envisaging such an outcome when he and his publisher Stanley Unwin agreed on the policy to adopt: [These films would be] "either a respectable treatment of the book, or else a good deal of money", or to quote Sir Stanley "the choice was between 'cash or kudos'" (Carpenter 228).

A number of Tolkien scholars, critics and fans have analyzed, praised, questioned or depreciated Peter Jackson's movies released between 2001 and 2003 and still watched by millions of people. As an example we can mention *Translating Tolkien: Text and Film* published in 2004 under the direction of Thomas Honegger. In "Humiliated Heroes: Peter Jackson's Interpretation of *The Lord the Rings*", Anthony S. Burdge and Jessica Burke, on the one hand, stressed their "utmost respect for the creative team behind the films—the actors involved, the geniuses who hold ground in the forges of WETA, and the artists who gave Tolkien's Middle-earth scope". The authors also granted "a measure of respect for Peter Jackson himself who took on the task, and without whom the project would have never seen fruition" (131). However, on the other hand, they had "issues" with "humiliated heroes" which were largely focused on "the

---

[1] The article was written by the journalist and literary critic, Raphaëlle Rérolle.

interpretations of Boyens and Walsh, and the attitudes of Boyens in particular (as seen in many documentaries and interviews concerning her work on the films)."

In *Understanding The Lord of The Rings: The Best of Tolkien Criticism* (2004), Rose A. Zimbardo and Neil D. Isaacs published an essay by Tom Shippey: "Another Road to Middle-earth; Jackson's Movie Trilogy". Shippey took into account the nature of the two media—narrative prose and cinema—and demonstrated how, to his mind, Jackson had done "exactly what Tolkien feared movie-adaptors would not do: subordinated noise to silence, heroes to hobbits, Subsidiary Action to Prime Action" (242). He showed to what extent the moviemaker had to adapt the rendering of Tolkien's novels to the expectations of a modern audience (255) and, at the same time, abide by "Tolkien's philosophic core" pervading "the whole structure of *The Lord of the Rings*", namely, the fact that "decision and perseverance may be rewarded beyond hope" (252). Although Shippey acknowledged Jackson's inability for example to "cope with all the ramifications of Tolkien on Providence", he explained why the moviemaker had "certainly succeeded in conveying much of the more obvious parts of Tolkien's narrative core" (254).

In 2006, in their *Tolkien Companion and Guide*, Christina Scull and Wayne G. Hammond observed how angrily divided Tolkien enthusiasts are over the adaptation: "(Though the lines are often blurred) some praise it highly; some accept its departures from its source as part of a legitimate interpretation of Tolkien's book, or as necessary changes to suit a different medium; and some feel that the film is a travesty as an adaptation and seriously flawed even when considered solely as a motion picture" (22).

In the seven-page entry on Jackson in Michael Drout's *Tolkien Encyclopedia* (2007), Daniel Timmons remarked that "films adapted from a book, even a masterpiece, should not be evaluated strictly on the fidelity to the source material" and that films can be appraised "on their artistic impression in terms of tone, story, character, and theme" (306). After circumscribing Jackson's adaptation as "a problematic blend of abridgment, compression, transformation, and addition", Timmons insisted that "the thematic core" of the novel is highly visible in the films (308). The many nominations and awards come as further evidence to its validation (309) and one cannot but come to the conclusion that "whatever one feels about the films..., Peter Jackson achieved phenomenal success with his adaptations" (309).

In the more recent French *Dictionnaire Tolkien*, directed by Vincent Ferré, Hervé Aubron, Associate Editor to the French *Magasine Littéraire*, sees the adaptation as "a fable", as "Peter Jackson's own quest": "that of a Hobbit moviemaker exposing himself to the temptations and dangers of Hollywoodian Mordor" (5). Aubron is also convinced that, Jackson, as a long-term fan, knew that he was likely to be "crushed between the hammer of Tolkienian orthodoxy and the anvil of Hollywood norms" (4).

So much has been said on the subject and the recent release of *The Hobbit* is going to fuel the debate even more. Nonetheless, if we consider Tolkien's continuing popularity, especially among the young generations, we can still wonder whether Peter Jackson deserves to be blamed for dumbing down, as Christopher feels, or whether this adaptation still acts as a key for many moviegoers who otherwise might never have been tempted to open the door to the written work.

Cash or Kudos: 2,352 Students' Points of View

In an attempt to shed more light on the subject, I decided to elaborate a questionnaire on Google Drive and target a wide segment of the population I am familiar with: students of higher education. After negotiating with the *ad hoc* authorities in Angers, France, I was given authorization to e-mail the Google link to students from a selection of local Universities, Undergraduate/Graduate Schools of Business and of Engineering[2].

The questionnaire—which was worded in French and whose purpose was clearly specified (the 2013 Tolkien Conference in Aachen)—contained more than 60 questions divided into six sections. Three sections were directed to all the students and the other three corresponded to different profiles, depending on whether they had read the books before or after seeing the films, or depending on whether they had just seen the films. The idea was to assess the impact of the films on the students' interest in Tolkien and to measure their appreciation of both the books and the films. The questions included rating scales, lists of choices and a number of open-ended questions.

It can be supposed that between 25,000 and 30,000 students received my e-mail and surprisingly enough within three weeks 2,352 replied, which corresponds to about 7.8 to 9.4% of the targeted population. The response came as preliminary evidence that Angers' students were eager to share their feelings on Tolkien's Middle-earth, even though they had no direct vested interest in replying.

---

2 The Universities and Undergraduate/Graduate Schools targeted: L'Université d'Angers, L'Université Catholique de l'Ouest, L'Ecole Supérieur des Sciences Commerciales d'Angers, l'Ecole Supérieure d'Electronique de l'Ouest, l'Ecole Supérieure d'Agriculture, l'Institut des Relations Publiques et de la Communication.

1. General Data[3]

1.1. Students' profiles

After collating the data it appeared that 57% of the respondents were female and 43% male, aged essentially between 16 and 29. More precisely, 51 % of them were between 20 and 22 years old. Their academic fields of study were mainly business and management (14.7%); health and medicine (12.3%), foreign languages (8.8%), agriculture (8,6%), psychology (8.3%) and, in descending order, came electronics, literature, law, computer science, history, biology, education, communication, environmental science, culture, math, heritage, human resources, sociology, catering, art, safety and security, music, theology, logistics, journalism and librarianship.

1.2. The films

To the question "How many times have you seen Peter Jackson's films?[4]" the dominant answer was "2 to 3 times". Few of them only saw the films once, which was nevertheless the case for 13.4% of the 2,352 participants for *Fellowship*, 15.7% for *Towers* and 15.8% for *Return*. Almost all the others saw the films between 2 to more than 10 times. As can be seen in Chart N° 1, *Return* seems to have slightly earned the favour of those who replied "10 times and more".

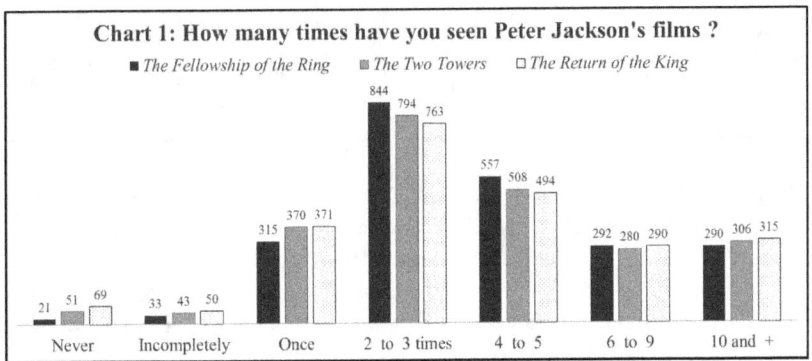

Apart from watching the adaptations, 78.7% of the 2,352 respondents explored Tolkien's world via other means, such as (in descending order): the books, the DVD appendices, video games, the internet, books and articles on Tolkien,

---

3 The questions asked in this section were compulsory to be allowed to continue with the following sections.
4 To simplify matters, *The Fellowship of the Ring*, *The Two Towers*, *The Return of the King*, will respectively be referred to as *Fellowship*, *Towers* and *Return*.

figurines/toys/objects, role plays, classes, forums, conferences, events around Tolkien and trips to New Zealand. A student even reported that he used to collect figurines of *The Lord of the Rings* from Kinder eggs and remarked that he had never eaten so many eggs in one week.

1.3. The books

A first glance at Chart N° 2 shows that accessing Tolkien's world via the books is not as popular as via the films, which is easily explained by modern cultural trends. Nevertheless more than half of the respondents have either tried to read or have read *Fellowship* (1,264)[5] and less than half have either tried to read or have read *Towers* (923)[6] and *Return* (848)[7]. Again, *Return* seems to have been slightly favoured by the keenest of them.

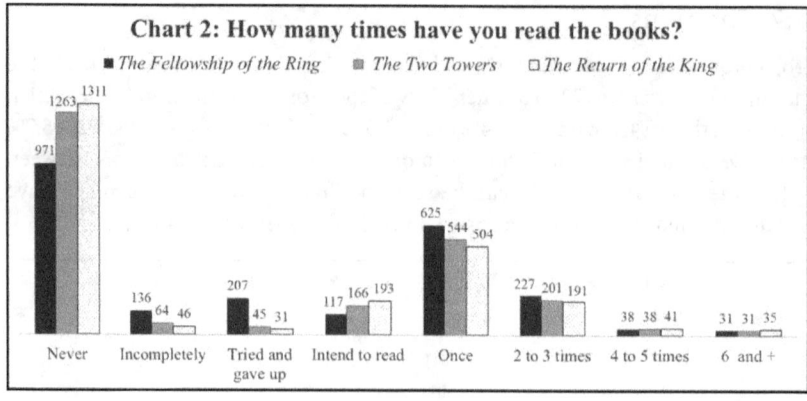

Their interest in other books by Tolkien (*The Hobbit, The Silmarillion, Unfinished Tales* …) is shown in Chart N° 3 and appears to be in keeping with the reading rate of *The Lord of the Rings*: nearly half of them (975, i.e. 41.45%)[8] ticked one or several titles. Among the 30 students who read other books by Tolkien than those given on the graph, 5 of them mentioned the 12 (or most) volumes of *The History of Middle-earth*.

---

5   1,264 = 136 + 207 + 625 + 227 + 38 + 31
6   923 = 64 + 45 + 544 + 201 + 38 + 31
7   848 = 46 + 31 + 504 + 191 + 41 + 35
8   975 = 2 352 - 1 377. This question was compulsory and they could tick several answers.

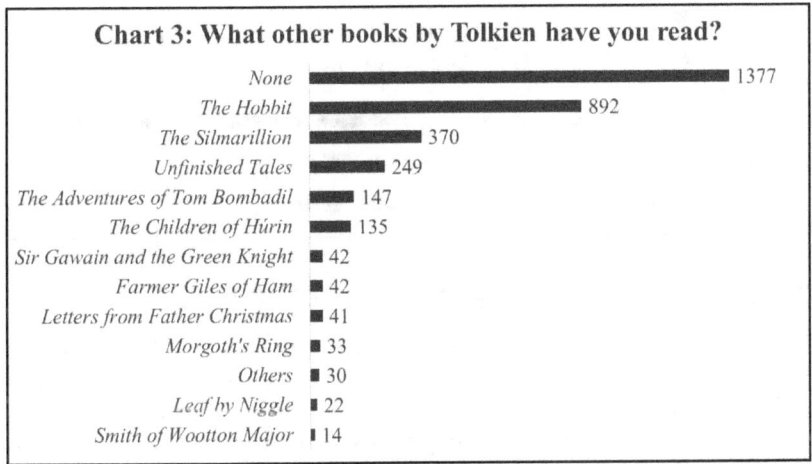

Although a little less than half the respondents claim that they have read books by Tolkien, the number of books bought—to tackle the more prosaic question of "cash"—is astonishingly large. If we can go by the answers gathered, 1,252 students bought at least 4,165 books by Tolkien, which is equivalent to 3.3 books per buyer. The most eager of them (66 students) claim that they bought at least 8 books by Tolkien.

When asked if they had read books and articles about Tolkien and his works, 157 participants referred to *Dictionnaire Tolkien* (V. Ferré, Ed.); 134 to *The Complete Guide to Middle-earth*, by R. Foster; 67 to Carpenter's *Biography* and 39 to *The Letters*. References were also made to the Canadian writer David Day for his illustrated books on Tolkien's life and works, geared towards a more general readership; to the French linguist Edward Kloczko for his books on Tolkien's invented languages; to Vincent Ferré's *Tolkien: Sur les Rivages de la Terre du Milieu*; to *Tolkien et le Moyen Âge*, directed by Leo Carruthers and also, among other authors and resources, to Lin Carter.

2. Three Profiles: Three Types of Data

More specific data were then collected from students who had read the books after seeing the films (22%), read the books before seeing the films (20%) or from students who had only seen the films (58%).

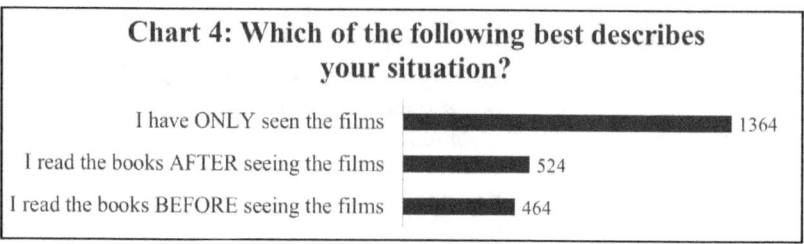

2.1. Books after films: 524 students out of 2 352

Nearly all the students who read the books after seeing the films highly enjoyed Jackson's adaptations (94.5%). This percentage clearly shows that the movies paved the way for the books as far as these particular students were concerned. 89.5% of them claimed that the films brought them to the books and 62% said that the films played a part in their understanding of the books. However their desire to further explore Middle-earth seems to stem from their interest in both the films and the books (61.7%) and not just in the films (15.6%) or just in the books (12.1%)[9].

Q.: Were you surprised when you read the books and if you were, why?
Out of the 524 who read the books after watching the movies, 174 admitted that they were surprised when they discovered the original story. Apart from commenting on the most obvious missing or altered elements (Tom Bombadil—mentioned by most of them—, the barrow-downs, the scouring of the Shire…), these respondents were mainly surprised by:
- The beauty of the written work; the profusion of details and descriptions for some and, for others, Tolkien's unexpected highly descriptive style at the expense of action; the invented languages; the scope of Tolkien's imagination; the gigantic work put in to make this world seem alive; the impression that this world has really existed; the depth of the story; the more pronounced philosophical scope; the songs; the poetry; the Elves; the characters' psychology (e.g. Faramir, Sam); the age of some of the characters (especially Frodo); a clearer delineation of temporal benchmarks; the discovery of whole chunks of history missing in the films (obviously due to concision) which unveil a historic, cultural, even philosophical richness and depth that the adaptations convey only partially.
- Some remarked that, in the books, we really enter Tolkien's world whereas in the films we remain spectators; they found it surprising that one man could invent such a complete and complex world; one student bemoaned the fact that our imagination is already filled with the films settings and has difficulty stretching

---

9   8.8% of the other students said that they did not want to further explore Middle-earth and 1.8% made 'other' comments.

in another direction (which can be said about most film adaptations). Someone said that "the profusion of details helps us to live with the heroes at all times: we travel the land with them, we get bored with them and we get tired with them. Reading *The Lord of the Rings* is exhausting." Another declared: "I was pleasantly surprised when I discovered the richness of the written work and all these stories which are not in the film. I really fell for Tolkien's way of writing. I would never have imagined such creativeness just by watching the films which have their own quality and coherence but they only touch upon the subject."

Q.: Are there elements in the books that you did not like?
Many respondents found the prologue too long. They said that *The Lord of the Rings* on the whole contains too many descriptions and too many details, which slows down the action and makes the story too difficult to follow for young readers who are looking for action and battles. However, some said that thanks to the films they managed to get into the story and did not get lost.

One student pointed out that "the abundance of details might seem an obstacle to begin with, but the more you read, the more you get into the story and all these details become essential and give the story and this particular world a feeling of veracity, truth, realism." Another one added: "I must admit that I got a little lost in the descriptions at times but apart from that it was real bliss".

Q.: Are there elements in the films that you did not like?
Most students regretted the absence of Tom Bombadil and his symbolic stance with regard to the ring. Some explained that his presence would have added a note of poetry, magic and mystery. They did not like Jackson's treatment of Faramir who is supposed to be a charismatic character and who is misrepresented and dark compared to the way he comes across in the books. A lot of them found the character of Legolas rather silly at times; they deemed his script was not worthy of an Elf; his skating performance on a shield looked more like a commercial trick to appeal to a young audience. In other words, a lot of them found that the adaptations are aimed at attracting a specific audience (as Christopher Tolkien pointed out in the article), rather than remaining faithful to Tolkien.

Some found the love-story between Arwen and Aragorn soppy, emotional and exaggerated. They did not like the alterations concerning Saruman's death (which, they remarked, has nothing to do with the books); someone said that the fight for freedom in the Shire in *Return* should not have been removed, because it was essential to show that the Hobbits could now manage to handle adversity by themselves. He added that it was all the more regrettable as it is an important lesson in the book.

They understand Peter Jackson when he said (in the DVDs appendices) that he had to shorten the plot for practical purposes. Nevertheless, a number of students wonder why he added so many new scenes and distorted the story to such an extent—why make so many unjustified changes, or focus on aspects of the story which are not particularly essential in Tolkien's books and which, all in all, add a lot of details to the story and make it longer? It does not seem to make sense to some of them.

Surprisingly enough, although a number of students deplored the alterations, what they found particularly interesting in both media (narrative prose and films) turned out to be very similar. Answers to the question "What did you find particularly interesting in *The Lord of the Rings* (books and films)?" were in the following descending order for both the films and the books: the characters, the genre, the atmosphere, the details, the history, the values, the action, the realism, and the aesthetics. It is interesting to note that this result closely resembles that of the students who had read the books before watching the movies exhibited in Chart N° 6 (page 35).

2.2 Books before films: 464 students out of 2 352

Reading the books before seeing the films seems to have decreased the students' appreciation rate of the film (by 15.5%). Out of the 464 students concerned, 78.9% (366) highly enjoyed the films (compared to 94.5% for the students who saw the films before reading the books), 10 did not really enjoy them or not at all, and 8 said that it depended on the films[10]. A student rated the three films separately: he did not like *Return*, found *Towers* a little over the top and declared *Fellowship* as his favourite. As can be expected, the extended versions are definitely favoured.

80.6% of the 464 students considered that the films respect the gravitas of the books, although some of them insist that the films should be solely regarded as an interpretation, as Peter Jackson's vision and therefore cannot be but different from the books. They regard the books and the films as two separate "masterpieces" in their respective fields. Asked about the beauty of the story, only 11% consider that it is lessened in the films, the others consider that it is rendered (62.7%) or even reinforced (25%)[11]. As far as the philosophical scope is concerned, 17.9% consider that it is highlighted in the films, 47.2% think that it is respected and that the story is not just reduced to that of an action film—compared to 30.4% who think that the adaptations do diminish the philosophical scope.[12]

The films did not seem to make much difference to most of these students' understanding of the books. Only 17.9% reported that the films helped them to better comprehend the books (compared to 62% for the previous group of students). However some added that, thanks to the films, they managed to better visualize the beauty of the scenery. Others declared that the music

---

10 Concerning the others, 57 were more or less satisfied with the adaptations and 23 did not answer.
11 The other students either did not answer or made alternative comments.
12 Idem.

reinforces the beauty and solemnity of the story. A student started reading *Fellowship* when he was 11 and gave it up because he found it too complicated. After watching the first movie he went back to the book and carried on with the other two volumes.

Although the films exerted a lesser impact on these students' interest in Middle-earth than on the previous section of respondents, the statistics show that, together with their long-lasting interest in the books, their enthusiasm for Middle-earth has been re-awakened, rekindled or reinforced by their exposure to the films[13].

Q.: **What did you find particularity interesting in *The Lord of the Rings* (books and films)?**
Chart N° 6 gives a rough idea of what these students most appreciated in both the books and the films with regard to the characters, the genre, the atmosphere, the details, the history, the values, the action, the realism, the aesthetics. They seem to find the details and the history more interesting in the books, whereas aesthetics, action and realism seem to be preferred in the films.

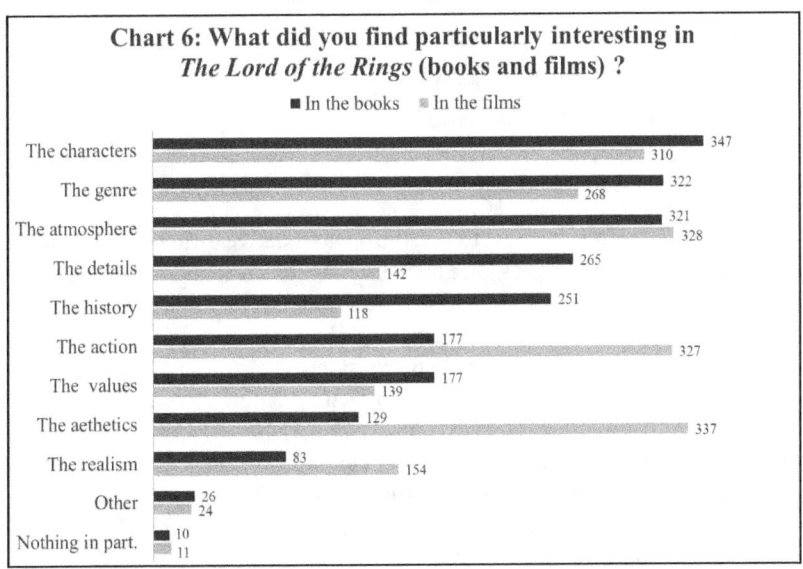

As far as the books are concerned, some participants added that they were sensitive to Tolkien's vision of man, as developed in his works in general; others were particularly interested in the poetry, the beauty, the purity, the style, the creation of languages and different cultures, the legends, the maps...

---

13 4.4% felt like further exploring Middle-earth thanks to the films only. 26.3% thanks to the books only, and 58.3% thanks to both the books and the films. 10.3% said they did not feel like further exploring Middle-earth and 0.7% gave other reasons.

As for the movies, some students added that they also particularly appreciated New Zealand scenery, the costumes, the music, the cast and the humour[14].

Chart N° 7 shows these students' general assessment of the films in relation to the books. Taking into account that they were allowed to tick as many items as they wanted, it appears that the majority went for the more positive comments. Only 11.6% of them considered that Peter Jackson's movies belittled the books as opposed to 38.1% who considered that the films are a credit to the books. A fair number of them (65.9%) agreed that the films increase awareness of Tolkien and his work.

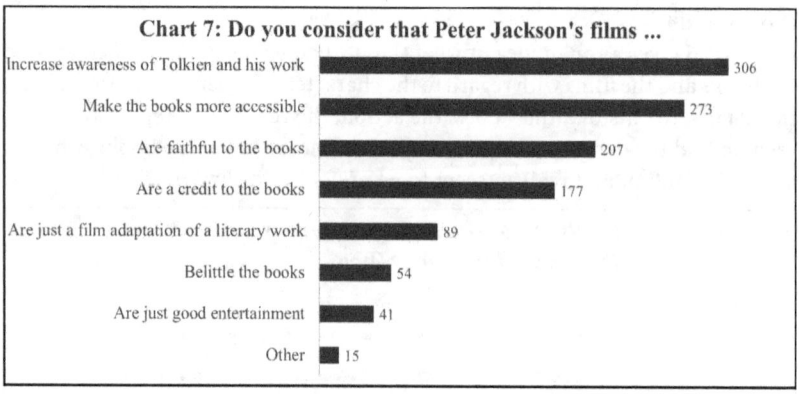

Among those (3.2%) who chose to tick the open-ended question ('other'), some stressed that although the films are obviously the screen adaptation of a literary work, they attest the film crew's passion for Tolkien, they make you feel like reading this author, and as was said previously by the first group of participants, both the books and the films should be considered as two separate entities, as part of a bigger ensemble belonging to Tolkien's imagination and his fandom.

Q.: Are there elements in the books that you did not like?
According to what they said, a lot of students were 9, 10, 11 or 12 when they first read *The Lord of the Rings*. Some found the story very complicated (too many descriptions, too many details, action too slow) even "for children who are used to reading a lot". They remarked that these books are far from being children's books and that you have to be older to really appreciate them.

---

14 These aspects were not offered as options considering that the suggested elements had to be more general and fit both the books and the movies.

The French translation seems to have disappointed some. One student did not like the translated version but was fascinated by the original English text. Some thought that the maps were essential to better follow the story owing to the multiplicity of descriptions (mainly scenery), characters and places.

Others said that the descriptions were necessary to better picture Middle-earth. As already pointed out by the first group of respondents, some considered that the Prologue can easily discourage the readers and others confessed to having skipped the songs. Some re-read the books after seeing the films and enjoyed them even more. One student said: "Nothing can be perfect in this world but Tolkien's books are, to me, what comes closest to perfection".

Q.: Are there elements in the films that you did not like?
Although 78.9% of the students who read the books before seeing the films highly enjoyed the adaptations and some still regard them as their favourite movies, they found fault with the following aspects:

As already mentioned by the group of students who read the books after seeing the films, most missing elements were generally regretted, namely the absence of Tom Bombadil. The addition of a number of details and the suppression of many appeared to disappoint the "purists". Again they wondered why so many scenes had been created in the films when the books were rich enough. They considered that the rendering of the characters' traits was often exaggerated and caricatured, e.g. Gimli's sense of humour.

Other comments concerned the characters of (and relationships between): Frodo and Sam, Legolas and Gimli, Arwen and Aragorn. Again, some found Frodo a little irritating at times and Legolas somewhat silly. A number of them deplored the "Hollywoodian" scenes like those with Legolas on his shield and the Oliphant, or those reducing a character to one facet of his personality, e.g. Gimli turned into the group's comic... The Elves were not physically in accordance with Tolkien's vision. They look too much like humans and appear "too nice" compared to the way Tolkien described them.

The music (although beautiful) is sometimes overloaded with emotion, which reduces the aesthetics and Americanizes the story. The films revolve too much around action scenes which are not essential in the books. There is too much focus on fights and not enough on songs and poems, which stand at the heart of the story.

Someone regretted the absence of Tolkien's theological foundation, which, among other missing elements, gives a superficial rendering of the book. The films appear to be aimed at the general public and do not provide the audience with better insight into the work, nor an objective approach to the work in general.

A student expressed her disappointment with the missing "Scouring of the Shire". She said that this chapter precisely highlights the deep changes the Hobbits went through during their journey and the way these changes guide their actions. It is "one of the rare moments in the films" which did not bring her "entire satisfaction".

Echoing a fair number of reported points of view, again some insisted that the films are just an interpretation. They remarked that all along we can feel the film director's admiration for Tolkien and see that he tried to do his best. A student declared: "Being a great admirer of Mr. Jackson, I won't say anything about the discordant notes". Another claimed that she had expected a "catastrophe" but was in fact pleasantly surprised for Peter Jackson has perfectly rendered the atmosphere of the books. She qualified the result as "very good".

2.3 Films only: 1,364 (58%) out of 2,352 students

These students enjoyed the movies slightly less (75.7%) than those who read the books beforehand (78.9%) and a lot less than those who read the book afterwards (94.5%). Nonetheless the figures are still high. They voiced their interest in the films by prioritizing the suggested items in the following descending order: the characters, the genre, the atmosphere, the action, the aesthetics, the details, the history, the values and the realism. Some added that they were also particularly interested in the beauty of the scenery, the music, the humour, the settings, the cast, the special effects, the invented languages, the psychology of the characters and the war scenes.

Even though the majority highly enjoyed the movies, nearly half of them (46.8%) have no intention of reading the books for the following reasons (in descending order): they do not feel the need; they have other books to read; they don't have time; they already know the end; they don't like reading; the films did not make them feel like reading the books. Among those who did not fit in the suggested items, some explained that they do not want to read the books because they don't like this literary genre or because they would have difficulty using their imagination now that they have all the pictures in mind. Finally a few of them said that they tried to read the books and gave up, because they found the story too long and the style too difficult to read.

Those who intend or are determined to read the books (52.3%)[15] gave the following reasons: they want to know the true story and to learn more about the mythology, the history, the peoples (especially the Elves for some), the characters (their psychology, their feelings, their origin), the whole cultural background which fuels the story, the invented languages, the true chronology, Tolkien's

---

15 The others (0.9%) did not answer.

descriptions of the battles. They seem eager to compare the books and the films in order to assess the quality of the adaptations and unveil mysteries.

Out of the 1 364 students who only saw the films, a little more than half of them (54.8%) feel like further exploring Middle-earth or have already started to do so by means of (open answer): conferences, classes, documentaries, video games, the Internet, websites, forums, films appendices, video games, board games, role plays, trips to New Zealand, discussions with friends, events around Tolkien, books and articles, magazines, computer graphics … Watching the movies undoubtedly triggered these students' interest in Tolkien's Middle-earth.

Q.: Are there elements in the films that you did not like?[16]
Only 17.5% of these students had precise elements to deplore and mainly referred to the following aspects: some scenes are a little tedious, the films drag on a bit at times; the French dubbing is not satisfactory. Others complained about excessive moralizing; the Manichean character of certain scenes; too much violence and too many fights (for just a few of these); the naivety of some characters.

Several respondents did not feel that the Elves were given enough importance (even though they have not read the books!). Others did not like the "Hollywoodian" or "blockbuster" aspects of the movies. Quite a number of them had difficulty putting up with Legolas (silly, effeminate, performing ridiculous stunts) and with Frodo (too emotional, soppy and effeminate). Some said that both Sam and Frodo whine too much. Given that the two previous sections of students made similar observations, one could argue that the films might be giving an impression of the story which can be prejudicial to the written work in certain aspects.

3. *The Hobbit*

Out of the 2,352 participants, 70.7% saw *The Hobbit*, among whom 2.2% went to see it at least 4 times. Out of those who saw the movie at least once, 63.4% highly enjoyed it; 21% enjoyed it a little; 9.7% more or less; 3.2% not really; 1.6% did not like it at all.[17] Concerning the book, 33.2% read it entirely, among whom 3.8% read it at least 4 times and 2.4% at least 6 times. Others admitted to just having browsed through it.

Further statistics also showed that they became interested in *The Hobbit* (book or movie), 1. because they enjoyed Peter Jackson's adaptation of *The Lord*

---

16 Open-ended question.
17 1.1% did not give their opinion.

of the Rings, 2. because they enjoyed both the books and the films of *The Lord of the Rings*, 3. because they were given the opportunity, fourthly because they enjoyed reading *The Lord of the Rings* and lastly for other reasons (studies …).

Those who did not like certain aspects of the film deplored the treatment of Radagast when he goes to Dol Guldur on his sledge pulled by the Rhosgobel rabbits. They observed that it is the kind of scene one might expect in a Walt Disney film or cartoon, but not in Tolkien's Middle-earth. A student wondered whether Peter Jackson had being smoking a special kind of weed before he shot these scenes. Another one commented that Radagast looked as though he had escaped from a lunatic asylum.

Some found the humour grotesque (contrary to the books); others considered that the fight scenes resemble those in *Die Hard*, or *Shrek* when the characters fall off cliffs, get back on their feet in no time at all and run away. Again, they commented that this is the kind of stunt you find in cartoons or video games. They considered that these scenes are unworthy of Tolkien's Middle-earth.

A lot of them found the story far-fetched, not true to the book and not credible. They pointed to a real lack of realism (contrary to the adaptation of *The Lord of the Rings*)—which obviously reminds us of Tolkien's insistence on suspension of disbelief in his essay *On Fairy-Stories* (40-41).

From that point of view, Peter Jackson's film production of *The Hobbit* does not seem to have matched their expectations. Quite a number of them said that it is too commercial. One opined that it is meant to have a huge mass appeal and that Tolkien readers must have felt abandoned. Another student remarked that you can feel that it is business-oriented and not made out of love for Tolkien's work and that it is an insult to Tolkien.

One said that it was when he saw *The Hobbit* that he realized the quality and the majesty of *The Lord of the Rings* adaptation. Another said "I read the book [*The Hobbit*] when I was 12 and I found it extremely good and beautiful. Although it was written for children, the film does not respect the seriousness and solemnity of the book".

Conclusion

One cannot but feel touched by Christopher Tolkien's apparent distress concerning his father's work to which he has devoted a considerable part of his life namely as the editor of thousands of pages left in umpteen boxes of archives. I often point out to my students how grateful we can be to him for giving us access to this valuable mine of information!

De facto the most visible part of the iceberg, i.e., *The Lord of the Rings* and now *The Hobbit* has been caught in a wind, or perhaps, in a gale of commercialization. As the journalist in *Le Monde* wrote, there seems to be an abyss between Tolkien's work and his commercial posterity.

Yet, the results of this survey are rather reassuring. They show that Peter Jackson did Tolkien a tremendous favour. And I am not just talking about "Cash" but about "Kudos". They prove Shippey right when he declared just after the release of *Fellowship*, "the mere rumour of the film has provided Tolkien with at least another generation of readers" (TLS 16).

As the answers to this questionnaire testify, the fans are not so easily duped. Many of them clearly draw the line between the written work and the adaptation of *The Lord of the Rings*. They appreciate both the books and the movies as two different entities. The majority highly enjoyed the films and what a number of them did not like, or what they liked less, was precisely what Peter Jackson had altered or added, i.e. the "serious 'dumbing down'" feared by Tolkien aficionados (TLS 16).

Furthermore, 469 out of the 2352 students read the books because they enjoyed the movies. Without the films, one could argue that they might never have developed an interest in Tolkien. 78.9% of those who had already read the books before watching the films highly enjoyed Peter Jackson's adaptation, especially the atmosphere, the action and the aesthetics. Moreover it clearly appears that the movies—adding to their already strong interest in Tolkien—rekindled, reawakened or reinforced their enthusiasm and curiosity for Middle-earth.

Similarly, 714 (52.3%) of those having only seen the movies either intend or are determined to read the books one day. Watching the films seems to have triggered their interest in Tolkien. Some even decided to study Tolkien as part of their curriculum even if they had not read the books.

I personally know a number of students in this situation. And these same students are sometimes very proud to tell you a few months later that they managed to read *The Silmarillion*. Had they not seen the films, they might never have even tried.

Nevertheless, one cannot fail to observe that a lot of students nowadays do not like reading or find Tolkien's style too complicated, with too many descriptions. One could argue that the films have provided them with a satisfactory "translation" since they watch the DVDs over and over again. One could also argue that, for some of them, Jackson has replaced Tolkien, even erased him as fear "some of Tolkien's defenders" (TLS 16).

The production that attracted the most criticism in this survey was the recent adaptation of *The Hobbit* which was frequently seen to leave an impression of lightheartedness, superficiality and betrayal. A student even qualified this adaptation as a "monumental catastrophe". Furthermore, the figures showed that a number of students having only seen the movie *The Hobbit* did not necessarily feel like reading the book

Nevertheless, what is most surprising is that, in spite of the negative comments, 63.4% of the students who saw *The Hobbit* said that they highly enjoyed it. Someone even declared: "The aesthetics in *The Hobbit* is breathtaking and I am prepared to forgive Peter Jackson for his infidelity".
To conclude, I would like to quote two students who discovered the books after watching the films — their testimonies reflect the general spirit of many respondents:

> The films awaken our curiosity and the books nourish it.
> Art student, female, 16-19 years old

And finally:

> When I read *The Lord of the Rings*, I was very surprised because I found the same "substance", the same "soul" as in the film, the same strength which emanates from the story but it was much more thorough. The questions raised were more complex and more numerous. It is as though Peter Jackson had opened the doors to Middle-earth and had given us a glimpse. When we read Tolkien's work, we penetrate fully into that world and we are delighted. We go from an appetizer to a delicious meal.
> Literature student, female, 20-22 years old

Bibliography

Aubron, Hervé. "Adaptations cinématographiques". *Dictionnaire Tolkien*. Ed. Vincent Ferré. Paris: CNRS Editions, 2012, 3-6

Burdge, Anthony S., and Jessica Burke. "Humiliated Heroes: Peter Jackson's Interpretation of *The Lord the Rings*". *Translating Tolkien: Text and Film*. Ed. Thomas Honegger. Zurich/Jena: Walking Tree Publishers, 2011, 129-158

Carpenter, Humphrey (Ed.). *J.R.R. Tolkien: A Biography* [1977]. London: Allen & Unwin, 1978

Carruthers, Leo (Ed.). *Tolkien et le Moyen Âge*. Paris: CNRS Éditions, 2007

Drout, Michael D.C. (Ed.). *J.R.R. Tolkien Encyclopedia*. New York: Taylor & Francis, 2007

Ferré, Vincent (Ed.). *Dictionnaire Tolkien*. Paris: CNRS Editions, 2012

---. *Tolkien, sur les rivages de la terre du milieu: Le Seigneur des Anneaux de J.R.R. Tolkien*. Paris: Bourgois, 2001

Honegger, Thomas (Ed.). *Translating Tolkien: Text and Film*. Zurich/Jena: Walking Tree Publishers, 2011

Rérolle, Raphaëlle. "Tolkien, l'anneau de la discorde". *Le Monde, Cahier du «Monde»* N° 20983 (July 7, 2012)

Hammond, Wayne G., and Christina Scull. *The J.R.R. Tolkien Companion and Guide*. New York: Houghton Mifflin Company, 2006

Shippey, Tom. "Temptations for All Time". Review of *The Fellowship of the Ring*, directed by Peter Jackson. *Times Literary Supplement* (Dec. 21, 2001), 16-17

---."Another Road to Middle-earth; Jackson's Movie Trilogy". *Understanding The Lord of The Rings. The Best of Tolkien Criticism*. Eds. Rose A. Zimbardo & Neil D. Isaacs. New York: Houghton Mifflin Company, 2004

Timmons, Daniel. "Jackson, Peter". *J.R.R. Tolkien Encyclopedia*. Ed. Michael D.C. Drout. New York: Taylor & Francis, 2007, 303-309

Tolkien, J.R.R. *The Hobbit: or There and Back Again* [1937]. London: Allen & Unwin, 1981

---. *The Fellowship of the Ring* [1954]. London: HarperCollins, 1993

---. *The Two Towers* [1954]. London: HarperCollins, 1993

---. *The Return of the King* [1955]. London: HarperCollins, 1993

---. *Tree and Leaf* [1964]. London: Allen & Unwin, 1964

Splatter in Middle-earth?
War and Violence between Book and Screen — a Comparison
Tobias Hock & Frank Weinreich

> "The canon of narrative art in any medium cannot be wholly different."
> J.R.R. Tolkien, Letter 120

1 Introduction

Fantasy is a violent genre; in its overwhelming majority it tells stories about conflicts at least partially solved by violent means. That is also true of the most influential piece of fantasy, J.R.R. Tolkien's *The Lord of the Rings*.[1] However, a study in 2009 found out that the sheer amount of violence in Tolkien's tale is not as great as one might believe. Only a fifth of the whole text contains violent material and only 8.2% of the story depict violence in a manner of actually describing how persons are harmed by the use of force (Weinreich, *Violence*). Since the three movies by director Peter Jackson are the most influential of the numerous adaptations of the narrative, it has been a desideratum ever since their appearance to compare movie and book in the most valid way possible. The given study does this concerning the topic of violence and with a first cursory look upon the composition of both plots, using quantitative and qualitative means of analysis.

2 Theoretical frameworks

2.1 Violence

The present content analysis of *The Lord of the Rings* focuses on the amount of violence in both versions of LotR. Violence in this study is understood according to the definition of the World Health Organization. It emphasises that violence is characterised mainly by the deliberate use of force with the result of harmful outcomes on the side of the people against whom this force is applied. The analysis of LotR limits itself to a comparatively narrow range of violent occurrences.[2] Violence in the narrative almost exclusively appears as

---

1. For a current account of the influence of Tolkien's *Ring*, see the proceedings of the DTG conference 2012 (*Hither Shore* 9). An overview of the research carried out on Tolkien: in Weinreich & Honegger; an exhaustive study concerning the actual amount of violence in the Ring-narrative: in Weinreich *Violence*.
2. A comprehensive discussion of violence as a general topic of research and the possibilities of limiting it in the analysis of LotR is given in the theoretical framework of Weinreich

interpersonal violence and it consists of physical and, to a much lesser degree, of magical and psychological violence.

2.2 Media Theory: Differences between literature and film

A comparison of Tolkien's novel and Jackson's cinematic adaptation must take into account the fundamental differences between literature and film. We will confine ourselves to elaborating upon aspects of particular importance to the subject and methodological approach of this paper.

The most crucial difference between the two media—especially with regard to a qualitative assessment of the violent material found in a story—is described very accurately by Tolkien himself in his essay *On Fairy-Stories*:

> The radical distinction between all art (including drama) that offers a *visible* presentation and true literature is that it imposes one visible form. Literature works from mind to mind and is thus more progenitive. It is at once more universal and more poignantly particular. If it speaks of *bread* or *wine* or *stone* or *tree*, it appeals to the whole of these things, to their ideas; yet each hearer will give to them a peculiar personal embodiment in his imagination…
> (159)

Tolkien's statement can be applied to his descriptions of violent scenes in LotR: As will be explained in more detail in section 4, Tolkien remains rather vague in his portrayal of actual fighting. Phrases like "Aragorn smote to the ground the captain that stood in his path" (LotR I 432), "Their onset was fierce and sudden, and the Orcs gave way before them" (LotR II 699) or "Beregond was stunned and overborne, and he fell" (LotR III 1169) typically provide no 'graphic' details of the act of killing. Instead, the particulars of fights and battles and their visualization are left to the reader's imagination. Within the framework of Reader-Response-Theory, such literary representations of violence can be said to create visual gaps that have to be filled by the reader's mind:

> What is said only appears to take on significance as a reference to what is not said; it is the implications and not the statements that give shape and weight to the meaning. But as the unsaid comes to life in the reader's imagination, so the said 'expands' to take on greater significance… (Iser 1527)

Violence, cf. 12-14. For the definition of violence:
http://www.who.int/violenceprevention/approach/definition/en/index.html.

By contrast, "film's portrayal of battles is, by definition, more graphic" (Dickerson 66). The director of a film must necessarily opt for one particular way of visualizing a violent scene, thus automatically limiting the audience's imaginative freedom to a high degree. As audio-visual representations of violence are commonly regarded as being potentially more harmful than verbal descriptions,[3] this medium-specific difference between literature and film must be kept in mind when it comes to a comparison between Tolkien's and Jackson's stance on violence.

Another important difference between literature and film is connected with the classical narratological distinction between story-time (i.e. the time the events in a story last) and discourse-time (i.e. the time it takes the narrator or reader to tell or read the story; cf. Neumann & Nünning 72):

> Whereas in novels, movements and hence events are at best constructions imaged by the reader out of words, that is, abstract symbols which are different from them in kind, the movements on the screen are so iconic ... that the illusion of time passage simply cannot be divorced from them. (Chatman 126)

This is important for a comparison between Tolkien's novel and Jackson's movie trilogy insofar as Weinreich (*Violence* 20) in a quantitative content analysis of LotR found out that approximately 20% of the text corpus consists of descriptive passages, during which "story-time stops though discourse continues" (Neumann & Nünning 74). However, a complete arrest of story-time is hardly achievable in films and "if it is the case that story-time necessarily continues to roll in films, and if description entails precisely the arrest of story-time, then it is reasonable to argue that films do not and cannot describe" (Chatman 125). Thus, when comparing the violent material in Tolkien and Jackson on a quantitative basis, one must take into account that several pages of description in the books may be adequately captured in a few seconds of screen time.

The last aspect we want to address are the different capabilities of film and literature to reflect differing points of view. Chatman observes that "[t]he fact that most novels and short stories come to us through the voice of a narrator gives authors a greater range and flexibility than filmmakers" and although cinematic techniques to create different perspectives on an issue do, of course, exist, "the visual point of view in a film is always *there:* it is fixed and determinate precisely because the camera always needs to be placed *somewhere*" (128).

In section 4 of this article, we will elaborate on the fact that Tolkien uses the individual viewpoints of different characters such as the Rohirrim, Faramir or

---

3   However, what media do to the audience is not the point of discussion in this study, so we will not elaborate on that. For a discussion of the effects of violence in the media on a basic level see for example Moser 175-196 or Tulodziecki 201pp.

the Hobbits to provide a balanced picture of war and violence. This "chorus of voices" (Croft 8) to illuminate a topic from different angles is a common tool in narrative literature. In the case of plots presenting multiple perspectives the specific kinds of focalization can be used to present differing values in a balanced manner. The use of different characters as focalising agents, which highlight the plot as a whole, or certain occurrences in the plot from their individual perspectives and their own set of values and convictions, suggests an equivalence of the various viewpoints which provide a reliable picture of a topic only when they are combined.[4]

Jackson, on the other hand, is basically confined to visualising battle scenes in a more presentational mode. Of course, a director also has several tools at hand in order to shed a more positive or a more negative light on scenes of war and violence, but there still remains a qualitative medium-specific difference to be considered.

3 Quantitative Analysis

3.1 Methodology

The system of categories applied to the content consists of three basic categories with differentiated sub-categories. The basic categories are classified as "Non-Violence", "Violence" and "In-between" as a third main category, into which fall descriptions, moments, or scenes of tension and suspense without actual violence. For the purposes of this study the category "In-between" can be subsumed under the department of non-violent content. "In-between" is, however, deliberately not omitted since this category will be extremely helpful in further analyses of the composition of the narratives, though only to a much lesser degree in the present article.[5]

The main categories are divided into more meaningful sub-categories. The category "Non-Violence" is split into two sub-categories, "Descriptions" and "Interaction". These sub-categories are then divided into more detailed parts. The main category "Violence" is split into actual violence on the one hand and indirect violence on the other, which consists of violent occurrences that are mentioned but not described in detail, for example historic events like the battle

---

4   See Gutenberg 125: "Gerade im Falle von multiperspektivisch konzipierten Romanplots kann die spezifische Art der (variablen) Fokalisierung als Verfahren der Werterelativierung eingesetzt werden. Wenn verschiedene Figuren als Fokalisierungsinstanzen fungieren und dieselbe Geschichte aus ihrer jeweiligen Perspektive und aus ihrem individuellen Voraussetzungssystem heraus schildern, kann damit eine Enthierarchisierung von Perspektiven nahegelegt werden, indem erst alle Versionen zusammengenommen (die Stimmenvielfalt) ein einigermaßen zuverlässiges Bild ergeben..."
5   See Weinreich *Violence*, p. 15, for a graphic representation of the system of categories. In that paper, the methodology is also discussed in greater detail. See another version here: http://polyoinos.de/tolk_stuff/violence_lotr.html.

of Mount Doom. The categories underwent peer discussion and were modified accordingly, intercoder-reliability was measured.

The basis for the analyses is on the one hand the novel *The Lord of the Rings* which amounts to a total of a little more than 2.5 million characters or 433,000 words, and on the other hand the films in their extended version on BluRay disc from 2011, consisting of 38,775 seconds or 10 hours 46 minutes. In the films credits were omitted, in the books the appendices and the chapter "Concerning Hobbits".

3.2 Results

The following results are descriptive first impressions out of a much greater number of possible analyses. But even these first results provide interesting details and encourage further examination.

3.2.1 Basic data: violent and non-violent content

The most basic findings concerning violence in *The Lord of the Rings* show that the book consists of 80% while the film is made up of 61% of non-violent content. Furthermore, the distinction between indirectly reported violence and the direct and graphic depiction of violence yields an amount of 8.2% of direct violence in Tolkien's original version of the story and 17% in Jackson's adaptation. This difference can roughly be observed throughout the whole plot, although some variances do occur which shed a light on slight distinctions in the plot construction and thus on the differing emphasis that is put on certain aspects. This aspect can only be reported very briefly in this paper, but the amount of violent and non-violent content according to the somewhat artificial[6] division of the story into the form of a trilogy may serve as an example for this.

While violent aspects—and thus elements of "action" in the story, which almost always are constructed around violent occurrences—amount to a mere 4% in the book LotR I, Peter Jackson obviously found a need to get the story going in a more violent manner with more than thrice the amount of violence, 14.2%. A qualitative indicator for this is the beginning of the movie with the battle of Mount Doom which in Tolkien is reported at a much later point and in an indirect way. This not-in-the-book-scene of 170 seconds also contributes 10% of the whole violence in Jackson's *Fellowship*. Another example of such differences are the fighting scenes in Moria which make up approximately 1% of the corpus of LotR I and 3% of the first film. Later on, book and film do not

---

6 As is known Tolkien did not mean to write a trilogy, although the division of a story into three parts later on became typical in fantasy (cf. Weinreich *Fantasy* 139).

differ as much, since on the one hand Tolkien provides more violent scenes, Peter Jackson on the other hand no longer shows actual violence in the same way he does in his *Fellowship*, although he still shows more than the book (see Table 1).

	non-violent content book / film	indirect violence book / film	direct violence book / film
LotR, overall	80% / 61%	11.8% / 24%	8.2% / 17%
LotR I	88.5% / 75.5%	7.5% / 10.3%	4% / 14.2%
LotR II	78.5% / 50.9%	11.5% / 31.4%	10.5% / 17.7%
LotR III	69.5% / 52.2%	19% / 29.7%	11.5% / 18.1%

Table 1, basic data

Non-violent content
The descriptive part of a fantasy novel is responsible for the creation of depth in the imaginary world and its occurrences (cf. Weinreich *Fantasy* 24-26). If these descriptions are imaginative, they allow for a sense of wonder and immersion into the fictional world. The given numbers, though, do not allow judgement of the quality of these descriptions.

There is a great discrepancy to be found regarding the amount of descriptive parts in the books and the films. The books consist to a third of descriptions of landscapes, people and customs and so on, while the films only show mere descriptions to an extent of 15% of their total length. However, that is mainly due to the fundamental differences in storytelling in literature and cinema as is discussed in part 2.2: films do not describe as books do. Although Jackson has much less descriptions in his films, this does not mean that he neglects his world-building, since many of the parts that drive the story on a second level also describe the world and provide depth to it. The layout of a city like Minas Tirith can be taken in by the viewer in a few seconds while Gandalf and Pippin are approaching it, but Tolkien has to stop story-time and invest quite an amount of discourse-time to 'display' the same thing (two pages in the book; reading this detailed part takes at least two minutes).

While on the one hand interaction in narratives has to drive the story, on the other hand it illustrates the characters, giving flesh to their bones. Thus, interaction plays a great part in the reader's ability to relate to the protagonists or to even identify with them. This is especially true of those portions of the interaction which do not have the main task of keeping the story going. It is thus presumably a strength of both versions of LotR that they do take their time of around one third of the whole story to tell or display people's behaviour and thus make them believable in a way which is kin to the giving of depth to the world in the descriptive parts (see Table 2).

	non-violent descriptions book / film	non-violent interaction book / film
LotR	34% / 15%	33% / 29%
LotR I	35% / 20.6%	38.6% / 27.1%
LotR II	34.9% / 12%	31.6% / 30.8%
LotR III	27.8% / 8.8%	27.7% / 29.9%

Table 2, non-violent content

It is important to point out that the placement of descriptions and interaction within the plot despite their quantitative differences is of remarkable similarity.

Violent content

The violent content is divided first into the actual description of violent occurrences—actual violence—which are depicted mostly as ongoing war and fighting, but also include actual threats, vivid reports, abuse and harmful magical influences. Secondly, violence-related material is coded as situations leading to violence (preparations for battle, strategic considerations), or situations after violence occurred (depictions of flight, death, wounds or mourning) and any kind of reported violence in a distant kind of depiction, for example stories from Middle-earth's violent history or reports of incidents which are not actually described, as in the case of the demise of Théoden's son in a skirmish far away. This distinction is made for two reasons:

- There is a differing quality in the experience of fictitious violence. It is most plausible that it is foremost the depiction of actual fighting, threats and abuse which affects the recipients. Further discussion on the effects of violence in LotR can thus be based on the findings in this category.[7]

- Indirect violence is much more suited to take a critical stance on violence than the depiction of violence. Jackson's impressions of people preparing for a fight, for example as shown before the battle of Helm's Deep with close-up shots of frightened boys and old men during the distribution of weapons, are unquestionably a condemnation of warfare. The same is true regarding most scenes of mourning or the depiction of dying and wounded combatants. While it is possible to achieve an arousing or glorifying effect by the use of indirect violence—Théoden's speech on the Pelennor Fields may be read in this way—in most cases in book and film indirectly reported violence and war are shown critically.

The difference in the extent of violence in LotR is great. As given above, the entirety of violent material amounts to 20%, which includes 8.2% of actual

---

[7] Possible effects of violence are, however, not scrutinised in this study, since it is important in this first step to just identify the occurrence of violence.

violence, while the numbers for Jackson are 41% and 17%. The fact that there is comparatively little violence in a story which tells the events of the Great War of the Ring is somewhat surprising but supports the observations of critics like Charles Williams or Matthew Dickerson, who argue that not war or heroism but friendship, beauty and the advantages of ordinary life lie at the centre of LotR.[8]

The composition of the plot in Jackson mostly shows more action and violence but remains true to the overall proportions. Where the films differ to a greater extent, this is due to the different requirements of films in general, as is discussed in part 2.2, or with regard to its role as a blockbuster, which requires following certain rules[9] of economically successful film-making. This explains for example that the first movie contains more than thrice the amount of violence than the book; a difference which is far greater than in the other films, which take less liberties compared to the original plot (see Table 1).

3.2.2 Composition of the stories

Both versions of LotR tell the same story or, as Peter Jackson has more than one time insisted upon, the movie tries to follow the plot of the original narrative to the most possible extent. But do the quantitative data verify this assumption?

Composition overall

A look at the trilogical division of the story at first glance shows a great difference between the novel and films. While the books become shorter in the telling, the films grow in length. Tolkien's LotR I encompasses 978,299 characters (without *Concerning Hobbits*), LotR II 826,264, and LotR III 718,200 (without appendices). Jackson's *Fellowship* lasts 11,755 seconds, his *Towers* 12,680, and the *King* 14,340 (each without credits). At first glance this is a remarkable difference in composition, which happens mainly because of two factors. First, Jackson (mostly for the sake of action and thus with a strong focus on mainly violent content) shows things or scenes which are not told as explicitly in the novel or were even invented for the movies. The attack of the Warg Riders on the fleeing Rohirrim in *Towers*, which is not told at all in Tolkien, may serve as an example, or the vivid depiction of battle scenes which are only reported in the book (the loss of Osgiliath, the attack on Isengard). Second, he does not have to interrupt story-time for the sake of discourse-time, which leads to comparatively longer scenes that drive the story, which take more room in LotR II an III. A more detailed look at the composition of both plots shows that the differences, however, are not so great anymore.

---

8 Cf. Dickerson chapter 1, esp. p. 27. Williams's opinion is quoted by Tolkien himself in one of his letters, in which he also declares that Williams's observation is right (Tolkien *Letters*, L. 93, p. 105).
9 See Julian Eilmann's article concerning this topic in this issue.

Composition in detail
The composition of the plots can be studied best by breaking up the story in smaller acts and then measuring the amount of words respectively the length of film in proportion to the story as a whole. LotR was split into eight acts: an intro, which leads up to the Old Forest (respectively Bree in the movie, since the Old Forest does not appear in Jackson), a first journey from Bree to Imladris, a second journey from Imladris to the breaking of the Fellowship at Amon Hen, a first part of the Aragorn-leg leading from Amon Hen to Helm's Deep (battle included), a first Frodo-leg from Amon Hen to Cirith Ungol, a second Aragorn-leg from Isengard to the Black Gate, a second Frodo-leg from Cirith Ungol to the slopes of Mount Doom, and a last part which begins on the Field of Cormallen and ends with Sam's "I'm back" (see Table 3).

	Intro	Journey 1	Journey 2	Aragorn 1	Frodo 1	Aragorn 2	Frodo 2	End
Book	9.9%	16.7%	11.9%	15.1%	14.5%	16.8%	6%	8.6%
Films	8.7%	7.8%	14.1%	22.5%	15.3%	23.2%	4.4%	3.4%

Table 3, composition of the story by division into eight acts (percentages are given in relation to the whole story)

The parts which are most important for the development of the story are quite similar in both versions, while deviations are due to an emphasis on action in the movies and a necessity to abbreviate a long story in certain parts in unison with the special properties of cinematic narration which allow for creating atmosphere and background while at the same time driving the plot, as is discussed above. So it turns out that Jackson can make much more haste in Journey 1 and the last act than Tolkien, but holds true to the original in both Frodo-legs. That action, and thus violence, plays a greater role in Jackson can be seen in the higher percentages of the Aragorn-legs, where the great battles of LotR are told. To a lesser extent this can also be seen in Journey 2, where the higher percentage in the film is due to longer sequences in Moria and at Amon Hen, both mainly showing attacks.

Selected scenes
The findings regarding the composition, which shed a light on the differing circumstances of writing and filming, are supported if one takes a look at selected scenes. The camp at Amon Sûl makes up 0.2% of the whole book and three quarters of this scene are of non-violent content before the Nazgûl attack. In Jackson the same scene makes up 0.6% of which three quarters show the violent skirmish. The chapter *The Council of Elrond* is the longest in LotR. In Tolkien it amounts to 3.4% of the whole narrative, while Jackson abbreviates it to 1.3%, telling the reports given therein much faster and with less detail. Tolkien lets 4.6% of the *Ring* play in Lothlórien, much of it descriptions of this wonderful

forest, which is responsible for a great part of the sense of wonder found in Middle-earth. Jackson's fellows stay in that place for 2.6%, but Jackson has the advantage to be able to show Mellyrn and Elvish life without the necessity to stop story-time. The Battle of Helm's Deep is a crucial but—regarding its length—minor event in Tolkien: 1.4%. Jackson makes that 5.4%, but he also enriches it with the Battle of Isengard, which in Tolkien is told in a few words by Merry and Pippin, and he lets Elves arrive at the scene—a crucial point in its own right since this shows the still existent friendship between Elves and Men in the form of one big sacrifice, embodied in Haldir and Aragorn; a friendship Tolkien had room to hint at in a more subtle manner on various occasions. The Battle on the Pelennor Fields is a major event even in Tolkien: 4.5% and nearly all of it actual violence. Jackson shows more, but he does not exaggerate in an undue manner: 8.3%.

As a last point the topics of Sex and Romance have to be mentioned: sex, since it sells in films, usually; Romance, since it is a motive abundant in the genre of fantasy literature. But there is no sex, neither in Tolkien nor in Jackson, although the latter quite as well could have shown some; elsewhere did he take liberties enough. Romance occurs in LotR at only[10] two occasions in one chapter: when Faramir and Éowyn get to know each other, and this amounts to 0.7%. Jackson instead shows romantic scenes of thrice that size (2.2%), and he distributes it all over the movies in twelve chapters spread throughout all films.

4 Qualitative Analysis

Interesting though they are, quantitative data can only provide some first hints and cautious hypotheses about Tolkien's and Jackson's individual representations of war and violence. Therefore, this section aims at a close examination of the medium-specific (i.e. literary and cinematic) means Tolkien and Jackson use. The underlying questions are: In how much detail are violent acts described? What aspects in the works highlight negative consequences of war and violence, thus functioning as a counterbalance to potentially brutal or glorifying depictions? How is violence morally justified in Tolkien and Jackson?

We want to begin by looking at the linguistic and narrative features Tolkien uses in those passages of LotR that contain violent material. So far, there has been no detailed analysis of the language Tolkien uses to describe battle scenes. Critics focusing on war in Tolkien's works usually deal with biographical aspects. Statements about linguistic issues are mostly vague. For example, Fawcett asserts

---

10 That does not mean that Middle-earth is not a romantic place. The appendices tell a highly romantic story describing the life of Aragorn and Arwen, but those were not included in this analysis. And the *Silmarillion*, of course, is full of romantic tales. It is well known that Tolkien depicted the love of his own real life, his wife Edith, in Middle-earth in various manners, but he did not tell romantic tales in the LotR.

that "[t]he actual battles are addressed with brevity, with as much description of character and setting given prior and following, passing over the clash itself with a sense of disgust" (200). Dickerson probably provides the most detailed examination of the great battles in LotR, continually repeating his observation that there are only few 'graphic' details (e.g. 23, 28 or 41). Basically, there are two important claims that can be extracted from Dickerson's elaborations that we want to corroborate with some textual examples:

(1) Tolkien very often focuses on the feelings of individuals experiencing the horrors of war rather than on the fighting itself.

(2) When fighting is actually mentioned, it is often "described in broad brushstrokes ... from a high and distant perspective" (23).

The first statement is especially apparent in the chapters on the Siege of Gondor and the Battle of the Pelennor Fields: Faramir's retreat from Osgiliath and the attack of the Nazgûl are observed by Pippin and Beregond on the walls of Minas Tirith. Comments like "Ah! I cannot stand it!" or "Help! help! Will no one go out to him?" highlight the characters' feelings; details of the fight are restricted to rather general descriptions like "the men are thrown" or "one of the foul things is stooping on him" (LotR III 1058-1059). Throughout the pages dealing with Sauron's attack on Gondor, the narrative focus switches to the feelings of the citizens, e.g. "The next day came with a morning like a brown dusk, and the hearts of men... sank low again" (LotR III 1067), and comparable scenes.

A similar effect is achieved in almost all battles (except for Helm's Deep) by the presence of at least one Hobbit. As it is stated in the prologue to LotR, Hobbits "love peace and quiet" (LotR I 1), and "[a]t no time had Hobbits of any kind been warlike" (LotR I 7). Of course, Bilbo, Frodo, Sam, Merry and Pippin become engaged in fighting during the course of the tale, but there remains a natural aversion to violence in them that is exploited to give a balanced picture to the battles in Tolkien's work, to "de-glorify [war] when others have glorified it" (Dickerson 33).

Another aspect is Tolkien's focus on the suffering experienced after a battle. As Fawcett observes, "[n]o battle... passes without the loss of a named or defined character, with the exception of the Black Gate" (200). A whole chapter (*The Houses of Healing*) is spent on the deep (physical as well as mental) wounds the characters have suffered during battle. The chapter *The Battle of the Pelennor Fields* ends with an enumeration of the fallen and a song composed to memorise them (LotR III 1111-1112).

We now want to focus on how Tolkien describes actual scenes of fighting. Dickerson observes that Tolkien typically provides few 'graphic' details of armed combat, but prefers to describe the battles from a distant perspective. This can be illustrated by analysing the Battle of Helm's Deep (LotR II 686-707).

A significant part of the chapter (LotR II 686-694) deals with the arrival of the Rohirrim at Helm's Deep, a description of the Hornburg and the characters' waiting for Saruman's army. After that the actual battle begins, but "[t]he greater part of the narrative is devoted to dialogue among the defenders during moments of respite" (Dickerson 41), e.g. when Aragorn and Éomer discuss how to defend the main gates (LotR II 697), what hope the dawn may bring (LotR II 700) or when Aragorn and Théoden prepare for the last attack (LotR II 702-703).

In his description of the actual battle, Tolkien often uses imagery from the semantic field of tempests (especially at sea). For example, the forces of Isengard "wavered, broke, and fled back; and then charged again... and each time, like the incoming sea, they halted at a higher point" (LotR II 695); at another point "they were swept away" (LotR II 696). "Against the Deeping Wall the hosts of Isengard roared like a sea" (LotR II 698) and finally "the last assault came sweeping like a dark wave upon a hill of sand" (LotR II 701), to name but a few examples. Similar images are found in the other battles. Tolkien's use of figurative language focuses the account of the battles on the masses, away from brutal hand-to-hand fighting. Even when Tolkien concentrates on individuals, he is typically sparing in giving violent details. For example, when Aragorn attacks the Orcs, it is merely stated that "Andúril rose and fell" (LotR II 696); the rest is left to the reader's imagination.

Another interesting observation is that very often when the narrative focuses on the killing of people, Tolkien confines himself to short clauses containing a single verb with the semantic meaning of 'to kill' or 'being killed'. A few examples (our emphasis):

> I beheld the last combat on the slopes of Orodruin, where Gil-galad *died*, and Elendil *fell*, ... but Sauron himself was *overthrown*...
> (LotR I 316)
> ... many *perished* at the crossing.   (LotR II 688)
> ... Beregond was stunned and *overborne*, and he *fell*. (LotR III 1169)

Of course, LotR also contains some passages in which Tolkien is more explicit regarding violent details.[11] However, such 'graphic' descriptions occur most often when Orcs, trolls or other beasts are involved and they are mostly restricted to one or two sentences.

Still, the general hate and brutality shown towards the race of Orcs by all the Free Peoples of Middle-earth remains very ambivalent. A particularly disturbing scene occurs during the Battle of Helm's Deep: Legolas and Gimli engage in a contest to determine who can kill more Orcs. This can reasonably be regarded as a belittlement of war.

---

11 For example, during the Battle at the Black Gate "Pippin stabbed upwards, and the written blade of Westernesse pierced through the hide and went deep into the vitals of the troll, and his black blood came gushing out" (LotR III 1169).

Also, any reader of LotR will remember that now and again there is a strong focus on heroic feats and the glory that a warrior can find in battle. Therefore, we want to take the Rohirrim's relation to war as a starting point to examine the various concepts of heroism in LotR and the different moral attitudes towards war and violence that are connected to them.

When it comes to the evocation of heroic feats in battle one of the most memorable scenes in LotR certainly is the attack of the Rohirrim at the Battle of the Pelennor Fields. When the Riders finally reach the besieged city of Minas Tirith, Théoden cries to his soldiers:

> *Arise, arise, Riders of Théoden!*
> *Fell deeds awake: fire and slaughter!*
> *spear shall be shaken, shield be splintered,*
> *a sword-day, a red day, ere the sun rises!*
> *Ride now, ride now! Ride to Gondor!*
> ... Suddenly the king cried to Snowmane and the horse sprang away. Behind him his banner blew in the wind, white horse upon a field of green, but he outpaced it... Fey he seemed, or the battle-fury of his fathers ran like new fire in his veins, and he was borne up on Snowmane like a god of old... His golden shield was uncovered and lo! it shone like an image of the Sun, and the grass flamed into green about the white feet of his steed.   (LotR III 1096-1097)

With this, Fawcett argues, "Tolkien catches the spirit of the medieval heroic society, including idealised valour and physical strength, which carries over into the presentation of battle" (199). Here Tolkien's use of the 'epic style' is most intense ('Fell deeds', 'slaughter', 'a sword-day, a red day'). The imagery of light ('His golden shield... shone like an image of the Sun, and the grass flamed into green') and the alliterative linking of singing and slaying ('sang as they slew'; a few lines further on, LotR III 1097) are but few examples of how Tolkien depicts a culture focused on war, glorious deeds and their remembrance in songs (Slack 119-120).

However, Tolkien is well aware of the fallacies of such heroism and also presents a kind of 'pragmatic heroism' which probably comes closest to his own stance on war and violence. Faramir for example says: "War must be, while we defend our lives against a destroyer who would devour all; but I do not love the bright sword for its sharpness, nor the arrow for its swiftness, nor the warrior for his glory. I love only that which they defend..." (LotR II 878). Moreover, he criticises that the men of Gondor "now love war and valour as things good in themselves, both a sport and an end; and though we still hold that a warrior should have more skills and knowledge than only the craft of weapons and slaying, we esteem a warrior, nonetheless, above men of other crafts" (LotR II 887).

This must obviously be read as a criticism of the glorification of violence and the appreciation of war for the sake of honour. Apart from the two types of heroism already mentioned, there is yet a third type to be found in LotR, namely that of the Hobbits.

Hobbits are not used to war and violence, they even profoundly disrelish them. Although Hobbits also have to fight at some points in the story, their heroism consists to a much higher degree in true loyalty towards their companions and their willingness to face any danger despite their fear. They are a reflection of the common man, having no extraordinary (e.g. physical or spiritual) strengths that would make them 'heroic' in the traditional sense. Hobbits embody the "heroism of the ordinary" (Vince 9); personal glory is completely alien to them.

One might easily be inclined to label the Hobbits' attitude as 'pacifist'. However, Tolkien objects to purely pacifist approaches to war and violence. There are two very good examples in LotR that illustrate what Nan C. Scott calls "the pacifist's dilemma" (quoted in Croft 130):

The first refers to Tom Bombadil. According to Tolkien, he represents a "natural pacifist view" (L 179). However, his existence depends on the heroic deeds of others: "Ultimately only the victory of the West will allow Bombadil to continue or even to survive" (L 179).

A similar problem arises during the Scouring of the Shire: Frodo is reluctant to use violence in order to free the Hobbits, but Merry and Pippin understand that the use of force might be necessary. Eventually, without their military efforts the Shire could not have been saved.

The issue these two examples raise is summarised best by Éowyn's statement that "those who have not swords can still die upon them" (LotR III 1256). Pacifism may be admirable as a moral conviction, but Tolkien makes it very clear that complete non-violence is ineffective if faced with the ultimate evil represented by Sauron.

In summary, LotR displays the tensions between "physical heroism" and "spiritual heroism" (Chance 147) and between traditional and modern concepts of the hero. Tolkien portrays societies in which war and feats of arms are central cultural components, but at the same time he relativises this attitude by creating characters such as Faramir, who regards war and violence as an inconvenient necessity, or the Hobbits, who show a natural aversion to physical combat.

All the different types of heroism can be subsumed under Slack's notion of "heroism of choice" (121). With regard to the topic of war and violence, Slack's hypothesis is that "Tolkien... suggests that the moral and spiritual capacity to... choose rightly must be the precursor to any deed in battle" (121). This is directly connected to issues of ethical justifications of violence, for it is above all moral principles that guide the characters' choices and their stance on virtue and war in particular. According to Slack, Tolkien uses the different concepts of heroism "as a way of exploring and re-envisioning a just war" (119).

While most critics seem to agree that Tolkien's picture of war and violence is differentiated, Peter Jackson is very often accused of too heavily focusing on action and fighting in his adaptation. The following quotations may serve as an exemplary selection of critical statements with regard to Jackson's cinematic representation of violence:

> "A book about imaginatively conceived characters on a lengthy journey interspersed with skirmishes has been turned into what some might see as a gallery of battles and monsters". (Thompson 54)
> Valente claims that the film features a general "toning down of majesty" and eliminates "fundamental moral and philosophical concerns". (quoted in Ricke & Barnett 276)
> "It is rather like an adaptation of *War and Peace* that omits peace". (Ricke & Barnett 276)
> "As for fights, the films' battle scenes go on and on… Tolkien's moral sense has been nearly completely lost, and the story reduced to a series of battles which are carefully avoided or distanced in Tolkien's narration, when they're in the book at all". (Bratman 29-30)

Criticism on Jackson can be divided into a quantitative and a qualitative component, i.e. in statements like "the films are almost exclusively about action and fighting" on the one hand and "the subtleties of Tolkien's moral comments on the topic of war and violence are lost in Jackson's trilogy" on the other. The quantitative aspects of this criticism have already been refuted or at least relativised in section 3. The following focuses on a qualitative assessment.

Verlyn Flieger summarises one of the key problems of modern film adaptations very nicely:

> The very pictographic opportunities of film, the ways in which photography can both enhance and manipulate reality, frequently tempt filmmakers to extend the visual beyond what the story needs simply because it is feasible to do so. The attitude seems to be that if it can be done it must be done—and all too often with computer-enhanced technology, done to death, resulting not infrequently in effect for the sake of effect rather than to support the story or the theme. (47)

Naturally, Jackson avails himself of a wide range of cinematic devices that enhance the impression of violence and brutality in a scene: sound effects (clanging of swords, war cries, the noises of the Orcs' death rattles) create a far more vivid and immediate picture of warfare than a distanced description in a novel possibly can. Moreover, Howard Shore's score highlights the epic and heroic moment of violence. Many critics have commented on the film's make-up and art design, which in some respects adhere to the conventions of the horror genre (where, after all, Jackson's roots as a filmmaker lie). There are also some explicitly brutal scenes in the films, e.g. Aragorn beheading Lurtz, Gothmog being hacked to pieces in the extended version of *King* or other Orcs being viciously stabbed. Still, the battle scenes could have been far bloodier than they actually are (after all, the films have received a PG-13 rating).

Apart from that, there are two further aspects in the criticism of Jackson's adaptation mentioned most frequently: several 'critical' character changes and the inclusion of fighting scenes which are either less prominent in the books or not mentioned in Tolkien at all. Since an exhaustive treatment of these changes and the reasons that led to them is not possible here, some crucial examples must suffice to illustrate Jackson's stance on violence:

In our view, one of the most serious diversions from Tolkien's moral attitude towards violence is Aragorn's commanding "Show them no mercy, for you shall receive none" before the Battle of Helm's Deep. While the lack of mercy may be compatible with Tolkien's treatment of Orcs to some degree, it nevertheless goes completely against the religious and ethical worldview established in the novel, especially the importance of pity and mercy (e.g. with regard to Gollum). Also, Tolkien's Aragorn would never simply kill an ambassador as he does in the extended version of *King*. Similar arguments are brought forth with regard to the characters of Gandalf (Bratman 50) and Faramir (Thompson 68-69). The latter case is also notable insofar as Faramir's 'War must be'-speech quoted above, which is arguably the most important passage in Tolkien concerning the topic of war and violence, is omitted in the film. Other examples are the duel between Gandalf and Saruman, the prolonged fighting in Moria or the Warg-attack (cf. section 3).

It would be unfair to finish this section without mentioning that Jackson, like Tolkien, also presents explicitly anti-violent attitudes in his films and does not forget to broach the issue of loss and suffering caused by war. The accusation that the characters in the films do not "pause often for reflection, lamentation, poetry, song, moral inventory, refocusing, wrestling with their consciences, and debating their commitment to the mission before them" (Ricke & Barnett 276) cannot be maintained considering scenes such as Gandalf and Frodo debating about the importance of mercy in Moria, Boromir's emotional death scene, the separation of a mother and her children during Saruman's attack on Rohan at the beginning of *Towers* or the obviously futile attack on Osgiliath into which Faramir is forced by his father, all of which are true to Tolkien's picture of war and violence. Moreover, Mikos et al. observe that Jackson frequently tries to add an emotional component to the otherwise technical aspects of warfare by including close-ups of frightened civilians, e.g. during the Battle of Helm's Deep (96-97).

Conclusion

The quantitative comparison shows that Jackson emphasises action and violence more than the novel, but taking into account the differences between the two media he does not seem to exaggerate in an undue manner. There is a certain bias towards action and violence, but the proportions of the story in the films are otherwise true to the book. The qualitative analysis—although to a greater extent a matter of interpretation—supports the quantitative analysis in the thesis that Jackson and Tolkien do differ in their stance on violence, but that the difference is not as significant as some critics suggest.

Eventually, master and adaptation do differ, but there are also many similarities: While they mainly differ in quantitative dimensions and in the intensity of their emphasis on the heroic dimension of war and violence, both are not that different in their outline of the negative consequences of war or in their portrayal of loss, suffering and anti-violent attitudes. However, the visually opulent battle scenes as well as some striking deviations from Tolkien's novel probably have a great impact on the audience, which might have sparked the criticism mentioned above.

Furthermore, the method of this study has proven to be an approach of literary analysis that in its combination of quantitative and qualitative data is able to produce remarkable results, which can be a valuable supplement in the research of literature and other media products. Further analysis of content—other books, films, computer games, audio dramas—is strongly encouraged, within the genre and across genre borders. Even a thorough analysis of just one story leaves one with the strong desire for further comparisons.

Bibliography

Bratman, David. "Summa Jacksonica: A Reply to Defenses of Peter Jackson's *The Lord of the Rings* Films, after St. Thomas Aquinas." *Tolkien on Film: Essays on Peter Jackson's* The Lord of the Rings. Ed. Janet Brennan Croft. Altadena, CA: The Mythopoeic Press, 2004, 27-62

Chance, Jane. *Tolkien's Art: A Mythology for England*. Rev. ed. Lexington: University Press of Kentucky, 2001

Chatman, Seymour. "What Novels Can Do That Films Can't (and Vice Versa)." *On Narrative*. Ed. W.J.T. Mitchell. Chicago, London: The University of Chicago Press, 1981, 117-136

Croft, Janet Brennan. *War and the Works of J.R.R.Tolkien*. London: Praeger, 2004

Dickerson, Matthew. *Following Gandalf – Epic Battles and Moral Victory in* The Lord of the Rings. Grand Rapids: Brazos Press, 2003

Eilmann, Julian. Erzählstrukturen in J.R.R. Tolkiens *Der Herr der Ringe* und Peter Jacksons Filmadaption. *Hither Shore* 10 (2013): 62-75

Fawcett, Christina. "Reluctant Warrior: Tolkien's conflicted language in *The Lord of the Rings*." *Proceedings of the Tolkien 2005 Conference: 50 Years of* The Lord of the Rings. *Vol. 2.* Ed. Sarah Wells. Coventry: Tolkien Society, 2008, 198-203

Flieger, Verlyn. "Sometimes One Word Is Worth A Thousand Pictures." *Picturing Tolkien: Essays on Peter Jackson's The Lord of the Rings Film Trilogy.* Eds. Janice M. Bogstad & Philip E. Kaveny. Jefferson, NC: McFarland & Company, 2011, 46-53

Gutenberg, Andrea. *Mögliche Welten: Plot und Sinnstiftung im englischen Frauenroman.* Heidelberg: Winter, 2000

Honegger, Thomas et al. *Eine Grammatik der Ethik. Die Aktualität der moralischen Dimension in J.R.R. Tolkiens literarischem Werk.* Saarbrücken: Verlag der Villa Fledermaus, 2005

Iser, Wolfgang. "Interaction between Text and Reader." 1980. *The Norton Anthology of Theory and Criticism.* Ed. Vincent B. Leitch. 2nd ed. New York/London: W.W. Norton & Company, 2010, 1524-1532

Mikos, Lothar et al. *Die »Herr der Ringe«-Trilogie: Attraktion und Faszination eines populärkulturellen Phänomens.* Konstanz: UVK, 2007

Moser, Heinz. *Einführung in die Medienpädagogik. Aufwachsen im Medienzeitalter.* Opladen: Leske & Budrich, 2000

Neumann, Birgit, and Ansgar Nünning. *An Introduction to the Study of Narrative Fiction.* UNI-WISSEN Anglistik|Amerikanistik. Stuttgart: Klett, 2008

Ricke, Joseph, and Catherine Barnett. "Filming the Numinous: The Fate of Lothlórien in Peter Jackson's *The Lord of the Rings*." *Picturing Tolkien: Essays on Peter Jackson's* The Lord of the Rings *Film Trilogy.* Eds. Janice M. Bogstad & Philip E. Kaveny. Jefferson, NC: McFarland & Company, 2011, 264-285

Slack, Anna. "Clean Earth to Till: A Tolkienian Vision of War." *Hither Shore 6* (2009): 116-129

Thompson, Kristin. *The Frodo Franchise. The Lord of the Rings and Modern Hollywood.* Berkeley/Los Angeles, University of California Press, 2007

Tolkien, J.R.R. "On Fairy-Stories." *The Monsters and the Critics and Other Essays.* 1983. Ed. Christopher Tolkien. London: HarperCollins, 2006, 109-161

---. *The Fellowship of the Ring – being the first part of The Lord of the Rings.* 1954. London: HarperCollins, 1991

---. *The Return of the King – being the third part of The Lord of the Rings.* 1955. London: HarperCollins, 1991

---. *The Two Towers – being the second part of The Lord of the Rings.* 1954. London: HarperCollins, 1991

---. *The Letters of J.R.R.Tolkien.* 1981. Eds. Humphrey Carpenter & Christopher Tolkien. London: HarperCollins, 2006

Tulodziecki, Gerhard. *Medien in Erziehung und Bildung.* Grundlagen und Beispiele einer handlungs- und entwicklungsorientierten Medienpädagogik. Bad Heilbrunn: Klinkhardt, 1997

Vince, Raymond M. *War, Heroism, and Narrative – Hemingway, Tolkien and le Carré, Storytellers to the Modern World.* Saarbrücken: VDM, 2008

Weinreich, Frank. *Fantasy. Einführung.* Essen: Oldib, 2007

---. "Violence in *The Lord of the Rings*". *Hither Shore 6* (2009): 10-26

Weinreich, Frank, und Thomas Honegger. »Die aktuelle Tolkienforschung im Überblick. Personen – Organisationen – Verlage – Werke«. *Zeitschrift für Fantastikforschung* 2 (2011): 63-89

World Health Organization (Ed.). WHO Definition of 'Health'. *World Report on Violence and Health.* 2009: http://www.who.int/violenceprevention/approach/definition/en/index.html (29/10/2103)

Erzählstrukturen in J.R.R. Tolkiens *Der Herr der Ringe* und Peter Jacksons Filmadaption

Julian Tim Morton Eilmann (Aachen)

Obwohl die Kinopremiere des letzten Teils von Peter Jacksons *Herr der Ringe*-Filmtrilogie inzwischen mehr als zehn Jahre zurückliegt und viele Filme eine Dekade nach ihrem Erscheinen bereits wieder in Vergessenheit geraten sind, hat Jacksons Filmadaption eines literarischen Klassikers doch eine erstaunliche Popularität bewahrt. Angesichts der andauernden Beliebtheit der *Herr der Ringe*-Filme lässt sich ohne Übertreibung sagen, dass Jacksons Filme als Gesamtwerk heute fest zum populärkulturellen Kanon gehören und somit selbst als (Film)-Klassiker wahrgenommen werden.[1] Zwar wurden die *Herr der Ringe*-Filme von Seiten der Tolkien-Forschung auch kontrovers diskutiert und mitunter abgelehnt, weil befürchtet wurde, durch den Filmhype gerate das literarische Werk aus dem Blick. Dennoch ändern diese Einwände nichts an der Tatsache, dass die Tolkien-Forschung im eigenen Interesse dazu aufgefordert ist, sich mit diesem Phänomen auseinanderzusetzen, werfen die Filme doch mehr als alles andere die Frage auf, was eine so große Anzahl an Menschen an dieser Literaturverfilmung fasziniert. Es bleibt also festzuhalten, dass an Jacksons wirkungsmächtiger Filmreihe kein Weg vorbeiführt, wenn man sich ernsthaft mit der Rezeption Tolkiens zu Beginn des 21. Jahrhunderts befasst.

Viel ist in den vergangen zehn Jahren darüber diskutiert worden, in welchen Aspekten Jackson von Tolkiens Vorlage abweicht. In den meisten Fällen ging es von Seiten der Tolkien-Leser darum, die Filme mit der literarischen Vorlage zu vergleichen, auf Abweichungen hinzuweisen und abzuschätzen, inwiefern solche Änderungen als gelungen oder verfehlt anzusehen sind (vgl. Rateliff 61ff). Um den Vergleich von Buch und Film geht es auch im Folgenden, allerdings liegt der Fokus hier auf den unterschiedlichen Erzählweisen der beiden Medien, d.h. Fragen der Dramaturgie. Viele Filmkritiker haben darauf hingewiesen, dass es selbstverständlich nicht möglich sei, die Geschichte eines Romans ohne Veränderungen in einem Film abzubilden und quasi nachzuerzählen. Die These, dass ein Film eine Geschichte anders erzählt als ein Buch – ja aufgrund der medialen Unterschiede sogar erzählen muss – scheint demnach eine Grundannahme zu sein, die selbst von den größten Gegnern der Filmadaption nicht geleugnet wird (vgl. ebd. 54). Wenn also weitgehend Konsens darüber herrscht, dass ein

---

[1] Die ungebrochene Popularität der *Herr der Ringe*-Filme wird u.a. durch die Bestenliste der Internet Movie Database dokumentiert. Dort rangieren die drei Filme unter den Top 20 der beliebtesten Filme aller Zeiten, *Die Rückkehr des Königs* sogar auf Platz 9 (Stand Mai 2013).

Film von der Buchvorlage abweichen muss, um in seinem Medium erfolgreich zu sein, stellt sich die Frage, worin genau jene filmische Erzählweise besteht, die für einen Film konstitutiv ist. Auf diese Weise werden wir hoffentlich nicht nur ein besseres Verständnis von Jacksons Adaptionsabsichten gewinnen, vielmehr wird es uns durch den Blick auf die Umsetzung des *Herrn der Ringe* im Medium Film möglich werden, ein besseres Verständnis von Tolkiens ureigener Erzählweise zu gewinnen.[2]

Versuchen wir zunächst, Peter Jacksons Ausgangspunkt genauer zu bestimmen, um seine dramaturgischen Entscheidungen besser einschätzen zu können. Hierzu erweist sich die Studie einer Autorengruppe um den Berliner Filmwissenschaftler Lothar Mikos als hilfreich, in der sich die Autoren besonders mit der Rezeption der *Herr der Ringe*-Filme beschäftigen, aber auch zu interessanten Ergebnissen im Hinblick auf die Filme selbst gelangen. So stellt Mikos fest, dass Jackson bei seiner Adaption einerseits vor der Herausforderung stand, Tolkiens »Markeninhalt« gerecht zu werden, d.h. den literarischen Stoff so aufzubereiten, dass ein Leser die geschätzte Geschichte als solche wiedererkennt. Andererseits galt es sich an den Erzählstandards zu orientieren, die für moderne Blockbuster-Filme relevant sind, da die Filme darauf ausgerichtet sind, nicht nur die Fans, sondern darüber hinaus ein weltweites Massenpublikum anzusprechen (vgl. Mikos 111). Zu diesen Standards gehören narrative Transparenz und Kohärenz, eine übersichtliche Konfliktlage, kausallogische Handlungsfolgen sowie eine psychologisch nachvollziehbare Figurenkonzeption (vgl. ebd.). Mikos ist sicherlich zuzustimmen, dass die Filmtrilogie diesen Standards in hohem Maße zu entsprechen versucht. Der zentrale Grund dafür, dass die Filmemacher die gewohnten Erzählnormen populärer Filme aufgreifen und ihrer Adaption des *Herrn der Ringe* zugrunde legen, ist, dass hierdurch Zuschauern, die Tolkiens Werk bisher nicht kannten, der Zugang zur Geschichte und der fantastischen Welt Mittelerde erleichtert wird. Will man die genannten Prinzipien ergänzen, dann bieten sich insbesondere die folgenden drei Begriffe an, um Jacksons Ansatz zu kennzeichnen: Reduktion, Vereinfachung und Verdichtung des epischen Stoffes gemäß den von Mikos genannten Kriterien. Mit diesen drei Begriffen lässt sich Jacksons Intention gut erfassen, Tolkiens Geschichte möglichst voraussetzungslos und nachvollziehbar zu erzählen. Es ist wichtig, diese Orientierung an narrativen Normen des Mainstream-Films zu betonen, denn angesichts der Tatsache, dass die *Herr der Ringe*-Filme für ein so breites Publikum offensichtlich so gut und reibungslos funktionieren, liegt die Vermutung nahe, dass dies in der literarischen Vorlage bereits angelegt ist. Tatsächlich ist

---

2   Angesichts der notwendigen Kürze des Artikels können nicht alle dramaturgischen Entscheidungen der Filmemacher im Detail vorgestellt werden. Weitere Aspekte sollen stattdessen in einem späteren Beitrag in den Blick genommen werden.

es jedoch so, dass der Regisseur die Romandramaturgie erst aufwendig umgestalten musste, damit diese in das bereits existierende Hollywood-Konzept passt. Anders ausgedrückt: Um eine möglichst erfolgreiche Adaption der Romanvorlage zu garantieren, wurde *Der Herr der Ringe* in ein filmdramaturgisches Korsett gepresst, was, wie im Folgenden deutlich wird, nur mit massiven Veränderungen der Handlungsstruktur möglich war.

Schaut man sich vor diesem Hintergrund verschiedene Drehbuchhandbücher an, mit denen professionelle Autoren in der Filmbranche arbeiten, zeigt sich, dass die Prinzipien und Grundsätze, die dort für erfolgreiche Drehbücher vorgeschlagen werden, sich teilweise wie Arbeitsanweisungen für Jacksons Filmadaption lesen. Eines der bekanntesten Drehbuchhandbücher ist beispielsweise David Howards und Edward Mableys *Drehbuchhandwerk*. Dort finden sich in dem Kapitel »Wie eine gute Geschichte zu einer gut erzählten Geschichte wird« die folgenden Empfehlungen für Drehbuchautoren:

1. Die Geschichte handelt von *jemandem*, mit dem wir ein gewisses Mitgefühl empfinden.
2. Jemand will unbedingt *etwas Bestimmtes* erreichen.
3. Dieses Etwas zu erreichen ist zwar möglich, aber *schwierig*.
4. Die Geschichte wird so erzählt, dass die *emotionale Wirkung* auf das Publikum und seine Anteilnahme so groß wie möglich sind.
5. Die Geschichte muss ein *zufriedenstellendes* Ende haben...

(Howard/Mabley 45)

Hier wird bereits auf den ersten Blick deutlich, dass dieses Drehbuchkonzept auch auf Jacksons *Herrn der Ringe* zutrifft. Wichtig erscheint insbesondere der vierte Punkt, denn eine Maximierung der emotionalen Wirkung scheint die Filmemacher in der Tat geleitet zu haben, wie im Folgenden erläutert werden wird. Denn unabhängig von der Tatsache, dass viele Leser Tolkiens Roman bereits als sehr bewegend wahrgenommen haben, war das durchaus schwierige Ziel, den Zuschauer emotional zu berühren, den Filmemachern ein besonderes Anliegen.

Schauen wir uns nach diesen einführenden Beobachtungen zu den Grundlagen von Jacksons Adaption die Spezifika der Filmdramaturgie näher an. Ein zentrales Merkmal der *Herr der Ringe*-Filmstruktur ist ein Aspekt, der von Jackson und zahlreichen Filmkritikern hervorgehoben wurde, der jedoch für unser Verständnis der Filme von zentraler Bedeutung ist: Gemeint ist die stringente Linearität von Jacksons Erzählung im Vergleich zu Tolkiens »blockartiger« Chronologie. Was ist damit gemeint? In den Filmen *Die Zwei Türme* und *Die Rückkehr des Königs*, in denen sich das Geschehen in verschiedene nebeneinander verlaufende Handlungsstränge aufspaltet, werden die Abenteuer der Gefährten mit dem Mittel der Parallelmontage, das weiter unten näher erläutert wird, erzählt. Jackson orientiert sich also an der fiktiven Chronologie der Ereignisse, wie sie Tolkien in Anhang B des *Herrn der Ringe* darlegt (vgl. LotR 1057-72). Die meisten Leser und Filmzuschauer werden eine lineare Erzählweise als die naheliegende Struktur ansehen, bietet diese doch zahlreiche Möglichkeiten der Spannungssteigerung und Herstellung von Bezügen zwischen den einzelnen Handlungssträngen. Umso erstaunlicher ist es mit der Kenntnis der Filmdramaturgie, dass Tolkien seine Geschichte auf eine Weise erzählt, die den Erwartungen vieler moderner Leser kaum entspricht. Wie sieht dies im Detail aus?

Nachdem sich die Wege der Gefährten am Ende von Buch II trennen, erzählt Tolkien in den Büchern III und IV jeweils voneinander getrennt die Erlebnisse der Figuren um Aragorn auf der einen Seite und Frodo und Sam auf der anderen Seite. Ein Leser, der Frodo und Sam demnach auf Seite 398 verlässt, muss ganze 200 Seiten warten, um in Buch IV zu erfahren, wie es mit den beiden weitergeht. Währenddessen hat er jedoch den gesamten Krieg um Rohan verfolgt, war Zeuge des letzten Marschs der Ents und begleitete Gandalf und Pippin auf dem Weg nach Minas Tirith. Das Schicksal von Frodo und Sam bleibt dem Leser also genauso wie den restlichen Gefährten verborgen. Dass der Erzählfluss demnach zahlreiche Brüche aufweist, wird dem Leser immer wieder offenbar, denn nachdem er die Abenteuer in Rohan in Buch III verfolgt hat und Gandalfs und Pippins Ritt nach Minas Tirith bis zum 5. März 3019 DZ gefolgt ist, springt die Handlung zurück zum 26. Februar, um von Frodos Erlebnissen in den Emyn Muil zu berichten.

Aber auch innerhalb eines Buches, d.h. eines weitgehend geschlossenen Handlungsstrangs finden sich einige bemerkenswerte Sprünge innerhalb der Chronologie. So endet das Kapitel »Riders of Rohan« damit, dass die drei Jägern jenen mysteriösen Zauberer treffen, bei dem es sich offensichtlich um Saruman handelt, der die Pferde stiehlt (ebd. 430-3). In Tolkiens Chronologie ist dies der 1. März. Die anschließenden Kapitel »The Uruk-hai« und »Treebeard« springen zeitlich wieder zurück zum 26. Februar und schildern die gesamten Erlebnisse Merrys und Pippins bei den Orks bis zum Marsch der Ents nach Isengart (Ende des Kapitels »Treebeard«). Dies ist der 2. März. d.h. in diesen zwei Kapiteln hat der Merry- und Pippin-Handlungsbogen denjenigen der drei Jäger überholt. Das anschließende Kapitel »The White Rider« setzt dann wieder am 1. März ein und schildert das Treffen mit Gandalf. In den darauffolgenden drei Kapiteln tauchen die beiden Hobbits nicht auf. Erst als die Gruppe um Gandalf in Isengart eintrifft, wird der Kampf der Ents gegen Saruman rückblickend erzählt (ebd. 549-58). Das Kapitel »Flotsam and Jetsam« dient somit dazu, rekapitulierend die Erlebnisse Merrys und Pippins zwischen dem 2. und 5. März zu erzählen.

Eine ähnlich paradoxe Erzählweise finden wir in den Büchern V und VI: Buch V erzählt die Abenteuer der Gefährten bis zum Ende der Schlacht vor dem Morannon und endet mit Pippins Sichtung der Adler. In Tolkiens Zeitlinie ist dies der legendäre 25. März, mit dem der Ringkrieg zu Ende geht. Nach Buch V springt die Handlung ganze zehn Tage zurück, denn Buch VI beginnt mit Sams Abenteuer in Cirith Ungol, d.h. am 14. März. In Tolkiens Chronologie tobt parallel dazu die Schlacht auf den Pelennor-Feldern. Buch VI ist darüber hinaus interessant, weil hier Tolkien vor der Herausforderung stand, die seit Buch III getrennten Erzählstränge wieder zusammenzuführen. Die ersten drei Kapitel des sechsten Buches erzählen den dramatischen Höhepunkt der Handlung, indem der Erzählbericht den Erlebnissen von Frodo und Sam folgt. An einigen Stellen gewährt uns der Erzähler jedoch einen kurzen Einblick in das Geschehen jenseits des Schattengebirges. So lesen wir zum Beispiel:

> But their [Frodo's and Sam's] luck held, and for the rest of that day they met no living or moving thing; and when night fell they vanished into the darkness of Mordor. All the land now brooded as at the coming of a great storm: for the Captains of the West had passed the Cross-roads and set flames in the deadly fields of Imlad Morgul. So the desperate journey went on, as the Ring went south and the banners of the kings rode north. (914)

Diese Ausführungen des auktorialen Erzählers vermitteln dem Leser zeitgleiches Geschehen. Sie sind das literarische Äquivalent zur Parallelmontage und im Film auch ähnlich umgesetzt, wobei die gefasst-sachliche Erzählhaltung im Roman nicht das Gefühl von Dringlichkeit aufkommen lässt, auf das zu erzeugen Jackson so großen Wert legt.

Nach der Zerstörung des Rings springt die Erzählung zurück zu den Hauptleuten des Westens und der Erzähler berichtet vom Ende der Schlacht (927-9). Hier am Ende der Erzählung finden wir zum einzigen Mal eine literarische Parallelmontage, d.h. einen raschen Szenenwechsel zwischen zwei gleichzeitig stattfindenden Ereignissen. Zuerst verfolgen wir Gandalfs Flug mit den Adlern in Richtung Schicksalsberg (ebd. 928f), anschließend erleben wir das Gespräch zwischen Frodo und Sam eingeschlossen in der Lava (929f). Interessanterweise wiederholt Tolkien hier dieselben Worte, die das vorherige Kapitel beendet haben (»›I am glad that you are her with me,‹ said Frodo. ›Here at the end of all things, Sam.‹«; 926 u. 929), sodass dem Leser unmittelbar klar wird, dass der zwischen beiden Textstellen eingeschlossene Erzählbericht zeitliches Nebeneinander wiedergibt. Dies ist für Tolkien an dieser Stelle aber nur möglich, da die beiden Erzählstränge sich sozusagen eingeholt haben. Auch der Ringträger-Plot hat die anderen nun eingeholt und wir schreiben den 25. März.

Es bleibt also festzuhalten: Tolkien wählt ein Erzählverfahren, das die übergeordnete Chronologie immer wieder aufbricht und mit gravierenden Rücksprüngen arbeitet, die teilweise mehr als eine Woche Handlungszeit überbrücken. Auch Tolkiens Erzählverfahren bietet Möglichkeiten, mit Spannungseffekten wie Cliffhangern zu arbeiten, beispielsweise bei der erwähnten Bewusstlosigkeit Pippins in der Schlacht am Schwarzen Tor (874) oder die Ungewissheit über Frodos Schicksal am Ende von Buch IV (725), aber im Vergleich zu den in den Filmen genutzten Mitteln der Verknüpfung sind dies bei Tolkien Einzelfälle. Im Vergleich zur Filmadaption lässt sich also festhalten, dass Tolkiens Erzählstruktur nicht auf maximale Spannungssteigerung, ein hohes Erzähltempo und einen möglichst hohen Grad an Emotionalisierung angelegt ist, zumindest nicht in der Form, wie dies bei der Filmversion der Fall ist (s.u.).

An dieser Stelle soll der Blick kurz auf andere Adaptionen des *Herrn der Ringe* geworfen werden, da auf diese Weise deutlich wird, dass Tolkiens Erzählstruktur nicht nur Jackson offensichtlich vor ein Problem stellte, sondern ebenso all diejenigen, die sich an eine dramatische Inszenierung von Tolkiens Roman wagten. So wählten sowohl Ralph Bakshi in seiner Filmfassung als auch die bekannten Hörspielversionen von BBC und WDR eine chronologische Handlungsstruktur, die von Tolkiens Ansatz des zeitlichen Nacheinanders signifikant abweicht. In vielen Fällen gelangen diese Fassungen auch zu ähnlichen dramaturgischen Entscheidungen wie Jackson.[3]

Es ist doch sehr erstaunlich, dass keine dieser Adaptionen des *Herrn der Ringe* die originale Erzählstruktur des Romans beibehält. Dass Hörspiel- und Filmregisseure die Romanstruktur verändern mussten, um sie darstellbar zu machen, ist somit ein Hinweis darauf, dass Tolkiens Roman keine einfach umsetzbare dramatische Struktur aufweist. Tolkiens Art des Erzählens erfüllt auf dem Papier offensichtlich bis heute in hohem Maße das Ziel, die Geschichte interessant, mitreißend und durchaus spannend zu machen. Wäre dies nicht der Fall, hätte der Roman wohl kaum über nunmehr 60 Jahre ein Millionenpublikum fasziniert. Für dramatische Inszenierungen ist diese Art der Dramaturgie aber ungeeignet.

Tolkien selbst vertrat in diesem Punkt jedoch eine gänzlich andere Sichtweise, denn in seinem viel zitierten Brief an Forrest Ackerman zum Filmscript von Ackerman, Zimmerman und Brodax betont er:

> **The canons of narrative art in any medium cannot be wholly different**; and the failure of poor films is often precisely in exaggeration, and in the intrusion of unwarranted matter owing to not perceiving where the core of the original lies.
>
> (L 270, Herv. JE)

---

3 So zeigt Bakshi ähnlich wie Jackson die Konfrontation zwischen Gandalf und Saruman, die im Roman nur rückblickend in Bruchtal erzählt wird. Auch die Parallelmontagen zwischen den Aragorn- und Frodo-Handlungssträngen ähneln sich in beiden Filmadaptionen.

Der Vorwurf der Übertreibung, den Tolkien hier Filmadaptionen im Allgemeinen macht, könnte sicherlich auch für Jacksons Fassung geltend gemacht werden. Auch sind die *Herr der Ringe*-Filme sicherlich nicht frei von überflüssigen Szenen, die am Kern des Textes vorbeigehen. Für meine Fragestellung ist aber insbesondere die hervorgehobene Aussage Tolkiens von Interesse, widerspricht diese doch grundlegend den Film- und Hörspieladaptionen seines Werks. Der Aussage, dass sich die narrative Darbietung einer Geschichte in verschiedenen Kunstformen nicht grundsätzlich unterscheidet, würden die Filmemacher Bakshi oder Jackson sicherlich vehement widersprechen – meiner Ansicht nach völlig zu Recht. Tolkien jedoch besteht darauf, dass sein Prinzip des zeitlichen Nacheinanders auch in der Filmadaption bewahrt bleibt:

> The narrative now [book III + IV] divides into two main branches: 1. Prime Action, the Ringbearers. 2. Subsidiary Action, the rest of the Company leading to the 'heroic' matter. *It is essential that these two branches should each be treated in coherent sequence.* Both to render them intelligible as a story, and because they are totally different in tone and scenery. Jumbling them together entirely destroys these things. (L 275)

Bezieht man diese Aussage Tolkiens auf Jacksons Adaption, würde dies den Filmen ein vernichtendes Urteil ausstellen, denn natürlich hat Jackson genau das getan: Er hat beide Handlungsstränge vermischt und hätte damit im Sinne Tolkiens das von diesem so bewusst gewählte Handlungskonstrukt zerstört. Umso spannender ist es deshalb, sich Jacksons Dramaturgie im Detail anzusehen, um die Frage zu beantworten, warum er und vor ihm Bakshi und die Hörspielregisseure so grundlegend von der Meinung des Professors abweichen.

Parallelmontage und ihre Wirkungsabsicht

Wie bereits erwähnt, stellt die dramatische Struktur den maßgeblichen Unterschied zwischen Buch und Film dar. Hinsichtlich der Problematik, wie die verschiedenen parallelen Handlungsstränge in den Büchern III-VI zusammengeführt werden können, beschrieb Jackson sein Vorgehen so, dass er zuerst die einzelnen Erzählstränge eigenständig geschnitten und erst danach durch Parallelmontage miteinander verknüpft hat. Dies verdeutlicht, dass der Prozess des Zusammenführens den Filmemachern nicht leicht gefallen ist, galt es hierbei doch sinnvolle dramaturgische Entscheidungen zu treffen, die eben nicht in der Vorlage angelegt waren. Peter Jackson erläutert dies in einem Interview so:

So we were always looking for ways where we could somehow create connections by feeling that events were happening simultaneously and just give the illusion that even though they weren't in the same space, there were times in the story where there was a cogency to the pacing of things. (zitiert in Goldsmith 63)

Die Schwierigkeit bestand also darin, dass die Handlung des Romans an verschiedenen Stellen unterbrochen werden musste, dass also sozusagen sinnvolle Bruchpunkte im Handlungsfluss gefunden werden mussten:

> We did have to create a timeline. One of the decisions we made early on was to not follow the fairly simplistic structure that Tolkien had devised himself. Right at the beginning, we decided that ... we'd intercut as much or as little as we deemed necessary. (ebd.)

Die Chance bei diesem Verfahren bestand darin, diese Brüche zu nutzen, um die übergeordneten Ziele einer solchen Filmadaption zu erreichen: Maximierung des emotionalen Gehalts und der Spannung, ein hohes Erzähltempo und damit einhergehend ein Gefühl von Dringlichkeit. Insgesamt wird das Ziel verfolgt, trotz der Handlungsbrüche einen möglichst gefälligen Erzählfluss zu gewährleisten, d.h. keinerlei Verständnisschwierigkeiten aufkommen zu lassen.

Ein gutes Beispiel für die Anwendung dieser Prinzipien ist der Beginn des zweiten Films. Er startet mit einem Erzählblock um Frodo und Sam (Jackson, *Towers* I 05:55-14:06). Diese Szenen, in denen wir den beiden Hobbits durch die Emyn Muil folgen, dienen neben der Einführung der wichtigen Nebenfigur Gollum vor allem dazu, den Zuschauern die Gefühlslage und Konflikte des Ringträgers zu vermitteln. Zwar handelt es sich bei den Tolkien-Filmen angesichts der Vielzahl an Figuren und Handlungsebenen um Ensemble-Filme, aber dass Jackson den zweiten und dritten Film jeweils mit einem Frodo-Erzählblock beginnen lässt, macht deutlich, dass wir diesen Handlungsstrang als emotionales Zentrum der Filmreihe verstehen sollen. Die Gestaltung der anschließenden Erzählblöcke zeigt, wie es Jackson gelingt, einen stringenten Erzählfluss zu gewährleisten. So folgt auf die Begegnung Frodos mit Gollum die Flucht der Uruk-hai mit Merry und Pippin (ebd. 14:07-16:24). Die Szene schließt damit, dass die Orks Menschenfleisch riechen und mit erhöhtem Tempo weiterziehen. Dabei sehen wir Pippins Gesicht in Großaufnahme mit nach innen gerichtetem Blick, wie er Aragorns Namen flüstert (ebd. 16:02). Diese Bemerkung Pippins wird letztlich eher für den Zuschauer gemacht und leitet geschickt die nächste Szene ein, in der uns zum ersten Mal im zweiten Film die drei Jäger gezeigt werden, die der Fährte der Orks folgen (ebd. 16:25-18:27). Jackson nutzt hier – dem Medium Film angemessen – eine visuelle Überleitung, die Verfolgte und

Verfolger eindeutig miteinander verbindet, denn auf das Bild der Elbenbrosche, die von Orkstiefeln in den Boden getreten wird, folgt eine Aufnahme des auf dem Boden liegenden und horchenden Waldläufers. Pippins Erwähnung Aragorns leitet also den Erzählfluss angenehm zu genau dieser Filmfigur weiter, sodass kein gefühlter Bruch zwischen den Szenen entsteht, sondern diese im Gegenteil inhaltlich und visuell miteinander verknüpft werden. Am Ende der Szene wendet Jackson dieses Verfahren erneut an, wenn Aragorn und Legolas sich Gedanken über das Ziel der Uruk-hai machen und Aragorn schlussfolgert: »Saruman!« Die Szene wechselt daraufhin nach Isengart, wo Saruman in der für die Filme typischen Weise über seine Weltherrschaftspläne monologisiert (ebd. 18:28-22:08).

Auch diese Szene endet wieder mit genau demselben Verknüpfungsprinzip: Eine Person kündigt durch ihre Worte die nächste Szene an und leitet damit zu einem neuen Handlungsort über. So hören wir am Ende der Saruman-Szene einen inneren Monolog des Zauberers, in dem dieser ankündigt, was parallel dazu auf der Leinwand zu sehen ist: »It will begin in Rohan. Too long have these peasants stood against you [Sauron]. But no more« (21:00-21:13). Interessant an dieser Stelle ist u.a., dass Sarumans innerer Monolog die Bilder der nächsten Szene überlagert und auf diese Weise als Kommentar derselben funktioniert. Bild und Text verschiedener Szenen verbinden sich zu einer Einheit, die den Erzählfluss erleichtert. Das hier geschilderte Verfahren, Szenen durch verbale und/oder visuelle Überleitungen miteinander zu verbinden, lässt sich in der ganzen Filmtrilogie an vielen Beispielen festmachen. Aber bereits die hier geschilderten machen deutlich, wozu diese Erzählstrategie dient: Sie soll genau das gewährleisten, was oben als Grundprinzipien der Filmadaption genannt wurde – hohes Erzähltempo, gefälliger Erzählfluss trotz Handlungsbrüchen, emotionale Dringlichkeit, Reduzierung von Verständnisschwierigkeiten.

Expositionen

Die Exposition erwies sich in allen drei Filmen als besonderes Problem. Wie sollte es gelingen, einem Publikum, das sich nicht mit Mittelerde auskennt, die notwendigen Informationen zu vermitteln? Peter Jackson entschied sich beim ersten Film für einen Prolog, eine Entscheidung, über deren Sinn und Notwendigkeit sich sicherlich streiten lässt. Viele Filmemacher und auch die oben erwähnten Drehbuchhandbücher raten von langen expositorischen Szenen am Anfang eines Films ab, da dies eine wenig elegante und allzu offensichtliche Form der Informationsvermittlung ist, eine Erzählstrategie, die schlimmstenfalls den Zuschauer langweilt. In Tolkiens Roman findet sich zwar auch ein Prolog, aber dieser beschäftigt sich vor allem mit der Hobbit-Kultur und widmet lediglich einen kurzen Abschnitt dem Ringfund (LotR 10-13). Im Roman werden die Informationen zur Vorgeschichte erst sukzessive enthüllt, insbesondere in den Kapiteln »The Shadow of the Past« und »The Council of Elrond«. Jackson und seinem Team erschien es aber offensichtlich als notwendig, die Hintergründe des Rings in einem Prolog zu erläutern, ein Erzählverfahren, das auch Bakshi in seinem Zeichentrickfilm wählte. An dieser Stelle soll der Blick aber nicht auf den ersten, sondern auf den zweiten Film geworfen werden, da wir anhand der Exposition von *Die Zwei Türme* sehen können, wie Jackson mit einem erzählerischen Problem gänzlich anders umgeht als Tolkien.

Im zweiten Teil des *Herrn der Ringe* wird mit Rohan ein neuer Schauplatz eingeführt, der in Buch III immer im Fokus steht. Tolkien und nach ihm Jackson mussten sich also mit der Frage auseinandersetzen, wie der Handlungsort und der dort vorherrschende Konflikt eingeführt werden. Tolkien selbst bleibt hier seiner vorherrschenden Erzählperspektive treu, denn der auktoriale Erzählbericht bleibt stets bei den Gefährten und verlässt niemals ihren Pfad. Der Leser entdeckt somit gemeinsam mit den Figuren das unbekannte Land, seine Bewohner und ihre Rolle im übergeordneten Konflikt des Ringkrieges. Die Helden bilden den Spiegel unserer Wahrnehmung. In diesem Sinne fungieren Aragorn und Gandalf als Informationsquellen für diejenigen Gefährten, die wie Legolas und Gimli die Kultur der Rohirrim nicht kennen (vgl. LotR 496f). Die Bedrohung Rohans durch Saruman erschließt sich dem Leser somit erst sukzessive. Die Begegnung mit Éomer gibt neue Einblicke, aber erst durch die Zusammenkunft mit Gandalf und das von ihm offenbarte Hintergrundwissen erschließt sich den Gefährten und dem Leser die nächste Aufgabe, die in Edoras wartet.

Jackson weicht im Falle der Rohan-Exposition grundlegend von Tolkiens Erzählfolge ab, denn er hält es offenbar für notwendig, der Einführung des neuen Handlungsorts und der Nebenfiguren mehr Raum einzuräumen. Aus diesem Grund wendet sich die Erzählung zu Beginn des zweiten Films nach den Erzählblöcken der Gefährten und Saruman ab und führt den Zuschauer nach Rohan, wo dieser Zeuge des Überfalls der Uruk-hai wird (Jackson, *Towers* I 21:00-22:09). Dem Prinzip der Emotionalisierung entsprechend versucht Jackson hier den Konflikt zu personalisieren, indem er die Rohan-Kinder Éothain und Freda als Nebenfiguren einfügt und das Leiden der Rohirrim so für den Zuschauer erfahrbar macht. Anschließend stellt uns der Film alle zentralen Figuren am Hofe König Théodens vor (ebd. 22:10-26:00). Der König wird als hilfloser und – wie sich später herausstellt – praktisch besessener Greis etabliert, dem der böse Geist Saruman durch Gandalf effektvoll ausgetrieben werden muss. In der Figur des Gríma Schlangenzunge findet der Regisseur schließlich den entsprechenden Widersacher, auf den sich der Zorn des Zuschauers richten kann.

Dass Jacksons langer Rohan-Exkurs Tolkien-Leser irritiert, liegt auch an einem Detail, das in den Beiträgen zu Tolkiens Erzählstruktur bisher kaum zur Sprache gekommen ist: Szenen dieser Art, in denen keiner der Gefährten anwesend ist, finden sich in Tolkiens *Der Herr der Ringe* so gut wie gar nicht.

Eine Ausnahme findet sich im Roman zu Beginn des Kapitels »A Knife in the Dark«, wo der Erzähler uns daran teilhaben lässt, wie Fredegar Bolger sich in Krickloch dem Angriff der Nazgúl erwehren muss (vgl. LotR 172f). Ansonsten ist die Erzählperspektive strikt an den Aktionen der Hauptfiguren ausgerichtet. Wenn in Jacksons Rohan-Szenen also periphere Handlungsstränge erzählt werden, bei denen noch dazu keine Hauptfigur anwesend ist, dann bedeutet dies ein grundlegendes Abweichen von Tolkiens Dramaturgie. In den Filmen finden wir entsprechend noch diverse andere Szenen ohne Beteiligung der Gefährten, etwa den Angriff auf Osgiliath im dritten Film (Jackson, *Return* I 58:22-1:01:51) und insgesamt alle Szenen mit Saruman. Zur Darstellung des gefallenen Istari in den Filmen ließe sich noch Einiges sagen. An dieser Stelle sei nur betont, dass es den Drehbuchautoren vor dem Hintergrund gängiger Filmdramaturgie (s.o.) wichtig war, den Antagonisten handelnd in Szene zu setzen, weshalb wir in den ersten beiden Filmen viele Szenen finden, in denen Saruman sein zerstörerisches Werk verrichtet und seine Pläne erläutert. Man muss dazu betonen, dass Saruman im Roman erst im Kapitel »The Voice of Saruman« als handelnde Figur auftritt. Vorher haben wir ihn nur durch Berichte und Kommentare anderer Figuren kennengelernt. Allesamt machen diese Beispiele die auktoriale Erzählhaltung der Filmadaption deutlich, bei der die von Jackson so kunstvoll eingesetzte bewegte Kamera praktisch die Rolle einer souveränen Erzählinstanz einnimmt, die uns mit großer Leichtigkeit zu den für die Geschichte relevanten Orten und Ereignissen führt.

Narrative Ökonomie

Abschließend soll auf einen Aspekt der Filmdramaturgie eingegangen werden, den ich als narrative Ökonomie bezeichnen möchte. Gemeint ist, dass Jackson daran gelegen ist, Informationen, die für das Verständnis der Handlung relevant sind, geschickt in den Erzählfluss einzubinden und Szenen zu vermeiden, in denen Figuren lediglich über vergangenes Geschehen berichten. Dies geschieht in Tolkiens Roman – dem Prinzip der Erzählblöcke entsprechend – recht häufig, wie z.B. beim Angriff der Ents auf Isengart, der im Roman nur rückblickend geschildert wird (s.o.). Da Jacksons Filme aber, wie eben geschildert, auf das übergeordnete Ziel ausgerichtet sind, die Geschichte mit einem hohen Tempo zu erzählen und die emotionale Wirkung zu maximieren, musste auch die Informationsvermittlung möglichst zeiteffektiv und wirkungsvoll arrangiert werden. Besonders war den Drehbuchautoren daran gelegen, die Filmexpositionen nicht mit zu vielen Hintergrundinformationen zu überfrachten, sondern diese der narrativen Ökonomie entsprechend an den effektvollsten Punkten innerhalb der Handlung einzustreuen. Besonders deutlich wird dies am Beispiel Gollums. Zwar wird bereits im Prolog des ersten Films kurz erklärt, wer dieser Ringfinder ist (Jackson, *Fellowhsip* I 05:33-06:22), aber die gesamte Hintergrundgeschichte Gollums wird noch nicht enthüllt. Dies geschieht erst zu dem Zeitpunkt, wenn diese Informationen für den Zuschauer relevant werden bzw. deren Enthüllung besonders eindringlich erscheint, nämlich genau zu Beginn des dritten Films (ders., *Return* I 00:00-06:08). Zu diesem Zeitpunkt hat man Gollum bereits als wichtige Figur innerhalb der Erzählung kennengelernt. Hinzu kommt, dass die Filmemacher die Analogie zwischen den Ringträgern Frodo und Gollum im Vergleich zum Roman vertiefen, um die emotionale Intensität dieser Beziehung zu erhöhen. Dementsprechend wird Gollum als potentielle Entwicklungsmöglichkeit Frodos präsentiert, d.h. als ein Ringträger, der der Versuchung des Rings erlegen ist und seine Freiheit und Persönlichkeit verloren hat. In dieser Form der nachgeschobenen Exposition übernimmt Jackson eine der Empfehlungen, die in zahlreichen Drehbuchratgebern gemacht wird. So schlagen die bereits zitierten Howard und Mabley vor, expositorische Szenen nicht mit einer Informationsflut zu überladen, sondern relevante Informationen erst später in einer handlungsreichen Szene zu vermitteln:

> Präsentiere notwendige Hintergrundinformationen in Szenen, die einen Konflikt enthalten... Verschiebe den Einsatz von der Exposition dienendem Material wenn irgend möglich auf einen späteren Zeitpunkt in der Geschichte und präsentiere es dann, wenn es die größte dramatische Wirkung erzielt.
>
> (Howard/Mabley 86)

Mit einem solchen Verfahren der dosierten Informationsvermittlung erreicht man also im Idealfalle zweierlei. Erstens wird die Informationsfülle, die in einer einzigen Szene vermittelt wird, reduziert und zweitens wird die dramatische Wirkung der isoliert präsentiert oft wenig interessanten expositorischen Informationen erhöht. Narrative Ökonomie zeigt sich an verschiedenen Stellen der *Herr der Ringe*-Filme. Besonders kunstvoll wird dieses Verfahren im Film *Die Zwei Türme* genutzt. Dort finden wir eine Szene, die Geschehen aus dem ersten Film ergänzt bzw. in einem neuen Licht erscheinen lässt. So sehen wir im zweiten Film eine Rückblende zu Aragorn in Bruchtal, wo dieser am Grab seiner Mutter kurz vor dem Aufbruch der Gefährten von Elrond zur Rede gestellt wird (Jackson, *Towers* II 05:33-06:27). Anschließend folgt ein Streitgespräch zwischen Arwen und Aragorn, in dem dieser seine Zweifel daran äußert, dass die Liebe zwischen Elbin und Mensch eine Zukunft haben könne (ebd. 06:28-07:43). Das Interessante an diesen beiden Szenen aus *Die Zwei Türme* ist, dass diese an eine Szene anschließen bzw. einer Szene vorausgehen, die nur in der Langfassung des ersten Films zu finden waren. Dort erweiterte Jackson die Bruchtal-Sequenz, indem er einerseits Aragorn am Grabe seiner Mutter zeigt (ders. *Fellowship* II 00:00-01:11), und andererseits die Verabschiedung der

Gefährten durch die Elben Bruchtals schildert (ebd. 02:50-04:04). Durch die ergänzenden Rückblicke im zweiten Film bekommt deshalb ein Blickwechsel zwischen Arwen und Aragorn beim Verlassen Bruchtals eine neue Bedeutung bzw. kann anders verstanden werden (ebd. 03:48-04:03). So scheint es sich bei dem Blickwechsel der beiden nicht einfach nur um den schmachtenden Blick zweier Liebender zu handeln, vielmehr scheint insbesondere Arwens Mimik auf das vorausgegangene Streitgespräch Bezug zu nehmen, das jedoch erst im zweiten Film zu sehen ist. Die Informationen und ihr dramatischer Gehalt wurden somit effektvoll auf den zweiten Film verschoben. Indem die genaue chronologische Szeneabfolge sich somit erst aus beiden Filmen zusammen ergibt, schlägt die Filmdramaturgie hier einen durchaus spannenden narrativen Zirkel.[4]

Zusammenfassung

Wie bereits erwähnt: In diesem Essay können nicht alle Aspekte analysiert werden, die mit Blick auf die Filmdramaturgie interessant erscheinen. So wäre es lohnenswert, sich mit der Frage zu beschäftigen, wie es Jackson gelingt, narrative Schlusspunkte in einem Roman zu finden, der hinsichtlich seiner Dramaturgie bekanntlich ein großes Gesamtwerk darstellt und eben nicht – wie die Filme – eine Trilogie mit jeweils in sich geschlossenen Spannungsbögen. Auch das Verhältnis von Zeit und Raum innerhalb der Filme und die Anwendung der Konventionen des Spannungskinos lohnen einen vertieften Blick. Der muss an dieser Stelle allerdings ausbleiben.

Deutlich wurde jedoch, wie stark sich die Erzählstruktur von Roman und Film im Falle des *Herrn der Ringe* unterscheidet, ungeachtet der Tatsache, dass es sich um ein und dieselbe Geschichte handelt. Dabei orientiert sich Jackson bei seiner Version des *Herrn der Ringe* an Erzählkonventionen, die für das Medium Film typisch sind. Auf diese Weise entstand eine Fassung des *Herrn der Ringe*, die zwar in weiten Teilen der Romanhandlung entspricht, die aber die Handlung gänzlich anders organisiert und arrangiert und so Tolkiens Forderungen nach Beibehaltung der Erzählstruktur im Falle einer Adaption widerspricht. Dass Jacksons *Herr der Ringe* hierbei mit anderen Dramatisierungen wie Bakshis Film oder den Hörspielen übereinstimmt, konnte nur angedeutet werden, ist aber ein Thema, das eine vertiefte Untersuchung verdient.

Weiterhin weist der Vergleich mit den Filmen darauf hin, dass Tolkiens eigene Erzählverfahren mit der starren Einhaltung von getrennten Erzählblöcken

---

4 Weitere Beispiele für narrative Ökonomie ließen sich nennen. So greift Jackson etwa die Geschichte um Isildurs Ringfund und die Konsequenzen daraus immer wieder auf und ergänzt sie um Aspekte, die im Laufe der Filmhandlung relevant werden. Auf diese Weise wird das Bild von Isildur und seinem Versagen als Ringträger sukzessive erweitert und vertieft. Ähnlich wie im Falle Gollums wird dies genutzt, um eine entsprechende Fallhöhe für Aragorn (als Isildurs Nachfahre) und Frodo (ebenfalls Ringträger) zu erzeugen.

modernen Konventionen des Spannungsromans und -films nicht entspricht. Zeitgenössische Erfolgsautoren wie Dan Brown oder George R. R. Martin würden bei einer Bearbeitung des *Herrn der Ringe* sicherlich ein Erzählverfahren wählen, dass Jacksons Erzählstruktur sehr viel näher kommt. Eine abschließende Einschätzung, die sich aus der Beschäftigung mit dem Thema ergibt, ist, dass die moderne Spannungsliteratur, sei es nun Krimi oder Fantasy, häufig Erzählkonventionen des Films übernommen hat, sodass viele Maßgaben des zitierten Drehbuchratgebers im 21. Jahrhundert auch für Romanschriftsteller gelten können. Ob dies eine Entwicklung ist, die man begrüßen oder bedauern sollte, muss natürlich jedem Leser selbst überlassen bleiben.

Bibliographie

Carpenter, Humphrey, Ed. *The Letters of J.R.R. Tolkien*. London: Allan & Unwin, 1981

Goldsmith, Jeff. "Return of the King." [Artikel mit Interviews der *Herr der Ringe*-Drehbuchautoren]. *Creative Screenwriting* 11 (2004): 62-67

Howard, David und Edward Mabley. *Drehbuchhandwerk. Technik und Grundlagen. Mit Analysen erfolgreicher Filme*. Übers. Matthias Schmitt. 2. Aufl. Leck: Emonts, 1998

Jackson, Peter. *The Lord of the Rings. The Fellowship of the Ring*. Extended Edition. 2 DVDs. New Zeeland: New Line Cinema, 2002

---. *The Lord of the Rings. The Two Towers*. Extended Edition. 2 DVDs. New Zeeland: New Line Cinema, 2003

---. *The Lord of the Rings. The Return of the King*. Extended Edition. 2 DVDs. New Zeeland: New Line Cinema, 2004

Mikos, Lothar, Susanne Eichner, et. al. *Die Herr der Ringe-Trilogie. Attraktion und Faszination eines populärkulturellen Phänomens*. Konstanz: UVK Verlagsgesellschaft, 2007

Rateliff, John D. "Two Kinds of Absence. Elision & Exclusion in Peter Jackson's *The Lord of the Rings.*" *Picturing Tolkien. Essays on Peter Jackson's The Lord of the Rings Film Trilogy*. Hg. Jane Chance & Philipp E. Kaveny. Jefferson: 2011, 54-69

Tolkien, J.R.R. *The Lord of the Rings*. London: HarperCollins, 1995

Angelsächsisches Rohan?
Tolkiens anti-normannischer Reflex unterstützt durch Peter Jacksons Film-Adaption
Annika Röttinger (Hannover)

Betrachten wir die Rohirrim in J.R.R. Tolkiens *The Lord of the Rings* etwas genauer und für sich genommen, so finden sich etliche Aspekte, die sie mit den Angelsachsen des 10. und 11. Jahrhunderts vergleichbar machen. Herrschaftsform, Kriegsführung, Ethos und nicht zuletzt die Sprache sprechen dafür, die Angelsachsen als historische Vorbilder der Menschen Rohans zu sehen. Eines jedoch spricht dagegen: das markanteste Element der rohirrischen Kultur, die Pferde. Die Tatsache, dass das rohirrische Heer eigentlich nur aus Reiterei besteht, spricht eher dafür, die Rohirrim den Normannen gleichzusetzen. Dass dies nicht der Fall ist, liegt an Tolkiens anti-normannischer Einstellung.

In Peter Jacksons filmischer Adaption von *The Lord of the Rings* (2001-2003) werden die angelsächsischen Elemente in der Kultur Rohans noch deutlicher. Diese visuelle Adaption bietet dabei eine zusätzliche Interpretationsmöglichkeit, da Beschreibungen im Buch oftmals keine konkreten Details liefern.

Im Folgenden werden angelsächsische Elemente näher betrachtet, die sich in der Kultur Rohans wiederfinden – mit besonderem Augenmerk auf der Erweiterung der Darstellung durch die Filmtrilogie. Abschließend soll kurz erläutert werden, warum die Rohirrim meiner Meinung nach keine Normannen sein können.

Rüstung und Waffen

Tolkiens visuelle Beschreibungen seiner Charaktere fallen oft etwas spärlich aus. Es sind Charakterzüge, Stimmungen und Verhalten der Figuren, die ihn mehr zu interessieren schienen:

> Tolkien's visual descriptions of his characters in *The Lord of the Rings* could be a little vague: he preferred to describe people as 'grim' or 'proud'. It was their mood, their attitude or their narrative function that interested him more. (Robinson 454f)

Daher bietet der Film hier eine wesentlich deutlichere visuelle Studie. Schon beim ersten filmischen Auftritt der Reiter Rohans fallen deutlich angelsächsische Elemente auf. Hier lohnt sich ein genauerer Blick vor allem auf Rüstung und Waffen: Die gängigsten Schilde der Angelsachsen waren Rundschilde aus Holz mit einer Aussparung für den Handgriff und beschlagen mit einem Eisenknauf. Im Buch wird zwar lediglich erwähnt, dass die Rohirrim bemalte Rundschilde haben, aber nicht das Material; der Film dagegen gibt wesentlich mehr Aufschluss: Die detailliert bemalten Holzschilde der Rohirrim sind oft und gut zu sehen. Sie sind rund und grün, bei den höheren militärischen Rängen zudem mit einem weißen Pferd oder dem Sonnensymbol der Rohirrim bemalt. Nichts von alldem, schon gar keine Muster, finden in der Buchvorlage Erwähnung.

Die gängigste Waffe der Angelsachsen war der Speer, vornehmlich aus Esche, wie die der Rohirrim. Schwerter waren die wertvollsten und unter gewöhnlichen Kriegern selteneren Waffen, die erst später, etwa um 1066 n.Chr., in der Zeit der Schlacht von Hastings, zur Standardausrüstung der Angelsachsen gehörten. Alle Rohirrim tragen Schwerter, aber ihre Hauptangriffswaffe ist der Speer. Mit dem Schwert kämpfen die Rohirrim in der Regel erst, wenn der Speer geworfen wurde und nicht mehr verfügbar ist.

Es sind lediglich vier angelsächsische Helme erhalten geblieben, da die gängigsten Helme nicht aus Eisen gefertigt wurden. Die erhaltenen Helme sind wohl Zierhelme – z.b. für Krönungszeremonien – gewesen, daher reicher verziert und aus höherwertigem Material: Sie sind teilweise mit Tiermotiven verziert, haben Silber- oder Kupfer-Ornamente. Auffällig sind Nasen- und beweglicher Wangenschutz sowie ein Nackenschutz aus Ketten. Im Vergleich zwischen diesen und den im Film gezeigten rohirrischen Helmen ist die Vorlage deutlich zu erkennen. Vor allem Éomers Helm lässt sich leicht mit einem angelsächsischen aus einer Grabung bei Coppergate vergleichen. Beide Modelle weisen einen erweiterten Wangenschutz auf sowie einen verlängerten Nasenschutz, der sich als Ornament im oberen Verlauf des Helms fortsetzt. Bei Éomers Modell ist der Nasenschutz in Form eines Pferdekopfes gehalten, was einmal mehr die Bedeutung dieser Tiere für die Rohirrim verdeutlichen soll.

Die blonden, geflochtenen Haare, die als besonderes Merkmal der Rohirrim herausstechen, unterstützen dabei das Bild, das die Moderne von germanischstämmigen Völkern hat.

Northern Heroic Spirit

Ein weiteres angelsächsisches Element in *The Lord of the Rings* bedarf einer genaueren Untersuchung: der Aspekt des *Northern Heroic Spirit*. Darunter versteht Tolkien »the doctrine of uttermost endurance in the service of indomitable will« (HB 143), also das Durchhalten und Kämpfen bis zum bitteren Ende, gewährleistet durch einen unbezwingbaren Willen. Dabei bezieht er sich auf eine Passage aus *The Battle of Maldon*, einem angelsächsischen Heldengedicht aus dem 10. Jahrhundert. Tolkiens eigene Interpretation des Gedichts findet sich in *The Homecoming of Beorhtnoth Beorhthelm's Son*. Sein Hauptaugenmerk richtet er auf den *Northern Heroic Spirit*, den er in einer Szene sieht, in der der Anführer bereits gefallen ist und einige wenige treue Untergebene seinen Leichnam in einer hoffnungslosen Lage gegen angreifende Wikinger verteidigen:

> ... Beorhtwold, as he prepares to die in the last desperate stand, utters the famous words, a summing up of the heroic code...:
> Hige sceal þe heardra, heorte þe cenre,
> mod sceal þe mare þe ure mægen lytlað.
> "Will shall be the sterner, heart the bolder, spirit the greater as our strength lessens." (HB 124)

Anstatt also zu fliehen oder sich den überlegenen Feinden zu ergeben, versuchen Beorhtwold und seine Männer, ihren gefallenen Anführer zu verteidigen, auch wenn sie damit ihren eigenen Tod wählen. Tolkien versteht den Ausspruch Beorhtwolds als fast reinen und unverfälschten Ausdruck des *Northern Heroic Spirit*.

Als fast reinen, denn, wie Tolkien in seinem Essay erklärt, könne der Northern Heroic Spirit selten vollkommen rein und unverfälscht sein, da der eigene Stolz nie ganz überwunden werden kann. Wie eine Legierung, die Gold weniger rein sein lässt.

> For this 'northern heroic spirit' is never quite pure; it is of gold and an alloy. Unalloyed it would direct a man to endure even death unflinching, when necessary: that is when death may help the achievement of some object of will, or when life can only be purchased by denial of what one stands for. But since such conduct is held admirable, the alloy of personal good name was never wholly absent. (HB 144)

Legen wir diese Vorstellung als Raster auf die Moralvorstellungen der Menschen Rohans, so ergibt sich ein weiterer Vergleichspunkt zwischen Angelsachsen und Rohirrim. Als Beispiel kann die Schlacht auf den Pelennor Feldern dienen: König Théoden wird vom Hexenkönig von Angmar unter seinem Pferd begraben. Seine Leibwache ist tot und die Lage absolut hoffnungslos. Und doch stellt sich Éowyn zwischen den übermächtigen Nazgûl und Théoden – und das nicht mit der Aussicht auf Ruhm, sondern aus reiner Liebe zu ihrem König.

Es ist die gleiche Situation, in der sich auch Beorhtwolds Männer befinden, die den Leichnam ihres gefallenen Anführers verteidigen. Éowyns Lage ist ebenso hoffnungslos, und auch wenn der Nazgûl ›nur‹ ein einzelner Gegner ist, so übersteigt seine Macht die der anstürmenden Wikinger bei Weitem. Aus diesem Blickwinkel betrachtet scheint Éowyns Tat sogar noch heroischer zu sein als die Beorhtwolds und seiner Männer. Die Aussicht auf Ruhm scheint bei den Rohirrim ohnehin nicht gegeben, da sie einer Übermacht gegenüberstehen, die bei einem Sieg die gesamte bekannte Welt zu beherrschen droht. Daher gehen die Rohirrim nicht davon aus, dass nach ihrem Scheitern noch jemand überleben würde, um Lieder über ihre Taten singen zu können.

Trotz drohender Vernichtung kämpfen sie unerbittlich weiter. In dieser Hinsicht sind sie den Angelsachsen heroisch ›überlegen‹, denn die Angelsachsen als ein Völkerverband sahen sich nie mit einer vollkommenen Ausrottung konfrontiert. Zudem hatten die Angelsachsen seit der Konversion zum Christentum die Aussicht auf ein Leben nach dem Tod, das den Menschen Rohans unbekannt war.

Tom Shippey erklärt in einem etwas weiteren Kontext:

> In a sense this Northern mythology asks more of people then Christianity does, for it offers them no heaven, no salvation... Even the heathen Valhalla is only a waiting-room and training-ground for the final defeat. Tolkien wanted his characters in The Lord of the Rings to live up to the same high standard, ... to make them conscious of long-term defeat and doom. (Shippey, Author 150)

Damit macht Tolkien die Rohirrim zu einer verzweifelteren und dadurch heroischeren Ausgabe der Angelsachsen. Er nimmt also dem historischen Vorbild sozusagen die Legierung, den eigenen Stolz und das Streben nach Ruhm – und übrig bleibt ein Volk, das einen reinen und unverfälschten Northern Heroic Spirit verkörpert.

Peter Jacksons filmische Adaption setzt Éowyns Handeln groß in Szene, mit einer Länge von ca. siebeneinhalb Filmminuten.[1] Musik, Kameraperspektive und Schnitte zu anderen Handlungssträngen bauen eine zusätzliche Spannung auf, die im Roman nicht gegeben ist. Allerdings sind bei einem solchen Vergleich auch die wesentlichen Kritikpunkte in Betracht zu ziehen. Die Szene an sich, Éowyn vs. Nazgûl, mag zwar im Film emotionaler und epischer wirken, das heroische Ausmaß wird Éowyns Tat allerdings dadurch genommen, dass kurz darauf Aragorn mit der Dwimorberg-Armee anrückt. Dem Zuschauer wird so das Gefühl vermittelt, Éowyn und Théoden hätten nur noch ein wenig durchhalten müssen und sich damit eine Menge Tragik ersparen können.

---

1   In der Extended Edition, gezählt ab dem Angriff des Hexenkönigs auf Théoden bis zu Théodens Tod.

Sprache

Die angelsächsische Sprache, die über Werke wie *Beowulf* erhalten geblieben ist, war Tolkien sehr wichtig. Bereits während seiner Schulzeit lernt er Angelsächsisch, vertieft es während seines Studiums und unterrichtet es später selbst. Die angelsächsische Sprache spiegelt sich in *The Lord of the Rings*, sowohl im Buch als auch im Film, in verschiedener Weise: durch Eigennamen, Waffen- und Pferdenamen, Ortsbezeichnungen und vereinzelte Ausdrücke und Redewendungen. Mithilfe eines altenglischen Wörterbuches sind rohirrische Namen und Ausdrücke leicht übersetzen, da sie meist wörtlich übertragen sind und dann aus zwei Wörtern zusammengesetzt ein neues ergeben.

Zum Beispiel bilden die angelsächsischen Wörter *eoh* (für Pferd) und *þeod* (für Volk) bei Tolkien *Éothéod* (Pferdevolk), den ältesten Namen der Rohirrim. Ebenso verhält es sich mit dem Namen, den die Rohirrim ihrem eigenen Land geben: *Riddermark*. Dieser erinnert an das altenglische *ridda* (für Pferdeherr) und *mearc* (für Grenze). Die Bedeutung der Pferde für die Kultur Rohans zeigt sich auch dadurch, dass das Wort *eoh* in den Namen von Adligen als Vorsilbe eingesetzt wird, wie zum Beispiel in Éomund, Éowyn, Éomer.

Im Buch wird die direkte Rede der Rohirrim kursiv wiedergegeben, um zu verdeutlichen, dass nun in der Landessprache gesprochen wird. Interessant hierbei ist, dass die Sprache bei diesen Gelegenheiten nicht mehr nur angelsächsisch *wirkt*, sondern auch *ist*. In der Filmtrilogie ist Angelsächsisch lediglich bei zwei Gelegenheiten zu hören, leider nur in der Extended Edition:

Die erste: Théodreds Beisetzung in *The Two Towers*. Éowyn singt ihr Klagelied auf altenglisch, das in Teilen sogar an *Beowulf* erinnert: »Bealocwealm hafað fréone frecan forth onsended / Giedd sculon singan gléomenn sorgiede / On Medusele þæt he ma no wære / His dryhtne dyrest und maga deorost«. Ins Englische übersetzt: »An evil death has set forth the noble warrior / A song shall sing sorrowing minstrels / In Meduseld that he is no more / To his lord dearest and kinsmen most beloved«[2].

Die zweite Begebenheit ergibt sich in *The Return of the King*, als Éowyn nach der Heimkehr aus Helm's Deep Aragorn einen Kelch reicht mit den Worten: »Westu Aragorn hál!«. Ins Deutsche lässt sich das nur schwer übersetzen. Im Englischen kann es mit »Aragorn, be thou hale« übersetzt werden, was im Hinblick auf die vielen Bedeutungen des Adverbs *hal* im Altenglischen eine gute Lösung ist.

---

2   David Salo übersetzte Phillipa Boyens englische Textvorlage ins Altenglische (Robinson 657).

Es sind natürlich wesentlich mehr Parallelen zwischen Rohirrim und Angelsachsen herzustellen, deren ausführliche Erläuterung allerdings den Rahmen dieser Publikation sprengen würde und die daher nur kurz Erwähnung finden sollen. In Gary Russells *Die Erschaffung eines Filmkunstwerks* zum Beispiel werden immer wieder angelsächsische Ausgrabungen wie Sutton Hoo als Vorlage für Rohan genannt. Die Goldene Halle ist nicht nur im Buch sondern auch im Film von *Beowulf* inspiriert. Oftmals sind die Ähnlichkeiten auch gar nicht an bestimmten Objekten festzumachen, sondern viel subtiler eingebaut und zeigen sich dann beispielsweise in der Ursprünglichkeit Rohans gegenüber Gondor.

Anti-normannischer Reflex

Nachdem nun einige auffällige Elemente analysiert wurden, die eine Parallele zwischen Angelsachsen und Rohirrim darstellen könnten, bleibt die Frage nach dem markantesten Element der Kultur Rohans: den Pferden. Die Tatsache, dass das rohirrische Heer fast ausschließlich aus Reiterei besteht, passt nicht zu ihren möglichen historischen Vorbildern, denn das angelsächsische Heer bestand zur Zeit der Schlacht von Hastings größtenteils aus Fußtruppen. Hingegen stellt sich mit Blick auf die in England einfallenden berittenen Normannen die Frage, ob diese als Vorbild für die Rohirrim nicht viel eher in Frage kämen.

Tolkien fand es sehr bedauerlich, dass England, ungleich den skandinavischen Ländern, keine eigene Mythologie vorweisen konnte. Also wollte er mit *The Silmarillion* und *The Lord of the Rings* eine Mythologie für sein eigenes Land schaffen. Wie schon erwähnt, war Tolkien nicht nur sein Land, sondern vor allen Dingen dessen Sprache sehr wichtig – um genauer zu sein: die altenglische Sprache. Diese hatte sich aber nach der normannischen Eroberung im elften Jahrhundert stark verändert. Eben diese Veränderung in der englischen Sprache und Kultur war es, die Tolkien so missfiel. Bereits während seiner Schulzeit scheint er eine ausgeprägte Meinung dazu gehabt zu haben. Als der schuleigene Debattierclub das Thema unter dem Motto *This House deplores the occurrence of the Norman Conques* (School Chronicle 94) diskutiert, hält der damals 18-jährige Tolkien dazu eine interessante Rede. In dieser stimmt er mit der Haltung der Schule überein und spricht sich vor allem gegen die Verdrängung der englischen Sprache durch die normannische Eroberung aus. In der *King Edward's School Chronicle* des Jahres 1910 findet sich im Bericht der Debating Society folgende Aussage:

> J.R.R. Tolkien rose, and in a speech attempting to return to something of Saxon purity of diction... deplored before the "worshipful fellows of the speechguild", the influx of polysyllabic barbarities which ousted the more honest if humbler native words.
> (School Chronicle 95)

Angesichts jedoch der Natur eines jeden Debattierclubs, nämlich das Debattieren an sich zu lernen, und des jungen Alters, in dem sich Tolkien zu dieser Zeit befand, ist diese Quelle nicht sehr zuverlässig. Weitaus verlässlicher ist ein Brief, den Tolkien 1967, also 75-jährig, an Amy Ronald schrieb. Darin:

> Personally I think one of the most unfortunate results of the French invasion of England was the adulteration of our own language. With the consequence that we have a large Franco-Latin ingredient, largely floating about like oil, and specially used when we are being "adult", stuffy or professional. So that French (to those who do not know it well) sounds often priggish in colloquial dialogue.
> (Auction Catalogue 37)

Über die Sprache, die ihm als Philologe so wichtig war, zeigt sich also bei Tolkien eine sehr starke Abneigung der normannischen Eroberung Englands. Dieser anti-normannische Reflex geht so weit, dass die Rohirrim, obgleich beritten, niemals Normannen zum Vorbild haben könnten. Tom Shippey meint in *The Road to Middle-earth* sogar, die Schlacht von Hastings habe deshalb nicht gewonnen werden können, weil die angelsächsische Infanterie die normannische Kombination aus Bogenschützen und Berittenen nicht hätte abwehren können:

> Hastings was lost, along with Anglo-Saxon independence, largely because the English heavy infantry could not (quite) hold off the combination of archers and mounted knights. (Shippey, Road 140f)

Sollte Tolkien diese Ansicht ebenfalls vertreten haben, könnten die Rohirrim aus diesem Grund als Berittene konzipiert sein. Somit würden sie eine Version der Angelsachsen darstellen, die um eine Reiterei als Hauptmerkmal erweitert das ›Plus‹ bekommen hätte, das ihnen 1066 n.Chr. zum Sieg gefehlt hatte. Tolkien sah sich selbst und seine Familie zudem als Nachfahren der Bewohner des angelsächsischen Königreichs von Mercia. Damit hätte er ein ganz persönliches Anliegen mit der normannischen Eroberung. Sein Biograph Humphrey Carpenter schreibt etwa:

> ... his Gallophobia (in itself almost inexplicable) made him angry not only about what he considered to be the pernicious influence of French cooking in England but about the Norman Conquest itself, which pained him as much as if it had happened in his lifetime. (Carpenter 175)

Betrachtet man dieses Zitat im Zusammenhang mit Tolkiens selbsternannter Urheimat Mercia vielleicht als eine Art Identitätssuche, wird seine starke Abneigung gegenüber normannischer Kultur etwas nachvollziehbarer.

Annika Röttinger

Allegory und Applicability

Seit seiner Veröffentlichung in den 1950er Jahren wurde *The Lord of the Rings* immer wieder als Allegorie für den Zweiten Weltkrieg interpretiert. Das brachte Tolkien schließlich dazu, der etwas überarbeiteten amerikanischen Neuauflage in den Mitt-Sechzigern ein Vorwort hinzuzufügen, das dieser Allegorie-Suche entgegensteuern sollte. Darin findet sich folgende sehr deutliche Aussage:

> I cordially dislike allegory in all its manifestations, and always have done so since I grew old and wary enough to detect its presence.
> (LotR I xi)

Es lasst sich allerdings nicht leugnen, dass sich viele Elemente der Weltgeschichte im Werk wiederfinden, wie zum Beispiel obige Ausführungen über die Ähnlichkeiten der Angelsachsen mit den Rohirrim. Um diesen Konflikt zu lösen, schlug Tolkien einen neuen Ausdruck vor: *applicability*. Nach diesem Prinzip lassen sich reale Strukturen auf die Zweitschöpfung anwenden. Auf obiges Zitat folgt sogleich die Erklärung:

> I much prefer history, true or feigned, with its varied applicability to the thought and experience of readers. I think that many confuse 'applicability' with 'allegory'; but the one resides in the freedom of the reader, and the other in the purposed domination of the author.
> (LotR I xi)

Mit Bezug auf den *Northern Heroic Spirit* wird noch deutlicher, wie Tolkien vorgegangen ist: Anstatt den Rohirrim diesen heroischen Ethos nur zuzuschreiben, tat Tolkien dies in seiner unverfälschten Form, ohne die bereits erwähnte ›Legierung‹. Das lässt sich auch auf die oben aufgeführte ›Erweiterung‹ der Angelsachsen um eine Reiterei beziehen. Von einem allegorischen Ansatz aus argumentiert bliebe nicht viel mehr als festzustellen, dass eine Ähnlichkeit zwischen Angelsachsen und Rohirrim vorherrscht. Das Element der *applicability* jedoch bietet dem Leser eine viel tiefere Interpretationsmöglichkeit.

Der Grund, warum die von Tolkien geschaffenen Kulturen in sich stimmig sind und trotz ihrer unterschiedlichen Vorbilder nebeneinander existieren können, liegt in der Art seiner *Subcreation*, seiner Zweitschöpfung. In seiner berühmt gewordenen Vorlesung *On Fairy-Stories* erklärt er:

> Fantasy is a natural human activity. It certainly does not destroy or even insult Reason; and it does not either blunt the appetite for, nor obscure the perception of, scientific verity. On the contrary. The keener and the clearer is the reason, the better fantasy will it make.
> (FS 144)

Das heißt, um die Zweitschöpfung so glaubhaft wie möglich zu machen, lassen sich bekannte Strukturen und Elemente aus der Primärwelt aufgreifen und im Werk verarbeiten. Indem Tolkien also die Rohirrim an ein Volk wie die Angelsachsen anlehnt, macht er ihre Kultur und ihren Ethos dadurch glaubhafter und verständlicher.

Bedenkt man die Tatsache, dass Tolkien Engländer war und für sein Land eine eigene Mythologie schaffen wollte, mit der sich die Leser identifizieren sollten, klärt auch dieser Aspekt noch einmal, warum die Normannen kein Vorbild für die Rohirrim sein konnten.

Fazit

> They are proud and wilful, but they are true-hearted, generous in thought and deed; bold but not cruel; wise but unlearned, writing no books but singing many songs, after the manner of the children of Men before the Dark Years. (LotR II 39f)

Durch Tolkiens spärliche visuelle Beschreibungen fällt es schwer, sich ein genaues und detailliertes Bild vom Aussehen der Rohirrim zu machen. Die Schilde beispielsweise sind zwar rund und bemalt, aber welche Motive zieren sie? Im Buch ist es schwer, darauf eine Antwort zu finden. Peter Jacksons filmische Adaption von *The Lord of the Rings* gibt darüber mehr Aufschluss. Die Paralellen zwischen Rohirrim und Angelsachsen werden durch den Film hervorgehoben, was ihre Bildlichkeit betrifft. Nehmen wir uns allerdings komplexerer Themen an, wie Ethos und Sprache, so werden wir im Film (zumindest in der Extended Edition) zwar auch fündig, jedoch gibt der Roman hier wesentlich tiefere und reichere Einblicke.

Interessant an den Filmen ist, dass die nichtvisuellen Ähnlichkeiten zwischen Angelsachsen und Rohirrim fast ausschließlich über Éowyns Charakter dargestellt werden. Aussehen, Waffen und Rüstung lassen sich natürlich durchaus auch an anderen Figuren festmachen. Aber wenn es um Sprache oder Ethos geht, welche Tolkien wichtiger gewesen sein dürften als das Aussehen, ist Éowyn die Quelle. Sie ist die Einzige im Film, die Altenglisch spricht und sie ist diejenige, die den *Northern Heroic Spirit* am deutlichsten verkörpert. Vielleicht lässt sich das als Hervorhebung der weiblichen Rolle im Film interpretieren. Vielleicht ist es aber auch unbeabsichtigter Zufall.

Abschließend lässt sich also festhalten, dass Peter Jacksons filmische Adaption Tolkiens anti-normannischen Reflex durchaus unterstützt und dadurch auch eine zusätzliche Interpretationsebene bietet. Für einen genaueren Blick auf angelsächsische Ideale in der Kultur Rohans können wir uns allerdings wie immer getrost auf die historische Fülle und erzählerische Dichte des Professors verlassen.

Bibliographie

Beowulf. A new verse translation, übers. von Seamus Heaney. New York: W.W. Norton, 2000

Carpenter, Humphrey. *J.R.R. Tolkien. A Biography*. London: HarperCollins, 2002 (1977)

Carpenter, Humphrey und Christopher Tolkien (Hg.). *The Letters of J.R.R. Tolkien*. London: HarperCollins, 2006 (1981)

Carver, Martin. *Sutton Hoo. A Seventh-Century Princely Burial Ground and its Context*. London: British Museum Press, 2005

Chance, Jane (Hg.). *Tolkien the Medievalist*. New York: Routledge, 2003

Christie's (Hg.). *Autograph Letters and Printed Books, including First Editions*, Auction-Catalogue. London: Christie's, 2000

Dawson, Deidre. "English, Welsh and Elvish. Language, Loss, and Cultural Recovery in Tolkien's 'The Lord of the Rings'". *Tolkien's Modern Middle-Ages*. Hg. Jane Chance & Alfred K. Siewers. New York: Palgrave Macmillan, 2009 (2005)

Honegger, Thomas. "The Rohirrim. 'Anglo-Saxons on Horseback'? An inquiry into Tolkien's use of sources". *Tolkien and the study of his sources. Critical Essays*. Hg. Jason Fisher. London: McFarland & Company, 2011

King Edward's School Chronicle. 'Debating Society', n. s. 26, no. 184. Birmingham: Oxford University Press, 1910

Robinson, Jeremy Mark. *J.R.R.Tolkien. The books, the films, the whole cultural phenomenon*. Maidstone: Crescent Moon, 2008

Russell, Gary. *Der Herr der Ringe. Die zwei Türme. Die Erschaffung eines Filmkunstwerks*. Stuttgart: Klett-Cotta, 2003

---. *Der Herr der Ringe. Die Rückkehr des Königs. Die Erschaffung eines Filmkunstwerks*. Stuttgart: Klett-Cotta, 2004

Shippey, Tom Allan. *J.R.R. Tolkien. Author of the Century*. London: HarperCollins, 2001 (2000)

---. *The Road to Middle-earth. How J.R.R.Tolkien created a new mythology*. London: HarperCollins, 2005 (1982)

The Anglo-Saxon Chronicle, übers. von G.N. Garmonsway. London: J.M. Dent & Sons, 1975 (1953)

The Battle of Maldon. Text and Translation, übers. von Bill Griffiths. Pinner: Anglo-Saxon Books, 1992 (1991)

Tolkien, John Ronald Reuel. *The Fellowship of the Ring*. Being the second part of *The Lord of the Rings*. New York: Ballantine Books, 1967 (1954)

---. *The Two Towers*. Being the second part of *The Lord of the Rings*. New York: Ballantine Books, 1967 (1954)

---. *The Return of the King*. Being the third part of *The Lord of the Rings*. New York: Ballantine Books, 1967 (1954)

---. "The Homecoming of Beorhtnoth Beorhthelm's Son". *Tree and Leaf*. London: HarperCollins, 2001 (1964), 119-150

---. *On Fairy-Stories*. *The Monsters and the Critics and Other Essays*. Hg. Christopher Tolkien. London: HarperCollins, 2006 (1983)

Music as a Narrative Element in *The Lord of the Rings* Radio Plays

Heidi Steimel (Scharbeutz)

Introduction

In the beginning was the word—what was said of the Biblical creation story also applies to Tolkien's sub-creation. His written words introduced us to Middle-earth. However, oral storytelling existed long before writing or printing, and it is therefore logical that his tales should be retold in audible form—as radio or audio plays.

Modern storage devices have made it possible to conserve and distribute productions which were originally conceived for one-time usage. Thanks to tapes, CDs and MP3s, we can today hear productions that were broadcast on the radio decades ago. The widespread popularity of the *Lord of the Rings* movies has rekindled interest in the radio plays produced in England and Germany—very likely in other countries as well, but I will concentrate on the two that I have heard myself. As a musician, I paid special attention to the music and its role in telling the story, and discovered that each version uses a very different style. I would like to compare both the style and the function of music in *Der Herr der Ringe* and *The Lord of the Rings*.

Is music essential for the retelling of Tolkien's stories? No—there are audio books of a number of them, which are straightforward readings without other elements. But the audio drama, with its different facets, uses music much as films do. As Young states in his analysis of the *Lord of the Rings* movie soundtrack, "...film music has the ability to influence an audiences' perception of a film, convey information to them, affect them emotionally, and aid in their memory of the events of the film" (Young 4-5). He notes that experts do not agree on the narrative function of music:

> Among these scholars, there are those who believe that the music itself can narrate; those who believe the composer is narrating through the music; those who believe the listeners hear the music as though it is narrating regardless of the composer's intent; and those who believe that music cannot narrate due to its inherent lack of a narrator. (Young 1)

However, he believes that "music does have the power to communicate information to the audience...", and adds: "At the very least, a film score's role as accompaniment to events occurring on-screen suggests the music's ability to reflect some sort of meaning to the audience" (Young 1).

These principles can be applied to the audio play, though it lacks the visual aspect of film. In his study of the music of the BBC radio play *The Lord of the Rings*, Paul Smith writes,

> The role music plays dramaturgically in radio and films is perforce different; the medium of radio invites the listener to use the mind's eye, while the television offers pictures for direct consumption. There are moments in the radio play where the music is the central means by which the drama is propelled forward and is the primary driver for the picture painted in the listener's mind. (Smith 243)

Mechtild Hobl-Friedrich's analysis of the dramaturgical role of music in audio plays states "that music in the audio play is not only a decorative accessory, sometimes even felt to be annoying, but has its own dramaturgy and is doubly indispensable as a statement" (Hobl-Friedrich 15).[1]

There are two basic categories of music used in drama, and since audio plays are closely related to both stage plays and movies, much of what can be said about one form also applies to the others. The first kind is that which comes from within the story and is called "diegetic". This refers to songs or instrumental pieces that are performed or heard by its characters in the context of the story. They belong to the narrative and their narrative function is within the story rather than independent thereof. Tolkien's tale includes numerous poems, many of which are sung in Middle-earth, so this category of music is important when dramatizing his work.

Sound effects can be produced by musical instruments at times and could possibly be included in this category.

The second category of music is non-diegetic and comes from outside the story. It is most often instrumental, though vocal music is also possible, and can function as an introductory theme, as a transition, and as a background underneath narrative or dialogue. "We can speak of music in an audio play when musical phrases are used in selected places for internal or external structure as scene dividers, introductory or closing music, interludes, in bridge functions or as sound effect substitutes" (Hobl-Friedrich 33).[2]

In the first function, as an introductory theme, it can help the listeners to identify the audio play by means of a recognizable melody at the beginning—an important method of getting them to focus on hearing, since there is no visible

---

1 Original: ...dass Musik im Hörspiel nicht nur schmückendes, manchmal ein als störend empfundenes Beiwerk ist, sondern eine eigene Dramaturgie besitzt und als Aussage in doppeltem Sinne unverzichtbar ist. (my translation)
2 Original: Von Musik im Hörspiel lässt sich immer dann sprechen, wenn musikalische Phrasen punktuell zur inneren oder äußeren Gliederung eingesetzt sind: als Szenentrenner, Einleitungs- und Schlussmusiken, Pausenfüller, in Brückenfunktion oder als Geräusch›ersatz‹. (my translation)

cue at the start. This music also sets the scene emotionally and prepares the listener for the story content.

The transitional function defines a change of location or time by setting the stage with a different music.

> It is used to close a scene and prepare a new one; it cushions the previous scene emotionally and catches the following mood in preparation. In this function it can frequently be found in traditional, conventional audio plays, such as those adaptations of epic literature or dramatic stage plays which have been prepared for radio. (Hobl-Friedrich 75)[3]

Background music adds emotional impact to the spoken word—an augmentation that is helpful, since the listeners do not have the visual factor of facial expression or gestures to aid in the interpretation of the audible narrative or dialogue. Both transitional and background music can be used to characterize persons or places, by use of *Leitmotifs*, for example—melodies or phrases that are consistently used when a character or location is present in the narrative.

> Typical for characterising music are examples in which persons are designated by a certain motive, the consistent use of the same instrument, or a recurring sound: Whenever this phenomenon occurs, the listener knows that this person is present, no matter which constellation of persons can be heard in the scene. In the same manner a change of location is indicated to the listener without having to resort to awkward verbal allusions.
> (Hobl-Friedrich 77)[4]

Non-diegetic music should add a narrative dimension to the spoken word—if it does not, it has little worth except as a pause or interruption.

---

3   Original: Sie wird verwendet, um eine Szene abzuschließen und auf eine neue vorzubereiten; sie federt die vorausgegangene Szene emotional ab und fängt die nachfolgende Stimmung vorbereitend ein. In dieser Funktion ist sie häufig in den traditionellen, konventionellen Hörspielen wie in den für den Funk erarbeiteten Adaptionen epischer Literatur oder dramatischer Bühnenwerke zu finden. (my translation)
4   Original: Für eine charakterisierende Musik typisch sind Beispiele, in denen Personen durch ein bestimmtes Motiv, durch das immer gleiche Instrument oder einen sich wiederholenden ›Sound‹ gekennzeichnet werden: immer, wenn dieses Phänomen eintritt, weiß der Zuhörer, dass diese Person gegenwärtig ist, gleichgültig, welche Personenkonstellation ihm die Szenerie hörbar macht. In gleicher Weise wird verfahren, wenn dem Hörer ein Ortswechsel signalisiert werden soll, ohne dass auf plumpe Art verbal darauf hingewiesen werden muss. (my translation)

Der Herr der Ringe

First, I would like to examine the German radio play *Der Herr der Ringe*. It was produced in 1991-92 by two state radio stations: Südwestrundfunk and Westdeutscher Rundfunk. It is 12 ½ hours long and considered one of the most complex productions in the history of German audio plays, as well as being one of the most continually popular (Ardapedia). The music was composed by Peter Zwetkoff, who also wrote music for other radio plays. His style, at least for this production, is quite modern and rather minimalistic. He uses few instruments, mostly those that are mentioned in the book, creating a sound that is not orchestral. At times the instrumental sound has an electronic character: either the original instrumental sound was electronically modified or synthesizers were played.

The introductory theme uses the beginning notes of the "Road goes ever on" song which we hear a bit later. It sets up the stylistic feeling of the play's music score. This is quite a change from the usual quasi-Mediaeval music heard in fantasy settings. Perhaps it is intended to denote the otherness of a different secondary world. Whether or not that idea functions depends on the reaction of the listeners.

The One Ring, which is pivotal to the story, has its own *Leitmotif*, a bell-like musical sound effect. It is heard when the Ring is used, or sometimes when it is spoken of.

Specific instrumentation is used to denote persons, peoples, and places throughout the production: the three primary female characters, Galadriel, Arwen and Éowyn are all characterized by flute melodies. Low-pitched instruments are frequently heard when danger and foes appear: we hear either a string bass or a bass woodwind instrument when the Ringwraiths, the Barrow-Wight, and the Paths of the Dead are encountered. Horns sound when the Rohirrim take the stage, especially when battles are fought.

Percussion instruments play at various times, prominently so when industrialization is indicated: accompanying Sam's Mirror vision of the despoiled Shire, for example. We hear metal percussion when Saruman is introduced, and wood percussion imitates the beat of the horses' hooves when the Rohirrim ride.

The use of instrumental music to indicate a change of location is frequent but not consistent throughout the production. A change of scene from Mordor to Rohan, for example, is signaled by horns. A change of time in the narrative is preceded by music when the story of Bilbo's previous adventure is retold.

Background music that heightens the emotional aspect of a scene can be heard in the chapter "The Shadow of the Past". Gandalf's monologue is accompanied by very evocative strains. Another passage which is underscored with emotional music is Theoden's death scene, backed by a funeral march.

As for the songs, those which are sung by the book's characters in this production have a typical style: unaccompanied, with one or more singers as mentioned in the narrative, sung by the actors without professional quality or even accuracy, just as they might have been sung by the Hobbits and others in their real life. The "Old Walking Song" is the first one which is recorded; the five-note motif of the series theme is heard at the beginning of the melody.

Considering the many poems that Tolkien wrote in his book, not very many songs were put to music by Zwetkoff. Some, like the Elven song in Rivendell, are used as background music, perhaps to save time. Other poems are recited or performed as *Sprechgesang*, spoken song. Treebeard and Gollum are two characters who do not sing a melody to their songs.

Sam's song about Gil-galad is one that was set to music in both the German and English productions. It serves the purpose of filling in history without resorting to the narrator.

"Durin's Day" is sung by Gimli. It too provides a historical background for the Dwarves in a concise and interesting way.

The German audio play has one very special feature which neither of the movie versions nor the BBC radio play has: the Hobbits encounter Tom Bombadil, Goldberry, and the Barrow-Wight! Bombadil's song utilizes the narrative function of anticipation—it begins in the background, under the narration, introducing the character before he becomes active in the storyline. Goldberry's song has the clearest melody of all the songs in this production. It is very modern in its tonality, wandering through several different keys, a technique that conveys the impression of flowing water to listeners—very appropriate for the River-daughter. The Barrow-Wight's poem is accompanied by very deep instrumental music—I say accompanied, but it is actually less that than a background music that runs parallel to the recitation without consideration of joint rhythm or any musical togetherness.

The composer once stated (Hobl-Friedrich 118) that he saw the role of music as subordinate to the words of the story, and that accurately sums up the concept of this production. A one-time listener would be hard put to sing or whistle any of the melodies—they are not so remarkable as to be easily remembered.

The Lord of the Rings

The BBC radio play was produced a decade earlier, in 1981. Its length is similar to that of the German production: 13 hours. The composer of the music is Stephen Oliver, who was chosen because the producers wanted someone to create a specifically English music for the story. That quality is most often mentioned by those who have written about it.

Paul Smith writes:

> The Middle-earth legendarium, and Tolkien's other stories, reflect his concepts of English society and pastoralism, which are summed up in the one short phrase, "a mythology for England." The BBC production team had sensed this and director Jane Morgan noted that "everyone was agreed that [the music of the play] must sound essentially English." (Smith 242)

David Bratman adds:

> The music to the BBC radio dramatization of 1981, written by Stephen Oliver, is much more interesting [than the film soundtrack]. It is startlingly derivative of modern British classical music of the generation immediately younger than Tolkien, but quite moving in context. The theme music is stodgy—it sounds like the march of the absent-minded professors—and could have been by any number of the followers of Benjamin Britten or William Walton. The vocal music is largely for counter-tenor and boy sopranos, and some of that is straight out of the English choral tradition... (Bratman 160)

Smith also says: "Much of this music can be characterised by generally quiet dynamics, consonant harmony, simple melodic contours, and often a "rocking" accompaniment in 6/8 or similar compound time signatures. It aims to evoke a particular atmosphere of place—'landscape in music'" (Smith 242). "... a particularly important aspect of Oliver's compositions; his settings take inspiration from the *whole* history of English music..." (Smith 243).

Greg Martin compares Tolkien's concept of a mythology for England to that of the composer Ralph Vaughan Williams, noting that "Both men were rooted in the pastoral idyll of late Victorian and Edwardian England..." (Martin 132), thereby confirming the choice of a specifically English style of music.

The basic principles of audio play music mentioned earlier apply here as well, though their use differs from the German production in some aspects. The recording begins with the theme, which uses more instruments and has a more lush orchestral sound than Zwetkoff's introduction.

There is less background music throughout the play, so that narrative and dialogue are often unaccompanied. However, Oliver composed melodies for more of the songs, and quite a few of those are memorable. Some are sung as if heard within the context of the story in Middle-earth, unaccompanied; in others, the voice is joined by instruments, combining diegetic and non-diegetic music.

The One Ring has its own *Leitmotif* in this production as well. It resembles the sound of musical glasses or a glass harp. Another motif is that used for Shadowfax—a theme of running notes that propels the action forward in the passages it underscores, taking on a very definite narrative role.

A five-note horn melody is used numerous times as a signal for Rohan. The melody to the song the Rohirric bard sings begins with those same five notes. Interestingly, Shippey notes that "Inside *The Lord of the Rings*, the horn of Rohan stands for a rejection of the despair which is Sauron's chief weapon…" (Shippey 220) The frequent use of the instrument in the radio play, though usually very brief, serves to remind the listener of the importance of hope.

A different horn melody is repeated as well—that of Boromir's horn is later heard in the background when Faramir speaks, reminding the listener that the two characters were brothers.

I consider some of these compositions for Tolkien's songs the best settings I have heard for his poetry. Oliver's tune for the "Old Walking Song", however, is not my favourite version—the minor key is not cheerful enough for a hobbit song, in my opinion, and the slow tempo defeats the purpose of a walking song for keeping one's feet moving. We first hear it sung by Bilbo, unaccompanied, as if we overhear it while he is walking. Later, when Frodo quotes the poem, the melody is heard in the background, establishing a connection.

There are several instances of *Sprechgesang* in which the poems are recited: by Aragorn and Gimli, for example, often accompanied by background music. Frodo speaks "There is an inn" rhythmically, but without singing a melody.

When songs are sung, they are often performed by the actors themselves, not by professional singers. One of the most beautiful, with a haunting melody, is Sam's song of Gil-galad, sung by Bill Nighy. "In Western Lands", sung by him later on, is another highlight.

However, Galadriel's song "O Lorien" is sung by a professional, and even more unusual, by a male, a counter-tenor! Tolkien wrote that she had a deep voice for a female (LotR I 462), and as Paul Smith conjectures, the composer may have chosen this option to denote "other-worldliness" for the Elf (Smith 246). The counter-tenor also sings the part of another character, the Eagle Gwaihir's song. In that case, the choice of the very high male register is quite appropriate for a speaking bird and also evokes "otherness" (Smith 245).

A professional boy soprano sings the poem that Boromir dreamt, "Seek for the sword that was broken". The high voice gives the song a dreamlike feeling and suits Tolkien's own description of the "voice, remote, but clear." (LotR I 320)

The narrative function of these songs is found within the story. In one case, however, a song is expanded to fulfill an additional narrative function—continuing the story in a concise fashion to compress the events into a short time. It is the song of the Rohirric bard, beginning with the lyrics we read in the book, but augmented by stanzas that carry on from there. Having a bard tell the tale in song is eminently fitting for the subject matter and very much in keeping with the spirit of Middle-earth!

Brundige's review of the radio play elaborates on this unique example of musical narrative:

> The Muster of Rohan and the Battle of the Pelennor Fields is presented in a highly original fashion, since of necessity it has too many action sequences to avoid a bland narrator giving a play-by-play. Yet the BBC version manages it. The sequence begins with a very traditional bardic performance (nothing like the cheesy Rankin-Bass minstrel, I promise) starting with *"Forth rode the king, fear behind him / fate before him. Fealty kept he..."* and goes through the end of that song, set to appropriately stately yet not overdone music. From then on until the battle's end, narrative is provided by stanzas of the ballad, linking together vignettes of live action and dialogue: Merry's introduction to Dernhelm, Théoden's arrival at the Rammas, his charge across the field, the whole Nazgûl sequence, and the other important incidents of that battle... The sequence concludes with *"Death in the morning and at day's ending / lords took and lowly"* through *"red fell the dew in Rammas Echor."* It is very powerful. But the true brilliance is that Sibley and Bakewell meticulously combed through Tolkien's narrative of the battle and adapted lines of its description, in meter, with appropriate alliteration, which fit so well that I had not realized lines had been added to serve as the play-by-play for the battle which in fact were not originally part of these songs.
>
> (Brundige)

The last example I would like to mention is unique to this adaptation of *The Lord of the Rings*: "Bilbo's Last Song". Though it does not actually belong to the original story, having been written by Tolkien some years later, it is a very appropriate closing highlight for the end of the radio play. It begins as Bilbo recites the poem, then continues, sung by the boy soprano, fitting for the passage of the ship to another world. Smith says:

> Oliver chooses to set this for treble rather than an adult male voice to emphasise the link with the divine and the universality of the experience of passing, as the Last Ship crosses the Sea and Bilbo reaches Elvenhome. As such it wraps up the narrative and underscores the emotional flavour of the final parting.   (Smith 248)

Conclusion

The same story can be told, not only in different languages, but also with different music. What works for one production would possibly not feel right for the other. Both composers succeeded in adding not only breaks to the play, but narrative value to their sound scores. Can one be said to be better than the other? A listener's evaluation is certainly a matter of personal taste.

In my case, I prefer Stephen Oliver's music for the BBC production for two reasons: firstly, I agree with the producers that a specifically English music fits the story best, at least as it is retold in its original language. It is my opinion that Tolkien would have approved of the score and enjoyed hearing that adaptation which many people consider the definitive dramatized version of *The Lord of the Rings*. Considering what we know of his taste in music, the music he might have composed could have sounded very similar to this, had he been a musician himself.

Secondly, the music of the BBC play holds more musical interest and value for me. As a musician, I appreciate the memorable and aesthetically pleasing song melodies—they provide me with a Middle-earth songbook that has considerable worth of its own, even apart from the audio play. As a matter of fact, a sound track CD that includes a number of songs and pieces was released in addition to the recording of the play itself.

Finally, I find a very Tolkienish aspect in Oliver's music: that of *eucatastrophe*. There is a "sudden and miraculous grace" (OFS 69) that touches my heart when I hear Sam's voice rising to sing "I will not say the Day is done" ("In Western Lands", LotR III 1189), full of hope that the quest will succeed in the face of overwhelming odds. I am also deeply stirred when Matthew Vine sings "I see the Star above your mast!" (BLS) with its high note in the final stanza of "Bilbo's Last Song".

This music does more than just supporting the words of the story—it adds an additional sub-creation to Tolkien's work. That is what the author hoped would happen—"other minds and hands, wielding paint and music and drama." (L 145) Had he the opportunity to see and hear the radio plays and other forms of art, visual and audible, produced by his readers, he would certainly be astonished over the extent to which this has actually happened. These two audio plays and their music continue to bring the joy of discovering Middle-earth to us, the readers and listeners.

Bibliography

Ardapedia. http://ardapedia.herr-der-ringe-film.de/index.php/Der_Herr_der_Ringe_ (H%C3%B6rspiel) (02.04.2013)

Bratman, David. "Liquid Tolkien: Music, Tolkien, Middle-earth, and More Music". *Middle-earth Minstrel.* Ed. Bradford, Lee Eden. Jefferson: McFarland and Company, 2010, 140-170

Brundige, Ellen. "A Masterpiece Worthy of the Masterpiece." Review. http://www.istad.org/tolkien/sibley.html (08.04.2013)

Hobl-Friedrich, Mechtild. *Die dramaturgische Funktion der Musik im Hörspiel. Grundlagen – Analysen.* Diss. Univ. Erlangen/Nürnberg, 1991

Martin, Gregory. "Music, Myth, and Literary Depth in the "Land ohne Musik". *Music in Middle-earth.* Eds. Heidi Steimel & Friedhelm Schneidewind. Zurich/Jena: Walking Tree Publishers, 2010

Shippey, Tom. *J.R.R. Tolkien - Author of the Century.* London: HarperCollins, 2001

Smith, Paul. "Microphones in Middle-earth: Music in the BBC Radio Play". *Music in Middle-earth.* Eds. Heidi Steimel & Friedhelm Schneidewind. Zurich/Jena: Walking Tree Publishers, 2010

Tolkien, John Ronald Reuel. *Bilbo's Last Song.* London: Hutchinson, 2002

---. "On Fairy-Stories". *Tree and Leaf.* London: HarperCollins, 2001

---. *The Letters of J.R.R. Tolkien.* Ed. Humphrey Carpenter. London: HarperCollins, 1995

---. *The Lord of the Rings.* London: HarperCollins, 2007

Young, Matthew. *Projecting Tolkien's Musical Worlds.* Saarbrücken: VDM Verlag Dr. Müller, 2007

Discography

Tolkien, J.R.R. *The Lord of the Rings.* Dramatised by Brian Sibley & Michael Bakewell. England: BBC, 1981

---. *Der Herr der Ringe.* Translated by Margaret Carroux. Dramatised by Peter Steinbach. Germany: SWF/WDR, 1992

"I feel as if I was inside a Song"

The Presence of Music in J.R.R. Tolkien's Middle-earth and Songs and Poems of *The Lord of the Rings* set to Music[1]

Tobias Escher (Bingen)

The references to music in J.R.R. Tolkien's *The Lord of the Rings*, both in terms of musical elements only mentioned indirectly in passing as well as music directly performed as part of the story are many and varied. Spanning nearly all cultures described by Tolkien in his work they arguably form an important part as to the cultural and historical background of the cosmos envisioned by the author. To a large extent, music serves as a major characterising force for the protagonists, remaining very realistic in its depiction and use as a believable part of the characters' behaviour and cultural background.

The most important aspect of music in Middle-earth are songs sung by characters during the course of the story as well as poems recited by them, with the boundaries between the two not always clearly separable. These texts range from traditional folk songs to—supposedly—art music as well as prophecies, riddles and verse. All of these are tightly interweaved with the actual narrative, not disrupting the storyline, but instead being part of it and are in some cases even necessary for understanding the plot.

Major Works

We will deal with three works, in which composers have tried to make the music of Middle-earth audible. What these works have in common is that clearly the artists responsible for their creation have carefully studied Tolkien's writings as well as his background rather than only loosely basing their art on Tolkien's universe.

The Tolkien Ensemble: Complete Songs & Poems

The Tolkien Ensemble is a Danish group of musicians, founded and led by composer Caspar Reiff. The ensemble came together in 1995 with the goal to create the first complete musical interpretation of all of Tolkien's poems in *The Lord of the Rings*. Composer Caspar Reiff explains the idea behind their four albums as follows (Reiff, *e-mail 1*):

---

[1] The full version of this paper is available at ww.middle-earth-music.info.

The four albums that led to the 4CD box were called *An Evening in Rivendell, A Night in Rivendell, At Dawn in Rivendell* and *Leaving Rivendell*. The reason for this is that the whole production could be seen as a fictive evening, night and morning in Rivendell where the main characters and the population meets up after the War of the Ring to share the songs and tales of the recent war.

Donald Swann: "The Road Goes Ever On" Song Cycle

The only published renditions of songs from *The Lord of the Rings* during the author's lifetime were written by British composer Donald Swann (1923-1994), who set a number of songs from the book to music along with one song from *The Adventures of Tom Bombadil*. Swann played the songs to Tolkien, who liked them with the exception of one single song. The songs are set for a solo vocalist with piano accompaniment and in their style draw from art song. The cycle is intended to be performed as a whole with key changes composed in and must be seen as separate from the book. The composer writes that his "music was not written in Middle-earth" (Swann, v).

The Lord of the Rings: The Stage Show

There have been a number of stage productions setting out to bring Tolkien's most well-known work. A big theatrical production of *The Lord of the Rings* premiered in 2006 in Toronto and, after mixed success, was shortened and with parts re-written reopened in London in 2007.

The music for the production was written by Indian composer A.R. Rahman in collaboration with Finnish world music group Värttinä. According to the producers, orchestrator Christopher Nightingale had a significant part in shaping the score (Russell, 77). The producers maintain their desire to be true to Tolkien: "'Was I ever tempted to use Tolkien's lyrics?' asks Shaun McKenna [Co-Writer]. 'No, it wouldn't have been appropriate here...'" (Russell, 75)

Prerequisites

The origins of music in Middle-earth—or in the whole of Arda for that matter—are clearly supernatural. It is hard to think of any universe in which music plays a more important role in its creation. By describing the creation of the world as an act of music, Tolkien implies its importance in the actual world. How can music—in a world created by music—not remain important?

In most writings, scholars have compared the music of Middle-earth in its general style to our medieval music. In his article *A Speculative History of the Music of Arda*, Steven Linden suggests an interesting theory about the development of music in Arda: to solve the dilemma how a music from an ancient world such as Middle-earth can sound very much alike to music tens of thousands of years later, while having completely different social and political as well as environmental, Linden proposes the concept of "reverse progress" (Linden 76f).

This means: we can assume that the stylistically most highly developed music was the music of the Ainur. This music, performed by gods, in its technical characteristics (use of counterpoint leading to perfect polyphony, choice of harmonies, melodic properties) can be considered as the ultimate peak of music. This perfect music was then passed on to the Elves, then to the Men and all the other peoples of Middle-earth. Ultimately, all music is therefore based on this First Music.

Selected Music

Songs found in *The Lord of the Rings* can be roughly divided into two groups.
1) Songs invented and sung by characters from the narrative during the course of the book or not a very long time before. A song from this group stands for its singer/composer, not necessarily for the race or culture he or she belongs to.

2) Traditional songs, whose origins very much predate the timeframe of the book (the end of the Third Age). These songs now are much more representative of the culture they originated from, by the fact of gradual textual selection: most of the songs and poems composed over time would have been forgotten, with only the most important and most valued ones remaining in cultural memory. These songs mostly deal with legends and past events or describe a certain state of the culture in a former time. Musically speaking, these songs also would be most representative of the accepted general style of that particular culture, since they would be passed on from one generation to another as a cultural heritage and therefore are unlikely to be changing much, if at all.

There is one general feature of all the songs presented: all the renditions are accompanied, even though in the book some clearly are not. The creators of the recordings clearly wanted to picture the common performance situation, not the special circumstances of the book. It is obvious that Gimli will not have had an 80 piece symphony orchestra at his disposal when singing the *Song of Durin*. But if we let such a performance stand as a representation of how such a song would usually be performed, we can and should analyse it as to the way this performance might be true to the book. Caspar Reiff, the founder of the Tolkien Ensemble confirms this:

> If you want to do a version that represents "the actual perform-ance in the book" our version obviously does not achieve that goal. Almost all songs would have to be single voice only. It was never the intension [sic!], though, to do so.   (Reiff, *e-mail 1*)

The instrumentation of pieces is a quite different topic, however, and can be treated somewhat more strictly. It is easily possible that in Rivendell there may have been an ensemble with musicians from different races or even cultures within the same race, providing the accompaniment to the songs. This would sufficiently explain the presence of some instruments in songs by cultures usually not likely to play these instruments. Nevertheless, there is no reason why any song should be accompanied by a "wrong" instrument at a retelling of the War of the Ring—just like in a modern ensemble these players could just have stayed silent for the song.

Namárië[2]

For a world so full of music and musical allusions, we have precious little first-hand information about how Tolkien imagined this music to sound like. There is one exception, though, where we not only have a description of the general stylistic qualities of a piece, but even a melody that goes with it by hand of the author. Galadriel sings *Namárië* after the Fellowship leaves her realm. The song is the longest Quenya text in the book. It deals with "things little known on Middle-earth" (LotR 377) and refers to the Undying Lands and Galadriel's desire to return there, something that was forbidden to her due to her being part of the group of Elves that went to Middle-earth against the wish of the Valar.

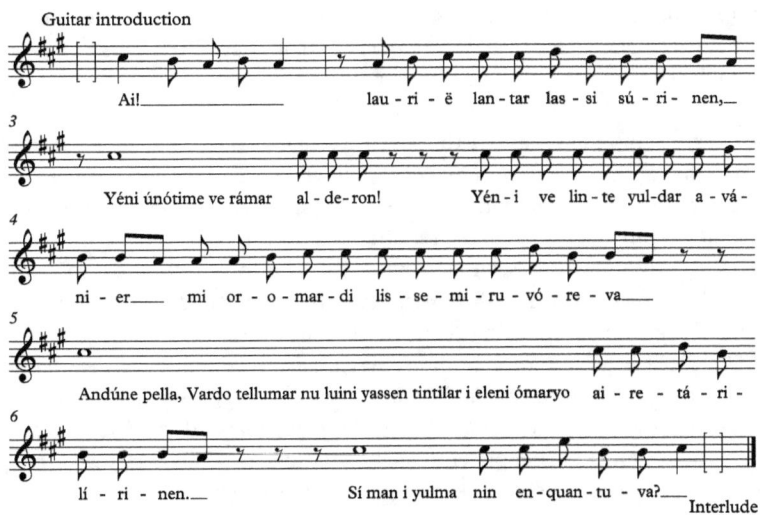

Excerpt: Namárië, Swann, 22

---

2 Donald Swann, *Namárië*, Swann, 22; Tolkien Ensemble, *Song Of The Elves Beyond The Sea / Galadriel's Song Of Eldamar (II)*, TE CD 2, Track 13, 6:13.

Donald Swann, who first set the poem to music, maintains that while Tolkien liked the rest of his renditions, he "bridled at my [Swann's] music for 'Namárië.' He had heard it differently in his mind, he said, and hummed a Gregorian chant" (Swann, vi). Swann therefore decided to use Tolkien's melody for the song and just print it in the way the author had told him, so technically speaking, Namárië is composed by Tolkien, not Swann.

Save for the introduction, the interlude and the ending of the piece, *Namárië* is performed unaccompanied; the tempo is given as "freely". Giving the Elves a musical language oriented towards plainsong makes sense if one sees them as the oldest, most traditional race. Nevertheless, if we think of the idea of "reverse progress", it seems strange for such an ancient and important piece of music to be quite so simple. We would expect rather rich polyphony in High Elven music, as it is nearest to the First Music.

One possible explanation would be that Galadriel simply preferred this mode of singing. Also if she only ever sang her lament to herself, there would have been no other musicians present for a polyphonic version. It is likely that Tolkien chose the plainsong approach to represent Galadriel's loneliness: far away from home, with no prospect to go back and the knowledge that when the Master Ring would be destroyed, her time to fade would come, too, due to her Ring loosing its power. So the most likely explanation for Tolkien's wish to see this song represented as plainsong is that he intended it as a representation of Galadriel's personality, not as a model of what High Elven music sounded like in general.

The Tolkien Ensemble has set this poem to music as the *Song Of The Elves Beyond The Sea / Galadriel's Song Of Eldamar (II)*. The rendition at the first glance does not use a Gregorian chant, but instead is oriented towards operatic music, similarly to the other renditions of Elvish songs by the Ensemble. It intelligently unites classical elements with plainsong technique, following Tolkien's conception of Elvish music, yet at the same time removing it from being purely based on existing "real-world" musical styles.

The piece begins with a tremolo marimba introduction, with a female soloist providing figures on "aah". In the whole piece, the voice constitutes a major source of momentum, driving the piece forward. Midway through the introduction, an arpeggiated marimba pattern is taken over by the harp. Low male voices and a string section provide a pad. The actual poem begins at 0:53:

Transcription (excerpt): Song Of The Elves Beyond The Sea / Galadriel's Song Of Eldamar (II), TE CD 2, Track 13

During the whole piece, the string and choir pad stays consistent; the harp plays its arpeggiated eights pattern with the first beat silent. Only occasionally for added impact, the accompaniment stays silent for a number of beats at the end of lines as well as mid-piece for single lines. These sparsely used passages of unaccompanied soloist singing strongly evoke a feeling of plainsong, thereby establishing a link between the Ensemble's mental image of what Elvish music sounds like ("something between folk music and classical music", according to Reiff, *e-mail 2*) and what we know of Tolkien's ideas of Elvish music from Swann's song cycle.

It may be argued that the Ensemble's approach of mixing learned classical music (including use of crafted instruments as a result of centuries of refinement of instrument families, establishing and suggesting an active development of instrument craftsmanship) with plainsong as described by Tolkien actually makes perfect sense by combining the author's vision of the sound of Elvish music with the background of a musical style developed over centuries and rooted in firm harmonic and melodic rules, thus complying to the idea of all music in Middle-earth directly being derived and based on the First Music.

The Old Walking Song[3]

The Old Walking Song, the very first song to be encountered by the reader in *The Lord of the Rings* is sung by Bilbo when leaving the Shire after the "long-expected party" and, with textual alterations, sung repeatedly later by Frodo.

---

3   Tolkien Ensemble, *The Old Walking Song (I)*, TE CD 1, Track 1, 5:09; Donald Swann, *The Road Goes Ever On*, Swann, 1; The Lord of the Rings Musical, *The Road Goes On*, LotR M, Track 2, 4:51.

The origin of the song is not completely clear: one might argue that it is derived from a similar poem spoken by Bilbo at the end of *The Hobbit*. Nothing suggests that he has invented it. Even though Bilbo is here described "saying" what would clearly be a good walking song, there is no reason to assume that even if he did not sing it when coming home, he would not make a song out of it later on. After all he had sixty years of time until the events of *The Lord of the Rings* to find a suitable melody.

The song is then again spoken by Frodo when crossing the border of the Shire and a final time by Bilbo as an old hobbit in Rivendell. The first two versions are nearly identical, with the only change being the line "Pursuing it with eager feet" in Bilbo's version, in which Frodo replaces "eager" with "weary".

> The Road goes ever on and on
> Down from the door where it began
> Now far ahead the Road has gone,
> And I must follow, if I can,
> Pursuing it with eager / weary feet,
> Until it joins some larger way
> Where many paths and errands meet.
> And whither then? I cannot say.   (LotR 73)

Bilbo's version from Rivendell, however, is noticeably different (LotR 987). It is best described as a textual adaption of the earlier song. The new text only uses the first three lines of the original poem, but by this (and presumably by using the same melody) Bilbo clearly draws upon the knowledge of the original song on the part of the reader. We may describe this new version as a musical summing-up of his part in the story to Frodo: He, as the Ring-bearer and the one who was responsible for the task of destroying it, has successfully taken over from Bilbo, who was originally responsible for the ring since the time he found it in *The Hobbit*.

The Tolkien Ensemble has set these three versions of the song to music, all three with the same melody and similar instrumentation.

The Old Walking Song (I) begins with a long plucked classical guitar introduction, with a solo violin coming in after 45 seconds, until the singer begins at 1:40. The instrumentation of the introduction, i.e. the use of a guitar poses some questions. There is no mention of guitars in the book, nor is it likely that any Hobbits played them, as a standard concert guitar would be very large indeed for a Hobbit. They could have used smaller versions, but this surely would have merited a mention by Tolkien. It is also doubtful that—if there indeed were guitars in Middle-earth—Hobbits would have kept using smaller versions without the chance of ever moving up to the full-size instruments.

Tobias Escher   *Hither Shore 10 (2013)*   103

Transcription (excerpt): The Old Walking Song (I), TE CD 1, Track 1

If we think about which instrument the Hobbits could have used instead of the guitar, the best alternative may be an octavo mandolin, which is tuned an octave lower than the regular mandolin. The instrument is much smaller than a guitar, while still having a tonal range allowing for chordal accompaniment as well as playing melodies. The inclusion of a guitar in the recordings is probably due to Caspar Reiff, the composer, being a guitarist. Reiff writes that he had "always thought of the guitar sound to be very close to a semi-sized-hobbit harp" (Reiff, *e-mail 2*). Indeed, a harp could take the place of the guitar in hobbit songs by providing chordal accompaniment as well as playing melodic fills.

The violin coming in during the introduction fits into the instrumentation, but we may question its playing style. The Tolkien Ensemble in its version has a violin, played with little vibrato, but still played in a classical style, not the folk style that is suggested by Tolkien. Even though we know he preferred the term "fiddle" in general, he nevertheless was certainly aware of the differences in style. Apart from a sometimes slightly flatter bridge, there is no visible difference between a fiddle and a violin, so the fact that Bilbo says "fiddle" and not "violin" when the Dwarves get out their instruments at his "unexpected party" suggests that Hobbits played fiddle style, not classical style. Lastly the introduction is very long. *The Old Walking Song*, as the name implies, is sung either while walking or before departing on a journey. In both cases, such a long instrumental introduction is not very likely. We may excuse this with Reiff's goal of presenting the songs as part of a retelling of the events of the War of the Ring in Rivendell, as outlined earlier.

When the voice comes in at 1:40, an orchestral string section accompanies the vocals until the end as a pad. This string section only makes sense in the situation of an after-the-war performance, because there is no reason to assume that at any performance of Hobbit music there was a string section present; maybe single instruments, but not a full (orchestral) section. After the poem has been sung once through, an interlude is played with violins con sordino (2:25), while the guitar and string accompaniment stays present. After this, the text is repeated identically (3:20). After that, we again hear the violin introduction, but this time accompanied by a string pad (4:07).

The whole piece is performed very slowly and with the string pad feels very much like a sad ballad. The slow tempo makes this song not ideal as a walking song. The melody itself is sufficiently catchy as to be memorable on the first pass. This version is sung when Bilbo embarks on his journey, so he supposedly is eager to go, which is also expressed in the book ("I am as happy now as I have ever been, and that is saying a great deal"; LotR 35). In the book, the song appears to be a happy, encouraging song, which should come across in any rendition even with the artistic license of adding an accompaniment. From the whole style of this rendition, it would better fit Bilbo's second version of the song at Rivendell.

Donald Swann also set this poem to music in his song cycle *The Road Goes Ever On* as the first piece in the cycle. He chose the second version of the song ("weary feet") for his piece and set it to a simple melody accompanied by a piano providing chordal harmony and most of the time doubling the melody.

Excerpt: *The Road Goes Ever On*, Swann, 1

Tobias Escher   *Hither Shore 10 (2013)*   105

Stylistically, the piece is heavily oriented towards art song and does not in any way display any specific characteristics that we could describe as belonging to Hobbit music. The melody is identically used for the *Elven Hymn of Elbereth Gilthoniel*, which supports the theory that it does not reflect typical Hobbit music.

The stage adaption of *The Lord of the Rings* does not use the song in its original form, but has a music number called *The Road Goes On*, which in its text draws images from Bilbo's song and essentially is used in the same manner.

There's a road call-ing you to stray.___ Step by step pull-ing you a- way.___
Un-der moon and star.___ Take the road no matt-er how far.___

[text continued (excerpt):]
[...] The Road goes on, Ever ever on
Hill by hill, Mile by mile
Field by field, Stile by stile.
The Road goes on, Ever ever on [...]

Transcription (excerpt): The Road Goes On, LotR M, Track 2

We can use this song to get a complete picture of how a hobbit could have performed the song during travel with instrumental and vocal accompaniment. While the text is only very loosely based on Tolkien's poem, nevertheless the connection between the songs is obvious. In the musical, the song is introduced with a fiddle pattern accompanied by a bouzouki. The latter, though not mentioned by Tolkien, would be small enough to have been used by Hobbits. The introduction with its repeated figures gives a solid sense of tempo and allows the singers to join in at the right spot with a violin playing a pickup line at 0:13 with the voice beginning at 0:18. This is important for an impromptu group performance at the campfire and of course in the stage show in order for the actor to know his entry. The melody (see excerpt for the first few bars) is as catchy as the version from the films and harmonically easy, so as to facilitate singing and playing along.

The musical also makes use of harmony singing, as suggested as a possible element of hobbit music before: in the theatrical performance, there is a short two-part harmony section after the first chorus. This section is not included on the cast recording, however.

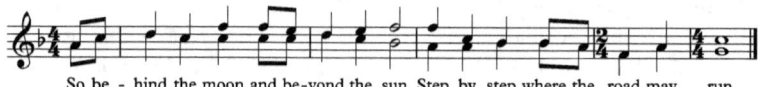

So be - hind the moon and be-yond the sun, Step by step where the road may run.

Transcription (excerpt): The Road Goes On, LotR M, not on the recording

This section could be representative of one of the vocal styles used by Hobbits, as this style of harmony singing lends itself to all catchy melodies with simple chord progressions, does not require any rehearsals and is simple enough to execute that a singer can play an instrument at the same time.

Song of Durin[4]

Fervently guarding their customs and language, the Dwarves most likely composed special Westron versions of their songs, or completely new songs in Westron, as well as (presumably) instrumental music for interaction with other cultures. Some of those pieces are very old, for example the *Song of Durin*, which Gimli sings after Sam spoke of Moria as "darksome holes" (LotR 315). The song speaks of Durin, one of the seven forefathers of the Dwarves, and arguably the most important of them. We do not know when the song was composed, but Gimli says that Durin is "still remembered in our songs", which means that there are several songs and implies that the one he is about to sing is not of recent origin and widely known. Maybe it belongs to the songs intended for representation when dealing with customers. The song may be regularly sung at such occasions for guests to introduce them to Dwarven history. It contains a number of musical references, which are written bold in the following text:

> Unwearied then were Durin's folk;
> Beneath the mountains **music woke**:
> The **harpers harped**, the **minstrels sang**,
> And at the gates the **trumpets rang**.
>
> The world is grey, the mountains old,
> The forge's fire is ashen-cold;
> **No harp is wrung**, no hammer falls...
>
> (LotR 315)

Not only can we learn from this song a lot about the appearance of Khazad-dûm in its early days after its foundation by Durin (the name Moria was later given to the place by the Elves), but also about the culture of the Dwarves who

---

4   Tolkien Ensemble, *Song of Durin*, TE CD 2, Track 9, 6:41; *Lord of the Rings* Musical, *Lament for Moria*, LotR M, Track 8, 1:38.

Tobias Escher   Hither Shore 10 (2013)   107

lived there. We learn of "golden roof and silver floor" and of "shining lamps of crystal". All this conjures up the image of a grand and very bright culture under the mountain—notably different from the way the place appears in the Third Age. We also hear of harps, minstrels singing and trumpets. The latter sound at the gates, which again suggests they are used for communication or to greet people approaching or leaving Khazad-dûm. It is no surprise that harps are mentioned—Thorin's magnificent harp is testament of the importance of the instrument to the Dwarves. The mention of minstrels is notable, however, because it confirms that Dwarves had professional singers, not just instrumentalists.

For our purpose, this means that vocal performances, either soloist or accompanied by instruments, have a high value in Dwarven society; otherwise minstrels would not be mentioned in such a song. It also means that songs or vocal performances in general were not just part of popular culture, but also performed at official events. Again: with the guardedness of the Dwarves, they would not mention minstrels in a song addressed to a non-dwarvish audience unless everyone would know of their existence when visiting one of their dwellings. Gimli clearly sings the song for the Fellowship to hear—specifically for Sam, who in a way insulted the memory of Khazad-dûm—to inform them of former times, so his choice of this particular song was certainly deliberate.

Of all pieces by the Ensemble, the *Song of Durin* stylistically stands out the most. While most of the other renditions by the Ensemble are not directly modelled after a particular style, the *Song of Durin* certainly is. Stylistically, it is very similar to Edward Elgar and Ralph Vaughan Williams. In fact, there is a striking similarity to sacred orchestral music from this period. We can find big similarities with Edward Elgar's orchestral arrangement of Hubert Hastings Parry's setting of the poem *And did those feet in ancient time*, written by Williams Blake.

Transcription (excerpt): Song of Durin, TE CD 2, Track 2

The pieces share the same key signature as well as time signature and are performed at roughly the same speed. The general shape of the melody is diametrically opposed—while *Jerusalem* first moves up, the *Song of Durin* moves down. Later on this is reversed. We may see in this an image of the subject matter: while *Jerusalem* is about Christ supposedly having set foot on the British Isles and such describes the lifting of the country to a higher state of being, only to question this act by referring to the "satanic mills" of the Industrial Revolution, the *Song of Durin* indirectly deals with Durin first going down into the mountains when founding Khazad-dûm, but then bringing the dwelling to fame—moving it up, one may say.

Large orchestra accompanies both pieces, with the *Song of Durin* bringing the brass in the foreground and mixing the strings more to the background as a pad. This supposedly is to differentiate dwarven music from Elvish music. Indeed, the song mentions trumpets and harps, so brass instruments seem more fitting to a dwarven hymn. In the middle of the *Song of Durin*, there is a percussive B-part (3:30). This part with a steady anvil beat (3:44) most likely represents the craftsmanship of the Dwarves and the work of Durin's folk. This part is followed by the last verse (4:15), which brings the piece to present time and mourns the loss of the splendour of the old days.

Caspar Reiff, who wrote the arrangement to the melody written by Peter Hall, confirms the music of Elgar being an inspiration for the *Song of Durin*:

> The Song of Dúrin [sic!] calls for grandeur. Peter Hall made the melody and asked me to do an "Elgarian arrangement". I had a look on the score of Elgar's first Symphony in A Flat Major, Op. 55—and pretty much did the same as Elgar in the arrangement.
> (Reiff, e-mail 2)

The stage version of *The Lord of the Rings* also has a song that deals with the former glory of Moria, called *Lament for Moria*. Once again the original text by Tolkien is not used, but a new text is created, drawing on Gimli's song with a duet by Gimli and Gandalf. This suggests that the song sung by the two is well known in the universe of the stage show, similarly to its status as a representative song in the book; otherwise Gandalf would not have been able to join in.

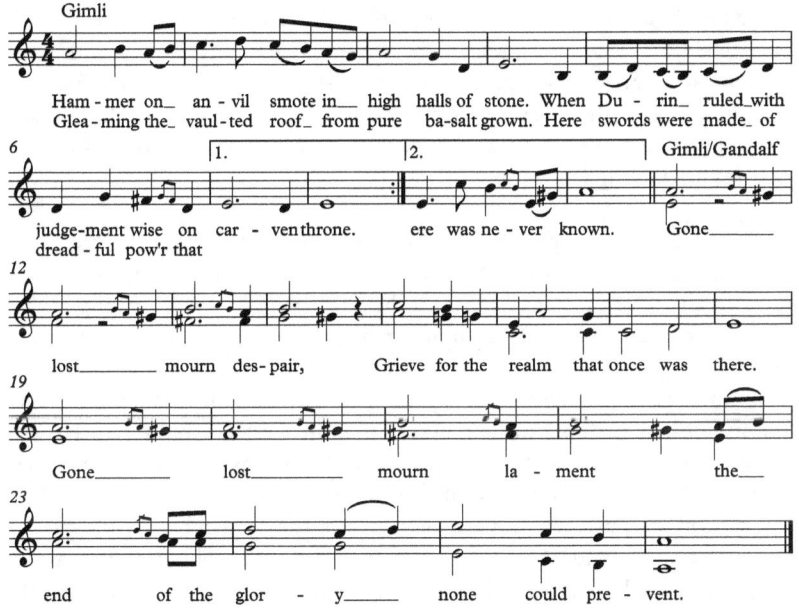

Transcription (excerpt): Lament for Moria, LotR M, Track 8

Like the *Song of Durin* from the book, the *Lament* deals with the former times and laments their passing. The Lament itself is a slow, hymn-like song, very sad and melancholic, but not pessimistic. It merely states the facts, but does not try to alter anything. On the contrary: it is expressly mentioned that no one could have prevented the things that happened. This suggests that maybe in the musical the Dwarves saw what happened as an accident. As they did not know of the Balrog, this is likely and would explain the making of such songs as a form of remembering the past.

Lament of the Rohirrim[5]

We have previously seen on the example of the *Song of Durin* how Tolkien characterized the dwarven culture by evoking similarities to sacred architecture and thought, most notably cathedrals (use of light, general architectural features, etc.) as well as values and socio-economic features (tradition, economic status as builders and craftsmen, etc.). Similarly, the Rohan culture draws heavily from the Anglo-Saxon Kingdom of Mercia, as Jason Fisher explains (Fisher

---

5   Tolkien Ensemble, *Lament of the Rohirrim*, TE CD 3, Track 9, 3:07.

7). The oral culture of the Rohirrim, with their language represented as Old English, is very similar to Mercian culture: "The Rohirrim sing and chant using an alliterative verse structure which is strikingly similar to that found in Beowulf... indeed the greater portion of surviving Old English poetry" (ibid.). Fisher in detail explains the workings of alliterative poetry as well as general features of Old English epics:

> While... the many other works... of the Old English corpus are usually thought of as poems by today's literal standards, they were really closer to songs, meant to be performed, chanted or sung, accompanied by the Anglo-Saxon harp. (Fisher, 9)

Aragorn sings the *Lament* when approaching Edoras with Gimli and Legolas, first in Rohirric (without the text given), then in Westron. Similar to the *Song of Durin*, the song speaks of the times of Eorl the Young, who built the Golden Hall, which goes back to the mead halls of the old epics.

The Tolkien Ensemble in their rendition of the song chose to not use any of the instruments mentioned to be employed by the Rohirrim. The lament begins with a solo plucked guitar introduction, maybe meant to represent the style of harps used by the people of Rohan, to set it apart from the elvish or dwarven harps. At 0:28, a string quartet plays a drone while the guitar plucks broken chords. This accompaniment stays the same over the course of the song with short melodic fills inserted between lines. The song does not group the lines into stanzas by means of a repeating melody, but instead has the singer declaiming the song with free use of melodic arches. The last two lines (2:05) are only accompanied by sparse guitar accents using arpeggiated chords. Only after the end of the poem the strings come in again, together with plucked broken guitar chords, which end the song.

The song gives us a good insight into Rohan culture: right at the beginning, we find the mention of the "horse and the rider", probably referring to Eorl the Young and his trusted steed Felaróf, the latter the ancestor of the Mearas and thus central to Rohan culture. Of the two musical instruments mentioned, the horn comes first – most likely in order to differentiate the Rohirrim from the Elves, who also use harps. The "hand on the harpstring" features in the same line as the "red fire", suggesting the use of the instrument in the hall for the accompaniment of epics. Again this makes the connection to Mercia. The song laments the days gone by similarly to the *Song of Durin* and is widely known among the Rohirrim ("So men still sing in the evening").

It is likely that the song was performed accompanied by harp at the fire. Music certainly plays a large role in Rohan society; in fact it is so important that immediately after Théoden's death, a lament is composed for him. Snowmane, his horse (presumably one of the Mearas, too), was buried on the battlefield with a poem set as inscription on his grave. This shows the intertwining of music/poetry and love of horses in Rohan culture; the two are inseparable and one of the traits making the Rohan culture unique.

Elven Hymn to Elbereth Gilthoniel[6]

The *Hymn* being the first elvish poetry heard by the Hobbits marks not only the importance of this particular piece, but also the importance of music in general in the context of different cultures meeting. Peter Wilkin remarks that "The first encounters between mortals and Elves that occur in *The Hobbit*, *The Lord of the Rings* and *The Silmarillion* are all initiated by the hearing of poetry and music." (Wilkin 48)

The Tolkien Ensemble has set all the versions of the poem to music. The *Elven Hymn To Elbereth Gilthoniel (I)* begins with a heavily reverberated violin solo preceded by orchestral chimes. Double bass and a guitar come in (0:17), the latter clearly associated with High-Elvish harp music by being played in a very harp-like, plucked style. The violin plays long melodic arches over the steady arpeggiated pattern of the guitar with the double bass providing sustained bass notes. A solo singer sings the four stanzas of the hymn (from 0:57), with the third stanza separated from the second by a violin interlude (2:31-3:13). The text is unchanged, only in the second and fourth stanzas the first exclamation (Gilthoniel! / O Elbereth!) is repeated to make the text fit better to the melody.

Transcription (excerpt): Elven Hymn to Elbereth Gilthoniel (I), TE CD 1, Track 5

---

6 Tolkien Ensemble, *Elven Hymn to Elbereth Gilthoniel (I)*, TE CD 1, Track 5, 5:32; Tolkien Ensemble, *Elven Hymn to Elbereth Gilthoniel (II)*, TE CD 2, Track 3, 2:10; Tolkien Ensemble, *Sam's Invocation of the Elven Hymn to Elbereth Gilthoniel*, TE CD 3, Track 17, 1:33.

The second time the hymn is sung is in Rivendell: after Bilbo presented his poem about Eärendil the Marine and Frodo and Bilbo leave for some quiet place to talk, "a single clear voice rose in song" (LotR 238). This version is sung in Sindarin and is the longest coherent text in the novel (LotR 238).

The Elves in Rivendell seem to have had solo singers. We do not learn who the singer is, but it is likely that Elrond had minstrels that sang these songs upon his request. Like in the book, the Ensemble's version, *Elven Hymn to Elbereth Gilthoniel (II)*, is monophonic and unaccompanied. Sung by a solo soprano with heavy reverberation it is very much reminiscent of plainsong, stylistically similar to *Namárië*.

Sam's Invocation of the Elven Hymn to Elbereth Gilthoniel was clearly recorded as a highly stylised version of the events. The book describes Sam's invocation very differently from the rendition by the Ensemble: the song begins with a choir of Elves chanting "Gilthoniel A Elbereth!" corresponding to the "music of the Elves as it came through his sleep in the Hall of Fire in the house of Elrond" (LotR 729). Then Sam sings the remainder of the song to a plucked guitar accompaniment in a very relaxed and laid-down manner (0:20)—exactly the opposite of the description in the book, where "his tongue was loosed and his voice cried in a language which he did not know". Midway through his verse, a soprano soloist comes in, probably signifying the help of Elbereth (0:48). The rendition by the Ensemble best fits an operatic performance of the events, but falls short as a literal representation.

The Eagle's Song[7]

After Frodo has succeeded in his task and the ring is destroyed, the glad tidings are brought to Minas Tirith by one of the mighty Eagles. The song is notable in that the Eagle in *The Lord of the Rings* is the only occurrence of an animal clearly speaking or even singing (LotR 963).

The Tolkien Ensemble clearly saw this song not as a mere report of a winged messenger bringing good news from the battlefield, but as a victory hymn. The rendition shows striking parallels to the *Song of Durin*: both songs use a large symphonic orchestra and are heavily modelled on late-romantic English sacred music. In the book nothing suggests that the people sang the same song as the Eagle after he relayed his message, though it is confirmed that they did indeed sing. The version by the Ensemble assumes this, though: after the introduction with signalling trumpets, evoking the trumpets of Gondor frequently mentioned in the text, the solo bass vocalist sings the first stanza (0:07):

---

7   Tolkien Ensemble, *The Eagle's Song (I)*, TE CD 4, Track 13, 3:24; The Lord of the Rings Musical, *The Final Battle*, LotR M, Track 16, 3:22, from 2:06.

Tobias Escher

Transcription (refrain): The Eagle's Song, TE CD 4, Track 13

This is then repeated by a mixed chorus in a four-part setting, probably representing the population of Minas Tirith (if the song is meant to represent the original performance in Minas Tirith), or all the free peoples of Middle-earth (if the Ensemble intends to represent the song as a victory song commonly sung by people to celebrate the victory over Sauron). After a repetition of the introduction and a modulation to the dominant of the dominant, the Eagle then sings the second stanza (0:44), with the phrase "sing and rejoice" repeated in the second line.

Transcription (verse 1): The Eagle's Song, TE CD 4, Track 13

The content of the lyrics speaks for the use of the song as a representative piece about the beginning of the reign of King Elessar: not only is his coming directly referred to, but also the renewing of the White Tree. The line "And he shall plant it in the high places" refers to the King not only bringing Gondor back to glory, but also to the re-establishing of the kingdom of Arnor. This is supported by the use of a signal call played by the trumpets both as an introduction as well as an interlude between verses and chorus.

Musically, as with the *Song of Durin*, it is unlikely that Middle-earth music completely sounded like Elgar. We may excuse this by seeing it as an outcome of the focus of the Tolkien Ensemble: to bring across the general ideas and concepts from the songs and poems, translated into modern musical idioms. For a celebration hymn that needs to be very festive, while at the same time having an air of eternity (after all those songs are hopefully remembered for centuries, as per Sam's wish on the way to Mount Doom), the choice of sacred music, which by its very nature conveys such a sense of tradition and perseverance, seems prudent.

The stage show has a similar moment of reflection and appreciation of the moment Sauron is vanquished: in the musical number *The Final Battle*, showing the destruction of the Ring in the Crack of Doom, Galadriel sings what can be described as a relieved comment to the fortunate outcome (at 2:06), when the Ring is destroyed. While most of the text is unique to the song, four lines from the song *Wonder* are included, which in turn is based on Galadriel's *Song of Eldamar* from the book:

Transcription (excerpt): The Final Battle, LotR M, Track 16

While the lyrics are completely different from the *Eagle's Song*, they nevertheless convey the same sense of relief. The "breath of healing" possibly refers to the White Tree, the re-establishing of the kingdom of Arnor or simply to the rebuilding of the free world in general after the reign of Sauron is over. The last line ("A new life will reign") can be taken as a reference to the reign of King Elessar. Galadriel in this musical therefore takes the role of the eagle messenger in the book. We can even find musical parallels to the way in which the song is structured both in the musical and the *Eagle's Song*: If we leave out the underscore in the stage show where the Ring is destroyed and begin with Galadriel's entrance, her singing the verse solo is similar to the Eagle singing the "refrain" in the *Eagle's Song*. In the *Eagle's Song*, the refrain is marked as such by being repeated by the choir representing the people; in the musical the refrain is recognized because the listener has heard it before—in the song *Wonder*. Galadriel then sings the last two lines while the choir repeats the chorus underneath her singing.

Both songs show the culmination of the efforts of the Fellowship—we might even interpret the line "destruction of pain" in the musical as an allusion to Sméagol, who is now liberated from the destructive force of the Ring and finally has peace.

Galadriel's *Song of Eldamar*[8]

One of the many songs of elvish origin, the *Song of Eldamar* is sung by Galadriel on her boat when the Fellowship leaves her realm. Galadriel stands on her boat and holds a harp in her hands. While it is nowhere stated that she played the harp, it is likely that she did – why else should she choose to carry it around with her? She sings a song before inviting the Fellowship to a farewell meal on the water (LotR, 372).

The Tolkien Ensemble has set the song to music as *Galadriel's Song of Eldamar (I)*, the piece being a good example of the Ensemble's perception of elvish music. The harp mentioned in the text is present in the song and Galadriel's voice certainly sounds "sad and cool" (LotR 372). The Ensemble wrote a sad, reminiscent melody, accompanied by plucked harp and string pads, evoking the movement of the water and the steady rustling of the trees of Lothlórien.

Incorporating the harp as mentioned by Tolkien was part of creating the realism of the performance, as Reiff notes: "If a specific instrument is mentioned by Tolkien to 'be a part of the actual performance in the book' we use it in our interpretation (like Galadriel and harp)" (Reiff, *e-mail 1*).

The song is built from single verses, each comprising of two lines. The first five of these are set to music in the form of AABBA. The melody of the A verses is introduced by a solo violin at the beginning of the piece: the first three bars are played twice, then the violin plays rhythmically similar phrases.

---

8   Tolkien Ensemble, *Galadriel's Song of Eldamar (I)*, TE CD 2, Track 12, 6:25.

Transcription (lines 1-10): Galadriel's Song of Eldamar, TE CD 2, Track 12

After Galadriel's verses (beginning at 0:45) as shown above in the excerpt follows a long interlude, with her singing textless long arches (3:24). The song closes with the last two verses in AA form.

The only textual change from the book is the insertion of an "aah"-bridge between the sentences. Thinking back to the highly skilful origins of music in Middle-earth in the First Music, we can see the use of the A/B model as a remnant of this high musical culture. The theory of reverse development supports this: The Song of Eldamar supposedly is an old song, so it makes sense that it is more oriented towards the former, higher form of music than for example Bilbo's walking song(s), which are of recent origin and not so much rooted in the traditional culture of such an ancient race as the Elves.

Conclusion

Because music is central to the very core of Middle-earth, all the cultures of Middle-earth possess a rich musical heritage, based on the First Music, which in turn is not only present in the physical world ("the sound of water"), but has also been passed on by the Valar themselves to the Elves in the Undying Lands. Their influence now seems to have made the musical cultures of Middle-earth largely compatible to each other because they are ultimately derived from the same source. In both *The Lord of the Rings* as well as *The Hobbit*, characters frequently sing songs or pass on messages by means of a song or poem. Some cultures, like the Dwarves, use songs as a means of representation to outsiders. Oral tradition seems prevalent; repeatedly characters express their hopes that their deeds will be "worthy of a song".

Bibliography

Media Sources

Rahman, A.R. *The Lord of the Rings: Original London Production*. A.R. Rahman, Värttinä, Christopher Nightingale. Kevin Wallace Music, 2008 (CD+DVD) (LotR M)

Swann, Donald *The Road Goes Ever On: A Song Cycle*. Boston: Houghton Mifflin, 1967

The Tolkien Ensemble & Christopher Lee. *The Lord of the Rings: Complete Songs and Poems*. Caspar Reiff, Peter Hall, Morten Ryelund. Hamburg: Membran, 2006 (4CD) (TE)

Score Manuscripts

The following score manuscripts were used for the creation of score extracts, courtesy of the composer:

Hall, Peter. *Song of Durin*, arr. Caspar Reiff, manuscript

Reiff, Caspar. *The Eagle's Song: Full Score*, arr. Gunner Møller Pedersen, manuscript, c2003

Reiff, Caspar. *Elven Hymn to Elbereth Gilthoniel*, manuscript

Reiff, Caspar. *Galadriel's Song of Eldamar – Ai! Laurie Lantar...*, manuscript, c1996-97

Works Cited

Fisher, Jason. "Horns of Dawn: The Tradition of Alliterative Verse in Rohan". *Middle-earth Minstrel*. Ed. Bradford Lee Eden. Jefferson: McFarland & Company, 2010, 7-25

Linden, Steven. "A Speculative History of the Music of Arda". *Music in Middle-earth*. Ed. Heidi Steimel & Friedhelm Schneidewind. Zurich/Jena: Walking Tree Publishers, 2010, 75-90

Reiff, Caspar. *The Lord of the Rings: Complete Songs and Poems*. CD-Booklet, Hamburg: Membran, 2006

---. *Electronic mail conversation between Caspar Reiff and Tobias Escher*, 7th August 2011 (e-mail 1)

---. *Electronic mail conversation between Caspar Reiff and Tobias Escher*, 8th August 2011 (e-mail 2)

Russell, Gary. *The Lord of the Rings: The Official Stage Companion*. London: HarperCollins, 2007

Tolkien, John Ronald Reuel. *The Book of Lost Tales 1*, ed. by Christopher Tolkien. New York: Del Rey, 1992

---. *The Hobbit or: There and Back Again*. London: HarperCollins, 2006

---. *The Lord of the Rings*. London: HarperCollins, 2007

---. *The Silmarillion*. London: HarperCollins, 1992

Wilkin, Peter. "Æfre me strongode longað: Songs of Exile in the Mortal Realms". *Middle-earth Minstrel*. Ed. Bradford Lee Eden. Jefferson: McFarland & Company, 2010, 47-60

Leben in Mittelerde: Tolkien-Adaptionen im Liverollenspiel

Stephanie Bauer (Augsburg)

Was ist LARP?

LARP ist sicher die gewöhnungsbedürftigste Form des Rollenspiels.
(Mogel 173)

Dabei kommt das LiveActionRolePlay, kurz LARP, dem, was in der Soziologie und Psychologie unter dem Begriff *Rollenspiel* verstanden wird, sogar recht nahe. Gemeinhin verwenden die Sozialwissenschaften ihn nämlich immer dann, wenn Kinder während ihrer Spiele in selbst gewählte Rollen schlüpfen. Dazu gehören die klassischen Cowboy-und-Indianer-Szenarien ebenso wie das Spiel mit dem Kaufladen. Während kleine Jungen angeblich Spiele bevorzugen, bei denen Kampf und Konflikt im Mittelpunkt stehen, legen Mädchen mehr Wert auf Szenen aus dem Familienalltag (vgl. Fritz 193). Egal, was im Zentrum des Spiels steht, die Kinder verkörpern Personen, die Dinge tun dürfen und können, die ihnen in der Realität selbst nicht möglich sind.

Auch wenn Mogel in seinem Überblickswerk *Die Psychologie des Kinderspiels* seinem Abschnitt über Rollenspiele die Bemerkung voranstellt, er werde im Folgenden eben nicht über die aus der Psychologie bekannten kindlichen Rollenspiele sprechen (Mogel 169), und zusammenfassend feststellt, es handle sich bei Rollenspielen, die für ältere Kinder und Erwachsene konzipiert seien, eigentlich um Regelspiele (Mogel 174), so sind starke Parallelen doch unübersehbar.

Im Liverollenspiel schlüpfen die Teilnehmer[1] in zumeist selbst gewählte Rollen, die sie für den vorgegebenen Zeitraum einer Con (abgeleitet vom englischen *Convention*), in der Regel ein Wochenende[2], verkörpern. Sie kleiden sich im entsprechenden Stil, schlafen häufig in Zelten und kochen am Lagerfeuer, sie sind Magier, Heiler, Waldläufer und Krieger und in dieser Funktion zaubern, heilen, spähen und kämpfen sie. Letzteres wird mit abgepolsterten Latexwaffen getan, die echten Schwertern, Hellebarden und ähnlichem nachempfunden sind. Die Verletzungsgefahr ist daher minimal, sehen wir einmal von einigen blauen Flecken ab.

---

1 Die Zahlen schwanken beträchtlich. Während die meisten Veranstaltungen für 80-150 Personen ausgelegt sind, gibt es sehr exklusive, kleine Treffen, aber auch solche mit über 4.000 Teilnehmern.
2 Die Zeitspannen variieren allerdings von kurzen Tavernenabenden, die nur wenige Stunden dauern, bis hin zu Großveranstaltungen, die inklusive Auf- und Abbau etwa eine Woche in Anspruch nehmen können.

Die dabei erlebte Rahmenhandlung wird von der Spielleitung grob vorgegeben und zumeist mithilfe sogenannter NSCs (Nicht-Spieler-Charaktere) in die vorgesehenen Bahnen gelenkt. NSCs unterscheiden sich dabei von SCs (Spieler-Charakteren) insofern, als sie sich Charakterzüge und Motivationen nicht selbst auswählen, sondern von der Spielleitung eine festgelegte Rolle zugeteilt bekommen. Oft stellen sie die »Bösewichte«, und nicht selten verkörpert ein NSC im Laufe einer LARP-Veranstaltung mehrere Rollen.

Spieler hingegen konzipieren die Figur, die sie für den Zeitpunkt der Veranstaltung darstellen, selbst und behalten diese auch durchgängig ohne Rollenwechsel bei. Diese Charaktere können nicht nur auf einer einzelnen Veranstaltung bespielt werden, viele von ihnen bleiben über Jahre hinweg bestehen. Dies ist vor allem auch deshalb möglich, weil ein Spieler mit ein und demselben Charakter jede beliebige Con aus einem passenden Genre besuchen kann, ohne dass im Vorfeld Absprachen mit den Veranstaltern nötig wären.

Allerdings existiert zumindest im Bereich der Fantasy-LARPs[3] keine stringente, allgemeingültige Hintergrundwelt; bespielt werden vielmehr einzelne Länder und Kontinente, teilweise aus der Literatur entlehnt, teilweise von der Spielleitung selbst erdacht. Auch die Charaktere der Spieler stammen dementsprechend aus verschiedensten Gegenden. Manche dieser Länder, die zumeist von Vereinen konzipiert und verwaltet werden, haben sich zu größeren Gruppen zusammenge-schlossen, eine übergreifende Rahmenhandlung erarbeitet und treten, etwa im Internet, gemeinsam auf.[4] In vielen Fällen aber existieren die Länder mehr oder weniger im luftleeren Raum und ihre geographische Lage zueinander ist völlig ungeklärt. Fragen danach, wie ein Charakter von einer Gegend in die andere gerät, sind daher oft schwierig zu beantworten und werden nicht selten gar nicht behandelt. Für die Spielrealität sind sie in der Regel nicht relevant.

Ausnahmen gelten bei geschlossenen Welten wie etwa Tolkiens Mittelerde. Wenn derartige Settings bespielt werden, so muss bei der Charakterwahl besondere Rücksicht auf den Umstand genommen werden, dass Reisen aus anderen Fantasywelten nicht möglich sind.

Rein formal gibt es verschiedene Möglichkeiten, die Spielwelt zu regeln. Die einfachste lautet vermutlich: Du kannst, was du darstellen kannst. Hier kann der Spieler seinen Charakter quasi frei erschaffen und ist nur durch seine eigenen körperlichen Merkmale und die schauspielerischen Fähigkeiten eingeschränkt. Sogar magische Fähigkeiten sind zu einem gewissen Grad möglich, wenn sie mittels Effekten überzeugend symbolisiert werden. Der Erfolg einer

---

3   Für andere Genres sieht die Situation naturgemäß anders aus: Western- und Endzeitspiele beispielsweise sind in der realen Welt – oder zumindest einer Parallelwelt – angesiedelt und richten sich nach deren geographischen Gegebenheiten, auch wenn der Ort der Handlung nicht mit dem realen Ort übereinstimmen muss.
4   Besonders umfassend sind hier die Mittel- und Südlande vernetzt: http://www.mittellande.org/ und http://www.suedlande.de/

Aktion ist dabei immer auch ein Stück weit davon abhängig, ob die Mitspieler die Darstellung als glaubwürdig akzeptieren.

Alternativ stehen diverse mehr oder weniger komplexe Regelwerke zur Verfügung, die es ermöglichen, gewisse Fähigkeiten zu erwerben und einzusetzen. Darin ist auch meist eine Anleitung enthalten, wie etwa ein magischer Effekt, das Lesen von Spuren oder auch das Knacken eines Schlosses darzustellen sind, denn das Regelwerk ersetzt nicht die Notwendigkeit des Schauspielerns. Es dient vielmehr dazu, die Machtfülle der Spieler zu beschränken und eine Charakterentwicklung im Sinne des Erlernens neuer Fähigkeiten zu ermöglichen.

Die Entscheidung für oder gegen ein Regelwerk ist Geschmackssache der Spielleitung, ebenso wie die Frage, ob Charaktere mit anderen Regelhintergründen für das jeweilige Spiel konvertiert werden müssen oder nicht. Dies ist meist relativ problemlos möglich, da die Regeln einfach gehalten und immer nach einem ähnlichen Prinzip aufgebaut sind.

Ohnehin wird das Spiel nicht von den Regeln bestimmt, sondern von der Darstellung der einzelnen Charaktere. Mogel geht sogar so weit zu sagen, das Spiel selbst stehe im Vordergrund, während die Rahmenhandlung und das Bestehen von Abenteuern eher zweitrangig seien (Mogel 173). Dies ist allerdings eine grobe Verallgemeinerung, denn was im Zentrum des Interesses steht, hängt stark vom Geschmack des einzelnen Spielers ab. Für viele Teilnehmer ist das intensive Erleben des gewählten Charakters tatsächlich die Hauptkomponente eines Cons, allerdings spielt der Plot für die meisten eine nicht unerhebliche Rolle, und viele Spieler sind durchaus bereit, eine konsequente Darstellung der Möglichkeit zu opfern, ein Abenteuer erfolgreich zu bestehen.

Bis hierhin scheint der Unterschied von LARPs zu den kindlichen Rollenspielen schwer fassbar, vor allem wenn man ein Beispiel aus Jürgen Fritz' *Das Spiel verstehen* heranzieht: Er beschreibt eine Mädchengruppe aus Vier- bis Fünfjährigen, die Einkaufen spielt. Im Vorfeld werden die verschiedenen Rollen verteilt und der grobe Handlungsverlauf abgesprochen, wobei ein Mädchen als »Spielführerin« auch immer wieder korrigierend in das laufende Spiel eingreift. Ziel ist es, in der selbst konstruierten Spielwelt einen Einkauf möglichst realistisch darzustellen. (Fritz 33)

Worin besteht der definierbare Unterschied, außer im Alter der Spieler? Die Reglementierung, wie Mogel meint (Mogel 174), kann es nicht sein, denn auch die Kinder einigen sich auf ein »Grundregelwerk«, das in gewissem Sinne sogar strenger ist als das »Du kannst, was du darstellen kannst« mancher LARPs für Erwachsene.

Erwachsene betreiben mehr Aufwand für ihre Rollenspiele, sie gestalten aufwändige Kostüme, kaufen teure Waffen und Accessoires, fahren teilweise weite Strecken zu Veranstaltungen und halten die Illusion einer anderen Welt oft über Tage aufrecht, weil sie, im Gegensatz zu den Kindern, die Möglichkeiten haben, dies zu tun. Im Prinzip aber handelt es sich um das gleiche Phänomen.

Man fühlt sich bereits hier an Tolkien erinnert, genauer gesagt, an seinen Essay *On Fairy-Stories*, denn die zugrundeliegende Problematik ist ähnlich: Genau wie *Fairy Stories* eben nicht für Kinder gedacht sind – auch wenn es durchaus solche für Kinder gibt (FS 35) –, sind auch Rollenspiele nicht *nur* für Kinder oder *nur* für Erwachsene gedacht. Und ebenso sehen kindliche Rollenspiele zwar anders aus als die der Erwachsenen, aber im Kern funktionieren beide gleich. Was hinter dem Versuch der Abgrenzung steckt, ist vielleicht weniger ein tatsächlicher Unterschied, als vielmehr das Bedürfnis, die leidenschaftliche Betätigung von Erwachsenen in einem »Kinderspiel« zu rechtfertigen. Tolkiens Aussage zur angeblichen natürlichen Verbindung von *Fairy Tales* und Kindern kann auf die Verbindung von Rollenspielen und Kindern übertragen werden:

> I think this is an error; at best an error of false sentiment, and one that ist therefore most often made by those who, for whatever private reason (such as childlessness), tend to think of children as a special kind of creature, almost a different race, rather than as normal, if immature, members of a particular family, and of the human family at large. (FS 34)

Warum Tolkien?

Die Verbindung zwischen Rollenspiel und Tolkien kann also bereits auf der Ebene der grundlegenden Problematik eines Genres gezogen werden, das sich zunächst von dem Gedanken, es sei für Kinder gemacht, emanzipieren muss(te). Und tatsächlich bieten sich die von Tolkien genannten Werte einer *Fairy Story*, für Erwachsene »Fantasy, Recovery, Escape, Consolation« (FS 46), auch im Rollenspiel an.

Generell wird daher heute noch Rollenspielern, ebenso wie den Lesern von Fantasy-Romanen gerne Eskapismus vorgeworfen, und das zu Recht, sieht man Eskapismus aus Tolkiens positivem Blickwinkel, der in *On Fairy-Stories* immer wieder betont wird:

> In what misusers of Escape are fond of calling Real Life, Escape is evidently as a rule practical, and may even be heroic. In real life it is difficult to blame it, unless it fails; in criticism it would seem to be the worse the better it succeeds. Evidently we are faced by a misuse of words, and also by a confusion of thought. Why should a man be scorned if, finding himself in prison, he tries to get out and go home? Or if, when he cannot do so, he thinks and talks about other topics than jailers and prison-walls? The world outside has not become less real because the prisoner cannot see it. (FS 60)

Auch weitere theoretische Aspekte zum Funktionieren von Erzählmechanismen aus *On Fairy-Stories* lassen sich problemlos auf das Feld der Spieltheorie übertragen. Tolkien beschreibt das Phänomen der *Willing Suspension of Disbelief*, also des bewussten Versuchs, sich auf eine Spielwelt einzulassen, im Gegensatz zum *Secondary Belief*, dem tatsächlichen Aufgehen in dieser Welt (FS 37f). Letzteres entspricht ziemlich genau dem, was Spieltheoretiker als *Flow-Theorie* bezeichnen (Fritz 99). Bezeichnenderweise wählt Tolkien als Beispiel hier ausgerechnet ein Cricket-Spiel, in dem er sich nicht wie ein wirklicher Enthusiast verlieren kann, für das er aber in der Lage ist, ein oberflächliches Interesse aufzubringen (FS 38) und verdeutlicht dadurch umso mehr die Relevanz der Phänomens auch für Bereiche außerhalb der Literaturwissenschaft.

Im Liverollenspiel, das ja bewusst darauf angelegt ist, ein »Aufgehen« des Spielers in der Spielwelt hervorzurufen, ist das Phänomen selbstverständlich ebenfalls bekannt und wird, in einer etwas anderen Spielart, als *Bleed* bezeichnet. Hier handelt es sich um den Effekt, dass reale Gefühle des Spielers in die Gedankenwelt seines Charakters übergehen *und umgekehrt*. Dies kann zu einem besonders intensiven Spielerlebnis führen, aber auch dafür sorgen, dass Konflikte aus dem Spiel in die reale Welt getragen werden (vgl. dazu Mosler 45).

Die in *On Fairy-Stories* getroffenen Aussagen zu *Escape* und *Secondary Belief* machen Tolkien als Theoretiker, über die Tatsache, dass er der Verfasser einiger der einflussreichsten Werke des Genres Fantasy ist, hinaus, für Rollenspieler prinzipiell interessant. Es ist jedoch auch völlig klar, dass *On Fairy-Stories* und die darin enthaltenen, durchaus nicht nur auf die literarische Fantasy anwendbaren, Aussagen wohl kaum rezipiert worden wären, gäbe es nicht das *Silmarillion*, den *Hobbit* und, vor allem, den *Herrn der Ringe*. Diese, und nicht die theoretischen Überlegungen, sind es, die das LARP nachhaltig geprägt haben.

Wieviel Mittelerde steckt in der Darstellung?

Wenn Frank Weinreich schreibt: »Fantasy in Film, Vertonung, Kunst, Brett-, Rollen- und Computerspiel unterliegt der gleichen Definition wie das Buch, ihre Herkunft und ihr Erfolg und ein Großteil ihrer Wirkung beruhen ebenso auf dem Mythos und mytheninspiriertem Denken und Fühlen und auch die Topoi sind keine wesentlich anderen« (Weinreich 87), dann könnte man an dieser Stelle fast geneigt sein, für alles Weitere einfach auf den Vorgängerband dieser Reihe zu verweisen, der *Tolkiens Einfluss auf die moderne Fantasy* thematisiert. »Was noch zu sagen bleibt«, setzt Weinreich jedoch nach, »bezieht sich auf medienspezifische Aspekte und deren Bedeutung für die Rezeption in anderer als in Buchform« (ebd). Gerade diese medienspezifischen Aspekte sind bislang für das Liverollenspiel nur rudimentär betrachtet worden. Die vorherrschenden Konventionen, die teilweise im Genre, teilweise im Medium begründet liegen, sind es durchaus wert, gesondert beleuchtet zu werden.

Die Welt

Wie in der Literatur schafft die Hintergrundwelt im Liverollenspiel den Rahmen, in dem sich die Geschichte abspielt. Es versteht sich von selbst, dass, anders als in der Literatur, die landschaftlichen Begebenheiten durch äußere Umstände, genauer gesagt den zur Verfügung stehenden Spielort, festgelegt sind. Das enthebt den Spielleiter jedoch nicht von der Verantwortung, sich Gedanken zur Hintergrundwelt zu machen, denn es gilt diesen real existierenden Ort in der Spielwelt zu verankern. Zum einen wird meist ein größerer geographischer Zusammenhang hergestellt, das Stück Wald oder die Taverne, die das Zentrum der Handlung bilden, werden in einem Land verortet, das wiederum, bestenfalls, Teil eines Kontinents ist. Exotischere Länder, die nicht unserem mitteleuropäischen Klima entsprechen, können im Hintergrund existieren und bieten mögliche Herkunftsorte, beispielsweise für verschiedene Wüstenvölker.

Nahezu jedes Land, sei es nur als Herkunftsort für einzelne Charaktere oder als in mehreren Kampagnen bespielter Ort einer Handlung, verfügt zumindest über eine Karte. Deren Erstellung erfolgt nach dem persönlichen Geschmack und den spielbedingten Bedürfnissen, die eben auch das Einbinden realer landschaftlicher Begebenheiten beinhalten, in der Regel ohne bewusste Adaption bestehender Vorbilder.

Neben der geographischen ist zum anderen aber auch die kulturelle Verortung von Bedeutung. Eine fiktive Welt braucht, zusätzlich zu ihrer Gegenwart, auch eine Vergangenheit, auf die sie fußen kann. Hier kommt es naturgemäß häufi-ger zur Verwendung mehr oder weniger bekannter Topoi, von denen einige bei Tolkien zu finden sind.

So werden beispielsweise in nahezu allen Welten, in denen Elfen vorkommen, diese als die schöpfungsgeschichtlich älteste »Rasse« betrachtet, deren Macht allerdings oft am Schwinden ist, da sie von den Menschen abgelöst wurden. Und auch wenn Religion, im Sinne von Kultausübung, in Tolkiens Mittelerde kaum eine Rolle spielt (vgl. L 193f u. 220), scheint sein Schöpfungsmythos doch Vorbild für einige Religionen im Liverollenspiel zu sein. Eine Vielzahl von LARP-Pantheons umfasst beispielsweise acht Götter, so dass von einigen Gruppen, quasi im Sinne einer *Interpretatio Romana*, Gleichsetzungen der Gottheiten verschiedener Namen aus verschiedenen Ländern vorgenommen werden. Da die klassische Zahl der Hauptgottheiten in der römischen und griechischen Antike zwölf war, ist die Inspirationsquelle wohl andernorts zu suchen. Ein meiner Meinung nach plausibles ursprüngliches Vorbild sind die

Aratar (vgl. S 32), wobei es sich in vielen später ausgearbeiteten Fällen sicher mehr um eine Übernahme bereits bestehender LARP-interner Konventionen als um eine bewusste Tolkien-Adaption handelt. Dasselbe gilt wohl auch für die Vorstellung einer übergeordneten, in einigen Fällen dem Großteil der Bevölkerung nicht bekannten und daher nicht verehrten, Schöpfergottheit, die sich ab und an findet.

Weitere Beispiele für von Tolkien inspirierte Versatzstücke ließen sich mit Sicherheit finden, alle Einzelbeispiele aufzulisten würde hier jedoch zu weit führen und ist wohl, in letzter Konsequenz auch gar nicht möglich. Prinzipiell bleibt an dieser Stelle festzuhalten, dass Tolkiens Mittelerde, ebenso wie die Werke anderer Fantasyautoren, diverse antike Mythologien, bestehende Rollenspielsysteme und Computerspiele, durchaus als Inspirationsquelle für die Schaffung von Hintergrundwelten für das Liverollenspiel dient, ohne dass seine Ideen unverändert übernommen werden. In diesem Fall ist also am ehesten von einer Adaption im Sinne von eklektischer Selektion zu sprechen.

Alternativ zur eigenen Schöpfung ist es aber möglich, eine bereits bestehende Welt als Hintergrund zu verwenden. Dies gilt, unter Vorbehalt, auch für Tolkiens Mittelerde. Überlegungen zu kulturellen Gegebenheiten und Geschichte entfallen hierbei großteils, dafür ist eine direkte Auseinandersetzung mit Tolkiens Werk und somit eine bewusste Adaptionsleistung, im Gegensatz zur Eigenkreation, in jedem Fall nötig.

Es gilt hier vor allem, sich in verschiedener Hinsicht logisch in die bestehende Welt einzufügen. Wichtig ist dabei nicht nur die Entscheidung für eine geographische Lage, die in ihrer Beschreibung möglichst gut zu den realen Gegebenheiten des bespielten Geländes passen muss. Auch eine zeitliche Einordnung in die Chronologie Mittelerdes will vorgenommen sein. Hier bieten sich abgelegene Orte oder Zeiten, über die wenig überliefert ist, an, auch um die Notwendigkeit des Auftretens von aus den Romanen bekannten Figuren zu vermeiden. Während es in selbsterdachten Hintergründen durchaus möglich ist, dass die Spieler durch ihr Handeln das Schicksal der Welt ändern, sind solche Eingriffe in das »historische« Geschick Mittelerdes unerwünscht.

Obwohl ein Spiel in Tolkiens detailliert ausgearbeiteter Welt für die Organisatoren den Vorteil bringt, auf einen reichen Fundus an Hintergrundmaterial zugreifen zu können, hält sich die Zahl der Cons auf diesem Gebiet in Grenzen. Neben den von einigen Tolkiengesellschaften ausgerichteten, größeren Veranstaltungen belaufen sich die meisten von ihnen auf sogenannte »Einladungscons«, bei denen nur eine geringe Zahl von der Spielleitung persönlich bekannten Teilnehmern zugelassen ist.

Dies hat verschiedene Gründe. Zum einen kann die Fülle an Informationen, die über Mittelerde verfügbar sind, einschüchternd und einengend wirken; die Angst, »Fehler« zu machen, ist groß. Zum anderen gibt es eine sehr handfeste Schwierigkeit: es ist nicht ganz einfach Spieler zu finden, denn eine solche

Veranstaltung ist nur für Charaktere zugänglich, die in Tolkiens Welt, zu der bespielten Zeit, beispielsweise kurz nach Ende des Ringkriegs, sinnvoll und glaubwürdig einzubinden sind. Charaktere aus anderen Welten sind nicht zugelassen, beziehungsweise ihre Hintergrundgeschichten müssten für diesen Zweck entsprechend abgeändert werden. Da dieses Problem jedoch auch in die andere Richtung funktioniert, sich Figuren aus Mittelerde also auf Veranstaltungen, die anderswo angesiedelt sind, schwer einbauen lassen, gibt es sehr wenige passende bespielte Charaktere. Die Hemmschwelle, für die wenigen angebotenen Veranstaltungen den beträchtlichen zeitlichen und finanziellen Aufwand der Konzeption und Ausstattung einer neuen Spielfigur zu betreiben, ist hoch. Bei dem daraus resultierenden Teufelskreis von Angebot und Nachfrage handelt es sich um ein sehr reales Problem, wie sich unter anderem daran zeigt, dass die sehr seltenen Cons teilweise aus Mangel an Anmeldungen abgesagt werden müssen.[5]

Die Charaktere

Betrachtet man die bespielten Welten, kann also der Eindruck entstehen, Tolkiens Werk habe keinen allzu großen direkten Einfluss auf die LARP-Szene. Ein anderes Bild ergibt sich jedoch beim genaueren Blick auf gängige Konventionen im Bezug auf einzelne Charakterkonzepte. Hier lohnt es sich in erster Linie, die gängigen Fantasy-»Rassen« gesondert zu betrachten.

Da Elfen, neben Menschen, am häufigsten bespielt werden, wird ihnen hier der größte Raum eingeräumt. Bemerkungen zu den anderen Völkern werden, sowohl um den Rahmen nicht zu sprengen, als auch aus Gründen des geringeren Referenzmaterials, kürzer behandelt.

- Elfen

    Elfen leben bevorzugt in Wäldern, im Einklang mit der Natur, sind wunderschön, schlank, unsterblich, androgyn, etwas zickig, manchmal arrogant, tolle Sänger, künstlerisch veranlagt und vortreffliche Bogenschützen. Verteilen gern magische Geschenke. In ihren Namen und ihrer Sprache werden viele Ls verwendet, damit sie weicher und harmonischer wirkt. Mögen keine Zwerge. Klaustrophob[6].

---

5   So geschehen beispielsweise mit dem Rohan-Con 2013.
6   Dieses von Metzeler aus Legolas' Aussagen gegenüber Gimli (LotR II 181) abgeleitete Klischee gibt zu denken, wohnen doch zumindest die Elben Mirkwoods bekanntermaßen in Höhlen. Auch an anderer Stelle wurde bereits Verwunderung geäußert, dass ausgerechnet Thranduils Sohn eine derartige Abneigung gegen enge Räume hat (Hammond/Scull 420). Da es sich hier aber um den einzigen Punkt in der Liste handelt, der meines Wissens im LARP keine Rolle spielt, muss an dieser Stelle nicht näher darauf eingegangen werden.

> Elfen sind irgendwie unergründlich, geheimnisvoll und wirken
> der Welt entrückt. (Melzener 136)

Diesen auch im LARP größtenteils gängigen, bei Axel Melzener genannten Klischees, die laut ihm alle aus dem *Herrn der Ringe* stammen, sind noch einige hinzuzufügen. Pflicht für Elfen sind, neben den spitzen Ohren, lange Haare und elegante Kleidung. Sie leiden unter Alkoholunverträglichkeit, haben einen feinen Geruchssinn, lachen nicht, sind bartlos und, zumindest wenn es sich um Hochelfen handelt, Vegetarier. Während die meist blonden Hochelfen besonders weise und erhaben sind und eher zaubern als kämpfen, sind Waldelfen naturverbundene Bogenschützen, die sich in Leder kleiden.

Insgesamt berufen sich die Spieler von Elfen meistens auf Tolkiens Elben als Vorbilder. Dessen konkrete Aussagen zu den Elben im Allgemeinen halten sich allerdings bekanntermaßen in Grenzen, die ausführlichste ist wohl die folgende:

> But I suppose that the *Quendi* are in fact in these histories very
> little akin to the Elves and Fairies of Europe; and if I were pressed
> to rationalize, I should say that they represent really Men with
> greatly enhanced aesthetic and creative faculties, greater beauty
> and longer life, and nobility... (L 176)

Diese Beschreibung umfasst einige, wenn auch bei weitem nicht alle der aufgeführten Klischees, die sich im LARP hartnäckig halten. Lassen sich vielleicht einige von ihnen zwischen den Zeilen herauslesen? Vor allem die vollkommene Ernsthaftigkeit zieht sich dabei als roter Faden durch die Darstellungen, insbesondere auch derjenigen Spieler, die sich explizit auf Tolkien als Vorbild berufen.

Auch wenn es wahr ist, dass die Elben im *Herrn der Ringe* nicht mehr die Scherzbolde aus dem *Hobbit* sind (vgl. Hammond/Scull lxxii u.103), so kann man ihnen doch nicht unterstellen, sie seien gänzlich humorlos. An dieser Stelle seien nur, als willkürliches Beispiel für die Fähigkeit der Elben, zu lachen, die Neckereien Lindirs gegenüber Bilbo in Bruchtal genannt. (LotR I 310) Für weitere »Beweise« möchte ich auf Heidi Steimels hervorragenden Beitrag *Humor bei Tolkien* verweisen. Dass lautes Lachen bei Elfenspielern verpönt ist, liegt wohl an dem Wunsch, besondere Erhabenheit und Abgeklärtheit überzeugend darzustellen.

Die von Tolkien selbst als Hauptunterschied zwischen den beiden »different aspects of the Humane« bezeichnete aus der Unsterblichkeit und Erdgebundenheit der Elben resultierende Geisteshaltung (L 236) darzustellen, ist in der Tat die wohl größte Herausforderung. Peter Jacksons Umsetzung in der Verfilmung der Trilogie, die wohl dem gleichen Gedanken geschuldet ist, tut als Vorbild ihr Übriges, um die Vorstellung von den humorlosen Tolkien'schen Elben zu verfestigen.

Belege für den Alkoholkonsum finden sich sowohl im *Hobbit* als auch im *Herrn der Ringe* derart zahlreich, dass es überflüssig erscheint, einzelne Stellen zitieren zu wollen. Ein Trinkwettbewerb zwischen Gimli und Legolas, der in der Extended Edition des Films *The Two Towers* zu sehen ist, zeigt, dass in diesem Fall eine Rezeption über die adaptierte Version Peter Jacksons ebenfalls auszuschließen ist. Es handelt sich hier wahrscheinlich aus einer Konvention aus dem Tischrollenspiel *Das schwarze Auge* (DSA), die sich so weit durchgesetzt hat, dass auch Spieler sie übernommen haben, die laut eigener Aussage nichts von diesem System halten.

Ohne auf jedes einzelne Klischee eingehen zu können, muss an dieser Stelle eines betont werden: Häufig scheinen sich die Spieler gar nicht bewusst zu sein, dass einige Punkte, die ihnen für ihre Darstellung von Elben »nach Tolkien« als wichtig erscheinen, gar nicht aus dem Werk zu begründen sind. Auch wenn der reale Tolkienbezug in einigen Fällen widerlegt werden kann, bleibt doch ein »gefühlter« Tolkienbezug, insofern als sich immer wieder explizit auf seine Werke als Vorbild berufen wird.

Besonders deutlich fällt die Existenz dieses Bezugs im Hinblick auf die Sprache auf. Die Homepage des Elbenlagers (http://www.elbenlager.de/), eine nach eigenen Angaben »übergeordnete Kommunikationsplattform für Elbenspieler«, gibt als mögliche Sprachen Sindarin, Quenya und Isdira, eine aus DSA stammende Sprache an. In der Realität wird letztere allerdings weniger gerne gesehen, vorherrschend ist in der Namensgebung für Personen und Orte klar Sindarin. Die Verwendung erstreckt sich auch in das Spiel hinein, die meisten Zauber werden auf Sindarin gesprochen und auch einige Floskeln, etwa Begrüßungsformeln in dieser Sprache sind bei Elfen gebräuchlich. Anhand dessen lässt sich relativ leicht erkennen, wie viele Spieler sich, bis zu einem gewissen Grad, dem Tolkien'schen Vorbild verpflichtet fühlen.

Wie problematisch andererseits die Verwendung von Tolkiens Aussagen im Bezug auf Elben im Sinne einer historischen Quelle sein kann, zeigt anschaulich das Beispiel eines Elfenspielers der, entgegen der Konventionen, seinen Bart nicht abrasieren will und sich auf die Tatsache beruft, dass ja auch die Elben Mittelerdes bärtig sein konnten, wie sowohl das Beispiel Cirdans (LotR III 377) als auch die Aussage »Elves did not have beards until they entered the third cycle of life« (Hammond/Scull 674) bewiesen. Mit der Berufung auf diese, nicht von der Hand zu weisenden Zitate unterlag der Spieler einer Versuchung, die auch bei der Verwendung historischer Quellen ein bekanntes Problem darstellt: Er suchte gezielt nach Beweisen für seine These, die er auch fand.

Dabei ging er aber nicht »quellenkritisch« vor, denn sonst wären ihm mehrere Argumente gegen seine Entscheidung ins Auge gefallen: Zum einen handelt es sich bei Cirdan um »the oldest elf living in Middle-earth at the time of the War of the Ring« (ebd.) und er, der im Gegensatz zu besagtem Spieler auch andere Zeichen des Alters aufweist, ist damit eine Ausnahme der ansonsten durchaus

aus Tolkiens Aussagen zu bestätigenden Regel, dass Bartlosigkeit gemeinhin ein Kennzeichen elbischen Blutes ist (vgl. Hammond/Scull 585).

Zum anderen setzt er sich damit, unabhängig von der »historischen Korrektheit« seiner Entscheidung, bewusst über geltende Konventionen hinweg und gerät so regelmäßig in Erklärungsnöte. Da die Legitimierung seiner Aussage nur anhand – im Sinne der Spielwelt – externer Quellen möglich ist, reißt sie ihn und diejenigen, die ihn darauf ansprechen, zwangläufig aus dem Spiel. Denn eines bleibt zu bedenken: die Elfen im LARP sind nicht die Elben Tolkiens, egal wie nahe sie sich dem Original fühlen. Adaption bedeutet eben auch Anpassung des Konzeptes an gewachsene Konventionen, selbst wenn diese möglicherweise einem anderen Hintergrund stammen.

- Orks

> Als ›böse‹ antropomorphe Kreaturen werden sogenannte ›Orks‹ eingesetzt, die hässlich, missgestaltet, lichtscheu und blutrünstig sind, nur über begrenzte verbale Ausdrucksmöglichkeiten verfügen und jede Hautfarbe haben können außer weiß. In ihren Namen – wenn sie überhaupt welche haben – und ihrer Sprache werden bevorzugt harte Konsonanten wie X, Z, G und K verwendet, um sie noch abstoßender wirken zu lassen. (Melzener 137)

Die Orks sind einfacher und zugleich schwieriger zu fassen als die Elfen. Die überschaubare Spielerschaft ist gut strukturiert und teilt sich klar in diejenigen ein, die sich am *Herrn der Ringe* orientieren, und diejenigen, die sogenannte Clanorks spielen. Erstere sind unter dem Namen *Grat u Murdur* in einem Dachverband organisiert[7].

Was bedeutet es aber, einen Ork »nach dem *Herrn der Ringe*« zu spielen? Rein optisch zunächst, dass eben nicht »jede Hautfarbe außer weiß« akzeptabel ist, sondern Braun- und Grautöne und Schwarz vorherrschen. Grüne Orks, wie es sie unter den Clanspielern ab und an gibt, werden nicht gerne gesehen, wenn dann handelt es sich allenfalls um ein gedecktes Olivgrün.

Tolkien beschreibt seine Orks als »corruptions of the ›human‹ form seen in Elves and Men. They are (or were) squat, broad, flat-nosed, sallow-skinned, with wide mouths and slant eyes: in fact degraded and repulsive versions of the (to Europeans) least lovely Mongol-types« (L 274). Während einige ältere Illustrationen, namentlich diejenige, die Klaus Ensikat für die deutsche Ausgabe *Der kleine Hobbit* von 1974 (H passim) schuf, diesem Bild sehr nahe kommen, ist das Vorbild der LARP-Orks ohne Zweifel ein anderes: Sie orientieren sich klar an der Darstellung aus Peter Jacksons Filmen, die ohnehin auf ästhetischer Ebene einen überaus großen Einfluss auf die gesamte Szene ausüben.

---

7 http://www.larpwiki.de/GratuMurdur

Über die Gesellschaft der Orks ist hingegen, außer ihrer sichtlichen Brutalität, wenig bekannt. Shippey weist darauf hin, dass sie offenbar durchaus ein Verständnis für Moral haben, über das sie sich jedoch hinwegsetzen und dass für sie »elbisch« ein pejorativer Ausdruck ist (nach Hammond/Scull 500f). Da über ihr Leben jenseits des Kriegshandwerkes nur spekuliert werden kann, stellen die Orkgruppen, die sich am *Herrn der Ringe* orientieren, in der logischen Konsequenz sämtlich kriegerische Verbände mit entsprechend rauen Sitten dar.

- **Zwerge und Hobbits**

Sowohl Zwerge als auch Hobbits sind im LARP selten, denn sie stellen ihre Darsteller vor ein Problem: Aufgrund ihrer Statur sind sie nicht für jeden spielbar. Im Prinzip wären sie sogar gänzlich unspielbar, würde nicht eine sehr konsequente Orientierung an den Klischees über den zu hohen Wuchs bis zu einem gewissen Grad hinwegtäuschen. Diese sind dankbarerweise in beiden Fällen recht eindeutig. Metzler fasst sie für die Zwerge folgendermaßen zusammen:

> Zwerge sind stämmig, stark, trinkfest, geschäftstüchtig an der Grenze zur Raffgier, kämpfen bevorzugt mit einer Streitaxt und fühlen sich unter der Erde sicherer als an der frischen Luft ... Mögen keine Elfen. (Melzener 136)

In dieser Liste fehlt freilich der Hauptpunkt, der lange Bart, ohne den ein Zwerg nicht komplett ist. Er ist, neben der Axt eine Art universeller Chiffre, um den Zwerg oder die Zwergin als solche zu kennzeichnen. Was aus Tolkiens eigenen Aussagen nur vermutet werden kann (vgl. Hammond/Scull 710f), wird damit im Rollenspiel zur unumstößlichen Gewissheit.

Was nun das Aussehen der Hobbits angeht, sind Tolkiens eigene Angaben so präzise, dass es kaum Deutungsspielraum gibt:

> I picture a fairly human figure...: fattish in the stomach, shortish in the leg. A round jovial face; ears only slightly pointed and 'elvish'; hair short and curling (brown). The feet from the ankles down, covered with brown hairy fur. Clothing: greenvelvet breeches; red or yellow waistcoat; brown or green jacket; gold (or brass) buttons; a dark green hood and cloak (belonging to a dwarf) ... leathery soles, and well-brushed furry feet are a feature of essential hobbitness. (L 35)

Gefestigt wurde dieses Bild durch die Filmtrilogie, die es nahezu Wort für Wort, bis hin zu den Farben der Kleidung, die sich in diesem Fall auf Bilbo Beutlin beziehen, übernimmt. Die wenigen LARP-Hobbits orientieren sich dementsprechend akribisch an den Vorgaben, da nur eine detailverliebte Umsetzung über die körperlichen »Defizite« hinwegtäuschen kann.

Auch was gesellschaftliche Topoi angeht, sind die Varianten bei den »Kleinwüchsigen« sehr gering: Zwerge sind in der Regel Krieger oder Bergleute, Hobbits quasi ausschließlich Köche oder zumindest Liebhaber guten Essens. Dies ist nötig, da jede Abweichung vom Klischee die Gefahr in sich birgt, nicht als Zwerg oder Hobbit erkannt zu werden. Bezeichnenderweise haben sich die meisten Spieler dennoch für ein selbst erdachtes, fiktives Land, also gegen Mittelerde als Herkunftsort, entschieden.

- Menschen

Die am meisten bespielte »Rasse«, Menschen, wird aus gutem Grunde hier zuletzt behandelt. Dass Menschenklischees sehr schwer fassbar sind, liegt in der Natur der Sache. Sehr schön verdeutlicht dies auch die Liste bei Melzener, in der er »Kulturen, die an Wikinger und/oder Kelten angelehnt sind«, »Kulturen, die an das mitteleuropäische Hochmittelalter angelehnt sind«, und »Kulturen, die an Afrika oder Asien angelehnt sind« (Melzener 137), anführt. Die Repräsentanten dieser Topoi sind laut ihm Rohan, Gondor und Haradrim und Ostlinge. Schon allein, dass er nicht sicher ist, ob die Rohirrim nun an Wikinger, Kelten oder beides angelehnt sind, zeigt, wie sehr er über das Ziel hinausgeschossen ist.

Natürlich umfassen diese Klischees, da sie sehr schwammig sind, die meisten der in der Fantasy verwendeten und somit auch einen Großteil der im LARP vertretenen Kulturen. Letztere orientieren sich allerdings nach eigener Aussage zumeist an ihren realweltlichen Vorbildern, ohne den Umweg über Mittelerde zu gehen. Eine Adaption von Tolkiens Welt kann hier nur bei den wenigen Gruppen oder Einzelspielern festgestellt werden, die tatsächlich Menschen aus Mittelerde darstellen.

Zwei dieser Gruppen, von den verschiedenen Fronten des Ringkrieges, können hier exemplarisch vorgestellt werden: die Dúnedain[8] und die Haradrim[9]. Erstere ist eine Gruppierung, die über das Cosplay zum Liverollenspiel gekommen ist. Nicht alle Mitglieder machen LARP, einige besitzen die entsprechenden Gewänder nur, um auf Veranstaltungen wie Tolkien-Tagen oder der RingCon darin aufzutreten. Entsprechend ist ihre Kleidung eng am Vorbild der Peter-Jackson-Filme orientiert, während ihr Hintergrund über die Informationen, die sich aus der Literatur ergeben, klar festgelegt ist. Sie besuchen die wenigen, ausgesuchten LARP-Veranstaltungen, die eine Verwendung des Hintergrunds ohne zu große Zugeständnisse an die Logik möglich machen. Dies ist vor allem auch deshalb kein Problem, weil das Rollenspiel ohnehin eher als Zusatzmöglichkeit gesehen wird, die bereits vorhandenen Gewandungen und Hintergrundgeschichten zu verwenden.

---

8   http://www.dunedain-germany.de/
9   http://www.pedes-inflati.de/haradrim.htm

Die Haradrim dagegen haben sich entschlossen, aus den spärlichen Informationen, die sich aus dem *Herrn der Ringe* ergeben, aus der Umsetzung im Film und Versatzstücken der orientalischen Kultur eine eigene Mixtur zu erschaffen, in der auch die Symbolik des roten Auges, mit dem sie ihre Anhängerschaft an Sauron verdeutlichen, eine gewisse Rolle spielt. Hier handelt es sich also um eine eher freie Adaption des Stoffes, der ja großen Interpretationsspielraum lässt.

Zusammenfassend bleibt festzustellen: Es zeigt sich, dass in keinem Fall eine Vorlage unverändert übernommen wurde. Adaption im Sinne von Interpretation findet statt, ohne notwendigerweise als solche wahrgenommen zu werden, wie besonders am Beispiel der Elben und Orks, mit einem großen Anteil an Spielern, die ihre Orientierung an Tolkiens Vorbildern sehr deutlich machen, gut zu sehen ist. Aus dem jahrelangen Zusammenspiel ergeben sich mit der Zeit neue ungeschriebene Regeln und feste Konventionen, die mit den aus dem literarischen Vorbild stammenden eng verwoben sind.

Schlussbemerkung

Zwar ist es unmöglich, festzustellen, was Tolkien vom Liverollenspiel gehalten hätte. Es ist jedoch zu vermuten, dass er diesem ebenso skeptisch gegenübergestanden hätte wie der Illustration und der cinematographischen Darstellung oder generell jeder anderen Kunstform, außer der Literatur, die er allesamt für zu präzise festgelegt und damit einengend hielt. (vgl. FS 49 u. Anm. E, 77f)

Andererseits spielt jeder Rollenspieler seinen eigenen, individuellen Charakter, egal, wie vieler Klischees er sich bedient, egal, wie nah er an eine literarische oder filmische Gestalt angelehnt ist. Seine Handlungen sind unabhängig von einem Drehbuch, er stellt nicht bestehende Geschichten nach, sondern erfindet, gemeinsam mit anderen, neue. Wenn Frank Weinreich sagt, die Aneignung von imaginären Welten geschähe wohl auf keine Weise so intensiv wie bei der interaktiven Teilnahme im Spiel (Weinreich 99), ist dies auf jeden Fall zu unterstreichen. Und aus diesem Grund wird vielen LARPern folgende Aussage als Beschreibung eines besonders intensiven Spielerlebnisses erscheinen:

> Now 'Faërian Drama' – those plays which according to abundant records the elves have often presented to men – can produce Fantasy with a realism and immediacy beyond the compass of any human mechanism. As a result their usual effect (upon a man) is to go beyond Secondary Belief. If you are present at a Faërian drama you yourself are, or think that you are, bodily inside its Secondary World. (FS 52)

Das Erlebnis des *Flows*, das sich bei einem konsequent aufrecht erhaltenen Charakterspiel im besten Fall ergibt, ist wohl die Erfahrung, die einer Teilnahme an einem tatsächlichen *Faërian Drama* in diesem unserem wahren Leben am nächsten kommt.

Bibliographie

Carpenter, Humphrey, Ed. with the assistance of Christopher Tolkien. *The Letters of J.R.R. Tolkien.* London: Allen & Unwin, 1981

Fritz, Jürgen. *Das Spiel verstehen. Eine Einführung in Theorie und Bedeutung.* Weinheim/München: Juventa, 2004

Hammond, Wayne G., und Scull, Christina. *The Lord of the Rings. A Reader's Companion.* London: HarperCollins 2005

Melzener, Axel. *Weltenbauer. Phantastische Szenarien in Literatur, Games und Film.* Boizenburg: Hülsbusch 2010

Mogel, Hans. *Psychologie des Kinderspiels.* Heidelberg: Springer ^{3}2008

Mosler, Astrid. »Bis einer heult ... Warum gespielte Verbrechen echte Konflikte erzeugen können«. *LARP Zeit* Sonderausgabe August 2013: 43-45

Steimel, Heidi. »Humor bei Tolkien«. *Der Flammifer von Westernis* (Vereinszeitschrift der Deutschen Tolkien Gesellschaft e.V.), in Vorbereitung

Tolkien, John Ronald Reuel. *Der kleine Hobbit.* München: dtv, 1974

---. *Das Silmarillion.* Stuttgart: Klett-Cotta, ^{3}1998

---. *The Fellowship of the Ring. The Lord of the Rings Part I.* London: HarperCollins, 1999

---. *The Return of the King. The Lord of the Rings Part III.* London: HarperCollins, 1999

---. "On Fairy-Stories". *Tree and Leaf.* London: HarperCollins, 2001, 3-81

Weinreich, Frank. *Fantasy. Einführung.* Essen: Oldib, 2007

Recreating *The Lord of the Rings* in Roleplaying and Board Games
A Narratological Analysis
Natalia González de la Llana (Aachen)

Introduction

Contemporary fantasy sagas are characterized by their permeability, which allows them to flow into different media. They are no longer exclusively a literary creation, but have been extended to other non-verbal discourses like cinema, comics, etc. through the sharing of narrative universes.

The Lord of the Rings is obviously no exception to this rule. On the contrary, it has been recreated in many ways. Tolkien's work can be considered the primordial fiction, the origin of the saga, that has given birth to a whole set of transfictions like the games we will be taking a closer look at in this paper.[1]

As García Rivera proposes, the paracosmos (a term born in psychology to refer to the stories created by children who make up islands, countries and all kinds of adventures up to building a complete new world) is the privileged form of the so-called speculative fiction, where the openness of the narrative model allows an expansion of the invented world into a really never-ending story. (García Rivera, *Paracosmos* 63-66)

The object of this paper is to analyze how Middle-earth, the universe brought to life by Tolkien, has escaped from the hands of its original author and taken form in two different kind of games: *The Lord of the Rings Role-playing Game* released by Decipher Inc. in 2002 and winner of the Origins Award for the Best Roleplaying Game of the same year, and *The Lord of the Rings Board Game* designed by Reiner Knizia and illustrated by John Howe.

In order to fulfil this goal, we have decided to compare these games from a narratological point of view, in both cases analyzing story, narrator, characters, time and space.

Story

The first thing we learn about our roleplaying game is that our objective as players is not to win, but to enjoy telling a fantasy story in which the characters we create accomplish noble and heroic deeds. It is like playing make-believe when you were younger, the *Core Book* explains to us, except that you have some rules to follow (Long 4). It is, no doubt, interesting to see how the

---
1 About the topic of sagas and transfiction, see García Rivera, *Sagas*.

instructions of the game refer directly to the inventive games of children as the origin of these stories confirming what we have pointed out before.

To play *The Lord of the Rings Role-playing Game*, we need characters which we create by defining their qualities, powers and personality. One member of the group is the Narrator, the person in charge of creating the outline of an adventure and of playing the part of those characters that nobody else controls. But all players influence the development of the story with their decisions and actions, so everybody cooperates as a group in creating the plot. Even if there are some rules, these are flexible or can be ignored altogether if necessary.

In opposition to other roleplaying games like the *Adventure Game* also by Decipher, where players had to take the role of a member of the Fellowship of the Ring based on the original story, they are not limited to playing Aragorn, Frodo, etc. any more in this game, as they get to make up their own characters. On the other hand, the adventures are not as rigidly defined here either.

The *Core Book* explains the rules of the game and gives advice to the Narrator. The first chapter describes the history of Middle-earth in the late Third Age, the time depicted in *The Lord of the Rings*, in order to provide the basic information needed to establish a context for the new stories.

The idea of this game, therefore, is to develop a narrative based on the background of Tolkien's trilogy (or Peter Jackson's movies, as the pictures that accompany the Book are taken from these), that is, it is placed in and inspired by his world, but with enough freedom to make up a totally different adventure. The players become active creators of characters and plots, and stop being mere spectators of the fight between good and evil.

The Lord of the Rings Board Game, on the other hand, pretends to reproduce the epic journey to try and destroy the Ring, as it is described in the original text. Players become members of the Fellowship and their collective aim is to take the Ring to Mordor and cast it into the volcano at the top of Mount Doom, while gathering as many of Gandalf's runes as possible. The runes symbolize each player's contribution to driving back the dark forces, and can summon the aid of Gandalf. There is actually no individual winner, the players act as a group.

At the end of the Rulebook, the story behind the game is briefly explained in connection with the key locations that the Fellowship has to cross in its path towards Sauron: Bag End, Rivendell, Moria, Lothlórien, Helm's Deep, Shelob's Lair and Mordor. The object of the game is clear: they have to get to Mordor and destroy the Ring, before Sauron reaches them, eliminates the Ring-bearer, and reclaims his Ring. In other words, pretty much the same thing that we find in Tolkien's narrative.

As is usually the case with board games, the freedom of the players is much more limited than in roleplaying games. They have to follow the road the Master Game Board outlines for them and they have to respect the rules. Besides, the important thing here *is* winning, not the storytelling, and it is, by the way, not easy at all, probably as a symbol of the perils and challenges the original Hobbits have to face during their journey. Evil is really strong. But there is still a possibility of scoring points at the end based on how close the Fellowship gets to destroy the Ring. These points allow the players to compare their performance with previous games.

We can also find some of the narrative elements of the novels translated with similar functions into the game. For example, the Ring can be used once during each Conflict – which is how some of the locations in their path are called - to advance one Activity Marker in such a way that spaces moved over or landed on are not carried out – i.e., the Ring makes the Hobbit invisible.

As a whole, we can affirm that this board game does try to reflect the spirit of *The Lord of the Rings*. It is also true that it could probably be played without knowing the novels or the movies, but a great part of its meaning would be lost as would be the pleasure of playing it.

Narrator

As we said before, the narrator is an essential figure in roleplaying games. He develops the plots and adventures the players have to go through, and plays the parts of those characters nobody else controls. Besides creating chapters, his main responsibility is to know the rules, to know the setting and to maintain the game balance.

Narrators in literature are considered to be a central element in a story because all other components experience, in one way or another, the effects of the manipulation he inflicts on the narrative materials. He has a greater or a smaller knowledge (depending on the kind of narrator) of the events that occur in the tale and organizes them as he wishes in a discourse (Garrido 105-106).

In our roleplaying game, however, the narrator has some interesting characteristics that we do not find in literary texts. In the first place, our narrator here is an oral teller who uses Tolkien's world and ideas to construct his own stories. His freedom is enormous, but, at the same time, the advice given to him in the *Core Book* suggests that he stay as near as possible to the original novels, keeping the spirit of Middle-earth as we know it. It further recommends, for instance, that the division between Right and Wrong typical for the trilogy be maintained not allowing the other players to choose characters with significant moral conflicts, or to avoid that they be heavily armed as true tolkienesque characters never are.

This narrator, therefore, is supposed to work on the basis of an already created world with concrete rules and values, think for himself of new chronicles that suit this world (or use the supplements prepared by the publishing company), and then to improvise during the course of the game in direct response to the reactions of the other players within the quests he proposes.

He has thus no absolute control over the story. In a novel, the narrator can bring us readers where he pleases. He can introduce the new information when he wants to. He is the master of the tale he is telling. This stands in marked contrast to the narrator in our roleplaying game who does not work alone and whose plots may and will develop in unforeseen ways, because the other players also cooperate in the invention of the adventure. So, even though one is the teller in this game, the others are not just "passive readers", but active constructors of the saga.

Besides, each role-play narrator will make up different stories expanding the possible history of Middle-earth, contributing to the paracosmos of Tolkien's land as writers of fan-fiction do in a similar way. His abilities to create the verisimilitude and epic feel needed, which can also be achieved with music, candles and other elements that help establish the right atmosphere, will be decisive in the success of the game.

In the board game dedicated to *The Lord of the Rings*, the presence of a narrator is not as obvious or central as in roleplaying. However, no story can be told by itself, there always has to be a narrator even if his presence is not tangible. As a filter of all materials in a story, Todorov says, the narrator has to be there (Garrido 110-111). The same happens in films. Every story, no matter how objective and impersonal it seems, shows the presence of an instance that conducts the narrative, choosing images and their point of view, combining them with sound, etc. (Neira 58-59).

There is a story in this board game, so there has to be a narrator who organizes the different materials and presents them to us. In fact, somebody has created the path to drive the players through the different scenarios in a quest to get the Ring destroyed.

The Rule Book explains to us the most important events in Tolkien's trilogy and our aim in this game: save the lands of Middle-earth, go to Mount Doom and get rid of Sauron's Ring forever. It explains to us how to play and the meaning of the different cards and boards, all of them closely related to the original novels.

There is no patent voice during the course of the game that tells us the story of the Hobbits' journey, but there is an organizing entity who gives us a particular selection of characters and adventures that we know through the books, and who is more clearly manifested while reading the Rule Book. There is a somebody, even if he reveals himself as extradiegetic and impersonal, who decides to tell his own version of *The Lord of the Rings* and offers it to the players to enjoy.

The narrator thus indicates the development of the tale, which necessarily has to pass through the fixed locations on the board, and must also follow very concrete rules. But, as it is not a literary text, his dominion is not complete either. The players who take the part of the Fellowship can fulfil their task or can fail and die. There is an open ending needed, of course, to keep up the interest in the game.

Characters

The characters in our roleplaying game do not have to be those that Tolkien created in *The Lord of the Rings*, as we have seen, but they do have to be coherent with his world. The various players have to invent a character and define his abilities, goals, etc. When they play out chapters in the chronicle made up by the narrator, they control their character's actions, speak their respective dialogues and so on, playing their part as an actor would do in a movie.

The steps a player has to take to give life to his character are quite similar in many aspects to the ones any writer must take when planning a story. The *Core Book* suggests to start by considering his appearance, his personality (traits and flaws), his goals and, therefore, the role he is going to play in the chronicle, even if it also offers the option of picking up one of the sample characters they propose, with the possibility of changing their name and background a bit, or simply leaving them as they are.

His identity, his behaviour and the relationship he maintains with others are some of the basic features that are needed to construct a character. The identity is mostly defined from the beginning on, but the other elements can be delineated—and sometimes modified—during the development of the action (Garrido 82-88).

In this game, the players have to decide on the race of their characters (Elf, Dwarf, Hobbit or Man), the order they belong to depending on what they do (warriors, magicians, craftsmen, mariners, etc.), their personality traits, skills and attributes (quantified in numbers). However, contrary to literary authors, these creators are meant to work as a group, considering what other players have in mind for their own characters and what kind of adventure the narrator is planning, so as to ensure that each player has a distinctive role to play within the group (Long 76).

It is interesting that the *Core Book* insists on the importance of creating heroes who embody the characteristics of Tolkien's world. Being true to the spirit of Middle-earth means creating characters whose qualities include: compassion, responsible free will, generosity, honesty and fairness, honour and nobility, restraint and self-sacrifice, as well as valour and wisdom (Long 50-51).

As in any other story, we can distinguish different character patterns here depending on the narrative abilities and the intentions of the players. Gemma Lluch reminds us that there are static characters (if their traits remain the same through the plot) and dynamic characters (if they change), flat characters (built around a main feature or idea) and round characters (defined by their complexity), and also individual and collective characters (Lluch 68).

All those types can be found in these fantasy tales, but players are above all encouraged to create epic heroes who begin their adventures in a quest full of perils to save the world. As in *The Lord of the Rings*, they have to work as a team to carry out a mission, so although they act individually, they need each other to achieve their victory. They embark on a journey that could last forever if they wanted to, a journey with different chapters and different goals by the end of which they hope to succeed in their ultimate objective of defeating evil.

It seems also important for the author of *The Lord of the Rings Board Game* to propose a collective aim that the players have to resolve as a group. This Fellowship, however, is composed exclusively of Hobbits, namely: Frodo, Sam, Pippin, Merry, and Fatty, who have innate special abilities described in their corresponding card. The main characters here are Hobbits, they represent the whole community of Middle-earth, but they receive help from their friends in the form of cards. For example, if the Fellowship gathers enough runes, Gandalf cards can be used to call the wizard to assist them with his magical powers.

The only other character who is explicitly present with a marker is, of course, Sauron, a constant threat on the path of corruption, always seeking to recover his Ring. Indeed, if a player's Hobbit encounters Sauron by being on the same space as he or beyond him on the Corruption Track, he is immediately eliminated from the game.

Frodo begins to play as Ring-bearer, but he does not stay it the whole time. After the end of a Conflict (there are four Conflict Game Boards which have to be resolved as the Fellowship progresses along the Master Game Board), a new Ring-bearer is determined following certain rules. The players should plan ahead as to who should become the new Ring-bearer. It is important that he is not very advanced in the Corruption Track, because if he gets to meet Sauron, the result is not just his elimination, but the end of the game.

These characters are not at all defined if we compare them to the ones developed in the roleplaying game. They could even be substituted by others (Aragorn, Legolas, etc.) and it would not be a great change, but it is also true that the player is supposed to know the story behind the game, and Tolkien's quest is also described in the Rulebook. Sauron is actually the only one who cannot be replaced, and his terrible eye constantly threatens the Hobbits with all the evil we can hope for.

The greatest achievement of this game in relation to the characters is, in our opinion, the need to work together to be able to defeat the enemy following the spirit of the original Fellowship. It is a challenge for the players to try and keep themselves alive at the same time that they work for the team. They want to go on playing, but they also know that their goal as a group is more important, because none of them will survive if Sauron wins, so they have to learn to make sacrifices for the common good.

Time

Applying the narratological distinction to our object of study, we can speak of an external time (the one during the playing of the game) and an internal time (the one inside the story). In the roleplaying game the chronicles can last as long as the players want them to, as there are infinite possibilities of new adventures to undertake, and it is usually played in many sessions over months or years. The process of playing is simultaneous for all players, there is no difference in the reception time, something the game has in common with films, but, on the other hand, contrary to these, the time is not concrete and limited, as we have just exposed.[2]

The internal time differs greatly from the original novels, as the literary texts are written in the past tense, while the narrator of the roleplaying game normally relates a current event to which the characters have to react as they find suitable. Therefore, the narrator uses mostly the present tense, although he could obviously also make use of the past to explain some background information, for example. The players are living their fantasy then and there. They do not have to reproduce events from the past, they have to create new ones deciding which path to take or what to do.

Inside the internal time, one also has to distinguish between the story (the complete series of events in chronological order) and the plot (the way the materials in the story are told). The transition from story to plot comes with the delimitation of a beginning and an end, a selection of the events presented and the importance given to them, the adoption of a point of view, etc. Time will also suffer a transformation, as the linear time of the story can be manipulated in the plot altering the chronological order, summarizing certain passages, and so on (Neira 180).

Even if this is true of any discourse, the stories invented for the roleplaying games tend to be more linear than the ones we read in literary texts. On the one hand, the fact that they are oral tales could explain why the narrator should not try to complicate the plots excessively (there can be, for example, simultaneous actions if the players decide to split, but it is not very common, as they are expected to try and work as a group). But on the other hand, and more importantly, the players are "living" their adventures in real time. It is not a time-honored epic story being told by one of them. It is their own story the narrator is telling.

---

2 "El proceso de recepción del film se enmarca, pues, en un tiempo concreto y limitado, que se caracteriza – a diferencia del tiempo de lectura de una obra literaria – por estar fijado en una duración determinada, sin posibilidad de variación de un espectador a otro." (Neira 179-180)

If we analyze *The Lord of the Rings Board Game*, we will see that the external time is clearly much shorter, just a couple of hours, and the internal time includes the same period in which Tolkien's trilogy takes place, beginning with the call for adventure in the Shire and finishing (if the Fellowship does not fail before) in the dark lands of Mordor.

The time of the story is also linear, as the players cannot but follow the track that has been designed for them, but there has been a selection of the main events that serve to represent all the battles and perils the characters have gone through in their fight against Sauron. Just as in the roleplaying game, the present is the time of the quest, in this case because the players are experiencing in real time the different steps needed to accomplish their journey successfully.

It is easy to understand why games do not usually present past, but ongoing events, something not so common in literature except in texts of the type "Choose your own adventure" that tend to blur the frontier between the extra-linguistic reality and the one created with language. The narrator addresses a "you" to whom he explains what is happening under the coordinates you/here/now, a stylistic resource that reinforces the presence of the reader in the narrative, creating a fiction in which he is at the same time the protagonist of the story (Lluch 58-59).

Although readers usually identify with the characters of the books they consume, the texts of the above-mentioned type and these games give them the opportunity of experiencing the stories more directly, of becoming the real heroes of their fantasies.

Space

The first difference in space that we can find between the reading of Tolkien's novels and the use of the roleplaying game is the situation in which the reader and the player respectively are. The reader stays alone with his book, entrapped in the world the author has created for him, while the player shares his fantasy with other people enjoying an oral storytelling they are improvising together. In roleplaying games, it is also common to intensify the feeling of being in the invented universe by using candles, music, pictures, etc. The maps[3] and pictures, that the narrator can include in the game to help the players introduce themselves into the story, outline the scenarios in which the action is taking place.

Once inside the tale, the abilities of the storyteller to describe landscapes and geographies are fundamental to make the narrative believable and interesting. The space is obviously that of Middle-earth, so much is done already,

---

3 For an analysis of maps in fantasy sagas, see Martos García.

but the narrator's freedom to create new places and fill them with details can be decisive in the success of his chronicle.

The *Core Book* provides in its first chapter a description of the various regions in Middle-earth: the Shire, Rivendell, the Old Forest... all of them possible spaces for adventures and quests. And it also recommends to emphasize the natural world, as it is an important element in epic fantasy, and one Tolkien stresses by devoting many passages to describe it.

The diversity of scenarios with a symbolic meaning is also very obvious in *The Lord of the Rings*: from the cozy little houses of the cheerful Hobbits to the elegance and refinement of the Elves' cities or to the dark and desolated territory that represents Sauron's power in Mordor.

Apart from the landscapes of the different regions in Middle-earth, the narrator can use diverse spaces to create a concrete atmosphere which could, at the same time, refer to a variety of states of mind in the characters and also respond to a manifest symbolism: the road, the tower, closed spaces vs. open spaces, and so on. In short, he can profit from the same possibilities of making up meaningful spaces that any writer has.

What is especially interesting here in comparison to the literary works the game is based on, is again the fact that even if both reader and player create Middle-earth through their imagination, in the first case this happens in solitude and the description of the scenarios is the same for every reader as the text does not change, whereas in the roleplaying game the players "visualize" simultaneously the places they are visiting within their minds when listening to the narrator inventing a living world for them in that very moment.

The Lord of the Rings Board Game is of course as well a collective adventure that takes place in Middle-earth. The space here, however, is not just "told", but "shown", and it serves as a real support for the story. In this game there are three boards, two of them double-sided, that represent the journey of the Hobbits to fulfil their task and destroy Sauron.

The Master Game Board contains the path the Fellowship will travel in their quest, as well as the Corruption Track, which indicates how close Sauron is to finding our main characters. The Activity Marker shows the movements of the Hobbits across the lands of Middle-earth. There are seven key locations: Bag End, Rivendell, Moria, Lothlórien, Helm's Deep, Shelob's Lair and Mordor. Some of these locations are Safe Havens (Bag End, Rivendell and Lothlórien), while the others are Conflicts, and each contains of specific actions the players must resolve before being allowed to the next step.

The Corruption Track points out each Hobbit's current level of corruption. The further a Hobbit is to the left, the purer his spirit has remained. The Sauron marker begins the game on space 12 (or on space 15 for beginners) and moves closer to the Fellowship in his search for the Ring, eliminating those whom he meets on his way.

This Corruption Track has a material place on the board, but has at the same time a symbolic meaning. This space is also a road that shows how deep the characters have been possessed by the darkness of evil, but this symbolism has also very real consequences for the players. If they become too corrupted, if Sauron reaches them, they are dead and expulsed from the game.

This road runs also parallel to the main journey of the Hobbits represented by the key locations named before. It indicates the dependence between the factual journey and the spiritual journey. When they begin their quest, Frodo and his companions are cheerful, quiet souls, but their intention to fight Sauron and destroy the Ring does not come without a price. The nearer they get to Mordor, the greater Sauron's influence is over them, and the danger of dying or being turned to the evil side is constantly present.

As we said before, some of the key locations are not safe places, but "Conflicts". These locations have a corresponding Conflict Game Board that is set up below the Master Game Board when it has to be played. Each Conflict Game Board has Activity Tracks for some or all of the following four types of activities: fighting, friendship, hiding and traveling. This choice indicates the elements of the quest the author of the game has wanted to emphasize by giving them their own space.

While the illustrations in the Master Board present a wonderful natural landscape that tries to remind us of the beauty of Middle-earth, the pictures in the different Conflict Game Boards are dark images of dangerous places, monsters and destruction.

The scenarios in this game, therefore, have their origin in Tolkien's world and count on the imagination of the players, but not as much as in the roleplaying game, as they also have a "physical presence" in the illustrated Game Boards.

Conclusions

In this paper, we have proposed a literary analysis of a roleplaying game and a board game, both based in Tolkien's *The Lord of the Rings*, by trying to show the most important narrative elements that they have used to "tell their own stories".

We have, in the first place, explained how the story of Middle-earth is presented in both cases: either new quests and characters are invented, as telling a fantasy story is the aim in the roleplaying game, or the journey to destroy the Ring is reproduced on a board.

The narrator is clearly an essential figure in a storytelling game. He knows the rules, invents the chronicles and chapters, and controls those characters played by none of the other players. Even if he is the creator of the adventures, the "character"-players can also introduce changes into his plans and the plot can develop other than he had first thought.

In the board game, the narrator is not so central and his presence is not that obvious, but every story has an instance which organizes the narrative materials and presents them in a concrete way. The players take here the part of the Hobbits who fight against the only other character with a marker: Sauron. These characters are not in the least defined, especially if we compare them to the ones developed in the roleplaying game, where everything has to be taken care of: appearance, personality, race, goals, etc.

The external time is quite different in both cases: in the board game it is just a couple of hours, while the roleplaying game can last until the players decide to stop. The internal time in the board game is, in principle, the same as in the novels (the war of the Ring), but represented only by a few key locations/battles, whereas the time in the role-play depends on the story the narrator makes up. In both cases, anyway, it is important that the present, and not the past tense, is the protagonist of the tales, as the players are supposed to be experiencing the events in real time.

The space in which the games take place is, of course, Middle-earth. In the roleplaying game, the places are visualized with the imagination of all players simultaneously and with the help of maps and pictures if the narrator thinks it appropriate, while Knizia's game offers different illustrated boards where the locations of the Hobbits' journey and their battles are represented, as well as their level of corruption during the quest.

Bibliography

García Rivera, Gloria. "Las sagas, entre la ficción y la transficción". *Primeras Noticias* 220 (2006): 49-56

---. "Paracosmos: las regiones de la imaginación (los mundos imaginarios en los géneros de fantasía, C&F y terror: nuevos conceptos y métodos)". *Primeras Noticias* 215 (2004): 61-70

Garrido Domínguez, Antonio. *El texto narrativo*. Madrid: Síntesis, 1996

Lluch, Gemma. *Análisis de narrativas infantiles y juveniles*. Cuenca: Ediciones de la Universidad de Castilla-La Mancha, 2003

Martos García, Alberto E. *Introducción al mundo de las sagas*, Badajoz: Universidad de Extremadura, 2009

Neira Piñeiro, María del Rosario. *Introducción al discurso narrativo fílmico*. Madrid: Arco Libros, 2003

Games

Knizia, Reiner and John Howe. *The Lord of the Rings. The Board Game*. Minnesota: Fantasy Flight Games, 2010

Long, Steven S. et al. *The Lord of the Rings. Role-playing Game. Core Book*. Los Angeles: Decipher, 2002

Summary

	Role-play	Board Game
Story	•Aim: to tell a fantasy story • The players have to create characters • A narrator develops the outline of the adventure • Narrative inspired by Tolkien, but with freedom	• Aim: to win (the Fellowship has to destroy the Ring) • Epic journey in key locations (Master Board Game) • Much less freedom • Game inspired by Tolkien, but it can be played without knowing the stories in detail
Narrator	• Essential (creates the story, knows the rules, etc.) • Oral teller • Freedom, but in keeping with the spirit of Middle-earth • No absolute control (the other players can change the course of action) • Expansion of Tolkien's world	• Not tangible, but implicit (organizing entity) • Selection of characters and events • No complete control (the players can fail and change the original story) • Open ending
Characters	• Not necessarily those created by Tolkien, but coherent with his world • Creation: appearance, personality, goals, skills and attributes, role within the group, etc. • Epic heroes (compassion, responsible free will, generosity, etc.) • Act as a group	• Hobbits: Frodo, Sam, Pippin, Merry + Fatty (each with special abilities) • Sauron • Undefined characters • Act as a group (the Fellowship)
Time	• Never-ending story (can last months/years) • Present tense (the players experience their fantasy in real time; they are the protagonists) • Linear stories	• A couple of hours to play - It covers the time described in *The Lord of the Rings* • Linear stories (selection of events) • Present tense (the players experience their fantasy in real time; they are the protagonists)

Space	• Inside the story:
	  - Middle-earth: landscapes, regions
	  - Symbolic spaces: roads, towers, etc.
	• Outside the story:
	  - The players share their fantasy
	  - Atmosphere: candles, music, maps, pictures, etc.
	• The players "visualize" simultaneously the places when listening to the narrator inventing a world at that very moment
		• Middle-earth (key locations)
		• Master Game Board:
		  - Path of the Fellowship towards Mordor: physical journey
		  - Corruption Track (it shows the Hobbits' level of corruption in relationship to their distance to Sauron): spiritual journey
		• Conflict Game Boards
		• Illustrations: wonderful landscapes on the Master Board; dark images of dangerous places on the CGBs
		• Scenarios: imagination+physical presence

Bringing Tolkien to the Table:
Blending and Conceptual Metaphor in the Board Game Adaptations *Der Herr der Ringe* and *Der Hobbit*

Timo Lothmann & Nicole Hützen

My heart tells me that he has some part to play yet, for good or ill, before the end
(LotR I 58)

1.

Due in particular to the impact of the film trilogy, *The Lord of the Rings* has turned into a pop-cultural phenomenon. The films had a multiplying effect on diverse other adaptations which have since arisen. Also, the plot of *The Hobbit* has recently joined in, proving to be an exploitable source. This paper focuses on selected board game adaptations of *The Lord of the Rings* and *The Hobbit*. We depart from the assumption that playing board games, and the group experience that is inherent to it, entail the construction of mental representations of the content. This includes the characters acting within the game plot and, importantly, their identity.

Taking a cognitive perspective informed by linguistics, literature and game studies, we claim that conceptual metaphors and the mapping of domains involved (cf. Lakoff/Johnson) can help to effectively set up an abstract, dynamic mental space. In this space, prevalent schemata are negotiated to the end of a blended identity construction (cf. Fauconnier/Turner) within the individual in the course of their playing a game. In other words: metaphors underlie the game characters' construct, and there is no gameplay without blending.

The theoretical framework will be tested against an analysis of the game adaptations *Der Herr der Ringe* and *Der Hobbit* (Knizia et al., *Herr*; *Hobbit*) which were designed for German-speaking markets. On this basis, we will point out sets of conceptual metaphors as elementary strategic tools for coming to terms with the (adapted) game-playing self. Eventually, we will propose a model which adequately acknowledges this constitutive nature of metaphor in gameplay.

In addition, empirical data samples will provide a glimpse at what may be termed 'game quality' beyond subjective notions. We intend to show that successful game design (in terms of a book adaptation) depends on the integrity of the blended space. The selected board games feature such to varying degrees.

2.

According to conceptual metaphor theory, metaphors are not primarily a rhetorical characteristic of erudite or poetic language. Prominent representatives of the theory assert that metaphors are pervasive in everyday life. Moreover, "[o]ur ordinary conceptual system... is fundamentally metaphorical in nature" (Lakoff/Johnson 3). In this view metaphors are not a matter of language in the first place. Rather, on a most basic level, they determine our actions and thought (cf. ibid.). One of the core assumptions of this theory is that abstract experience is understood in terms of knowledge which is already well-established and stable, i.e. we understand and categorise one thing in terms of another. This key mechanism of making sense of new information works largely subconsciously (cf. ibid. 4; 272).

From the perspective of textual realisations, linguistic metaphors are seen only as evidence for underlying cognitive categories, reflecting deeply ingrained conceptualisation strategies. For instance, the contemporary conceptual metaphor TIME is MONEY can have various realisations in language, such as "I've *invested* a lot of time in her" or "That flat tire *cost* me an hour".[1]

Two domains are involved here: the conceptual structures of the (concrete) source domain MONEY are mapped onto those of the (different, more elusive) target domain TIME. The language here reveals how TIME can be viewed in a particular context by highlighting certain aspects of the concept and hiding others (cf. ibid. 10). In general, our conceptual system plays a central role in structuring our everyday experience.

In this context, the theory of conceptual blending (Fauconnier; Fauconnier/Turner) is related to conceptual metaphor theory. Conceptual blending is described as a basic mental operation for the construction of meaning and thus for our conceptualisation of reality (cf. Fauconnier/Turner 18). In this framework, meaning construction runs via the partial mapping of so-called mental spaces. Mental spaces can thus be seen as hypothetical constructs which contain general knowledge about particular situations or scenarios, including culture-specific knowledge. The knowledge that is culture-specific can be assumed to consist of a dynamic set of cultural models, i.e. idealised cognitive subcategories which are shared within a social group (cf. Stockwell 33). With regard to the TIME is MONEY example, the conceptual domains involved can also be conceived of as two mental spaces contributing to a blended space.

These two input spaces, or mental domains, are partially merged (or mapped) and thus create the new blend which joins different aspects of the time and money concepts. This merger is assumed to facilitate the understanding of new experience and creates new meaning. Conceptual metaphors may activate or enforce the blending, while the mental spaces, central to the construction

---

[1] The examples are taken from Lakoff/Johnson (8).

of meaning, are subject to constant change triggered by the mapping process (Fauconnier/Turner 102-106). Let us consider a Tolkien-related blend example: the statement "Bilbo is a traveller" can be meaningfully exploited only on the basis of a blending of components of two distinct mental spaces (cf. Fig. 1).

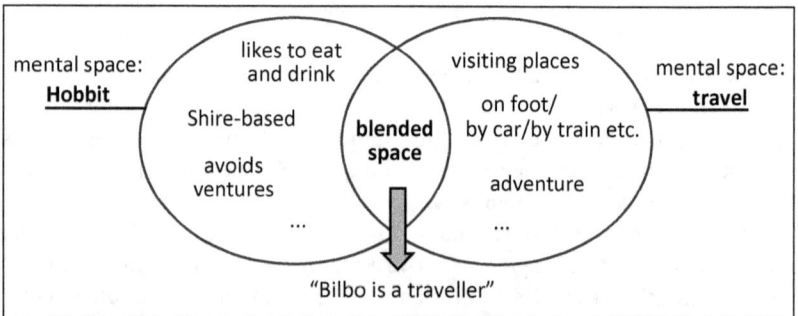

Fig. 1: The blend as an abstract mental model: example

While the fictional character Bilbo is originally constructed to be firmly rooted in the Shire (cf. H), he may, via blending, 'become' a passionate wayfarer in a given context and act according to our culturally influenced, 21st-century conceptualisations of TRAVEL.

In the present study we are concerned with gameplay and identity construction during a game via the blending of spaces activated by means of the conceptual metaphors underlying the game design. The identity blend will be outlined as a new, individually meaning-constitutive mental space supplied with information from the contributing domains. Consequentially, narration in a game develops on the basis of the characters acting and interacting in the blend. From a cognitive psychology perspective on the matter, we agree with Lindley: "Playing the game is… performing the gameplay gestalt" (9). In actual fact, however, the blend cannot be predicted purely on the basis of the input spaces,[2] as it remains the result of a creative process with various possible effects.

3.

As a deep-seated facet of human cultures, games are multi-purpose systems encompassing (educational) training, research (cf. Klabbers 55) and, most definitely, entertainment. Games are groups of narrative media, i.e. the narrative structure influences game and game time structure. The player manipulates the "narrative architecture" (Jenkins 118) by performing moves for the characters

---

2 Fauconnier/Turner comment that "[b]lending is neither deterministic nor compositional" (254), i.e. there is always an individual way of constructing the blend.

embedded therein. In other words, the player is supposed to implement individual actions which contribute to larger game plot events (cf. Lindley 12). Common game characteristics comprise a rule-based challenge or contest with a variable and evaluable outcome which can be actively influenced by the players, and their emotional attachment respectively (cf. Juul 34). Thus, there is a 'contract' at the core of playing a game. The context of action provided and represented by the game design meets the players' consent that, on this basis, their effort is worthwhile. We want to take these general assumptions into our analysis of board game examples adapted from a book original.

Here, we advocate using the term 'adaptation' in a broad sense. In this vein, adaptations are derivations from a source of various kinds within or across media, subject only to target medium conventions and to a generally assumed transposability of narrative structures. This typically makes adaptations stand-alone products which are substantially less constrained than translations are, for instance (cf. Bastin). Further, they deserve specific and measured treatment.

Let us now turn to the actual board game adaptations. As outlined above, we will focus on metaphors as vital tools to conceptualising the framework underlying both gameplay design and experience, particularly with regard to game character identity, which is assumed to be created in an abstract blend space. Due to inconsistent terminology in game studies so far, it is our goal to apply linguistic terminology to game analysis.

4.1
Der Herr der Ringe

In what follows, the structural resources and the game plot features of this KOSMOS publication (Knizia et al., *Herr*) will be delineated very briefly. Subsequently, essential underlying metaphors and concepts will be elucidated.

The players move game pieces representing the main Hobbit characters (e.g. Frodo, Merry), who feature individual skills, on a 'journey board'. In every turn, i.e. during the intended behavioural routine within the game, events can be induced on the basis of cards and casting a particular die. If negative outcomes are at hand for the Hobbit party, which are ideally supposed to cooperate and to protect the ring-bearer among them, the characters move towards Sauron, the antagonist non-player character (NPC), who himself may proceed towards the party. In sum, an encounter is fatal and will end the game. The actual action, however, takes place on four 'adventure boards' (e.g. 'Moria', 'Shelob's Lair'[3]) which are played one after the other.

---

3   For consistent understanding, German terms have been re-translated into English in line with LotR and H.

Game time is multilayered. The Hobbits usually follow the 'main quest' paths on the adventure boards;[4] their journey progress means diegetic (in-game) time progress. Yet, the game also contains optional 'subquest' paths where parallel fellowship actions are represented, e.g. the siege of Minas Tirith when playing the Mordor board. By this means, narrative threads from the book source are taken up in a filtered form. The narrative element is strengthened by small, causally connected cut-scenes, as it were. In chronological order, these highlight selected small-scale story events, e.g. 'Balin's tomb' and 'Fly, you fools!' on the Moria board. As such, the adapted narration is a significant part of the gameplay experience. Depending on the characters' success, it is they who develop the narration, thus blurring original author, game designer, and players.[5]

Metaphors and concepts
We observe on the journey board that life is conceptualised as a journey from bright (fields) to dark (fields), with brightness visualising 'the good' and darkness representing 'evil'. These dichotomies prevail as basic principles, while the shades-of-bright vs. shades-of-dark colorisation clearly contributes to the aesthetic appeal of the game design. The party members' shared life episode 'realises' as a sequence of adventures; their success conceptualises global redemption. The representatives of good, which in fact is a moral and thus highly relative category, require being active, while evil is designed to be passively confined to reaction. The good characters oppose Sauron in a timeless conflict. Sauron, who like the Hobbits is metaphorically rendered by a playing piece, is omnipresent danger and impending death personified, as it were. The 'being' of the game characters results in their being represented as objects. These objects serve as both the material and narrative anchors (cf. Fauconnier/Turner 195; Hutchins 1562, Dancygier 42) for the taking-up and the development of the gameplay.

Likewise, events, actions and narration are objects. Examples of this are, among several others, game cards enabling the party to move forward, 'shields' that can be collected and used for protection,[6] a playing piece indicating the narrative focus, a feet symbol showing a travelling action and sun coins conceptualising the individual power to withstand evil. The latter example shows different layers of metaphors at work: while the sun is power, it is an object realised via another object, namely the playing coin, which is needed during gameplay.

---

4   The 'Helm's Deep' board is an exception here.
5   With regard to gameplay, positive results are harder to attain than dire consequences. The challenge is high—more often than not, the final board, or the final boss fight respectively, is hard for less experienced players to reach. In this case, the distance travelled to Mount Doom up to that point represents their final score.
6   Interestingly, Gandalf cards can be 'bought' to call him to protective action. In a deus-ex-machina manner, this NPC interferes with the course of the narration similar to jokers in card games.

While metaphors such as LIFE is JOURNEY and EVIL is DARK are in conventional use beyond *The Lord of the Rings* and the game adaptation, others are more particular and subject to game design. Above all, they enable the player to create, on the basis of their real-world experiences and the game resources, a blended space where the game characters gain a life. Ideally, they do so within a narrative framework into which the player can immerse. Indeed, gameplay shows itself to be only the player's mindwork—including the overarching, intra-cultural metaphorical given that life, or an episode thereof, can be rendered via a game.[7]

Before we present the underlying metaphors in a more structured way (cf. 5.), let us consider a Hobbit board game adaptation.

4.2

Der Hobbit

In this game (Knizia et al., *Hobbit*), like *Der Herr der Ringe* a KOSMOS publication, the players are supposed to move a Bilbo playing piece on a board that depicts a single journey route from Hobbiton to the Lonely Mountain. In this respect, journey length corresponds to in-game time. Bilbo, virtually an NPC with streamlined traits and skills, is aided by a party of anonymous dwarves embodied by the players themselves and specified by individual skill bars. The game structure to be followed is moves and events on the basis of dice and game cards along which the narration develops rather randomly.[8] Items can be collected and skills can be raised while the aim is to reach Dale before the antagonist NPC Smaug does so. Only after completing 'adventure fields' along the journey, which results in gaining reward in the form of colourful plastic 'gems', can the players tackle and, ultimately, defeat Smaug. The player with the most gems wins, which adds an overall competitive notion to the common goal of the game.

Metaphors and concepts

Bilbo and Smaug represent the archetypes of opposite normative morality in the game. The good-vs.-evil principle is thoroughly at work while life is conceptualised as a (unidirectional) journey characterised by adventure and the omnipresent conflict between the opposing norms. Smaug represents evil and

---

7   The LIFE is GAME metaphor is apparent, for instance, in everyday expressions such as 'in life, you have to play the hand you are dealt' or 'all life is a quiz—and we are mere candidates'.
8   Some cards contain quotes from H, which may be read out to intensify the narrative of the game. While such intensification can be assumed to have been well-intentioned by the game designers, the quotes remain fragmentary and are not necessarily in line with the chronology of the book original. For informed players, this can result in perceiving the narration as artificially implemented, leaving the impression of randomness.

death. If the dragon is overcome, global redemption is at hand. Dark is danger and threat, which shows for instance in the deliberately gloomy depictions of an Orc and a Warg, both in league with Smaug and thus opponents of the party. Due to the resources of the game, beings and events are objects (e.g. playing pieces and cards).

So far, we can detect parallels between the two games in terms of their metaphorical foundation.

There are additional, more game-particular conceptualisations. For instance, wealth is a desirable, if not the ultimate, goal. This wealth in the form of gem-shaped objects is implemented as guarded by the dragon, which reappraises the Nibelungen saga motif contained in H.[9] The ring is indeed conceived of as a burden, since the ring-bearer—remarkably, one of the dwarves and thus deviating from the book source—suffers a character trait decrease. The trait 'wisdom', for instance, is metaphorically visualised by a fox, which is not the only peculiar choice in terms of an inconsistent implementation of the players' prevalent cultural experience.[10] Further, the rules stipulate that food (coins) serve as admission fee to take part in the adventures during the journey.

We now want to proceed to a summary of the metaphors and, building on this, to a model that integrates our findings into a larger framework for game adaptation analysis.

5.

The following main metaphor groups can be identified: life **(a)**, good/evil **(b)**, and other **(c)**. The compilation below includes examples of subtypes, as particular conceptual constituents are highlighted (e.g. the unidirectionality of the journey) or hidden (e.g. a life's journey starts at birth) according to the game design.[11] The metaphors, functionally intertwined as they are, enter the blended space as assets which can be drawn upon for effective gameplay.

---

9   "[Bilbo] stole from the shadow of the doorway, across the floor to the nearest edge of the mounds of treasure. Above him the sleeping dragon lay, a dire menace" (H 216); compare LSG (110).
10 From a German-based perspective, foxes are associated rather with cunningness, while the owl may be used more effectively when it comes to metaphorical conceptualisation of 'wisdom' which is clearly positively laden. These conceptualisations of abstract entities as animals are rooted in folk mythology, i.e. culturally modelled.
11 The list is meant to provide a selection of relevant examples, not an exhaustive compilation of (minor) conceptualisations that underlie the gameplay. On highlighting and hiding in metaphor, cf. 2.

Conceptual metaphors	Examples of subtypes
(a) LIFE is JOURNEY	LIFE is JOURNEY INTO DARK FULL OF OBSTACLES
	LIFE is UNIDIRECTIONAL MOVEMENT TOWARDS AN END POINT
	HONOURABLE LIFE is JOURNEY
LIFE is ADVENTURE	LIFE is QUEST
LIFE is CONFLICT	LIFE is TIMELESS CONFLICT BETWEEN OPPOSITE MORAL NORMS
	LIFE is THREAT
LIFE is OBJECT/ANIMAL	LIVING BEING is OBJECT
	CHARACTER TRAIT is OBJECT/ANIMAL
LIFE is GAME	LIFE EPISODE is BOARD GAME
(b) GOOD is PARTY	GOOD is INTERACTION OF PARTY TOWARDS A (COMMON) GOAL
GOOD is BRIGHT/EVIL is DARK	SAURON is DARK (DRAWING NEARER)
EVIL is DANGER	EVIL is OMNIPRESENT THREAT
	SAURON/SMAUG is THREAT/DEATH
(c) EVENT/ACTION is OBJECT	EVENT/ACTION is GAME CARD
	PROTECTION is SHIELD,
	SHIELD is PLAYING COIN
	NARRATION PROGRESS is OBJECT
	GAME PROGRESS is NUMBER
WEALTH is GOAL	MATERIAL WEALTH is DESIRABLE GOAL
DRAGON is GUARDIAN	SMAUG is GUARDIAN OF TREASURE FOR LIFE
FOOD is CURRENCY	BREAD (COIN) is ADVENTURE ADMISSION FEE
RING is BURDEN	RING is CHARACTER TRAIT IMPAIRMENT

Both game designer[12] and players are decisive in creating the game-related blended space. The designer provides the game context including rules and structural-aesthetic resources, while the players, who are supposed to engage with the game representation and to perform within this framework, bring their individual socio-cultural background and world experience, i.e. game-external factors, to the game. Among these factors are expectation and affective disposition, motivation to play, and knowledge and social skills of a various kind.

Clearly, for the game adaptations under consideration, it matters whether or not the players are (either more or less) acquainted with the book originals, translations thereof, the film adaptations, etc. If so, a selective projection of the respective memory will influence the individual approach to the game. The playing pieces provided, such as Bilbo in *Der Hobbit*, are the material anchors that enable a visual link between the designer's and the player's spheres. The playing piece is the fictional *non-person*, which emblematically incorporates particular game-inherent (narrative) factors, while the real-life player repre-

---

[12] We use 'designer' here to denote all those responsible for authoring the game, including illustrators.

sents the *person* component in the character construction model we are putting forward (cf. Fig. 2).

Fiction and reality meet in an abstract blend. Only there can the game characters receive, maintain and, if required, change their identity. On this basis, gameplay can evolve and exclamations like "Oh no, Sauron is approaching! Heal me!" are character utterances that make perfect contextualised sense.

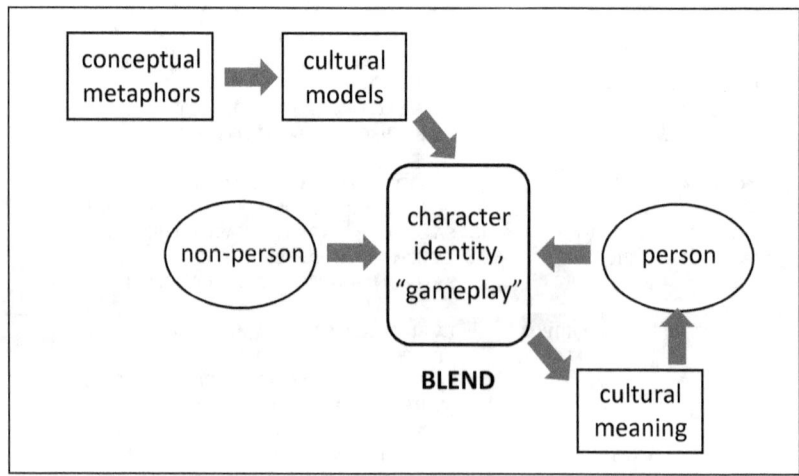

Fig. 2: The integrative model for character construction in board games

The blend as a shared generic structure thus is the site of game plot and game time/space which are narratively filtered[13] and confined by rules. It is this ludic space (cf. Lindley [2]), a locus of agreement and negotiation, which is the source of actual gameplay. As gameplay 'occurs', it will likely result in cultural meaning which, in turn, influences the players' re-playing the game. Examples of this are an evaluative report of the gameplay experience in online social networks and, not least, this academic approach to the matter.[14] The more rigid or intact the shared blend is, the more identity can ensue and the more immersion of the player into the game world can happen.

If the blend is inconsistent or, more figuratively put, porous, the opposite happens, with detrimental effects on motivation. Blend inconsistency and, ultimately, failure, may be due to a variety of reasons, among which an unappealing

---

13 We refer to a necessary limitation, or narrowing, of narrative complexity in adaptations of novels in particular (such as LotR and H). Narration is a main 'software' feature in board games, yet its implementation underlies medium specificity. It thus usually undergoes selection processes in order to comply with the game 'hardware'.
14 Here, the term cultural meaning is meant to include all game-specific effects that are imported in extra-game domains (or group contexts).

design, an ambiguous rule set, illogical challenges, inconclusive narration and culturally heterogeneous or distracted players are the most prominent ones.

Thus, a game that is 'balanced'[15] and positively effective is characterised by a high degree of blend integrity (which is assumed to be the goal of the game designer in spite of commercial pressure).

The model we propose is completed by including conceptual metaphors as a constitutive mainstay of the blend. Metaphors as exemplified above trigger and are part of shared cultural knowledge organised in cultural models (cf. 2.) which, as abstract pre-shaped canvases, help to structure the ludic space along with the more concrete, blend-stabilising *non-person* and *person* determinants.

6.

Based on a questionnaire, we have collected assessments of individual gameplay experiences. Non-representative as the data are, they show a notable tendency which complies with the model above. Parts of the results will be presented in the following. At the outset, we identified *narration* and *(character) identity* as quantifiable key factors of gameplay in board games adapted from a book original.

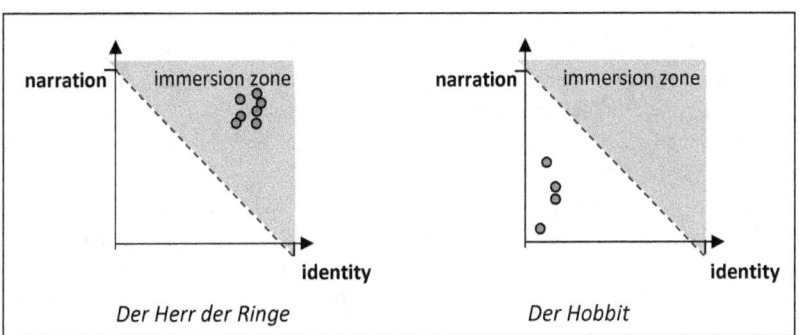

Fig. 3: Evaluation of game player data[16]

The answers show that there is no trade-off between narration and identity, but both factors contribute positively to the players' immersion and, in terms of the model, to the integrity of the blend. We suggest a so-called immersion

---

15 On balance and emotional adaptivity in games, cf. Andrade et al.; Tijs et al.
16 All players were native German adults with an academic background; most were acquainted with the LotR and H originals as well as with the Peter Jackson film adaptations. We are greatly indebted to Julia Dinn, Jennifer Fest, Stephan Helling, Frauke Intemann, Aljoscha Merk, Paula Niemietz, Antje Schumacher, Tatiana Serbina, Julia Vaeßen and Peter Wenzel, who shared in gameplay experiences and/or provided invaluable feedback and support.

zone above the hypotenuse of the *narration* and *identity* zero axes. If a game tends to score there for a group of players who at the same time enjoyed the (cooperative) group activity as such, we can assume that the blend has been sufficiently stable, and immersion can happen and last.

This, again, has a multiplier effect on (re-)play motivation and the evaluation of the game as 'worthwhile' and 'high-quality'. In this regard, the data show a gap between both board game adaptations. Though attempts at coherent design can be observed across the board, as it were, gameplay that can be called successful developed only in *Der Herr der Ringe* experiences, and not with *Der Hobbit* to any significant extent.[17]

Interestingly enough, the sales figures of the games under concern correspond to our findings. While *Der Herr der Ringe* has been a top-seller in view of its complexity, *Der Hobbit* has lagged far behind the expectations of the publisher.[18] Bluntly put, blend integrity appears to pay off as a qualitative sine qua non in board game design. In this context, it has been our task so far to suggest the validity of the presented model and evaluation toolset as applicable to assess literature-based board game adaptations in general.

7.

Gameplay is living in the blend, and conceptualisation via metaphors (in shared intra-cultural use) is a prerequisite to accessing it. The possibility of running, i.e. 'elaborating' a blend (cf. Fauconnier/Turner 44) is the motor for the entire game activity. The degree of its integrity correlates with immersion and motivation.

After all, a blend question par excellence remains: what would Tolkien say? We know that he, as a storyteller-linguist, had a clear view of the intricacies and fallacies of translation (cf. MC; LotR A) and claimed the final authority over translations of his work; cf. L 188 (in Smith 1992). Yet what about adaptations, in particular those which involve a medium transfer? Moving away from the authority of the original, we retain the position that such adaptations are artistic pieces in their own right, characterised by a considerable amount of freedom to derive the original in terms of content and form (cf. 3). The original author's or

---

17 In this respect, the recent board game *Der Hobbit – Das Spiel zum Film* (Schmidt et al.) is an in-between case. This game is not included in more detail here as it is an adaptation of the first film adaptation of the novel, thus representing yet another layer of blend complexity.

18 *Der Herr der Ringe* (Knizia et al., *Herr*): more than 300,000 units sold (2000-2007); *Der Hobbit* (Knizia et al., *Hobbit*): 7,500 units sold (2009-2013). The data were kindly supplied by Bärbel Schmidts, Franckh-Kosmos Verlag (personal communication, 16/05/2013).

any other emotional stance towards adaptations is inappropriate when it comes to serious and expedient considerations of the matter.[19]

With respect to blends, it is notable that Tolkien himself had an idea of these dynamic abstract, mind-borne spaces which are construed by both author and recipient:

> [The] story-maker... makes a *Secondary World* which your mind can enter. You... believe it, while you are, as it were, inside. The moment of disbelief arises, the spell is broken; the magic, or rather art, has failed.
> (MC 132, emphasis ours)

The ideal is what he calls *Secondary Belief* (cf. ibid.), namely the successful mind state of the story-recipient on the basis of the effort of the story-maker, which is, in principle, in line with current research (cf. e.g. Fauconnier/Turner) and the game analysis approach presented here. We have stated that such a successful blend, made up of designer, player, and culturally effective metaphor, is at the core of gameplay.

The board games discussed here accompanied the respective film releases, which renders them elements of a larger commercial trend realised via adaptations characterised by individual economic and aesthetic constraints. While a development towards 'merchandisation' is open to criticism, we can state that Tolkien's work has come a long way through series of translations and adaptations which, irrespective of qualitative assessment, degree of intervention, and economic success, were created for more or less particularised audiences in subsequent generations. This tradition—in the truest sense of the word—is most likely to continue, and even grow, in the near future. The "brand Tolkien" will be zeitgeistily exploited with no saturation of demand in sight.[20] With *Hobbit* films in our cinemas until 2015 and the *Silmarillion* yet to be adapted, however, we can look forward to opportunities for the whole breadth of adaptation media, not only board games.

---

19 Authors who claim that a particular adaptation is not "faithful to the spirit of the original text" (e.g. Høgset 168) miss the point. Notions such as "faithfulness", "spirit" or "truth" in this context foster the ill-view of the myth-like, absolute original which is meant to be interpreted in one way, however elusive it may be. In this respect, Gambier warns against a "'fetishization' of the original text" (in Bastin 6).
20 This has, so far, resulted in occasional peculiarities. One example out of many are recent LEGO LotR adaptations; cf. LEGO Group. Further strands of game adaptations not discussed here are, for instance, card games, (online) computer games and pen-and-paper roleplaying—these deserve detailed treatment of their own.

Bibliography:

Andrade, Gustavo et al. "Dynamic Game Balancing: an Evaluation of User Satisfaction." In John E. Laird et al. (eds.): *Proceedings of the Second Artificial Intelligence and Interactive Digital Entertainment Conference*. Menlo Park: AAAI Press, 2006, 3-8

Bastin, Georges L. "Adaptation." In Mona Baker et al. (eds.): *Routledge Encyclopedia of Translation Studies*. 2nd ed. London et al.: Routledge, 2011, 3-6

Dancygier, Barbara. *The Language of Stories: a Cognitive Approach*. Cambridge et al.: Cambridge University Press, 2012

Fauconnier, Gilles. *Mappings in Thought and Language*. Cambridge et al.: Cambridge University Press, 1997

--- and Mark Turner. *The Way We Think: Conceptual Blending and the Mind's Hidden Complexities*. New York: Basic Books, 2003

Høgset, Øystein. "The Adaptation of 'The Lord of the Rings': a Critical Comment." In Thomas Honegger (ed.): *Translating Tolkien: Text and Film* (Cormarë 6). 2nd ed. Zurich/Jena: Walking Tree, 159-175

Hutchins, Edwin. "Material Anchors for Conceptual Blends." *Journal of Pragmatics* 37, 2005, 1555-1577

Jenkins, Henry. "Game Design as Narrative Architecture." In Noah Wardrip-Fruin et al. (eds.): *First Person: New Media as Story, Performance, and Game*. Cambridge et al.: MIT Pr., 2004, 118-130

Juul, Jesper. "The Game, the Player, the World: Looking for a Heart of Gameness." In Marinka Copier et al. (eds.): *Level Up: Digital Games Research Conference, 4-6 November 2003*. Utrecht: Utrecht University Press, 2003, 30-45

Klabbers, Jan H. G. "The Gaming Landscape: a Taxonomy for Classifying Games and Simulations." In Marinka Copier et al. (eds.): *Level Up: Digital Games Research Conference, 4-6 November 2003*. Utrecht: Utrecht University Press, 2003, 54-68

Knizia, Reiner et al. *Der Herr der Ringe*. [Stuttgart]: KOSMOS, 2000, Board Game

---. *Der Hobbit*. Stuttgart: KOSMOS, 2010, Board Game

Lakoff, George and Mark Johnson. *Metaphors We Live by*. Chicago et al.: University of Chicago Press, Repr. 2011

LEGO Group. *The Lord of the Rings*. 2013. http://thelordoftherings.lego.com/de-de/default.aspx (03/06/13)

Lindley, Craig A. "The Semiotics of Time Structure in Ludic Space as a Foundation for Analysis and Design." *Game Studies* 5(1), 2005, [1-17] http://www.gamestudies.org/0501/lindley/ (17/03/2013)

Schmidt, Andreas et al. *Der Hobbit: Das Spiel zum Film*. Stuttgart: KOSMOS, 2012, Board Game

Smith, Arden R. "Transitions in Translations: Tolkien on Translation." *Vinyar Tengwar* 21, 1992, 21-24

Stockwell, Peter. *Cognitive Poetics: An Introduction*. London et al.: Routledge, 2002

Tijs, Tim et al. "Creating an Emotionally Adaptive Game." In Scott M. Stevens et al. (eds.): *Entertainment Computing – ICEC 2008: 7th International Conference Pittsburgh, PA, USA, September 2008. Proceedings* (LNCS 5309). Berlin et al.: Springer, 2008, 122-133

Tolkien, John R.R. "On Fairy-Stories." In Christopher Tolkien (ed.): *The Monsters and the Critics and Other Essays*. London et al.: Allen & Unwin, 1983, 109-162

---. *The Hobbit: or There and Back Again*. New York: Ballantine Books, rev. ed. 1982

---. *The Legend of Sigurd and Gudrún*. Christopher Tolkien (ed.). London: HarperCollins, 2009

---. *The Lord of the Rings*. London: HarperCollins, 1995

---. *The Silmarillion*. London: HarperCollins, new ed. 1992

Kein Kinderspiel: Brettspiele als Adaptionen des *Herrn der Ringe*

Christian Weichmann (Braunschweig)

Einleitung

Brettspiele kommen uns nicht unbedingt als erste in den Sinn, wenn wir an Adaptionen eines Romans denken. Das hat verschiedene Gründe: Brettspiele werden häufig nicht als eigenständige Werke wahrgenommen. Zum anderen ist eine Buchadaption als Brettspiel meist in erster Linie kommerzieller Natur, was oft zu einer eher oberflächlichen Umsetzung führt. Hinzu kommt, dass gerade bei *Der Herr der Ringe*-Brettspielen oft keine direkte Adaption des Buches vorliegt, sondern eine Adaption einer Adaption des Buches, also etwa ein »Spiel zum Film« (zum Buch). Aber gerade weil Gesellschaftsspiele so selten als eigenständige Adaptionen wahrgenommen werden, ist die Frage interessant, was denn speziell diese Adaptionen von anderen (wie etwa Dramatisierungen oder Werken der Bildenden Kunst) unterscheidet.

In diesem Artikel werden sowohl die Motivationen einer Brettspieladaption als auch die spezifischen Schwierigkeiten einer solchen untersucht. Weiterhin werden einige Informationen gegeben zur historischen Entwicklung und zum Phänomen der indirekten Adaption.

Was ist ein Brettspiel?

Zunächst muss geklärt werden, womit sich dieser Beitrag überhaupt beschäftigt. Von Brettspielen haben zwar die meisten von uns eine intuitive Vorstellung. Aber wenn wir eine Definition versuchen, zeigen sich Schwierigkeiten bei der Abgrenzung gegenüber ähnlichen Dingen, wie anderen Spielen und auch spielartigen Lehrmitteln oder Nicht-Spielen.

Dass schon allein die Definition von »Spiel« nicht einfach ist, zeigte Henning Poehl, der als Fazit seines Artikels zu folgender Spieldefinition kommt:

> Ein Spiel ist eine **interaktive** *freiwillige* Tätigkeit, die im »Hier und Jetzt« stattfindet, deren Ausführung oder Ausgang aber keine reale Bedeutung/Konsequenz für das »Hier und Jetzt« hat.
> Die Bedeutungslosigkeit des Ausgangs für das »Hier und Jetzt« schließt nicht aus, dass die durch das Spiel gewonnenen Erfahrungen reale Bedeutungen und Konsequenzen in der Zukunft haben können.

Die Interaktion kann dabei mit einem realen oder einem nicht realen Mitspieler, der nur in den Vorstellungen oder virtuell im Computer existent ist, stattfinden. (Poehl 37)

Diese Definition ist natürlich für unsere Zwecke viel zu weitgehend. Denn hier soll es allein um eine spezielle Art von Spiel gehen: das Brettspiel. Wenn wir aber die Poehl'sche Definition zugrunde legen, brauchen wir die Brettspiele nur noch gegen andere Spiele abzugrenzen. Das offensichtlich kennzeichnende Kriterium für *Brett*-Spiele ist ein Spielbrett. Dieses hat dabei mehr Bedeutung als einfach nur eine Fläche, um Figuren abzustellen, und es ist ein notwendiger fester Bestandteil des Spiels. Daher werden in diesem Artikel zusätzlich zur allgemeinen Spieldefinition von Poehl noch folgende Kriterien zur Definition eines Brettspiels herangezogen:
Das Spiel hat ein festes Regelsystem. Das Spiel hat eine eigene Spielfläche, die ein notwendiger, regelrelevanter Bestandteil ist.

Das zweite Kriterium bedeutet: Das Spiel lässt sich ohne das Brett nicht spielen. Und das Brett enthält für die Regeln wichtige Informationen und Beziehungen (Nachbarschaften, Wege usw.).

Warum adaptiert man Bücher als Brettspiele?

Natürlich gibt es hier verschiedene Gründe, die zum Teil auch allgemein für Adaptionen gelten:

Aus einer Vorliebe für Brettspiele und den *Herrn der Ringe* ergibt sich die Annahme, dass ein Brettspiel zum *Herrn der Ringe* noch besser ist als beides zusammen. Dieser Grund gilt besonders für inoffizielle Fan-Adaptionen, wie *Anno Domini – 3. Zeitalter* oder *Die Jagd nach Gollum*, das *Scotland Yard*-Regeln verwendet.

Brettspiele eignen sich als hochwertiges Merchandise, um aus oder mit einer Lizenz zum Thema *Der Herr der Ringe* Geld zu machen. Wobei dieser Grund gerade bei den Filmen relevant wird, da diese stärker übergreifend vermarktet werden.

Brettspiele brauchen neben einer (Regel-)Mechanik auch ein Thema, um die Käufer anzusprechen. Es gibt sehr wenige Brettspiele, die so abstrakt sind, dass kein Thema erkennbar ist oder zumindest das Thema nur noch sehr schwach ist. Und diese Spiele sind typischerweise traditionelle Spiele wie *Dame* oder *Halma*. Selbst *Schach* hat schon ein deutlich erkennbares Kriegsthema. Neue Spiele hingegen müssen, um aufzufallen, zumindest ein Designthema haben, das häufig dann auch als allgemeines Spielthema aufgebaut wird. Dafür eignet sich der *Herr der Ringe* aufgrund seiner Bekanntheit sehr gut.

Die beiden letzten Punkte überlappen sich in gewisser Weise. Wobei bekannte Spiele, die mit einem *Herr der Ringe*-Thema neu herausgebracht wurden, definitiv zum Merchandise gerechnet werden müssen. Bei neuen Spielen fallen eindeutig die als »Spiel zum Film« herausgebrachten in diese Kategorie. Bei anderen lässt sich oft der dritte Grund als stärker annehmen.

Wie lässt sich ein Buch in ein Brettspiel adaptieren? Generelle Ansätze

Bei der Adaption von Büchern als Brettspiel ist es klar, dass eine sehr starke Anpassung zwischen den sehr verschiedenen Medien vorgenommen werden muss. Allerdings zeigen sich bei Betrachtung der Spiele, die zum *Herrn der Ringe* entstanden sind, unterschiedliche Ansätze in Bezug auf die Herangehensweise beim Adaptieren.

Natürlich gibt es Spiele, die in einem gewissen Sinne dem Geschehen des Buches folgen, wie Reiner Knizias *Der Herr der Ringe* (Knizia, *Herr*). Diese entsprechen also Dramatisierungen. Trotzdem unterscheiden sie sich von diesen insofern, als dass der Spielcharakter eine Herausforderung für den Spieler und damit einen offenen Ausgang der Handlung erfordert[1]. Je nach Können und Glück der Spieler ist ein Sieg Saurons nicht nur möglich, sondern auch wahrscheinlich.

Andere Spiele konzentrieren sich auf einen Teilaspekt des Buches, wie zum Beispiel die Kriegshandlungen während des Ringkriegs[2]. Auch hier gilt, dass das Ende offen ist und dass häufig der Verlauf des Spiels mit dem im Buch vorgegebenen Verlauf nur wenig übereinstimmt. Denn hier macht im Gegensatz zu den nachvollziehenden Spielen die Spielmechanik keine Vorgaben, die eine bestimmte Reihenfolge der Ereignisse fordert: Es steht einem Sauronspieler also durchaus der Versuch offen, über den Norden das Auenland anzugreifen und Gondor in Ruhe zu lassen.

Ein dritter Typ Spiele abstrahiert noch weiter von der Vorlage. Es handelt sich um Spiele, die zwar Elemente aus dem Buch nutzen, aber nicht oder nur sehr grob versuchen, die Handlung wiederzugeben. Das kann bedeuten, dass zwar vielleicht der Weg von Frodo und Sam zum Schicksalsberg nachvollzogen wird, der Spiel-Hauptaspekt aber woanders liegt, wie im *Meisterquiz* (Petersen), bei dem der Weg mehr eine Fortschrittsleiste darstellt. Oder es kann bedeuten,

---

1 Dies ist kein Teil der Definition von Spiel/Brettspiel und auch nicht wirklich definitorisch. Aber ein häufiges Kriterium für die Beurteilung von Spielen ist der sogenannte »Wiederspielwert«, also wie stark die Motivation ist, das Spiel mehr als einmal zu spielen. Spiele ohne offenen Ausgang haben es da natürlich schwerer.
2 Z.B. *War of the Ring* (Barasch)

dass Elemente aus dem Buch übernommen werden, wie die Karte und einzelne Personen, diese aber in eine Handlung eingebaut werden, die nicht direkt mit dem Buch zu tun hat, wie bei *Abenteuer in Mittelerde* (Konieczka).

Ein noch ganz anderes Vorgehen findet sich bei *Der Herr der Ringe*-Lizenzausgaben von bekannten Spielen, die zwar auch Elemente aus dem Buch übernehmen und für andere Zwecke nutzen, die aber durch die Vorgaben des Ausgangsspiels noch weiter vom Buch entfernt sind. Die Spielhandlung von *Monopoly* könnte kaum weiter vom *Herrn der Ringe* entfernt sein[3]. Und auch wenn *Trivial Pursuit – The Lord of the Rings Movie Trilogy Collectors Edition* (Trivial Pursuit) und *Der Herr der Ringe – Das Meisterquiz* (Petersen) sich insofern ähneln, als dass sie Quizspiele mit dem Thema *Der Herr der Ringe* sind, hat ersteres doch durch die Übernahme der Regeln der Standard-Ausgabe inklusive der Spielbrettform (ohne dass deren Ring-Form thematisiert wird) nur optisch und im Inhalt der Fragen einen Bezug zu den Jackson-Filmen, während letzteres klar zum dritten Typ gehört, da es den Weg von Frodo und Sam nutzt. Außerdem unterscheiden sie sich dadurch, dass *Trivial Pursuit* eine indirekte, *Das Meisterquiz* aber eine direkte Adaption ist.

In vielen Fällen gibt es allerdings auch für diesen letzten Typ neben einer hauptsächlich optischen Anpassung des Spiels auch noch eine *Herr der Ringe*-bezogene Regelvariante, die neben den Standard-Regeln angegeben wird und typischerweise den Ring einbezieht. Beim *Lord of the Rings Stratego* gibt es sogar zwei Regelvarianten: Die eine erlaubt bestimmten Figuren besondere Züge, die andere vernichtet einen großen Teil der Figuren der »bösen Seite«, sobald Frodo das Schicksalsberg-Feld erreicht und somit den Ring vernichtet.

Wie lässt sich ein Buch als Brettspiel adaptieren? Details

Nachdem wir vier verschiedene generelle Ansätze zur Adaption unterschieden haben, wollen wir betrachten, welche Elemente eines Buches sich für eine Adaption im Brettspiel eignen und welche Elemente des Brettspiels dafür adaptiert werden. Denn im eigentlichen Sinne kann man ein *Herr der Ringe*-Brettspiel als doppelte Adaption ansehen:

---

3   Obwohl Immobiliengeschäfte im LotR mit dem Verkauf von Bag-End an die Sackville-Baggins (LotR 65, 67-68) und Frodos Kauf des Hauses in Crickhollow (LotR 65-66) eine eher kleine Rolle spielen. Tatsächlich ist Beutelsend eines der erwerbbaren Grundstücke im *Monopoly*. Aber der Verkauf des Schicksalsbergs oder Barad-dûrs oder ein Festungsbau in Beutelsend sind im Roman-Kontext eher unwahrscheinlich. Crickhollow kommt im *Monopoly* nicht vor, stattdessen gibt es die Bockenburger Fähre, was (neben dem Design) klar zeigt, dass es sich hier um eine Adaption der Jackson-Filme und nicht um eine direkte Roman-Adaption handelt.

1. Adaption des *Herrn der Ringe* im Medium Brettspiel.
2. Adaption eines abstrakten[4] Brettspiels zum Thema *Der Herr der Ringe*.

Entsprechend lässt sich auch die Adaption von den beiden Seiten her betrachten.

Ein Buch enthält eine Reihe von Elementen, die bei einer Adaption berücksichtigt werden können. Dies ist natürlich nicht spezifisch für die Adaption als Brettspiel, sondern kann entsprechend auch für die Umsetzung in andere Medien als Grundlage dienen.

→ Handelnde Personen, ob Protagonisten, Nebenfiguren oder nur Gruppenmitglieder (etwa namenlose Orks), sind ein wichtiger Punkt, der bei der Umsetzung berücksichtigt werden muss. Natürlich je nach Ansatz unterschiedlich stark, aber keine der *Herr der Ringe*-Adaptionen verzichtet völlig auf Personen aus dem Roman. Diese sind also augenscheinlich eine essentielle Quelle.

→ Orte/Landschaften sowie insgesamt die Landkarte sind ebenfalls wichtige Quellen. Selbst bei Spielen, die wenig mit der Geographie Mittelerdes zu tun haben, wird die Landkarte als Design-Element gern verwendet. Aber häufig ist die Geographie in einem gewissen Abstraktionsgrad auch wesentliches Element des Spiels. Das reicht von einer Aufreihung von Orten, die ein Teil der Roman-Charaktere besucht hat, wie beim *Meisterquiz* (Petersen) oder der willkürlichen Auswahl wesentlicher Orte aus dem Film wie bei *Monopoly* (*Monopoly*) bis zur kompletten spielrelevanten Übernahme der Karte von Mittelerde wie bei *Risiko* (*Risiko*).

→ Sprachen, Begriffe und die Terminologie sind gerade bei Tolkien, der ja seine Bücher als „*fundamentally linguistic* in inspiration" (L 219) einstuft, bedeutsam, um ein Spiel als *Herr der Ringe*-Spiel zu kennzeichnen. Wobei häufig die Verwendung der Begriffe Ork, Nazgûl, Hobbit, Elb, Waldläufer, Númenorer, Rohirrim, Haradrim[5] ausreicht.

---

4   Die Abstraktion kann dabei sehr unterschiedlich sein. Bei originären *Herr der Ringe*-Brettspielen, wie denen von Knizia (Knizia, *Herr*, Knizia, *Entscheidung*, Knizia, *Kinderspiel*) handelt es sich tatsächlich um abstrakte Regelmechanismen, die an das *Herr der Ringe*-Thema angepasst werden, wobei allerdings das Thema schon bei der Entwicklung der Mechanismen eine Rolle spielt. Bei *Risiko* hingegen handelt es sich um ein sehr konkretes Spiel, das an das Thema angepasst wird, was in diesem Falle allerdings recht einfach erscheint, da man nur die Landkarte übertragen muss. Die tatsächliche Schwierigkeit ist aber, die Landkarte so einzuteilen, dass ein einerseits faires andererseits den Vorgaben entsprechendes System entsteht (Mittelerde im dritten Zeitalter hat ja viele leere Flecken, was bei *Risiko* nicht geht).

5   Dies auch fehlerhaft mit dem Gruppenplural für Einzelpersonen

→ Ziele und Motivationen der handelnden Personen werden oft entsprechend als Spielziele für die Spieler übernommen.

→ Am schwierigsten gestaltet sich oftmals der Versuch, das Thema oder den Gesamteindruck des Buches zu übernehmen. Denn hier wäre eine genaue Untersuchung nötig, was überhaupt das Thema des Buches ist, und der Gesamteindruck ist in erster Linie subjektiv.

Umgekehrt gibt es bei Brettspielen vier Bereiche mit einzelnen Elementen, die adaptiert werden können, um ein vorgegebenes Thema (wie *Der Herr der Ringe*) widerzuspiegeln:

→ Die Regeln bzw. der eigentliche Spielmechanismus
  • Das Spielziel: was von den Spielern erreicht werden soll.
  • Die Zugfolge: die Abfolge der einzelnen Aktionen der Spieler.
  • Die Interaktions- und die Bewegungsregeln: wie sich die Figuren der Spieler auf dem Feld bewegen können und wie die Spieler miteinander interagieren. Diese Regeltypen sind oft nicht voneinander zu trennen, da Bewegungen zu Interaktionen führen können (»rausschmeißen«) oder Interaktionen Bewegungen beeinflussen (»Blockaden« o.ä.).
  • Der Spielplan als der regelrelevante Anteil des Spielbretts: Nachbarschaftsbeziehungen und Wege auf dem Feld.
  • Die Anpassung der Nomenklatur: vorhandene Spielelemente mit Namen und Begriffen aus dem Thema belegen.[6]

→ Das Design
Brettspiele liegen in einer materiellen dreidimensionalen Darstellung vor. Diese wird bei einer Adaption natürlich auch durch das adaptierte Werk in einem gewissen Maße vorgegeben. Die zu gestaltenden Elemente sind:
  • Die Verpackung, also typischerweise der quaderförmige Karton, der alles zum Spiel gehörende Material enthält. Das Design kann von der einfachen Bedruckung bis zu einer speziellen Form des Kartons reichen.
  • Das Spielregel-Heft/-Blatt, das mit passenden Illustrationen versehen werden kann und ggf. auch Schriftarten und Satz passend zum adaptierten Werk wählt.

---

6 Was nicht so einfach ist. So werden im Monopoly (*Monopoly*) die »Bahnhöfe« durch »Pferde« ersetzt. Aber die Spielanleitung verwendet nach der ersten Einführung doch den Begriff »Bahnhof«.

- Das Spielbrett, das die physische Realisierung des Spielplans darstellt, und teilweise weitere Elemente, wie Zählleisten oder Ablagebereiche enthält, ist meist eben nicht abstrakt gestaltet, sondern mithilfe von Bildern oder Symbolen aus dem gewählten Thema.
- Figuren und Material müssen eine bestimmte Form haben. Natürlich sind Spielfiguren oft einfache Kegel [mit Köpfen], aber bei Themen-Spielen werden sie meist auch dementsprechend gestaltet.

→ Das Material
Ein weiterer Aspekt der materiellen Darstellung ist, dass die Spielelemente als tatsächlich gefertigte Objekte vorliegen. In welcher Art, kann auch durch die Adaption bestimmt werden. Mögliche Unterschiede sind hier:
- Spielelemente können geometrisch oder figürlich dargestellt sein, also z.B. als Spielplättchen oder als richtige Figuren.
- Die Wiedererkennbarkeit des Materials hat zwei Aspekte, die u.U. gegeneinander abgewogen werden müssen:
Die spieltechnische Wiedererkennbarkeit: ob beim Betrachten des Spielmaterials, ohne die Spielregel zu lesen, für alle Teile des Materials zu erkennen ist, welche Funktion sie jeweils im Spiel haben werden (also Spielfigur oder Zählmarker oder etwas ganz anderes, beziehungsweise bei der Umsetzung von bekannten Spielen wie etwa *Schach*, welcher Figur aus dem Originalspiel die Schachfigur entspricht).
Die thematische Wiedererkennbarkeit: ob ohne weitere Erläuterung klar ist, welchem Element aus dem adaptierten Thema das Material entspricht (z.B. welche Figur aus dem Buch durch die Spielfigur repräsentiert wird).

→ Der »Fluff«
Dieser Begriff beschreibt alles, was zur Einstimmung in das Spiel beziehungsweise das Thema hilfreich ist.

Abbildung 1 zeigt die Anzahl der Spiele, die als *Herr der Ringe*-Adaptionen zwischen 1977 und 2011 erschienen sind. Dabei sind nur vollständige Spiele und keine Erweiterungen zu existierenden Spielen erfasst. Allerdings ist die Grafik speziell in den Jahren 2001 bis 2004 unvollständig, da es zu den Peter-Jackson-Filmen national begrenzte Lizenzen gab, so dass in anderen Ländern andere »Spiele zum Film« herauskamen. Auch sind nicht alle zum Thema erschienenen Schachspiele eingeflossen, da es hier ganz unterschiedliche Qualitäten und Verfügbarkeiten gab. Die wesentlichen Trends lassen sich aber trotzdem erkennen.

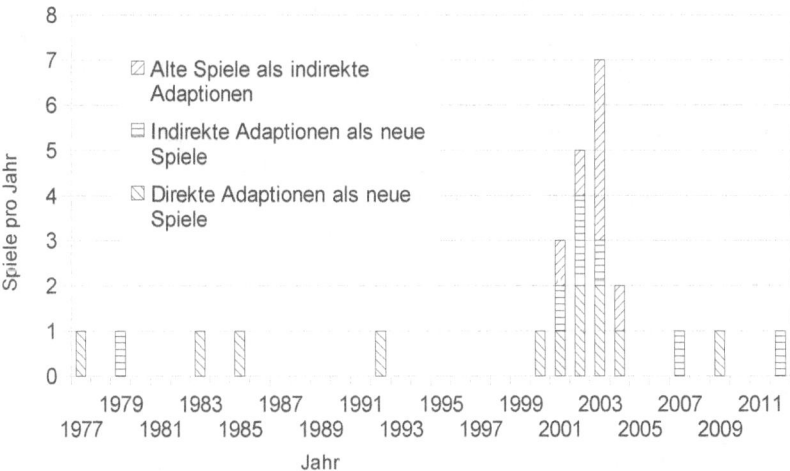

Abbildung 1

Die Abbildung unterscheidet auch, ob es sich um direkte Buch-Adaptionen handelt oder indirekte Adaptionen, das heißt Adaptionen von Adaptionen des Buchs (Filmen und Musicals). Außerdem wird aufgeschlüsselt, ob es sich um neu entwickelte Spiele handelt oder um bestehende Spiele, die thematisch an den *Herrn der Ringe* angepasst wurden.

Es ist natürlich nicht verwunderlich, dass rund um die Peter-Jackson-Filme (2001-2003) besonders viele Brettspiele mit *Herr der Ringe*-Thematik erschienen sind, und zwar hauptsächlich indirekte Adaptionen (also Adaptionen der Filme). Insbesondere die Anpassungen bestehender Spiele an ein *Herr der Ringe*-Thema konzentrieren sich auf diesen Zeitraum. Das ist natürlich dem Merchandising geschuldet.

Aber auch sonst zeigt sich eine zunehmende Erscheinungsdichte der Spiele im Laufe der Zeit[7]. Neben der durch die Filme erhöhten Aufmerksamkeit für das Thema gibt es dafür auch andere Gründe:

---

7   Ein Phänomen, das noch verstärkt wird, wenn man die Spiele zum *Hobbit* dazu nimmt. Andere Tolkien-Bücher wurden meines Wissens bisher nicht in kommerzielle Brettspiele umgesetzt.

Der wichtigste dürfte eine allgemeine Entwicklung im Spielbereich sein. Seit den 1980er Jahren haben sich (Brett-)spiele deutlich »emanzipiert«: Bis dahin gab es im wesentlichen Kinder- und Familienspiele. Deren Spielmechaniken zeichneten sich eher selten durch besondere Originalität aus. Lediglich einige wenige etablierte Klassiker, wie etwa *Schach* oder auch *Monopoly*, galten als taktisch ausgereift bzw. anspruchsvoll genug, um auch in reinen Erwachsenenrunden gespielt zu werden. Ab den 1980er Jahren entstanden aber immer mehr Spiele, die (auch aus ökonomischen Gründen) gezielt ein erwachsenes Publikum ansprechen sollten. Diese mussten neue anspruchsvollere Spielmechanismen bieten und brauchten dabei noch dezidierter als Kinderspiele ein Thema, das die Zielgruppe anspricht. Daher nahm der Rückgriff auf bekannte und beliebte Themen, zu denen auch *Der Herr der Ringe* gehört, zu.

Eigenständige Herr der Ringe Spiele

Konfrontativ und Kooperativ

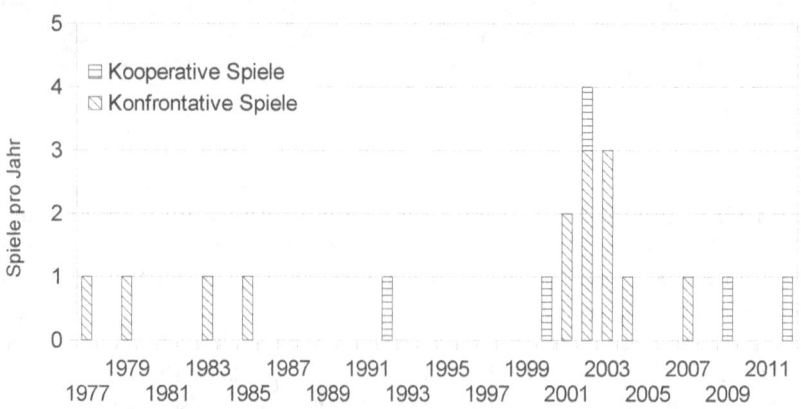

Abbildung 2

Interessant ist es, die neuen Spiele[8] zum Thema *Der Herr der Ringe* nach traditionell-konfrontativ (gegeneinander spielen, um zu gewinnen) und kooperativ (miteinander gegen das Spiel spielen und nur durch Zusammenarbeit gewinnen) zu unterscheiden. Abbildung 2 zeigt diese Verteilung[9]. Hier zeigt

---

8 Bei Anpassungen bestehender Spiele ist dies schon durch das ursprüngliche Spiel (üblicherweise als konfrontativ) vorgegeben.
9 Dabei habe ich *The Lord of the Rings Nazgûl* (Kinsella/Tyson), das als semi-kooperativ vermarktet wird, aber auch eine vollkooperative Regelvariante enthält, als kooperativ eingeordnet.

sich, dass doch die meisten Spiele nach wie vor konfrontativ sind[10]. Allerdings gibt es in den späteren Jahren immer wieder kooperative Spiele, die damit argumentieren, dass die Kooperation der Gefährten ein wesentliches Element des Buches ist[11]. Tatsächlich setzten diejenigen konfrontativen Spiele ohne eine große Abstraktion (also nicht aus der oben genannten dritten Gruppe) darauf, dass bei zwei Spielern einer die Seite Saurons und einer die seiner Gegner spielt und dass bei mehreren Spielern zwischen den durch die einzelnen Spieler dargestellten Gruppen eine gewisse Rivalität zumindest auch in der Vorlage (Buch oder Film) erkennbar ist.

Welche Elemente des *Herrn der Ringe* werden wie in Brettspiele umgesetzt?

Um von den oben angeführten allgemeinen Elementen einer Adaption Buch -> Brettspiel speziell zum *Herrn der Ringe* zu kommen, betrachten wir, wie *Herr der Ringe*-Spiele bestimmte Romanelemente umsetzen[12]:

→ Personen des Buchs:
 • Die (Gefährten-)Hobbits werden oft als Spielfiguren dargestellt (Barasch; Petersen; Knizia, *Herr*; Knizia, *Entscheidung*; Knizia, *Kinderspiel*; *Trivial*; *Stratego*; *Monopoly*; *Schach*; Hartwig; Hering, *Gefährten*; Neugebauer, *Suche*; Hering, *Türme*; Wallace, *Rückkehr*; *Adventure*; Charlton/Neidlinger; Califf/Walker; Maggi/Di Meglio/ Nepitello; Siggins), können aber auch Ereignisse *(Zwei Türme)* oder Ressourcen sein (Kobbert) oder selten auch Hindernisse (Kinsella/Tyson).
 • Die anderen Gefährten werden ebenfalls als Spielfiguren umgesetzt (Barasch; *Monopoly*; *Schach*; *Stratego*; Knizia, *Entscheidung*; Hartwig; *Adventure*; Charlton/Neidlinger; Maggi/Di Meglio/ Nepitello; *Trivial*; Neugebauer, *Duell*; *Risiko*), Ereignisse *(Zwei Türme)* oder Ressourcen (Petersen; Knizia, *Herr*; Knizia, *Kinderspiel*; Hering, *Gefährten*; Hering, *Türme*; Neugebauer, *Suche*; Wallace, *Rückkehr*; Kobbert; *Trivial*; Califf/Walker; Siggins; Konieczka/Petersen/Uren). Sie können aber auch Hindernisse sein (Kinsella/Tyson).

---

10 Selbst beim kooperativen *Der Herr der Ringe* (Knizia, *Herr*) gibt es mit der »Sauron«-Erweiterung eine teilkonfrontative Variante.
11 Auch ein Trend, der durch die *Hobbit*-Spiele eher noch gestützt würde.
12 Für eine vollständige Auflistung aller umgesetzten Elemente reicht der Platz hier nicht.

- Gollum kann eine Spielfigur (Barasch; *Schach*; Hartwig; Wallace, *Rückkehr*; *Stratego*; Charlton/Neidlinger), ein Ereignis (Maggi/Di Meglio/Nepitello; Petersen), eine Ressource (Maggi/Di Meglio/ Nepitello; Kobbert; Califf/Walker; Neugebauer, *Suche*; Konieczka/ Petersen/Uren) sein[13].
- Orks können Spielfiguren (Barasch; *Schach*; Knizia, *Entscheidung*; *Risiko*; *Stratego*; Maggi/Di Meglio/Nepitello; Charlton/Neidlinger), Ereignisse (*Zwei Türme*; Petersen; Knizia, *Herr)*, Hindernisse (Knizia, *Kinderspiel*; Hering, *Gefährten*; Hering, *Türme*; Wallace, *Rückkehr*; *Adventure*; Neugebauer, *Suche*; Siggins) oder in Spielen, in denen ein Spieler auch Saurons Seite spielt, eine Ressource (Maggi/Di Meglio/Nepitello; Kobbert; Kinsella/Tyson, Califf/ Walker, Konieczka/Petersen/Uren) sein.
- Nazgûl treten als Hindernisse (Hering, *Gefährten*; Knizia, *Kinderspiel*; *Adventure*; *Trivial*; Neugebauer, *Suche*; Siggins), Ereignisse (Knizia, *Herr*), Spielfiguren (*Stratego*; Barasch; Knizia, *Entscheidung*; Maggi/Di Meglio/Nepitello; *Risiko*; Hartwig; *Adventure*; Kinsella/Tyson; Charlton/Neidlinger; *Trivial*; Califf/ Walker; Konieczka/Petersen/Uren) oder eben auch für »Sauron«-Spieler als Ressourcen (Knizia, *Entscheidung*; Kobbert; Maggi/Di Meglio/Nepitello; Konieczka/Petersen/Uren) auf.
- Sauron tritt als Spielfigur (Knizia, *Herr*), Hindernis (Siggins), Ereignis (Knizia, *Herr)* oder Ressource (Kobbert) auf. Er kann aber auch ins Spielziel einfließen (Konieczka/Petersen/Uren), wie in »Nazgûl« (Kinsella/Tyson), wo Saurons Wohlwollen errungen werden soll.
- Gondorianer und Rohirrim treten als Spielfiguren (Barasch; *Stratego*; Maggi/Di Meglio/Nepitello; *Risiko*), Ereignisse und Ressourcen (Hering, *Türme*; Knizia, *Herr*; Wallace, *Rückkehr*; Kobbert; Califf/Walker; Siggins, Konieczka/Petersen/Uren) oder für »Sauron«-Spieler als Hindernisse (Kinsella/Tyson) auf.
- Haradrim werden als Spielfiguren (Barasch; *Stratego*; Maggi/ Di Meglio/Nepitello), Ereignisse oder je nach Seite als Ressource (Kinsella/Tyson; Califf/Walker; Konieczka/Petersen/Uren) oder Hindernis (Charlton/Neidlinger) umgesetzt.

→ Orte, Landschaften und Karten:
- Die Landkarte findet sich oft auf dem Spielbrett *(*Barasch; *Zwei Türme*; Checkers; *Risiko*; Maggi/Di Meglio/Nepitello; Petersen; *Monopoly*; *Schach*; Kobbert; Charlton/Neidlinger; Hering, *Türme*;

---

13 Manchmal auch Ressource und Hindernis gleichzeitig, wie bei Knizia, *Herr.*

Trivial; Kinsella/Tyson; Califf/Walker; Konieczka/Petersen/Uren) und auf der Verpackung (*Zwei Türme*; *Checkers*; *Monopoly*; Hering, *Gefährten*; Hering, *Türme*; *Risiko*; Wallace, *Rückkehr*; Kobbert; *Trivial*) wieder. Aber sie beeinflusst auch den Spielplan (Barasch; Maggi/Di Meglio/Nepitello; *Adventure*; Knizia, *Entscheidung*; Hering, *Türme*; *Risiko*; Charlton/Neidlinger; Califf/Walker; Konieczka/Petersen/Uren*)*.

- Das Auenland ist typischerweise der Ausgangspunkt des Spiels (Neugebauer, *Suche*; Knizia, *Entscheidung*; Petersen; Hering, *Gefährten*; Knizia, *Herr*; Knizia, *Kinderspiel*; *Adventure*; Siggins).
- Die Nebelberge oder Moria sind ein Hindernis (*Adventure*; Knizia, *Herr*; Charlton/Neidlinger; Knizia, *Entscheidung*) oder ein Ereignis (Petersen; Siggins; Neugebauer, *Duell*).
- Mordor beziehungsweise der Schicksalsberg kann ein Ereignis (Petersen; Siggins) oder Hindernis (Knizia, *Herr*; *Adventure*) sein. Oft ist es auch das tatsächliche räumliche Spielziel (Neugebauer, *Suche*; Knizia, *Entscheidung*; Maggi/Di Meglio/Nepitello; Petersen; Knizia, *Herr*; Knizia, *Kinderspiel*; *Adventure*; Charlton/Neidlinger; Califf/Walker; Siggins).

→ Gegenstände
- Der Eine Ring kann sowohl Ressource (Barasch; Neugebauer, *Suche*; Petersen[14]; Hering, *Gefährten*; Knizia, *Herr*; *Adventure*; Charlton/Neidlinger; *Trivial*; Califf/Walker) als auch Hindernis sein. Außerdem ist natürlich oft das Spielziel die Vernichtung des Rings (Barasch; *Stratego*[15]; Neugebauer, *Suche*; Maggi/Di Meglio/ Nepitello; Knizia, *Herr*; Knizia, *Kinderspiel*; Wallace, *Rückkehr*; *Adventure*[16], Charlton/Neidlinger; *Trivial*[17]; Califf/Walker; Siggins). Manchmal tritt er auch als eine Art Fortschrittsmarker auf (*Monopoly*; *Risiko*). Häufig ist er Designelement der Verpackung (Neugebauer, *Suche*; Maggi/Di Meglio/Nepitello; Knizia, *Herr*; *Monopoly*; *Risiko*; Hering, *Gefährten*; Wallace, *Rückkehr*) bzw. von Verpackung und Spielbrett (*Zwei Türme*; *Schach*; Kobbert; *Trivial*; Siggins). Ein Sonderfall ist das Damespiel, wo der Eine Ring als Spielfiguren umgesetzt ist (*Checkers*).

---

14 Hier allerdings sehr symbolisch, so dass es sehr viele davon gibt.
15 Zumindest in einer Regelvariante
16 Seltsam hier: Es gibt mehrere Ringe, von denen einer vernichtet werden muss.
17 Zumindest in der optionalen Regel

→ Sprachen, Begriffe, Terminologie
- Völkernamen gehen in die Spielanleitung (Barasch; Maggi/Di Meglio/Nepitello; *Risiko*; Hering, *Gefährten*; Charlton/Neidlinger; Califf/Walker; Konieczka/Petersen/Uren) ein und bilden oft einen nicht unwesentlichen Teil des »Fluff« (Knizia, *Herr*; Califf/Walker; Konieczka/Petersen/Uren)
- Personennamen finden sich in der Spielanleitung (Barasch; Knizia, *Entscheidung*; Maggi/Di Meglio/Nepitello; *Monopoly*; Knizia, *Herr*; Hartwig; Wallace, *Rückkehr*; Charlton/Neidlinger; Califf/Walker; Kinsella/Tyson; Siggins; Konieczka/Petersen/Uren), bei Ereignissen (Neugebauer, *Suche*; Knizia, *Herr*) oder auf den Spielfiguren (Barasch; Knizia, *Entscheidung*; Knizia, *Kinderspiel*; Wallace, *Rückkehr*; *Adventure*). Auch sie gehen in den »Fluff« ein (Knizia, *Herr*; Califf/Walker; Siggins; Konieczka/Petersen/Uren).

→ Zitate
- Zitate aus dem Buch werden in der Spielanleitung zur Charakterisierung von Ereignissen (Petersen) oder Spielfiguren (*Checkers*; Charlton/Neidlinger) und im »Fluff« verwendet (Konieczka/Petersen/Uren).

→ Ereignisse
- Die Über-/Unterquerung der Nebelberge sind Hindernisse (Hering *Gefährten*, Knizia *Entscheidung*, Knizia *Herr*, *Adventure*) oder Ereignisse (Kinsella/Tyson, Petersen, Siggins, Neugebauer *Duell*).
- Die Zerstörung Isengarts kann speziell bei »Die zwei Türme«-Spielen zum Spielziel gehören (Hering *Türme*).

→ Ziele und Motivationen
- Das Ereignis der Ringvernichtung lässt sich natürlich auch als Motivation oder Ziel auffassen. Dafür gilt bei der Umsetzung dann das oben Gesagte.
- Die Freundschaft als Motivation geht in Interaktionsregeln (Neugebauer, *Suche*; Knizia, *Herr*; Hering, *Gefährten*; Siggins) und Ressourcen (Knizia, *Herr*) ein, ebenso bei der Entscheidung, ob das Spiel kooperativ (Hering, *Türme*; Knizia, *Herr*; Siggins) oder konfrontativ ist.
- Ähnliches gilt für die Feindschaft zwischen Personen oder Völkern (Barasch; *Zwei Türme*; *Stratego*; Knizia, *Entscheidung*; Maggi/Di Meglio/Nepitello; *Schach*; Knizia *Herr*; Knizia, *Kinderspiel*; Hartwig; Hering, *Gefährten*; Hering, *Türme*; Wallace, *Rückkehr*; *Adventure*; Charlton/Neidlinger; Califf/Walker; Siggins;

Konieczka/Petersen/Uren), die aber eher als Hindernisse denn als Ressourcen umgesetzt wird.

→ Das »Thema«
 • Der Konflikt Gut vs. Böse geht in die Interaktions- und Bewegungsregeln (Barasch; Neugebauer, *Suche*; Knizia, *Entscheidung*; Knizia, *Herr*; Hartwig; Hering, *Gefährten*; Wallace, *Rückkehr*; Charlton/Neidlinger; Califf/Walker; Siggins; Konieczka/Petersen/Uren), die Spielfiguren (Konieczka/Petersen/Uren) und natürlich in das Spielziel (Knizia *Herr*, Charlton/Neidlinger) ein.
 Die Versuchung (speziell durch den Ring) tritt in den Interaktionsregeln (Maggi/Di Meglio/Nepitello; Knizia, *Herr*; Konieczka/Petersen/Uren), als Hindernis (Siggins) und für »Sauron«-Spieler auch als Spielziel auf (Maggi/Di Meglio/Nepitello; Konieczka/Petersen/Uren).
 • Krieg ist für einige Spiele natürlich das Hauptthema, was sich vor allem in den Interaktionsregeln und im Spielziel widerspiegelt (Barasch; *Stratego*; Knizia, *Entscheidung*; *Risiko*; Maggi/Di Meglio/Nepitello; Kinsella/Tyson; *Schach*; Wallace, *Rückkehr*; Hering, *Türme*; Charlton/Neidlinger; Califf/Walker).

Probleme der Adaption bei Brettspielen

Ein Problem, das die Brettspiele mit den meisten anderen Adaptionen teilen, ist der unterschiedliche Spielraum der Vorlage und der Adaption. Soll ein Brettspiel gut spielbar sein, kann es nicht so viele Elemente enthalten wie das Buch. Es muss also immer eine Wahl getroffen werden. Gerade Spiele mit starker kommerzieller Ausrichtung (wie Anpassungen bestehender Spiele) neigen dazu, einfach die bekanntesten Elemente (Figuren wie Frodo, Gandalf, Legolas und Gollum, Orte wie Beutelsend, Moria und Mordor) zu übernehmen.

Ein spezielles Problem bei Brettspielen als Adaptionen (vor allem wenn bestehende Spiele angepasst werden) sind die Aspekte der Wiedererkennbarkeit: Einerseits müssen die übernommenen Elemente (z.B. Personen) aus dem Buch wiedererkennbar sein, andererseits soll man auch gleich ihre Rolle im Spiel erkennen können und nicht irregeleitet werden.

Ein gutes Beispiel für dieses Problem ist das *Schach*: Hier werden der weiße König durch Gandalf, die weiße Königin durch Galadriel dargestellt. Durch die Größe der Figuren (und ihr Geschlecht[18]) ist die Wiedererkennung in Bezug

---

18 Das wirkt auf der schwarzen Seite allerdings nicht, da hier die Königin durch Lurtz dargestellt wird.

auf ihre Rolle im Spiel gegeben. Aber wenn man diese Rollen aus der Sicht des Buches betrachtet, kann man sie nicht wirklich wiedererkennen: Dem König, der im Schachspiel ja die zu beschützende Figur ist, deren Verlust zur Niederlage führt, würde im Buch am ehesten Frodo entsprechen. Und der Königin, die über das ganze Spielfeld wandert und die mächtigste Figur ist, würde im Buch am ehesten Gandalf entsprechen[19].

Direkte gegen indirekte Adaptionen

Viele Spiele zum Thema »Der Herr der Ringe« basieren nicht auf dem Roman *Der Herr der Ringe* (HdR), sondern selbst auf einer Adaption des Buchs. Der Grund hierfür liegt in den Lizenzen für diese Umsetzungen, die zusätzliche Einnahmen über Zweitverwertungen erlauben. Speziell die Umsetzungen bekannter Spiele (*Monopoly*; *Trivial*; *Stratego*; *Checkers*; *Schach*; Kobbert) sind ausschließlich Adaptionen der Filme Peter Jacksons (Jackson, *Gefährten*; Jackson, *Türme*; Jackson, *Rückkehr*), denn diese haben eine wesentlich stärkere kommerzielle Aufmerksamkeit als die Bücher.

Ein Vorteil von indirekten Adaptionen ist für den Umsetzenden, dass das Design zumindest bei Dramatisierungen wie den Filmen (Jackson, *Gefährten*; Jackson, *Türme*; Jackson, *Rückkehr*; Rankin/Bass) oder dem Musical (Wallace, *Lord*) schon vorgegeben ist. Es muss also nicht neu entwickelt werden. Auch ist das Design dann entsprechend allgemein bekannt und gewährleistet einen großen Wiedererkennungseffekt. Wenn das Design allerdings wie beim Musical nicht unbedingt den Mainstream-Vorstellungen von Lesern entspricht, ist dieser Vorteil natürlich nur für Musicalbesucher wirksam.

Unterschiede zwischen direkten und indirekten Adaptionen ergeben sich im Wesentlichen aus den Unterschieden zwischen dem Buch selbst und der Adaption, von der sich das Spiel ableitet. So finden sich in indirekten Adaptionen bestimmte Elemente nicht, die beim adaptierten Werk weggelassen wurden. Da aber Adaptieren immer auch Weglassen bedeutet[20], kann es natürlich vorkommen, dass in zwei verschiedenen direkten Adaptionen (also einem Spiel und einem Film) auf dieselben Elemente verzichtet wird. Ein deutlicherer inhaltlicher Hinweis auf eine indirekte Adaption ist die Übernahme von Elementen, die in der als Vorlage dienenden Adaption hinzugefügt wurden, Beispiel: Lurtz (Jackson, *Gefährten*).

---

19 Eine geschlagene (getötete) Königin kann ja sogar wiederkommen (wenn ein Bauer umgewandelt wird), was noch mehr zu Gandalf passt.
20 Speziell Brettspiele bieten oft einen viel kleineren Raum der Möglichkeiten, als er für eine vollständige Umsetzung eines so umfangreichen Buches wie *Der Herr der Ringe* notwendig wäre.

Fazit

Spiele, die das Thema *Der Herr der Ringe* auf unterschiedlichste Art und Weise umsetzen, gibt es in großer Zahl. Dabei werden immer nur ausgewählte Elemente aus der Vorlage übernommen, wobei einige fast notwendig erscheinen, während andere nur in einzelnen Spielen vorkommen. Eines der Hauptprobleme ist dabei, die Erwartungen, die die Kenntnis der Vorlage beim Spieler in Bezug auf ein adaptiertes Element weckt, mit der Rolle des Elements im Spiel zu verbinden.

Außerdem sind Brettspiele oft zweifache Adaptionen, bei denen neben dem Buch auch ein bereits vorhandenes Spiel adaptiert wird. Dies führt oft zu besonderen Problemen bei der Zuweisung von Elementen des Buches zu Elementen des Spiels bei gleichzeitiger Wiedererkennbarkeit.

Im Gegensatz zu anderen Formen der Adaption geht ein sehr großer Anteil der Brettspiele nicht auf die literarische Vorlage zurück, diese Spiele sind also indirekte Adaptionen.

Schließlich steht der kommerzielle Aspekt bei der Adaption als Brettspiel sehr häufig stark im Vordergrund und die Adaptionen fallen recht oberflächlich aus.

Bibliographie

Carpenter, Humphrey (Ed.). *The Letters of J.R.R. Tolkien*. London: HarperCollins, 1995

Poehl, Henning. »Anhang: Von der Evolution der Spiele – eine kritische Auseinandersetzung mit dem Begriff ›Spiel‹ und eine neue Definition«. *Spiele Entwickeln 2007*. Hg. Marcel-André Casasola Merkle, Christwart Conrad, Friedemann Friese, Andrea Meyer, Henning Poehl, Andreas Wetter. Berlin: Pro BUSINESS, 2007, 30-37

Tolkien, J.R.R. *The Lord of the Rings*. London: HarperCollins, 2001

Diskographie

Wallace, Kevin. *The Lord of the Rings*. London: Kevin Wallace Music, 2007

Filmographie

Jackson, Peter. *Der Herr der Ringe – Die Gefährten* Special Extended DVD Edition. Hamburg: Warner Bros. Entertainement, 2002

---. *Der Herr der Ringe – Die Zwei Türme* Special Extended DVD Edition. Hamburg: Warner Bros. Entertainement, 2003

---. *Der Herr der Ringe – Die Rückkehr des Königs* Special Extended DVD Edition. Hamburg: Warner Bros. Entertainement, 2004

Ludographie

Der Herr der Ringe – Die zwei Türme. Frankfurt: Ferrero, 2002
Der Herr der Ringe Risiko. Soest: Hasbro Deutschland, 2002
J.R.R. Tolkien's *The Lord of the Rings Adventure Game.* Springfield: Milton Bradley, 1979
Lord of the Rings Collector's Chess Set. Sterling: Noble Collection, 2001
Lord of the Rings Stratego – Trilogy Edition. Pawtucket: Hasbro. 2004
Monopoly – Der Herr der Ringe Sonderedition zur Filmtrilogie. Soest: Hasbro Deutschland, 2003
The Lord of the Rings Checkers. Encinitas: USAOPOLY, 2003
Trivial Pursuit – The Lord of the Rings Movie Trilogy Collector's Edition. Pawtucket: Hasbro. 2003

Barasch, Howard und Berg, Richard. War of the Ring. New York: Simulation Publications, 1977
Califf, John und Walker, William A. *Riddle of the Ring.* Charlottesville: IRON CROWN ENTERPRISES, 1985
Charlton, Coleman und Neidlinger, Bruce. *The Fellowship of the Ring.* Charlottesville: IRON CROWN ENTERPRISES, 198
Hartwig, Jo. *Die abenteuerliche Reise der Hobbits ins Reich der Ringgeister.* Hamburg: Laurin, 1992
Hering, J.R.R. *Der Herr der Ringe – Die Gefährten – Spiel zum Film.* Stuttgart: Kosmos, 2001
---. *Der Herr der Ringe – Die zwei Türme – Spiel zum Film.* Stuttgart: Kosmos, 2002
Kinsella, Bryan und Tyson, Charlie. *The Lord of the Rings Nazgûl.* Hillside: WIZKIDS/NECA, 2012
Knizia, Reiner. *Der Herr der Ringe.* Stuttgart: Kosmos, 2000
---. *Der Herr der Ringe – Die Entscheidung.* Stuttgart: Kosmos, 2002
---. *Der Herr der Ringe – Das Kinderspiel.* Stuttgart: Kosmos, 2003
Kobbert, Max J. *The Lord of the Rings Labyrinth.* Ravensburg: Ravensburger, 2003
Konieczka, Corey und Petersen, Christian T. mit Uren, Tim. *Der Herr der Ringe – Abenteuer in Mittelerde.* Stuttgart: Kosmos, 2009
Maggi, M., Di Meglio, R. und Nepitello, F. *Der Herr der Ringe – Der Ringkrieg.* Weesp: Phalanx Games, 2004
Neugebauer, Peter. *Der Herr der Ringe – Die Suche.* Stuttgart: Kosmos, 2001
---. *Der Herr der Ringe – Das Duell.* Stuttgart: Kosmos, 2002
Petersen, Christian T. *Der Herr der Ringe – Das Meisterquiz.* Stuttgart: Kosmos, 2003
Siggins, Mike. *The Lord of the Rings Board Game.* Cambridge: Sophisticated Games, 2007
Wallace, Martin. *Der Herr der Ringe – Die Rückkehr des Königs – Spiel zum Film.* Stuttgart: Kosmos, 2003

Mittelerde als Kartenspiel: Ist das möglich?

Thorsten Werner (Hamburg)

Sammelkartenspiele in der Spielewelt

Der HdR sorgte schon in den 1970er Jahren für eine Vielzahl von Adaptionen in der Spielebranche. So ist nicht zuletzt die Entwicklung des ersten »Pen & Paper«-Rollenspiels *Dungeons & Dragons* auch auf Inspirationen aus dem HdR zurückzuführen (vgl. Gygax). In den 1990er Jahren brachte eine neue Kategorie von Spielen einen Umbruch in der Fantasy-Spielewelt: Sammelkartenspiele. Sie wurden von Richard Garfield als *Magic: The Gathering* erfunden, der ein kurzes, aber abwechslungsreiches Spiel für unterwegs entwickeln wollte. Das von ihm initiierte Spielprinzip basiert auf drei Säulen: Sammeln, Anpassen und Tauschen (vgl. *Wizards of the Coast*).

Aus einer Vielzahl Karten (je nach Spiel mehrere hundert bis tausende) wählt der Spieler nach bestimmten Regeln Karten aus und bildet daraus den eigenen Spielstapel (Deck) mit dem er (meist) gegen einen Gegner antritt. Die Karten gibt es dabei in der Regel in unterschiedlicher Seltenheit in den kommerziell erhältlichen Basis- und Erweiterungspackungen, sodass Spieler die Karten sammeln und mit anderen Spielern tauschen können. Dieses Spielprinzip wurde nicht nur im Fantasy- und SciFi-Genre angewendet, sondern auch auf bekannte Filme und Serien wie *Die Simpsons*, *Die Ritter der Kokosnuss* oder *Akte X*.

Ein wesentliches Element der Sammelkartenspiele ist die Abbildung auf jeder Karte, die typischerweise die obere Kartenhälfte abzüglich eines Rands einnimmt. Unterhalb dieses Bildes enthält die Karte einen Text, der die Spielmechanik der Karte erläutert. Der umgebende Spielkartenrahmen kann weitere Eigenschaften meist in Form besonderer Symbole anzeigen. So kann beispielsweise die Rahmenfarbe eine bestimmte Funktion repräsentieren. In der Regel werden die Texte für eine einfache, schnelle Spielweise kurz gehalten und ggf. um ein begleitendes Zitat ergänzt.

Typischerweise ist ein Spielzug eines Sammelkartenspiels in mehrere Phasen unterteilt: Es beginnt mit dem Wiederherstellen der Karten, dabei werden die Karten in horizontaler Anordnung (tapped) in die vertikale Anordnung gedreht (untap). Dann folgt das Ziehen neuer Karten und schließlich das Ausspielen, Auslegen und/oder Benutzen von Karten. Beim Benutzen ausliegender Karten werden diese gedreht (tap), um den Zustand der Karte zu markieren. Mit diesen Karten wird dann eine Form von Konflikt ausgetragen. Am Ende des Zuges werden überzählige Karten abgeworfen.

1995 erschien das Sammelkartenspiel *Middle-earth: The Wizards* (ME:TW), herausgegeben von Iron Crown Enterprises (ICE), damaliger Lizenznehmer für Spiele basierend auf HdR und H. Außerdem erhielt ICE eine Genehmigung des Tolkien Estate, die Istari Alatar und Pallando aus den UT zu verwenden (vgl. ICE, ME:TW *Rulesbook*). Neben dieser Basisausgabe erschienen bis zum Jahre 1998 sechs weitere Ausgaben des Spiels, die zusammen das *Middle-earth: Collectible Card Game* (ME:CCG oder »Mittelerde Sammelkartenspiel«) bilden. Anschließend verlor ICE die Rechte an Spielen in Mittelerde, so dass aus urheberrechtlichen Gründen keine neuen Ausgaben erscheinen konnten (vgl. Applecline).

Neben dieser Sammelkartenadaption des HdR erschienen bis zum jetzigen Zeitpunkt (April 2013, Anm. der Redakt.) zwei weitere Adaptionen: das Spiel *Der Herr der Ringe Sammelkartenspiel* (LotR TCG), das sich stark an den filmischen Adaptionen von Peter Jackson orientiert und von 2002 bis 2007 von Decipher herausgegeben wurde (vgl. Decipher), sowie das kooperative Setsammelspiel *Der Herr der Ringe – Das Kartenspiel*. Hierbei erhält man in einer Box alle Karten einer Ausgabe. Es wird seit 2011 von Fantasy Flight herausgegeben (vgl. Fantasy Flight).

Das Mittelerde-Sammelkartenspiel: Prinzipien und Ausgaben

Das grundlegende Spielprinzip von ME:CCG ist bereits an anderer Stelle ausführlich dargelegt worden, so dass hier nur ein kurzer Abriss folgt, um eingehender auf die Besonderheiten dieses Kartenspiels eingehen zu können (vgl. Buchs, Näf).

Als Spieler übernimmt man die Sicht eines Avatars. Dies ist im Basisspiel die Sicht eines der fünf Istari. Der Spieler versucht mit seinen Gruppen, bestehend aus Charakteren wie Aragorn und Beregond, Mittelerde zu bereisen, um mächtige Artefakte zu erlangen, wichtige Heere und Verbündete für sich zu gewinnen oder besondere Ereignisse auszulösen. Der eigene Avatar kann dabei später ausgespielt werden und so selbst am Geschehen teilnehmen. Während der Reise durch Mittelerde kann der Gegner Gefahren auf die Gruppen spielen. Diese Gefahren können Kreaturen sein, wie etwa eine Gruppe Orks oder Crebain, oder besondere Ereignisse wie ein Fluss oder verschiedene Versuchungskarten. »Versuchung« ist ein Konzept, das die Korruption durch Macht aufgreift und durch gegnerische Ereignisse und insbesondere das Tragen mächtiger Artefakte verstärkt wird.

Ziel des Spiels ist es, entweder den Einen Ring im Schicksalsberg zu vernichten oder mehr Siegpunkte zu erlangen als der Gegner. Über die Siegpunkte soll ermittelt werden, welcher der Istari am ehesten geeignet ist, die freien Völker anzuführen, um in die Schlacht gegen Sauron zu ziehen. Je mächtiger ein Artefakt ist und je wichtiger ein Charakter, Verbündeter, Heer oder Ereignis ist, umso mehr Siegpunkte erhält der Spieler für das Ausspielen.

Als Zufallselement werden zwei normale Würfel (2 W6) verwendet. Diese werden beim Ermitteln von Zufallswerten im Kampf, bei Versuchungswürfen und beim Beeinflussen von Heeren (sowie bei weiteren Karten) verwendet, sodass neben der Auswahl der geeignetsten Karten auch der Zufall sowohl beim Kartenziehen als auch bei verschiedenen Aktionen über Sieg oder Niederlage entscheidet.

Bedingt durch die Komplexität des ME:CCG weicht dieses vom gängigen Schema der kurzen Kartentexte ab. In der Regel enthalten Aktionskarten (kurzfristige, längerfristige und permanente Ereignisse) einen längeren Kartentext, der den kompletten unteren Bereich der Karte einnimmt. Insgesamt ist die Schriftgröße geringer als im Durchschnitt der Sammelkartenspiele, trotzdem musste bei einigen Karten die Schriftgröße zusätzlich herabgesetzt werden, damit der vollständige Text überhaupt auf eine Karte gedruckt werden konnte (vgl. ICE, *Companion*).

Ausgehend von der Basisausgabe *Middle-earth: The Wizards* wurden insgesamt sieben offizielle Kartenserien von ICE herausgegeben. Die Basisausgabe ermöglicht das Spielen eines der fünf Zauberer als Avatar und umfasst einen Großteil des aus HdR und H bekannten Teils Mittelerdes. Einige Illustrationen auf den Karten sind vorher schon für Rollenspielbücher, Buchcover oder Tolkien-Kalender verwendet worden und stammen von namhaften Fantasy- und Tolkien-Illustratoren. Als erste Erweiterung wurde *Middle-earth: The Dragons* herausgegeben. Diese widmet sich besonders Drachen: Bei diesen handelt es sich um (Namens-)Erfindungen von ICE und besonderen Schätzen, die sich an Drachenhorten finden lassen. Als zweite Erweiterung war *Middle-earth: Dark Minions* erhältlich. Diese Erweiterung bereitet mit den als Agenten getarnten Schergen schon die nächste Serie vor, wie dies durch Lutz Farning oder Grima Schlangenzunge im HdR verkörpert ist. Zusätzlich gibt es eine neue Kategorie Orte: die Unter-Tiefen. Diese befinden sich unterhalb der Erdoberfläche und sind über unterirdische Labyrinthe miteinander verbunden. Die zweite Basisausgabe und dritte Erweiterung ist *Middle-earth: The Lidless Eye*. Sie ist ohne die vorhergehenden spielbar, dabei spielt man als Avatar einen der Ringgeister. Dementsprechend enthält die Ausgabe alle nötigen Karten, um ein komplettes Spiel aus der Sicht der Schergen zu ermöglichen. Ein direktes Spiel von Helden gegen Schergen ist erst seit der fünften Ausgabe *Middle-earth: Against the Shadows* möglich. Diese Erweiterung ergänzt sowohl die Zauberer als auch die Ringgeister um die nötigen Karten, damit beide Ausrichtungen auch im Wettstreit gegeneinander stehen können. Die vorletzte Ausgabe *Middle-earth: The White Hand* ermöglicht die Kombination beider Ausrichtungen in einem Deck durch Spielen von »gefallenen Zauberern« als Avatar. Wie Saruman im HdR kämpft der Spieler nun nicht mehr für die freien Völker, sondern für sich selbst. Mit der siebten und letzten Ausgabe *Middle-earth: The Balrog* wird das

Spiel um den Balrog von Moria als Avatar ergänzt, der auf der Schergen-Seite für sich selbst kämpft (vgl. ICE).
Weitere Ausgaben waren zwar geplant, konnten jedoch durch den Verlust der Lizenz seitens ICE nicht herausgebracht werden. Einige der Ideen und Karten wurden aber von der Spieler-Gemeinschaft aufgegriffen und im Internet veröffentlicht.

Schergen, gefallene Zauberer und der Balrog von Moria

Insbesondere die Ausgaben seit *The Lidless Eye* erweitern das Spiel um Möglichkeiten, die selten in Spieladaptionen zu finden sind: das Spielen von Schergen. So finden sich in einigen Spielen sowohl Helden als auch Schergen, jedoch beschränken sich die Möglichkeiten zum Spielen der Schergenseite in der Regel auf Kampfhandlungen. Im Mittelerde-Sammelkartenspiel besteht jedoch ein in den Möglichkeiten ebenbürtiges Spiel der Schergen-Seite. Es bestehen für Schergen die gleichen Möglichkeiten wie für Helden, Siegpunkte zu erlangen. Einige Völker Mittelerdes lassen sich jedoch nicht durch die Helden-Seite spielen, wie Orks und Trolle, während andere nicht von der Schergen-Seite gespielt werden können, wie Elben und Hobbits. Dies zieht sich entsprechend durch alle Kartentypen. Es besteht somit keine Kongruenz zwischen Helden und Schergen, obwohl sich eine Vielzahl von Überschneidungen ergibt. So sind Orte und Gegenstände nahezu übereinstimmend in allen Ausrichtungen vorhanden. Dies erlaubt ein, innerhalb des Spielrahmens, freies Spielen der Schergen-Seite inklusive eines Wettstreits (über Siegpunkte) innerhalb der Schergen und zwischen Schergen- und Helden-Seite. Weiterhin lässt sich über »gefallene Zauberer« auch das Abwenden eines Zauberers von der »Guten Sache« hin zu seinem eigenen Zielen spielen, wobei der Avatar dabei durch Versuchung korrumpiert wird. Diese Option ist zwar eher theoretisch, jedoch lässt sich so der Fall Sarumans vom wichtigen Zauberer im Weißen Rat hin zu Sharkû nachspielen. Alternativ lässt sich auch gleich als »gefallener Zauberer« starten, der für seine eigene Sache kämpft und sich dafür der Ressourcen auf beiden Seiten bedienen kann. Einschränkend kann er sich jedoch nicht der mächtigeren Charaktere bedienen, da diese nur für ihre Sache (Held oder Scherge) eintreten. Diese dritte Ausrichtung als Mischung aus Helden- und Schergen-Seite ist einzigartig – ebenso wie die Möglichkeit, den Balrog von Moria als Avatar zu spielen. Dieser ist auf Orks und Trolle als Charaktere beschränkt und er selbst darf sich normalerweise nur unterirdisch bewegen, so dass sich ein eher Moria-zentriertes Szenario ergibt.

Während der Sieg über Siegpunkte mit jeder neuen Ausrichtung leichter zu erreichen war, so dass jahrelang Balrog- und »gefallene Zauberer«-Decks die Turnierszene beherrschten, ist der »absolute Sieg« durch Vernichtung bzw.

Beherrschung des Einen Rings praktisch nur Helden, also Zauberern, zugänglich. Um den Einen Ring zu erlangen, muss ein goldener Ring gespielt werden, der dann in einem zweiten Schritt geprüft werden (per Würfelergebnis) und sich dabei erst als der Eine Ring erweisen muss. Erst anschließend kann dieser im Schicksalsberg vernichtet oder nach Barad-dûr (bzw. Isengart, Moria usw.) gebracht werden. Ein Heldenspieler benötigt bei der Ringprüfung niedrigere Würfelergebnisse als ein Schergenspieler. Und Heldenspieler verfügen über bessere Unterstützungskarten als Schergen, während diese an einigen Orten zusätzlich Malus auf den Würfelwurf erhalten. Ein gefallener-Zauberer- bzw. Balrog-Spieler muss nach Erhalt des Einen Rings zusätzlich den Einen Ring beherrschen, um zu gewinnen. Dabei hat er eine 50-prozentige Chance zu sterben (und damit zu verlieren) und nur eine 25-prozentige Chance, das Spiel sofort zu gewinnen. In einem normalen Spiel ist es daher nur für einen Heldenspieler realistisch, durch Vernichtung des Rings zu gewinnen.

Vergleich mit den Romanvorlagen

Die Frage der Qualität bzw. Legitimität einer Adaption lässt sich an vielen Stellen diskutieren. Betrachten wir zunächst das Ziel des Spiels, so muss zwischen zwei verschiedenen Siegmöglichkeiten unterschieden werden: Dabei ist die Vernichtung (bzw. Beherrschung) des Rings unbestreitbar eine direkte Übertragung aus der Romanvorlage. Der Wettstreit innerhalb einer Ausrichtung über Siegpunkte als zweite Möglichkeit lässt sich durchaus rechtfertigen, wenn die Istari betrachtet werden: Gandalf hat sich durch die Gewinnung vieler Charaktere, Heere und wichtiger Gegenstände als der geeignetste Istari zum Führen der Freien Völker herausgestellt, während Radagast sich »nur« um die Natur kümmert, Saruman seine eigenen Ziele verfolgt und die beiden blauen Zauberer den Osten erkunden. Auch ein Wettstreit innerhalb der Ringgeister scheint durchaus möglich, so hat sich der Hexenkönig von Angmar als fähigster Führer in der Romanvorlage ergeben.

Der Wettstreit der verschiedenen Ausrichtungen mittels Siegpunkten ist dagegen eine deutlichere Abweichung von der Vorlage. So sagt Gandalf im *Herrn der Ringe*: »Ich sagte, der Sieg könne nicht mit Waffen errungen werden... Wird der Ring vernichtet, dann wird er stürzen; und er wird so tief stürzen, daß niemand voraussehen kann, ob er sich jemals wieder erhebt« (HdR III 173). Ein solcher Wettstreit stellt dabei am ehesten dar, wer den Sieg auf dem Schlachtfeld erringt, jedoch nicht die Vernichtung des Gegners.

Die Gesamtszenerie des Spiels erstreckt sich räumlich auf die aus dem HdR und dem H bekannten Teile Mittelerdes zuzüglich einiger Teile rund um Mordor, dabei treten viele bekannte Orte Mittelerdes in Erscheinung. Einige neue Orte wurden erfunden, um die Spielbarkeit zu erhöhen. In den meisten

Fällen handelt es sich um Orte, wie die »Hauptstadt« eines Volkes (z.b. das Lager der Ostlinge) oder Horte erfundener Drachen, die sich in der Regel nahtlos in Mittelerde einfügen. Mittelerde selbst ist in Regionen eingeteilt, die zum einen für Spielmechanismen wichtig und dafür in verschiedene Gefährlichkeitsstufen eingeteilt sind und zum anderen politische Bereiche abgrenzen (z.b. Rohan oder Ithilien). Auch wenn einzelne Orte, wie Osgiliath, unverständlicherweise fehlen und einige Regionen in ihren Grenzen bzw. ihrer Gefährlichkeitseinstufung fragwürdig sind, so ergibt sich ein stimmiges Gesamtszenario, das mit den Romanvorlagen gut übereinstimmt, auch wenn die Unter-Tiefen sich nur sehr bedingt in den Quellen finden (vgl. Fonstad & ICE, *Companion*). Ein ganz anderes Bild ergibt sich jedoch bei der Betrachtung der Zeit. Hier hat J.R.R. Tolkien insbesondere mit den Anhängen zum HdR sehr genaue Fakten geschaffen, so dass ein Zusammentreffen von Bard und Pippin bei Tolkien nicht möglich wäre. Beides sind jedoch im ME:CCG spielbare Charaktere. In *The Dragons* ist sogar Thrain enthalten, der die Großtat Bards nicht mehr erlebte. Dieser Umstand ist natürlich der Spielbarkeit und Vielfalt geschuldet, damit möglichst viele aus den beiden Romanen bekannte Charaktere im Spiel verwendet werden können (vgl. Tolkien, HdR A).

Beide Romanvorlagen beschäftigen sich sehr lange mit Reisen, sie ließen sich wohl auch als Reiseromane charakterisieren. Dieser Aspekt wird im Spiel direkt übernommen. Ebenso wie in den Romanvorlagen ist die Reise selbst von Gefahren durchdrungen: Neben natürlichen Gefahren, wie Schneestürme oder schwer überwindbare Flüsse, können die Gemeinschaften auch auf physische Gegner treffen, etwa Orks, Trolle oder Drachen, oder auf andere Weise, wie z.B. durch Versuchung, von ihrem Weg abkommen. Durch Kampf oder Versuchung können Charaktere (und Avatare) auch eliminiert werden, so dass diese dann aus dem Spiel genommen werden. Durch die Verwendung von Orten und Regionen auf einer Landkarte wird das Reisen der Gemeinschaften gut vermittelt. Die möglichen Gefahren verstärken diesen Eindruck noch.

Während Kämpfe auch in den Romanvorlagen einen hohen Stellenwert einnehmen, so wird die Lösung dieser Konflikte dort häufig auf ungewöhnlichem Wege erreicht. Offene Schlachten finden sich auch im Roman, doch im Spiel wird tendenziell häufiger auf die physische Austragung eines Konflikts zurückgegriffen. Zum einen geben die Regeln vor, dass sich unter den Gefahrenkarten mehr als ein Drittel Kreaturenkarten befinden müssen und zum anderen fehlt beim Spielen häufiger die passende Karte, um sich geschickt aus einem Konflikt manövrieren zu können. Jedoch gibt es auch Decks, die versuchen, komplett ohne physische Konfrontationen auszukommen.

Während Gegenstände und Heere sich leicht aus den Vorlagen ableiten lassen, ist die Einteilung für Verbündete deutlich schwieriger. Hierbei handelt es sich um Personen im weitesten Sinne, die jedoch nur eine weniger aktive

Rolle einnehmen und in ihren Möglichkeiten beschränkt sind. Dabei mag die Einteilung von Baumbart oder Tom Bombadil durchaus vertretbar sein, aber bei Lobelia oder Gollum ist die Grenze zu einem Charakter sehr fließend. Die größte und gleichzeitig schwammigste Gruppe ist: Ereignisse. Dabei können Ereignisse Reaktionen auf besondere Situationen sein, z.b. ein Versteck bei einem Angriff, oder aber auch besondere Ereignisse sein mit einem weitergehenden Einfluss auf das Spiel, wie die Rückkehr des Königs mit der Krönung Aragorns. Trotz dieser Bandbreite sind beides Beispiele von Ereignissen, die sich aus den Romanen ableiten lassen.

Ein sicherlich wichtiger Aspekt des Spiels ist das Konzept der Versuchung. Hier haben die Autoren den Versuch unternommen, das immerwährende Thema der Korruption im HdR in einen Spielmechanismus zu übertragen. So erhält jeder Charakter Versuchungspunkte durch das Tragen von Gegenständen, wobei besondere, mächtige Gegenstände besonders viele Versuchungspunkte geben. Zusätzlich kann er durch Gefahrenkarten weitere Versuchungspunkte erhalten und durch sie zu einem Versuchungswurf gezwungen werden. Dabei muss dann eine größere Zahl erreicht werden, als die Versuchungspunkte ergeben. Besondere Charaktere oder Ereignisse können die Versuchungswürfe modifizieren, z.b. haben alle Hobbits einen Bonus auf diese Würfe. Das Konzept ist deutlich einfacher gestrickt als Korruption und Versuchung im HdR, jedoch lassen sich über diesen Spielmechanismus diverse Handlungsstränge aus den Romanen direkt nachstellen.

Kategorisierungen bergen inhärent die Gefahr, die Vorlage nicht ordentlich abzubilden, weil eben nicht alle Facetten der Vorlage beachtet werden können. In seiner Gesamtheit bildet ME:CCG die Romanvorlage trotz all seiner Kategorisierungen gut ab und wartet mit einigen interessanten Umsetzungen der Romanvorlagen in Spielmechanismen auf, wie etwa Ringprüfung oder Versuchung.

Neben diesem qualitativen Vergleich lässt sich auch ein quantitativer Vergleich anstellen. Dazu werden die Karten in drei Kategorien eingeteilt: originalgetreu, möglich und erfunden. Wird diese Methodik auf die Karten angewandt, so lassen sich deutliche Unterschiede zwischen den einzelnen Ausgaben erkennen. Während die Basisausgabe ME:TW noch in allen Kategorien über eine hohe Originalität verfügt, zeigt sich schon in der nächsten Ausgabe eine stark abnehmende Tendenz, die sich dann zwischen 20 und 30 Prozent einpendelt. Genau andersherum nimmt der Anteil an erfundenen Karten zu, der nur bei ME:TW unterhalb zehn Prozent liegt. Innerhalb der Kartentypen selbst ist die Verteilung wiederum sehr unterschiedlich: Während die Charaktere der Basisausgaben eine etwa 90-prozentige Originaltreue aufweisen, sind es bei den Schergen keine 20 Prozent. In allen Kategorien übertrifft der Anteil an originalgetreuen Karten den der erfundenen Karten (außer bei den Schergen-Heeren). Jedoch sind die Stichproben zum Teil sehr klein (n < 15), so dass sich keine detaillierten Schlüsse ziehen lassen. Insgesamt lässt sich jedoch von einer guten quantitativen Übereinstimmung sprechen, da die starken Abweichungen vor allem im Bereich der Schergen zu finden sind, über die einfach sehr wenig veröffentlicht wurde, so dass naturgemäß der Anteil an erfundenen Karten höher sein muss.

Ein gutes Spiel für Zwischendurch?

Neben den reinen Aspekten der Werktreue muss eine gelungene Adaption auch in ihrem Genre erfolgreich sein. Somit muss das ME:CCG auch als Spiel spielbar sein. Neben der immer noch großen Fangemeinde mit jährlich mindestens zwei internationalen Veranstaltungen finden auch noch regelmäßig neue Spieler zu dem Spiel – und das obwohl seit 1999 die Unterstützung seitens der Spielverlage weggefallen ist und dadurch auch keine neuen Karten mehr gedruckt werden können. Der Reiz des Spiels liegt sicherlich auch begründet in der guten Übertragung der Welt Mittelerde in ein Kartenspiel, aber im Gegensatz zu einer Vielzahl anderer Sammelkartenspiele bietet das ME:CCG selbst mit einer nicht mehr steigenden Kartenauswahl (im Gegensatz zu *Magic: The Gathering*) immer wieder neue Möglichkeiten: Einerseits können neben der Standard-Variante (einem Turnierformat) verschiedenste Szenarien gespielt werden (z.B. Beschränkung auf Karten aus dem H), andererseits sind die Kartenfunktionen teilweise sehr komplex, so dass immer wieder neue Varianten und Wechselwirkungen ausprobiert und ausgenutzt werden können. Diese hohe Komplexität sorgt dafür, dass dieses Sammelkartenspiel (im Gegensatz zu vielen anderen) eine sehr steile Lernkurve hat und isolierte Spielgruppen die Regeln z.T. anders interpretieren als vom Verlag beabsichtigt. Auch dauern durchschnittliche Spiele etwa anderthalb Stunden und sind nicht mit den kurzen Spielrunden von *Magic: The Gathering* oder *Pokémon* vergleichbar.

Unterm Strich ist den Autoren des Spiels jedoch ein kurzweiliges, abwechslungsreiches Spiel gelungen, das erfahrene Spieler auch nach vielen Jahren zu neuen Partien reizt. Die fehlende Unterstützung durch Verlage und das Fehlen neuer Karten regt die Fangemeinde an, eigene Karten zu entwerfen und ganze eigene Ausgaben zu erstellen (vgl. Council of Elrond). Zusätzlich wurde die Möglichkeit geschaffen, mittels eines Computerprogramms ME:CCG auch über das Internet zu spielen (vgl. Ronkainen).

Zusammenfassung

Ebenso wie sich Tolkiens Werke als komplex und tiefschürfend charakterisieren lassen, handelt es sich beim ME:CCG um ein komplexes Spiel. Dabei haben die Autoren ein Spiel geschaffen, das auch fast zwanzig Jahre nach seinem Erscheinen in seiner Fangemeinde ungebrochen beliebt ist – auch wegen der Möglichkeit, nicht nur die Heldenseite auszuspielen – und darüber hinaus eine werktreue Adaption darstellt.

Bibliographie

Appelcline, Shannon. *A Brief History of Game #9, ICE, Part Two: 1993-Present*. rpg.net , 2006 (http://www.rpg.net/columns/briefhistory/briefhistory9.phtml)

Buchs, Peter. "Middle-earth: The Wizards - the Representation of Tolkien's World in the Game". *News from the Shire and Beyond - Studies on Tolkien*. Hg. Peter Buchs & Thomas Honegger. Zürich/Jena: Walking Tree, 2004, 103-160

Council of Elrond, Hg. *Council of Elrond*. http://www.councilofelrond.org, 2013

Fonstad, Karen Wynn. *Historischer Atlas von Mittelerde*. Stuttgart: Klett-Cotta, 1994

Gygax, Ernest Gary. "On the Influence of J.R.R. Tolkien on the D&D and AD&D Games". *Dragon* 95 (1985): 12-13

ICE. Hg. *Middle Earth: The Balrog. Rulesbook*. Charlottesville, Virginia: Iron Crown Enterprises, 1998

---. Hg. *Middle Earth: The Lidless Eye. Rulesbook*. Charlottesville, Virginia: Iron Crown Enterprises, 1997

---. Hg. *Middle Earth: The Wizards. Rulesbook*. Charlottesville, Virginia: Iron Crown Enterprises, 1995

---. Hg. *Middle Earth: The Wizards Companion*. Charlottesville, Virginia: Iron Crown Enterprises, 1996

---. Hg. *Middle Earth: White Hand. Rulesbook*. Charlottesville, Virginia: Iron Crown Enterprises, 1997

Media Factory, Hg. *Pokémon Trading Card Game*. Shibuya, Tokyo: Media Factory, 1996

Näf, Patrick. "Middle Earth: The Collectible Card Game - Powerplay in the World of Tolkien". *News from the Shire and Beyond - Studies on Tolkien*. Hg. Peter Buchs & Thomas Honegger. Zürich/Jena: Walking Tree, 2004, 83-102

Ronkainen, Tommi. *Generic Collectible Card Game*. gccg.sf.net, 2013

Tolkien, John Ronald Reuel. *Der Herr der Ringe*. Stuttgart: Klett-Cotta, 1995

---. *Der Herr der Ringe. Anhänge*. Stuttgart: Klett-Cotta, 1995

---. *Der kleine Hobbit*. München: DTV, 1995

Wizards of the Coast, Hg. *Magic: The Gathering*. Renton, Wahington: Wizards of the Coast, 1993

Fan Fiction as Criticism
Renée Vink (Hilversum)

Let me begin with a brief and broad definition of fan fiction as a genre: fan fiction is storytelling that uses pre-existing worlds and characters to create new fictions[1]. It can be based on a book, a play, a movie, a TV-series or even the life of a celebrity.

Tolkien fan fiction is a widespread phenomenon. At this moment, the most popular hosting site for fan fiction, FanFiction.net, contains about 55.000 stories based on Tolkien's works. Most of them were inspired by *The Lord of the Rings* (and since December 2012 by *The Hobbit*), but the site also lists more than 3.300 *Silmarillion* fanfics. Tolkien's world turns out to be the third most popular setting for stories written by fans, after *Harry Potter* and *Twilight*. Besides FanFiction.net there are other archives, including many personal ones, and the total number of Tolkien 'fanfics' may amount to perhaps 60.000.

Before I concentrate on Tolkien fan fiction only, a brief historical note is in place. The term arose in the 1960s when *Star Trek* fans started writing stories about their beloved series, but the phenomenon itself is much older. It has been argued that Vergil's *Aeneid* is essentially a fanfic of the *Iliad*; something similar has been said of medieval Arthurian romances, Shakespeare's plays and many other works of world literature whose authors built on existing tales. Even if some of these examples are discounted because their authors may have believed they were using historical material, this still leaves many other instances of people consciously working within someone else's fictional universe, especially from the 19th century onward.

People changed the endings of Jane Austen novels or wrote sequels to the works of Dickens. The world is rife with Sherlock Holmes fan fiction, a recent example being *Skrinet* (*The Shrine*, 2012) by the Norwegian Tolkien linguist Kåre Helge Fauskanger. Established authors like Jean Rhys, J.M. Coetzee and former British poet laureate Andrew Motion wrote a prequel to *Jane Eyre*, respectively a *Robinson Crusoe* novel and a sequel to *Treasure Island*. [Margaret Atwood used the *Odyssey* as a basis for her novella about Penelope], Christa Wolf wrote about Kassandra, the Trojan seer in the *Iliad*, while Christoph Ransmayr's novel *Die Letzte Welt* is built on Ovid's *Metamorphoses*. The list could go on, but let me only mention two more works: J.R.R. Tolkien's epic poems about Sigurd and Gudrún and his soon to be published *The Fall of Arthur*.

The only reason why these works are not formally labelled as fan fiction is that they are inspired by non-copyrighted texts and can be published legally.

---

1   For an alternative definition and some background information:
    http://www.themillions.com/2012/04/fifty-shades-of-fan-fiction.html (18-1-2013)

The original authors, known or unknown, have been dead for seventy years or more, meaning that their works are in the public domain. Contrary to popular belief, quality is not a criterion here. Established authors have created fan fiction: Neil Gaiman wrote a story based on C.S. Lewis' *Narnia* chronicles[2]. His writing did not suddenly deteriorate because it could not be published legally. Beginning authors have made a name by publishing stories inspired by works in the public domain, or by altering stories based on copyrighted works just enough to avoid violating the law, but this does not automatically mean they are better than others of their kind. I only have to mention *Fifty Shades of Grey* here.

The thought that people are basing stories on their works does not please all authors. Unlike J.K. Rowling and Neil Gaiman, to name a couple of authors who allow or applaud fan fiction, others reject or despise it, like George R.R. Martin and Diana Gabaldon[3]. As for Tolkien, the question inevitably arises what he would have thought of it. He did make several statements regarding the matter. In late 1951, he wrote to Milton Waldman:

> Once upon a time (my crest has long since fallen) I had a mind to make a body of more or less connected legend, ranging from the large and cosmogonic to the level of romantic fairy-story—the larger founded on the lesser in contact with the earth, the lesser drawing splendour from the vast backcloths... I would draw some of the great tales in fullness, and leave many only placed in the scheme, and sketched. The cycles should be linked to a majestic whole, and yet leave scope for other minds and hands, wielding paint and music and drama. Absurd.   (*Letters* 145)

The 'absurd' is generally taken to refer to the enterprise as a whole, not to the contribution of other minds and hands. On the contrary, not a few fan fiction authors are familiar with these words. They consider them an indication that his views on the phenomenon must have been favourable. The archive *Stories of Arda* quotes the statement on its main page, adding: "We take the cultures, races, histories, geography and languages he created and weave in our own creativity."[4] This is just one example.

However, fan writers may be deluding themselves if they truly believe Tolkien would have applauded them. Firstly, his "other minds and hands" do *not* wield story or film for that matter, but this aside. Secondly, Tolkien's response to

---

[2] http://www.dailydot.com/culture/10-famous-authors-fanfiction/n (15-1-2013)
[3] See this list: http://ohnotheydidnt.livejournal.com/68332629.html (18-1-2013). It also mentions Rowling as favourable to fan fiction. For Neil Gaiman: http://journal.neilgaiman.com/2002/04/in-relation-to-current-burning-topic.asp (18-1-2013)
[4] http://www.storiesofarda.com/about.asp (17-1-2013)

proposed dramatizations of his published works was generally negative (see Hammond & Scull, *Chronology*, 623, entry of 11 September 1964). Apparently the theoretical licence did not withstand the test of reality. Thirdly, in the two known cases Tolkien was approached by people proposing to write a sequel to *The Lord of the Rings*, he was outraged, calling one of them "a young ass". What disturbed him most was the idea of anyone publishing this "tripe", as he labelled it (*Letters*, 371).

Now it can be argued that he specifically objected to the idea of a sequel to a work as complete as his *Rings* epic. Unlike *The Lord of the Rings*, the writings set in the Elder Days had once been intended to leave gaps to be filled. Still, the vehemence of his reactions to the proposed sequels, his use of the word "tripe" and his general aversion to dramatisations do not point to a fan fiction friendly attitude on Tolkien's part. It would seem that writers of stories based on his works do not have much of a case when they claim to have the support of the Professor himself. This notwithstanding possible objections that not all fan fiction is tripe, that some writers capture the style and spirit of the originals quite well and that imitation is the sincerest form of flattery, to name a few widespread arguments in favour of the genre.

Not that this would deter the average fan writer. For most, it would probably take the threat of a lawsuit to do so. And that is the only thing I am going to say about the legal aspects of the matter, about which I know very little. Nor am I going to say a great deal on the ethical aspects of writing fan fiction. This is a matter that should be left to the individual. My position is that as fan fiction exists, it can be used as a basis for further investigation of the kind I will conduct here. Stories written by fans, whether commercially publishable or not, are simply a time-honoured and perfectly normal response from readers to works of fiction.

They are, in fact, the ultimate form of readers' response as discussed in the school of literary theory known as 'reader-response criticism' (*Rezeptionsästhetik* in German). This school, which established itself in the late 1960s and early 1970s[5], focuses on the way the public reacts to a text, instead of on other aspects like content, style, or on the author. Fan fiction is usually treated as a form of intertextuality with its notion about the meaning of texts being shaped by other texts[6], but reader-response theory also offers an inroad to the study of this phenomenon. In the famous essay in which he declared the author to be dead, Roland Barthes wrote that 'what meaning there is to a text was made

---

5   Well-known names in this field are Stanley Fish, Wolfgang Iser and especially Roland Barthes. A precursor is C.S Lewis with *An Experiment in Criticism*, 1961.
6   The Wikipedia article about intertextuality contains a list of literary works of which several qualify as fan fiction, such as the novel Wide Sargasso Sea by the above-mentioned Jean Rhys, http://en.wikipedia.org/wiki/Intertextuality (18-1-2013).

by the reader' (Barthes 148, quoted in Hellekson/Busse 242). From there, it is but a small step to readers presenting their own meanings to the audience in the shape of fiction.

Seen like this, fan fiction can become a form of literary criticism, a view on a work of fiction presented, not as a discourse, but as a secondary work of fiction derived from and built on the primary one. As Deborah Kaplan puts it:

> The same fans who analyse character in the source text so closely will be writing fan fiction that plays into that interpretive and critical activity. Character analyses, rather than being constructed in a nonfiction essay, are constructed in a fictional environment... Because both the producers and consumers of the fan works are aware of the source materials that are extratextual to the fan productions, a rich interpretive space is created...
>
> (Hellekson/Busse 151)

In the following, I intend to analyse a number of Tolkien-inspired fan stories to show what results these interpretative activities can have in practice, not only with regard to character analysis but also with regard to other aspects such as social and political constructs. From there, I will move on to argue that the reflection aimed at creating fan fiction can turn from literary interpretation via literary criticism into critique, which I shall illustrate with a few additional examples.

That authors lose some degree of control over their works after publication is a given; whether all interpretations are equally valid is debatable, but readers are free to create their own meaning. This interpretative freedom can be taken a step further by calling an author's own rendering of his fictional universe into question, either tongue-in-cheek or seriously. In an afterword to a new edition of Thackeray's *Vanity Fair*, for instance, the published author and literary critic V.S. Pritchett wrote of the heroine, Becky Sharp: "it is plain that Thackeray is wronging her and at three points he is actually lying" (q. by Pugh 16). In Tolkien's case, this kind of approach is facilitated by his presentation of the texts as being based on accounts written by others, and by his insistence that Middle-earth is essentially our own world. These conceits leave room for doubts regarding the "trustworthiness" of the texts he "made available" to the audience (especially where *The History of Middle-earth* is concerned). They also invite a closer scrutiny of the world Tolkien described from writers bringing expertise from various fields of knowledge to the fore. This critical and sometimes even suspicious attitude towards the source texts leads fan writers to "correct" and/or subvert these texts in their own stories. Much of this remains implicit; many fan writers never expand on their motives and it isn't necessary to have a theory. Yet several of the critical writers show themselves aware of what they are doing, adding fore- or afterwords, footnotes or even essays complementing their stories.

My first example of an interpretative story by a fan writer is *Like the Heathen Kings of Old*[7]. In this *Lord of the Rings*-based fanfic, the billowing black smoke of Denethor's pyre reminds Beregond of the tales Faramir told him about Númenor before its fall: "of the great temple at Armenelos and of the never-sated fires that feasted first on the wood of the old White Tree and then on the flesh of the faithful. Faramir had described the great black cloud that hung over the Temple..." What it boils down to, Beregond says to himself, is that intentionally or not, Denethor was making a human sacrifice of his son by trying to burn him. With that, "the heathen kings of old" are identified as the renegade Númenoreans who made human sacrifices in the temple of Melkor in Armenelos with Sauron as a high priest—the same Sauron under whose shadow Denethor had fallen. In a comment to someone else's blog post, the author writes that she let some Jesuit priests on her dissertation committee, among them published Tolkien scholars, read the story. They told her they would never have made this connection, but found that it had "enriched their understanding of what *Tolkien* was saying"[8]. Fan writers in creative mode see connections that do not occur, or not as easily, to scholarly writers, purely because the former often have to imagine a situation they are writing about, including what characters may have been thinking, in order to get it right.

Another example of an interpretative fanfic is Nath's *Old Man Willow*[9]. This is a typical "what-if" scenario; in fan fiction such stories are labelled "Alternative Universe", because the change of one element gives rise to a narrative universe diverging from the original one. This particular story was inspired by the question "What if Old Man Willow's motives in trying to trap four hobbits were more sinister?" Old Man Willow, sensing the presence of the One Ring, pushes Frodo into the river Withywindle and manages to put a root through the Ring. Discovering this Sauron tries to do something about it, but "all trees are connected through the earth in which they stand, and so the news spread quickly. The trees in the great dark wood far beyond the mountains and the river rejoiced, for their forest would be theirs again at last." Serving Old Man Willow, they repel Sauron's attack. One by one Old Man Willow conquers the powers of Middle-earth until all civilisations are overgrown with vegetation. Then, at the end of the story

---

[7] https://dl.dropbox.com/u/11470456/Fanfic/Like%20Heathen%20Kings%20of%20Old.pdf (22-2-2013)

[8] http://dawn-felagund.livejournal.com/313086.html, comment of 18/10/2012, 18:43 (22-2-2013)

[9] http://www.henneth-annun.net/stories/chapter.cfm?stid=7247 (21-1-2013)

...he wondered what lay beyond the Sea. How far would the mangrove forests, so far sunwards that pushed towards the Sea be able to take his Will? Perhaps, he should start with the humble seaweeds that grew near the coasts...

The link between this story and a statement made by Treebeard in *The Two Towers* is easily made. Noting that many trees are waking up, he tells Merry and Pippin: "When that happens to a tree, you find that some have *bad* hearts. ...there are some trees in the valleys under the mountains, sound as a bell, and bad right through... There are some very dark patches" (LotR II 489). Old Man Willow obviously has a bad heart, as he uses the Ring to conquer the world. At the same time, this is simply what nature will do if no one puts a halt to it. Seen this way, the story re-emphasises the fact that the Ring is a metaphor for the "will to power" (to use Nietzsche's term, referred to by Tolkien in *Letters* 160). Remembering that nature has power over man as much as man has power over nature, we will have to wonder to what degree Tolkien really was on the side of trees and nature in general. How funny is it to contemplate a world taken over by Old Man Willow?

Whereas Nath is purely a writer of stories, Tyellas also writes scholarly essays about Tolkien's works. One of these, *The Unnatural History of Tolkien's Orcs* (Tyellas 2012) is intertwined with a story about the same subject, *A Question of Breeding* [10]. Both were "written in the same mental headspace over several weeks"[11]. The essay discusses everything Tolkien ever wrote about orcs and concludes that they are the embodiment of what Tolkien calls "Arda marred". This gives rise to the question if they can be redeemed. Although Tolkien does not rule this out they are not present in Arda renewed in his *legendarium*—yet they are 'part of the world, which is God's and ultimately good', as he writes in a letter (*Letters*, 195). This orcish conundrum has perplexed many a reader, and Tyellas wrote the story partly because she considered this lack of clarity unsatisfactory.

In *A Question of Breeding*, Elrond's sons, Elladan and Elrohir, discuss the nature of orcs with successively Saruman, Radagast and Gandalf. Saruman suggests that orcs may be redeemable, though he is more interested in their breeding habits—a sinister foreshadowing. Elrond's sons are troubled. They hunt the orcs like beasts to avenge their mother, who was tortured so badly by them that she could find no more solace in Middle-earth. But "if Saruman the Wise thinks their evil might fade," as Elrohir muses, "have we been doing the wrong thing all along?" The next wizard, Radagast, fails to reassure them: he

---

10 http://www.henneth-annun.net/stories/chapter.cfm?stid=3237 (25-2-2013)
11 E-mail correspondence with Tyellas, 27-3-2013

knows for certain that orcs are *not* beasts: to think so is an insult to animals. Gandalf, finally, offers a tentative answer: orcs were once good, but their will was taken from them. Neither he, nor the sons of Elrond, nor anyone in Middle-earth can save orcs by trying to remake them, but there is something else they can do. "If an orc asks for mercy—give it," he advises them. "You cannot force redemption. It must come of their own wills. If an orc ever has enough will to want to be redeemed, then it should be. And no doubt, it will." Relieved, the sons of Elrond resume their orc hunt, realising they would pursue anyone who had perpetrated the kind of evil done to their mother, not just orcs.

This story, being reminiscent of a folk tale with its three wise men of whom the third turns out to be the wisest, does several things at once. By projecting the conundrum on the sons of Elrond, it personalises the problem of the orcs in a way the essay could not do, turning it into a matter of conscience. It acknowledges the concerns of readers who object against Tolkien's seemingly one-sided vilification of an entire race, refusing to call them irredeemable[12]. At the same time, it makes these readers wonder about free will and the redemption of the deeply corrupt, refusing to offer easy solutions. Lastly, it integrates one of Tolkien's little known musings, about orcs having to be granted mercy if they ask for it (MR 419), with the wider history of the One Ring and the end of the Third Age: it is put in the mouth of the only character having the knowledge, the integrity, the humility and the wisdom to say such a thing. "It was reading the HoME volumes and Tolkien's letters, with their many ambiguous and complex statements, that made me think about this,"[13] as Tyellas writes, but it feels like it could have been said in *The Lord of the Rings*.

Marnie's fan fiction about Celeborn constitutes an example of a character analysis in the form of fan fiction. This writer also supports her stories with theoretical writings, and the first essay on her favourite character Celeborn, *That tall fellow next to Galadriel*[14], is quite relevant for this paper. Marnie explains that she started writing fan fiction about Celeborn because she was unable to find any stories doing him justice. Most people considered him either a doormat or a jerk—the latter for questioning Gandalf's wisdom and retracting his welcome to Gimli on hearing the Dwarves have roused the Balrog again (LotR I 374-5). Trying to correct this negative impression, Marnie brings the entire history of the Sindar and their relations with the Dwarves into play. Also, she points out that Sindar are not Noldor; as Sam says, "there's Elves and Elves," (380), and notes that Celeborn resembles the Elvenking from *The Hobbit*, another Sindarin

---

12 Which Tolkien himself did as well in a letter to Peter Hastings (*Letters*, 195) but not in his fictional texts.
13 E-mail-correspondence with Tyellas, 21-4-2013
14 http://www.henneth-annun.net/stories/chapter_view.cfm?stid=1372&spordinal=1 (25-2-2103)

no-nonsense type, more than he resembles Galadriel, Elrond or Gildor. In *The Hobbit,* Tolkien contrasts the Elves that went to the West favourably with the ones who did not, whom he calls "more dangerous and less wise" (162). Marnie, however, compares the Elves of Middle-earth, including Celeborn, favourably with the Noldor: "They are guiltless of the kind of atrocities to which the Noldor seem prone. They have not murdered their own kind in kinslaying, nor have they rebelled against the Valar and been cursed for it," she writes, calling the Noldorin superiority strongly suggested by *The Silmarillion* into question, even using the term "Elvish racism".

These reflections on different groups of Elves spill over into several of stories written after the essay. The novel-length fanfic *The Battle of the Golden Wood*[15] describes the attacks on Lothlorien from Dol Guldur, and the victory of the Elves. At the end, Thranduil joins forces with Celeborn and Galadriel. Having laid bare the pits of Dol Guldur with her song, Galadriel begins to sing of springtime and new beginnings. Thranduil, however, cuts her short: "Of destruction you may sing, for destruction you have brought on many a realm. But you will not sing of beginnings or times to come. I will not have your curse rest upon my wood" (Ch. 22). This antagonism between the Sindar and Noldor pervades the First Age story *Oak and Willow,* written still later[16]. Here, the Noldor look down on the "savages" of Beleriand, and everywhere but in Doriath the Sindar become their servants and subordinates. "How much Noldor glory was built upon the menial labour of their Sindar subjects?" Galadriel wonders at some point (Ch. 15). Even the wise and sympathetic Finrod talks condescendingly to the Grey Elves, while Curufin announces that they are no longer Thingol's people now that the Noldor have come. In short, the attitude of the Noldor towards the Sindar resembles that of Europeans towards the indigenous people of the territories they colonised – or on that of the Norman conquerors towards the Anglo-Saxons.

Is this still Tolkien, one may wonder, or is this already a subtle form of correcting the original? That the kinslaying at Alqualondë led to Sindarin antagonism towards the Noldor is obvious in *The Silmarillion,* but when we read about Light and Dark Elves in the tales of the Elder Days, are these descriptive terms, or do they imply a judgement? If so, is it Tolkien's judgement, that of anonymous Noldorin chroniclers looking down on Elves not of Aman, or a bit of both? Perhaps the author's "partisan" attitude towards Celeborn leads her to overstress the darker sides of the Noldor[17]. But we also have the Dark Elf Eöl's

---

15 http://www.henneth-annun.net/stories/chapter.cfm?stid=957
16 http://www.henneth-annun.net/stories/chapter.cfm?stid=1559
17 The fan writer Darth Fingon does not think so. He depicts the Noldor as colonialists of doubtful character, pointing out that 'the Elves of the *Silmarillion* did lie, steal, fight, discriminate, kidnap, covet, attempt rape, betray, murder, and so on' (Never Speak nor Sing http://www.henneth-annun.net/stories/chapter.cfm?stid=6515, Story Notes). In an even more subversive story, *Children of Lindorinand,* the Sindar are the oppressors of

harsh words to Turgon: "No right have you or any of your kin in this land to seize realms or to set bounds... This is the land of the Teleri, to which you bring war and all unquiet, dealing ever proudly and unjustly" (S 137). Granted, shortly afterwards Eöl commits murder, but does that invalidate his words? Is depicting the Noldorin exiles as the Middle-earth equivalent of a colonial power a step away from what Tolkien wrote, or is this a correct reading of the text? If the latter, what can we conclude from this regarding his ideas about colonialism[18]?

Ultimately the question is one of bias, a theme that comes up frequently in discussions about Tolkien's works. In most cases, however, the parties are more strongly opposed and more clearly on opposite ends of Tolkien's scale of good and evil. When fan writers question this fairly rigid dichotomy, they often depart from a suggestion present in the original, but tend to move beyond it. One such writer is Soledad, who repeatedly used the viewpoint of Sauron's minions. Her story *The Face of the Enemy* [19] shows the Battle of the Pelennor Fields from the perspective of the Haradrim commander. She roots Sauron's Haradric allies firmly in a well-elaborated culture inspired by the (semi-)nomadic Asian realms of the early Middle Ages and the mythology of Ancient Iran to give them an identity of their own. Now in *The Lord of the Rings* the Haradrim chiefly exist in the moral space between Gollum's assessment of them as "very cruel, wicked men" (LotR II 672) and Sam's musings on seeing one of their fallen warriors: "He wondered what the man's name was and where he came from; and if he was really evil of heart, or what lies or threats had led him on the long march from his home" (LotR II 687). The latter seems a much-needed counterbalance of Gollum's statement, and Soledad's story is partly meant as an answer to Sam's question. But seen as a comment by Tolkien-the-author, these musings, though well-intended, seem a little condescending: either Sauron's human allies are evil, or they must have been misled or coerced into joining his cause; there can be no other explanation.

Soledad does not entirely go with this suggestion. Instead, she gives the Haradrim, or at least their leaders, a political motive to side with Sauron: they serve Mordor to further their own aims (or so they think). They are not evil at heart, but neither merely nice but misled people: they have an agenda of their own and are willing to kill for it. They sincerely believe the other side are the bad guys—and not entirely without reason. They are, in fact, perfectly human. The commander from Harad genuinely mourns his fallen blood-brother and

---

the Silvan Elves (http://www.henneth-annun.net/stories/chapter.cfm?stid=7919). Stories accessed 23-2-2013.

18 For a discussion about Tolkien as a post-colonial 'Anglo-Saxon' rejecting the Norman colonisation of England, see Hiley. I'd like to point out that fan writer Marnie addressed the subject of colonialism in Tolkien's works almost ten years earlier.

19 http://www.fanfiction.net/s/1589452/1/Face-of-the-Enemy (22-2-2013)

considers the orcs foul creatures, but though he is basically a decent guy, he resolves to set honour aside until the war is won. This way, the writer not only gives the enemy a face, but also briefly lifts him out of the dichotomy of good versus evil dominating the original work, while at the same time showing the dehumanising effect of war on the individual.

The enemy also acquires a face in Kirill Yeskov's novel *The Last Ringbearer*[20]. This is an officially published, Russian work of fan fiction that acquired some reputation outside Russia after it was unofficially translated into English. Yeskov, a professional paleontologist, started out by wanting to correct some geographical errors in Tolkien's world. This lead to the question: What if this world were as real as our primary one? History is written by the victors; the losers may have quite a different story to present. The first part of the novel retells LotR from the perspective of Mordor. Orcs are not monsters but a human race, the Dark Tower is really a bastion of enlightenment, art and scientific progress, the Elves are power-hungry manipulators, etcetera. According to Jim Clarke, who presented a paper about this novel at the "Return of the Ring" conference in Loughborough (2012), Yeskov attempted to subvert Tolkien's narrative by reconstructing

> the War of the Ring as a culture clash between industrial progress and multicultural liberalism and the fascist and arcane power of supernatural magic... Yeskov's recasting of Lord of the Rings as the propaganda of the victor illuminates a rare blindspot of Tolkien's—the idea that industrialisation and science could be liberal and progressive.[21]

Yeskov is by no means the only scientist who balks at what they consider Tolkien's suspicion of science and technology. An American biochemist writing as Pandemonium_123[22] does the same. She openly states that much of what she writes is heresy and flagrantly un-canonical, meant to criticise some of Tolkien's philosophies. In her stories and also in her essay *The Tolkienian War on Science* she attacks his relentless punishment of the Noldor (especially Fëanor) and his condemnation of Sauron—Arda's scientists and technologists. Some of her stories recast Tolkien's creation account in an evolutionary mould, even using scientific terminology. In *Ulmo's Wife* (the Sea), we read:

> She wrapped him [Ulmo] in her waters and led him back in time to when the sky churned with vapors and was rent by lightning, back

---

20 http://ymarkov.livejournal.com/270570.html (31-3-2013)
21 http://www.returnofthering.org/timetable_items.php (31-3-2013)
22 http://www.silmarillionwritersguild.org/archive/home/viewuser.php?uid=44 (15-3-2013)

to her little wombs, the warm, silent pools where the beginnings of life danced, born of her substance and star-semen. The twisted strands of molecules gyrated wildly, crashing into one another and reeling apart, but gradually they stepped with stately order until they shimmied on fins out of her waters, carrying her blood within them as they grew to fly, to walk, and to make rocks into tools and name the stars.

In another of her stories, *Cat's Paws*, Sauron (as Annatar) changes the colour of a rose and turns cat's paws into tiny human hands by "molecular manipulation", as he tells Celebrimbor. He then explains to him how the process works, introducing the term neurotransmitters, and suggesting the possibility of grafting "the molecular configurations of the mind into metal alloys". This is not too far removed from the kind of analyses Henry Gee presents in a more positive way in his book *The Science of Middle-earth*[23] But in story form and illustrated with the examples Pandemonium gives it has a bigger impact on the imagination, illustrating what fan fiction can achieve if it takes a critical distance from Tolkien's own way of thinking.[24]

The same applies to the Númenorean arc by Gadira[25]. Her criticism is rooted in a different field of scholarship, Classical Studies, in which she has a PhD[26]. The main story in this arc, still in progress, is *Full of Wisdom and Perfect in*

---

23 Cold Spring Harbour, NY: Cold Spring Press, 2004
24 Pandemonium also wrote a story, Trinity, in which Fëanor and Sauron (as "Fionn" and "Saunders") have a conversation with Robert T. Oppenheimer, who to her mind bears some resemblance to Tolkien's characters. First she refers to a letter in which Tolkien calls Oppenheimer and his likes "lunatic physicists" for "calmly plotting the destruction of the world", admits that their inventions helped to end the war but adds that God "does not look kindly on Babel-builders" (*Letters* 116). Pandemonium then uses statements made by Oppenheimer himself to show that his thoughts about the matter were a great deal more nuanced than the epithet "lunatic" suggests. Her—subversive—conclusion is that Fëanor and Sauron must have been "far more morally complex individuals than JRRT's historians (Rumil, Pengolodh, Baggins, et al.) were letting on. History is full of revisionism." (Notes to *Trinity*)
25 http://www.fanfiction.net/u/1242973/Gadira (2-4-2013)
26 For this PhD, the author of these stories researched on a subject including the Atlantis story and cultural relations between the Phoenicians and the Greeks. She writes: "I could see that Tolkien had contracted a great debt with Plato's Atlantis (I even wrote a paper about it), at such a deep level that even what the Atlantis tale had of the Greek mind's ambiguous consideration of Eastern civilizations, great but corrupt, lived on in Tolkien's Atlantis through the very Eastern influences of the Semitically-inspired Adûnaic language of the evil kings, the expanding nature of the Númenoréan Empire ... and the fire sacrifices to a god named Melkor, in whose Semitic root we recognize both the Phoenician god Melqart and the evil 'Moloch' of the Hebrew *Bible*, the other major Eastern influence in Tolkien's Númenor." The paper referred to is Fernandez Camacho.

Renée Vink

Beauty, set during the final days of Númenor. The following, lengthy quote, is taken from Gadira's own analysis of the story and her motivation to write it[27]:

> From the point of view of the writer, it is very challenging to deal with a period of Middle-earth history so little explored in Tolkien's works. All we have is the general outline of how things were supposed to unfold, in the *Akallabêth*, the chronologies of the kings and a few, very fragmentary later developments which Christopher Tolkien published in *The Peoples of Middle-earth*. But even those contradict each other often, and after reading them all we are not much advanced concerning crucial information like Amandil and Elendil's chronology (the former didn't even exist in all versions), the exile of the Faithful, Inzilbêth's parentage or the nature of Ar-Pharazôn's and Ar-Zimraphel/Tar-Míriel's relationship... It is a scenario which encourages the philological impulse to find the "correct" version of each event and "fix" the text, and the writing impulse to build my own story around those choices, justifying them and bringing them to life. I wonder if Tolkien did it on purpose: to leave behind so many unfinished and contradictory texts so future generations would become philologists of his work such as he was a philologist of the works of others.
>
> However, this "positive" pleasure of reconstruction was connected to another one, more "negative" meaning, critical and polemical. It is the pleasure of subversion, of picking up notions in Tolkien's work... that bothered me, in order to highlight them or tear them down. [My chief problem] is Tolkien's general reluctance to show religions as part of his world. It is known why he did this. However, in the POV of a readership [that] does not necessarily share his personal beliefs, the lack of religion, except as a very negative force, is a major stumbling stone when it comes to suspend one's disbelief and see Middle-earth as a viable world with its own history... I have always been quite interested in History of Religions, and this story of a monotheistic Númenor which lost its faith in Eru and then spent an entire religion-free millennium before they were influenced by the bad guy into worshipping an [inevitably evil god], became a really irritating and insurmountable difficulty whenever I tried to figuratively touch late Númenor with a less-than-10-inch pole. These people were human, not Hobbits or Dwarves or Elves, and their civilization looked historical on the surface, but I could not make

---

27 E-mail correspondence, 31-3-2013

sense of it... [T]o flesh out the society and the characters, I had to address what Tolkien did not want to address: religion, evolution, culture, and all those little concrete aspects of Númenórean society that would reveal specifical historical influences—influences whose origins were clear to me, though not to many others who read Tolkien with a different set of coordinates in mind... I discovered then that fan fiction could be more than a literary exercise, or a way of going deeper into something you enjoy or connecting the dots: it could be a form of expression, a creative way to "antagonize" the author and add what you feel is lacking in his worldview...

Anyone who reads my Númenórean story arc will notice that these religious, cultural and world-building issues are central to the story, and not merely accessory to the plot. They inform the personality, the thoughts, the actions of every character involved, sometimes pushing them in different directions from those that Tolkien had outlined for them... [T]hat is what happens, for example, to the evil king Ar-Gimilzôr and his good, reformist successor Tar-Palantir, once that it is established that the non-monotheistic religious cults in Númenor predate Sauron (who is only another reformist) by centuries. The notion that Ar-Gimilzôr is protecting something that Númenor has achieved through evolution and historical changes, something which, in the eyes of himself and others, may be worth protecting, and [the notion] that Tar-Palantir, on the other hand, might not be seen as right in his attempt to impose a set of beliefs in Númenor, inspired by the non-human society of the Elves and "entirely new" and extraneous for almost everyone who lives there now..., informs most of the story and transforms the original conflict in many significant ways. In line with this, I drew my inspiration for the figure of Tar-Palantir from the Roman emperor Julian the Apostate, who is seen today as a romantic figure who tried to fight his own times and inevitably failed. This implies a sympathetic view of the character, but also reinforces the futility, and the error, of his efforts, too intellectual and disconnected from reality to triumph in a real world. Therefore, others who oppose him can be seen as sympathetic, too, like his sucessor Ar-Pharazôn, who has a different view of the future of Númenor. The Faithful, like Tar-Palantir, are disconnected from the world they live in, and this is symbolized and reinforced by their long periods of lonely exile in which they only interact with one another, following traditions and speaking a language of their own which nobody else can understand... Almost everything that happens in the story hails back, in last instance, to an important, culturally game-changing event from a more remote past: the accession to the throne of Ar-Adunakhôr, who, like Constantine the Great, introduced Eastern (Middle-earth) cults to Númenor (that of Melkor and that of the Mother Goddess which the Númenoreans identified with the Maia Uinen) to support his legitimacy after a civil war with his cousin. This was the period in which the different sides, beliefs and loyalties are established as we see them later, ...This is why I generally introduce it as a "subversive story"... [But] In fact, nothing is so truly anti-modern as a story based on ancient religious forms of thought. At the end of the day, and in spite of the introduction of new coordinates based on the study of history of religions, languages and civilizations, it remains an old story about an old society where old tropes like the largely unmapped world, predestined children, prophetic visions, Elves and even dragons are firmly entrenched, connected the subversion to Tolkien's own canon.

Here, Gadira nicely turns the idea on its head that it is Tolkien who is the anti-modernist with his 'old-fashioned' values and beliefs. Compared to really ancient mindsets and religions, his approach turns out to be quite modernist.

This concludes my list with examples of Tolkien criticism in the shape of fan fiction, going from the interpretative via the mildly critical and questioning to the outright subversive. I have deliberately omitted any stories subverting the absence of almost all overt references to sexuality in Tolkien's works into various kinds of eroticism, and notably homo-eroticism—despite the fact that they are very numerous and very popular with readers. This subject would take a paper of its own (and has in fact done so[28]).

Of whatever kind, in the end a surprising number of fan fiction stories is rooted in the desire to engage with Tolkien's work on more than one level simultaneously, melding critical assessment and creative inspiration into a—sometimes very well-crafted—unity. This aspect of Tolkien criticism can yield results worth taking note of and therefore deserves more attention, as I hope to have argued here.

---

28 Anna Smol discusses slash, stories involving male/male pairings.

Bibliography

Fernandez Camacho, Pamina. "Cyclic cataclysms, Semitic stereotypes and religious reforms: a classicist's Númenor". *Lembas-extra* (2012): 13-25

Hellekson, Karen and Kristina Busse. *Fan Fiction and Fan Communities in the Age of the Internet.* Jefferson NC: McFarland, 2006

Hiley, Margaret. "'(Re)'Authoring History: Tolkien and Postcolonialism". *Sub-creating Middle-earth. Constructions of Authorship and the Works of J.R.R. Tolkien.* Ed. Judith Klinger. Zurich/Jena: Walking Tree Publishers, 2012, 107-125

Kaplan, Deborah. "Construction of Fan Fiction Character Through Narrative". *Fan Fiction and Fan Communities in the Age of the Internet.* Eds. Karen Hellekson & Kristina Busse. Jefferson NC: McFarland, 2006,134-152

Pugh, Sheenagh. *The Democratic Genre. Fanfiction in a Literary Context.* Bridgend: Poetry Wales Press Ltd., 2005

Scull, Christina and Wayne G. Hammond. *The J.R.R. Tolkien Companion and Guide. II. Chronology.* London: HarperCollins, 2006

Smol, Anna. ""O... oh... Frodo!" Readings of male intimacy in *The Lord of the Rings*". *MFS Modern Fiction Studies* 50 No. 4 (2004): 949-979

Tolkien, J.R.R. *The Hobbit*, 2nd edition. London: Allen & Unwin (Unwin pb), 1975

---. *The Lord of the Rings*, De Luxe Edition. London: Allen & Unwin, 1969

---. *The Silmarillion*, London: Allen & Unwin, 1977

---. *The Letters of J.R.R. Tolkien.* Ed. Humphrey Carpenter, with the assistance of Christopher Tolkien. London: Allen & Unwin, 1981

---. *Morgoth's Ring. (HoMe X).* Ed. Christopher Tolkien. London: HarperCollins, 1993

Tyellas. "The Unnatural History of Tolkien's Orcs". *Lembas-extra* (2012): 75-85

Van Zon, Cecile (Ed.). *Lembas-extra.* Leeuwarden: Tolkien Genootschap Unquendor, 2012

Relevant fan fiction archives on the internet (accessed between 12-1-2013 and 20-4-2013):

www. fanfiction.net
www. henneth-annun.net
www. silmarillionwritersguild.org

A Vision of Middle-earth: Contemporary Views in Peter Jackson's *Lord of the Rings* Trilogy

David Goldie (Aix-Marseille)

In *The Gods Return to Earth*, C.S. Lewis (1082) opens his review of LotR[1] by acclaiming the return of Heroic Romance, comparing Tolkien's work with stories stretching back to *The Odyssey* (and beyond). Indeed he goes on to make the claim that the book also represents a revolution for this genre. This point of view in fact reflects a dialectic argument which has faced artistic creation since ancient times. Should we look backwards taking classical inspiration, "standing on the shoulders of giants", as Isaac Newton[2] put it, or forwards, always aiming to "make it new" as Ezra Pound[3] proclaimed, with a modern approach? Of course our own reaction probably says more about us than the work in question. This artistic opposition is still relevant today however. As far as Tolkien's works are concerned, it now relates to six movies. Firstly, there is a new version of LotR in Peter Jackson's original trilogy from 2001 to 2003 and more recently another three based on H, scheduled for annual release between 2012 and 2014[4]. The "right" approach becomes a lot more than just a philosophical or aesthetic argument when you are in charge of major Hollywood productions, particularly ones aiming to adapt two of the most popular books in the world.

While many of the aesthetic points we intend to raise here would apply to both the adaptations of LotR and H, we will concentrate our analysis on *LotR* and consider the implications of approach in three ways. Firstly, we examine the question of fidelity in relation to the original texts. Secondly, we analyse how Peter Jackson responds to some of the major differences between text and image. Finally, we take a thematic approach to focus on changes to two important characters. The overall aim is to see how far we can find a modernising or "Romantic" spirit running through Jackson's vision of Middle-earth.

---

1 To distinguish between the identical titles of Tolkien's books and Jackson's movies, the following abbreviations are used: LotR = the book series; *LotR* = the film series. Individual films are abbreviated in italics accompanied by the year of their release in brackets. For example: LotR I = The Fellowship of the Rings by J.R.R Tolkien; *LotR I* (2001) = The Fellowship of the Rings by Peter Jackson.
2 In a letter to Robert Hooke (15th February 1676)
3 The title of a collection of essays from 1935
4 At the time of writing only *An Unexpected Journey* (2012) has appeared in cinemas.

1. The Problem of Fidelity

The *LotR* trilogy forms a central part of the Hollywood movement of "family" movies as described by Brown (2). This includes other series like Disney's *The Chronicles of Narnia* and Warner Brothers' *Harry Potter*. According to Brown *LotR* represents classic Hollywood narrative cinema focussing on spectacle, emotion, an overall optimistic message and broad audience suitability. In addition to enormous commercial success[5], the films received widespread recognition within the cinematic industry, winning a total of 17 Oscars. Among critics, the website *metacritics.com* lists a total of 110 positive reviews to just 3 negatives for all three films.[6] *Empire Magazine*, for example, gave all three films 5 star "classic" status, Alan Morrison hailing *LotR* (2003) as "The resounding climax to a landmark in cinema history." Hannah McGill sums up this mainstream appeal thus:

> Shot back-to-back, the three instalments have a glorious stylistic unity. With imaginative casting, superb special effects, gorgeous landscape photography and nail-biting action, this is riveting stuff, even for those not customarily drawn to elfin fantasy. (356)

On the other hand, Scull and Hammond, in *The J.R.R. Tolkien Companion and Guide,* acknowledge the popular success of the series yet also highlight sharp divisions in the reception of the trilogy among Tolkien enthusiasts. These range from high "praise" to "travesty".

> Points frequently argued include the diminishing or alteration of characters in the film relative to their portrayal in Tolkien's book, emphasis on violent action, the over-use of special effects, and the omission of scenes from the book while incidents invented by the screenwriters have been inserted. (22)

Criticisms of the movies relate chiefly to missing or changed elements of the story. In other words, viewers expecting a close fidelity in terms of a copy of events and dialogue from the original text were inevitably disappointed.

Fidelity requires clarification. Philosophically speaking, should *mimesis* be the aim of artistic endeavour, a perfect reproduction of reality or is art in fact too far removed from the original idea to be able to represent it accurately?

---

5 At the time of writing, *LotR III* (2003) is 9th in the list of all time worldwide box office earnings with $1,119.9m, *LotR II* (2002) is 23rd with £926m, *LotR I* (2001) is 31st with $871.5m. See: http://boxofficemojo.com/alltime/world/ (25/04/13)
6 It also gives 1,153 positive user reviews to 174 negatives (25/04/13)

If we regard the original source text as the "real" version, we return to this philosophical problem. Which is more important: the object or the idea? Dudley Andrew (99) identifies three basic approaches to adaptation.

1. Transforming: the film creates a *mimetic* copy of the events of the text.
2. Borrowing: the film represents the themes and ideas of the text.
3. Intersecting: the text defies either of the approaches above.

We could equate *transforming* with a classical approach, maintaining the primacy of the text over the film, whereas *borrowing* could be said to be a more modern approach, unafraid to break with the original source to create a new version. It may be reasonably assumed that an audience with knowledge of the text would prefer the transforming approach in deference to the source. Film theorists and academics, on the other hand, often tend towards the borrowing approach. Cinema takes the essence (in other words, the most important elements) of the narrative and makes use of its specific visual and sensory qualities to "improve" on the book.

Kate Egan and Martin Barker (83-103) analyse the rhetoric employed by Jackson and his production team in DVD bonus documentaries and interviews to present their versions of the story. Initially wary of alienating their audience, the filmmakers erred on the side of caution. As such, a spirit of "deference" was applied to producing *LotR I* (2001). Following its success, their confidence gradually grew to the point that they felt justified in making stark changes. By the time *LotR III* (2003) was released they were able to claim not only to have found the heart of the narrative but to have improved on it (91-8). Therefore, while the films begin by *transforming*, they move increasingly towards *borrowing*.[7]

How can we define fidelity? Is a cinematic copy reproducing the action and dialogue of a book any more faithful to it than a movie which focuses more on getting to the heart of the text? Here we find a choice which can only reflect our personal taste. However, we should perhaps note the logical conclusion as highlighted by Brian McFarlane (26) that the likelihood of any one reader's mental image of the text corresponding with that of its film adaptation's director is extremely small. While he argues that film adaptation should be regarded in the context of intertext and therefore not unjustly compared with literature, it is nonetheless unsurprising that the process and the product of adaptation in general is so often and so fiercely criticised. An adaptation of such a popular

---

7   This trend continues to an even greater degree with the release of *An Unexpected Journey* (2012). The much shorter original story is now a trilogy, cinematically, at least, of as grand a scale as LotR.

work as LotR would inevitably split audiences, according to their own taste and point of view. Any number of individual commentators could find any number of points with which they would not agree. Martin Barker underlines these tensions in his essay *On Being a 60's Tolkien Reader*. In his own views and criticisms (82-85), as well as in his discussion of interpretative communities (85-91), he points out that since the story means so much to so many people and in so many different ways, it would be impossible to find one "true" way to appreciate it.

Tom Shippey's[8] contributions to documentaries accompanying the DVD releases of the films provide them with critical credibility. While recognizing some of the essential differences between cinema and literature, his appraisals of the films elsewhere in his essay "Peter Jackson's Film Versions"[9] (409-30) also provide comparison of the text and the films. Shippey dismisses a number of the changes in the action and the characters as merely "playing to the gallery". Events such as Legolas firing off arrows while surfing on a shield down the outer steps of Helm's Deep in *LotR II* (2002), and more importantly, the increased role of Arwen are examples of unnecessary concessions to a contemporary and youthful audience (412-13).

In their own interviews to be found on the same DVD releases, Jackson, the cast and production team take great pains to underline the authenticity of the films in relation to Tolkien's vision. This can be seen in the care and attention devoted to making weaponry and costumes for orcs and men at WETA Workshop, the natural proximity of New Zealand's landscape to Middle-earth or by highlighting the "Prime Action" of Frodo's journey with the Ring while providing insight on the "Subsidiary Action" concerning battles and heroes.

However, given the age in which the films were made, a more contemporary feel is hard to avoid. While the Medieval setting of the books is recreated in sometimes painstaking detail, many of the most dramatic scenes could only have been made with the most modern of special effects technology. Jackson has acknowledged in interview the debt he owes to special effects pioneers like Ray Harryhausen[10]. Yet he has also pointed out that he is glad to be working in cinema now with the benefits that twenty-first century technology brings to the process of image creation. For example, the scale of the battles at Helm's Deep and Pelennor Fields was only possible with the invention of the *Massive*[11] artificial intelligence program while Gollum was the first CGI character brought to life by motion-capture of an actor.

---

8   Shippey, "Tolkien" & "Book to Script".
9   See also: Shippey, *Another Road*
10 His numerous works include: *The 7th Voyage of Sinbad* (1958), *Jason and the Argonauts* (1963), *First Men in the Moon* (1964), *One Million Years B.C.* (1966), *The Golden Voyage of Sinbad* (1974), *Sinbad and the Eye of the Tiger* (1977), *Clash of the Titans* (1981)
11 Multiple Agent Simulation System in Virtual Environment

We will concentrate the next part of our analysis on some of the perhaps more visually obvious differences between the text and the films. With this in mind, we now turn our attention to the problems created for a filmmaker by some of the more essential differences between cinema and literature.

2. Showing and Telling: from the Sublime to the Ridiculous?

While both cinema and literature are narrative arts, the fact remains that cinema can only show what literature has to tell. Hamburger (187-207) demonstrates the limits of images as narrative. Even if an extract of text contains no dialogue and consists entirely of description of setting or objects which can be filmed, there will always be something missing from the text in the on-screen image. She demonstrates this with an example of an extract from *Joseph and His Brothers* by Thomas Mann. Word play and associations create linguistic effects which quite simply can never appear in an image, even with an exact representation of the setting and objects within the passage. In this way Hamburger highlights, very effectively, the fundamental opposition and problems that exist between telling a tale and showing its events.

In an article for *CinémAction: Contes et légendes à l'écran* , the French aesthetician, Isabelle Smadja, praises the high quality of landscape photography in LotR I (2001) which frequently creates a vision of the Sublime (238). At the same time, however, she also highlights the challenge for Jackson of representing the beauty and depth of Tolkien's language. In her opinion, Jackson cannot match it and therefore replaces it with the recurrent theme of sublime and grandiose landscapes, striking in their savage beauty. The landscapes evoke a journey towards the infinite, just like the journey that Frodo is on. The fertile cultivated land of the Shire is opposed to the wild and untamed lands into which he travels. In another striking example from the opening shot of *LotR II* (2002), the audience is treated to a vision of magnificent mountains while hearing Gandalf defying the Balrog in Moria from *LotR I* (2001) as a voiceover. In Smadja's opinion, instances such as these give a visual expression of Rilke's phrase: "For beauty is nothing but the beginning of terror".

Smadja continues by highlighting the importance of fairytale (240). The Medieval setting of LotR serves to enhance the atmosphere of an ancient tale that yet contains hidden depths and universal truths. This is true for the early part of Peter Jackson's trilogy. The idyllic Shire shares many of the characteristics of a marvellous fairytale setting. Describing the genesis of the book, Carpenter (256) highlights the fact that as the narrative progresses, the aesthetic turns darker, reflected not only by the passage of the characters towards greater danger and darker times, but also a linguistic development in Tolkien's prose towards more archaic terms, indicating the growing seriousness of the situation and the themes treated by the text.

To some extent these changes are reflected in the films. Mirroring the characters' individual journeys the general aspect of the landscapes and settings changes over the course of the trilogy. At the beginning, the viewer is struck by the verdant lushness and simple beauty of the Shire which gives way to progressively darker and more desolate landscapes. In *LotR III* (2003) rapid shifts of time and place are accompanied by radical shifts of colour and atmosphere. For example Gondor's defeat at Osgiliath is represented in harsh grey, followed similarly in tone by Frodo and Sam on the Stairs of Cirith Ungol, before warmer colours return as the forces of Rohan muster at Dunharrow, where hope, albeit slim, remains.

From the moment the hobbits leave the Shire in *LotR I* (2001), the narrative continues almost exclusively in darkness. A pleasant walk through Farmer Maggot's field in the sunlight ends abruptly with Frodo, Sam, Merry and Pippin being chased onto the Road and their first encounter with a Black Rider. The whole environment darkens in reaction to the presence of evil. The film cuts to night as the hobbits are chased through thick forest before a temporary reprieve at the Buckland Ferry. From now on darkness reigns almost exclusively until the arrival of Arwen. Making her appearance after Frodo is struck on Weathertop, she appears like an angel in white, bathed in glorious light. Day has dawned again as she outrides the Black Riders to Rivendell. The contrast in luminosity upon Frodo's re-awakening there is striking. This continues for the majority of the time the hobbits spend in Rivendell, firmly contrasting this place of temporary rest with the evil to be encountered in the world outside.

This technique serves to underline one way in which Jackson answers the problem of showing rather than telling. The natural world of Middle-earth consistently reflects the tone of the narrative. Both Isengard and Mordor are represented predominantly in the dark. Saruman's evil industry takes place in the depths of the earth and it is almost pitch black when Frodo and Sam climb the stair of Cirith Ungol to enter Mordor. Despite the apparent hurdles presented by the description of Tolkien's settings in print, the images should not be automatically considered inferior to the text. Jackson manages to give authentic physical portrayals of place while at the same time create differing and contrasting atmospheres which do reflect the overall development of the narrative.

In 1956, George Bluestone highlighted a central paradox of literary adaptations when he classified their relationship as "overtly compatible, secretly hostile" (2). For Bluestone particular problems arise in the representation of thought and time on film. The reader is in a privileged position compared to the film viewer. Through his words an author can choose precisely what information to give. The director is at a disadvantage in this respect as his images can only show a scene. He will never be able to provide the direct access to a character's inner life as is possible for the author. In cinema, rather than seeing through the eyes of a character, it may be more accurate to say that we are invited to try to see into their eyes. Close-up views and other visual effects may give clues to their thoughts but otherwise the limits of the image for representation of thought are plain to see.

Smadja (242) feels that Jackson may have struggled with this aspect, almost trying too hard to fit modern concerns into the Tolkien's narrative context. She criticises the way Jackson chooses to show the Ring's effect on those who come into contact with it. For example, when Bilbo and Frodo experience sudden feelings of jealousy over it, their voices, eyes and faces begin to eerily resemble Gollum. These physical transformations on screen in reaction to the Ring seem almost comical caricatures, like cartoon animations of shock.

Yet this is a rather harsh judgement. Physical transformation accompanying psychological anguish around the Ring is a repetitive visual element in the trilogy. Jackson provides a full representation of Gollum's story that allows the viewer to make a definite comparison between him and his former self in Sméagol. The full physical horror of the Ring's power is thus demonstrated in a way that is implied in the text. Gollum in fact represents one of Jackson's major successes. His duality is rendered very effectively on screen. At several points his inner battle is made obvious as he talks to himself; Sméagol arguing with Gollum. At one time this is done through reflection in a pool; at another the screen is effectively split by a tree trunk where each half of his personality addresses the other. Here as much is imparted by the construction of the image as the dialogue.

Finally, as Frodo refuses to throw the Ring into the Crack of Doom in *LotR III* (2003), we recognise that it has finally taken possession of him. The text gives a precise description, without recourse to monstrous transformation. In the films, it is possible to compare the innocent young hobbit of the Shire with the emaciated individual we now see. However, Jackson does not treat the viewer to visual pyrotechnics here. The image of Frodo before the Crack of Doom does reflect Tolkien's text while adding an expression in his eyes suggestive of demonic possession and transformation. This is reminiscent of the look we see in Isildur's eyes as Elrond recounts the first failure to destroy the Ring in *LotR I* (2001). In the end though, perhaps it is the fact that Frodo has undergone a prolonged and subtle change, progressively portrayed over the three films, which makes this final realisation that he has succumbed all the more powerful.

Despite the comparatively limited possibilities of description in film images, Jackson makes a real attempt to live up to the heights achieved by the text. However the characters' relationship with their surroundings is only partially successful as it leads simultaneously towards conclusions about their inner lives and also serves to highlight one of the inherent problems of translating text into images.

3. A Romantic Spirit?

How far then could we regard the film versions as modern interpretations of Tolkien's original and does a *borrowing* approach automatically mean something is lost from the original source? Lewis invites us not to overlook the "Romantic" spirit running through LotR and indeed makes a claim for Tolkien's own revolutionary status within the genre of Romance. Let us consider briefly how nineteenth century Romanticism could relate to a *borrowing* approach.

In contrast to the idea of educating people through literature and classical studies, the nineteenth century Romantics wished for a return to nature. They tried to rediscover the lost world of tales, legends and folklore of the Middle Ages. Inasmuch as they sought to break with the past, the Romantics were taking the first steps towards Modernism, reaching beyond classicism and elevating a revived medievalism. Tolkien's universe clearly has much in common with the aims of the nineteenth century Romantics. Could we say that Peter Jackson has, in some ways, adopted an equally "Romantic" spirit in his vision of Middle-earth in comparison with Tolkien's original source? His *borrowing* approach already places him in rupture with the text. We have also seen how his use of sublime landscape photography seeks to point out certain themes.

We will now consider the effect of some of the most radical changes made in the films and ask whether they automatically mean concession to a new audience or in fact serve the story better. Since Shippey provides much analysis on a variety of themes (Shippey, *Film Versions*), we propose to take up one of his points: the position of women, a theme on which Tolkien's works have received much criticism, to discuss the potential significance of such changes in the films.

The story of Aragorn and Arwen is played out on screen via flashbacks and insertions into the main narrative. From a commercial point of view, a love interest caters for the female viewers and therefore significantly increases the potential audience, thereby creating a completely new interpretative community. Yet is the elevation of a female character in respect of her position in the text merely a commercial ploy? The female characters, as a whole, are substantially different in the films and we should not forget that while Jackson directed the trilogy he co-wrote the screenplay with his wife Fran Walsh and their collaborator Philippa Boyens. Were their decisions based on demographics or a real will to "correct" the narrative in a way they saw would better serve the story?

Arwen's role is significantly altered in the films. She appears much more regularly and in two guises. The first is as an ethereal being. Frodo sees her in a vision after his wounding at Weathertop. She calls to him, giving him the strength to withstand the poison of the Morgul blade. She appears again in a similar fashion to Aragorn in an event invented for *LotR II* (2002). As the people of Rohan come under attack by Warg Riders on their way to Helm's Deep, Aragorn is lost in battle, seemingly tumbling to his death over a cliff. We soon learn, however, that he is floating unconsciously down a river, eventually coming to rest on a shore, far from his comrades. It would seem that he is seriously injured and while still unconscious Arwen visits him in a vision. She apparently breathes life back into him with a kiss. Though this may just indicate the deep union of Aragorn and Arwen's souls, this episode also inverts the story of *Sleeping Beauty*. Peter Jackson here reverses the roles traditionally ascribed to the princess and the handsome prince, while also adding another layer of interest to Arwen's character as she seems to possess magical healing powers.

At these times, she appears as an ethereal Pre-Raphaelite beauty, a fairy tale princess bathed in a soft white light. She maintains these qualities when we see the story of her love for Aragorn on screen. She also becomes a somewhat tragic heroine. She is willing to give up her mortality for the man she loves and even disobeys Elrond's wishes when the elves begin their exodus from Middle-earth. Under these circumstances we can see her both as an ideal of feminine beauty and a woman asserting her own opinion over her father's, no matter the consequences. This aspect of her character may not be vastly different from the books. However the reality of choosing mortality is seen on screen in a lucid vision which brings vividly home to the viewer the consequences of aging and losing her lover.

Although not actually present at the muster of Rohan in either the book or the film of *LotR III* (2003), Arwen contributes symbolically to Aragorn accepting the mantle of the King. She asks Elrond to re-forge "The sword that was broken" and thus, like Arthur and The Lady of the Lake, becomes instrumental in calling Aragorn to meet his destiny. From this point onwards Aragorn will increasingly take his rightful place as Isildur's heir. Producing Andúril in front of the King of the Dead proves his right to command the Army of the Dead which is decisive in the battle of Pelennor fields. Following this, Aragorn increasingly takes a lead in decisions. In fact in the film he (and not Gandalf) instigates the final march on the Black Gate.

This chain of events is again somewhat different from the book where Halbarad the ranger arrives in the aftermath of the battle at Helm's Deep bringing a gift by Arwen. She has remade the King's banner which will eventually be unfurled as Aragorn arrives by river to save Gondor. Substituting both the object and the time it is presented in the film serves a dramatic purpose. While a coat of arms is of course symbolically significant, it is probably not as strikingly powerful an object as a sword.

In another instance we see Arwen in a substantially different way, as active against the forces of the Dark Lord as the male characters. She takes the place of Glorfindel in *LotR I* (2001). She has gone out to search for Aragorn and the hobbits despite the danger of the Ringwraiths. She then proceeds to outride the nine Black Riders and causes their downfall by invoking the power of the Ford at Rivendell. This is the first time the viewer meets Arwen in person. Dressed like a ranger she strikes the viewer as adventurous and heroic, in stark contrast to the ethereal beauty we see at other times. As the Ringwraiths begin to ford the river she sits on her white horse, sword aloft, defying them, shouting that if they want Frodo they will have to come and take him by force.

Gender politics being substantially different now than at the time of Tolkien's writing, Shippey consigns this incident in particular to the level of "playing to the gallery". However in conjunction with the other instances previously mentioned, it seems clear that Arwen's enhanced role is more than simply symbolic. Despite this, the increased presence and participation of the female characters is perhaps even more remarkable with Éowyn.

In her commentary on LotR, Smadja is scathing of Tolkien's treatment of women (119-23), arguing that he uses the Medieval context to portray an outmoded and outdated view of them. Concentrating her analysis on Éowyn in LotR II, Smadja emphasises how she is required to stay in Edoras while the Riders go out to face Saruman's forces at Helm's Deep. In other words, it is the women's duty to stay at home while the men decide their futures on the battlefield. In response to such charges, Curry's reply is "guilty as charged". However, he goes on to point out that, "...there are the characters of Galadriel and Éowyn, without whom *The Lord of the Rings* would be seriously impoverished..." (81).

The screenwriters go some way to try to redress this problem. In the films, Éowyn's role is promoted. While the book narrative does allow her to assert herself and join the men, albeit secretly, it also places a good deal more emphasis on her love interest. After this initially remains unrequited with Aragorn, she eventually falls for the courtly love of Faramir. This is all but removed in the films. The audience is therefore guided to focus on her as an assertive female. She rejects the suggestion of being forced into union with Wormtongue and once he has been disposed of, we see her increasingly as a warrior princess. She knows how to ride and fight. Her attraction to Aragorn could even be described as assertive, since she recognises him as a kindred spirit and chooses to make her feelings known.

As Edoras is evacuated in the film, the whole of the city moves to Helm's Deep, including the women and children. Despite the fact that she is left in charge, Éowyn is left behind in the book and her role is diminished as the battle rages. Furthermore, in the film, leadership is thrust upon her, when the company comes under the attack of Warg riders. As the Riders of Rohan fly to the attack, King Théoden asks Éowyn to lead the rest of the company through the wilderness to Helm's Deep. Although she wishes to join the attack, she responds with firm action and immediately begins marshalling the convoy. Finally, perhaps more symbolically significant than anything else, Théoden chooses to name her (and not Éomer) as his successor before the ride to Gondor. We should note, however, that the effect of this is slightly undone by him then wishing her happiness in love and that this twist in the plot remains undeveloped.

Of course Tolkien had already allowed Éowyn to be integral to the plot when she secretly accompanied the Riders to the Battle of Pelennor fields. It is foretold that no man can defeat the Witch-King yet two apparently weak individuals, a woman and a hobbit, are chosen to defeat the leader of the Nazgûl. Quantitatively in comparison with the deeds of the male characters, this may seem like a small concession. However, placing Éowyn and Merry in such crucial roles could be seen to be particularly forward-looking by Tolkien. He was not some sort of proto-feminist of course. Yet one of the most important messages coming through the narrative is not to underestimate anyone, especially those outwardly appearing weak and insignificant. The reader is constantly reminded how hobbits have hidden resources and resolve. Ultimately they are the ones upon whom the whole future of Middle-earth depends. Through affirmative action a female character is able to empathise with another marginalised one, joining forces with them. Éowyn is recognised as being as courageous as any man, she possesses the essentially feminine quality of empathy which gives her another kind of strength and permits her to ultimately succeed where men would have failed.

As one of the most technically and politically audacious of the New Wave directors, Jean-Luc Godard helped to create a rupture with cinema's past, rewriting the rules of narrative. After collaborating with Godard on *Le Mépris* (1967), Fritz Lang was recorded in conversation with the French filmmaker. Among the subjects of their conversation were their differing styles of filmmaking and Lang, who was a classical narrative director, labels Godard a "Romantic". Brown (2) reminds us that the *LotR* trilogy is part of this classical tradition. Jackson admits his aim is to "entertain", yet his vision of Middle-earth is unafraid to make changes to the original text and to modernise it. Morrison underlines this in his review of *LotR III* (2003): "Jackson has also proved that notions of risk and ambition needn't be confined to the low-budget, indie end of the spectrum". Whether this is a result of essential differences between cinematic and literary narrative, a desire to reach the heart of the story or a pragmatic approach to attracting a contemporary audience, it seems clear that this "Romantic" spirit also prevails in his interpretations.

Does this mean that in C.S. Lewis' eyes, the film versions of LotR would be regarded as equally revolutionary as the original texts? In the book, when Frodo and Sam discuss their own story on the Stairs of Cirith Ungol, the point is made that each of us has our favourite versions of tales. We attach our own significance to them and characters which attract us. Underlining the role of our personal taste in such questions reminds us that whether it is a case of an aesthetic opposition such as classicism versus modernity or something as simple as preferring one character over another, our appreciation of any work of art is subjective.

"Fidelity" is a hazardous notion, inevitably mixed with subjective reactions based on our own relationship with the original text. Texts are rarely entirely independent from previous creations. Even if a director wants to stamp his own mark on his creation, it is impossible to erase the traces of what has gone before. Genette (556) points this out by using the term *palimpsest* to discuss the concept of intertext. In the Middle Ages, when parchment was in short supply, scribes would use pieces with text already on them. Carefully erasing the original text left a fresh page. However, the traces of what had been written before still existed under the surface. Cinematic adaptation of literature further demonstrates Genette's point and requires the audience to consider the question of intertext. Writers, their texts and their readers are inter-dependent and not separate from directors, their films and their audience. Making a judgement of the adaptation of a literary work based entirely on our own conception of "fidelity" is therefore not necessarily the most fruitful way to proceed.

The question of adaptation reveals that there are many factors involved in bringing a literary work to the screen, not the least of which are the essential differences between literary and cinematic narratives. Peter Jackson has made a huge effort in this respect. Although not always successful, he has managed to introduce a certain psychological depth to the characters despite the problem faced by showing the story rather than telling it. While it may be difficult for us to accept Jackson positioning himself as a "corrector", emboldening Tolkien's original vision, he is not merely "playing to the gallery". Jackson's vision of Middle-earth certainly demands serious consideration and should not be dismissed simply because of a lack of fidelity to our own. Even if we do not agree with all his changes, the fact that we notice them and react to them cannot fail but to reengage us with Tolkien's story. As such, the discussion and evaluation of the text that the changes in the films provoke can only be positive.

Bibliography

Andrew, Dudley. *Concepts in Film Theory*. Oxford: Oxford University Press, 1996, 99-104

Barker, Martin. "On Being a 60's Tolkien Reader". *From Hobbits to Hollywood: Essays on Peter Jackson's* Lord of the Rings. Eds. Ernest Mathijs & Murray Pomerance, New York: Editions Rodopi B.V, 2006, 81-100

Bluestone, George. *Novel into Film*. Berkeley: University of California Press, 1957, 1-61

Brown, Noel. "'Family' Movies and Contemporary Hollywood Cinema". *Scope: An Online Journal of Film and Television Studies* 25 (2013), 1-22: http:// www.scope.nottingham.ac.uk/feb_2013/Brown.pdf (09/04/2013)

Carpenter, Humphrey. *J.R.R. Tolkien: A Biography*. London: HarperCollins, 2002, 244-277

Curry, Patrick. "Tolkien and His Critics: A Critique". *Root and Branch: Approaches towards Understanding Tolkien*. Ed. Thomas Honegger. 2nd ed. Zurich/Jena: Walking Tree Publishers, 2005, 75-139

Egan, Kate, and Martin Barker. "The books, the DVDs, the extras and their lovers". *Watching the Lord of the Rings: Tolkien's world audiences*. Eds. Martin Barker & Ernest Mathijs. New York: Peter Lang Publishing, 2008, 83-103

Genette, Gérard. *Palimpsestes. La Littérature au second degré*, Paris: Editions du Seuil, 1982

Hamburger, Käte. *Logique des genres littéraires*. Paris: Editions du Seuil, 1986, 187-207

Jackson, Peter. *The Fellowship of the Ring*, New Line Cinema, 2001

---. *The Two Towers*, New Line Cinema, 2002

---. *The Return of the King*, New Line Cinema, 2003

---. *The Hobbit Interview Special*, Interview, Film 4, UK, broadcast 12/01/13

---. On *The Lord of the Rings Trilogy*, Interview, Film 4, UK, broadcast 27/03/13

Labarthe, André S. *Le dinosaure et le bébé, dialogue en huit parties entre Fritz Lang et Jean-Luc Godard*, from the television documentary series, *Cinéastes de notre temps* (1964-72), episode 29, broadcast 15/03/67

Lewis, Clive Staples. "The Gods Return to Earth". *Time and Tide*, 14 August 1954, 1082-3

McFarlane, Brian. "Reading film and literature". *Literature on Screen*. Eds. Cartmell & Whelehan, Cambridge: Cambridge University Press, 2007, 15-29

McGill, Hannah. "100 Most Notable Films". *The Chambers Film Factfinder*. Ed. Camilla Rockwood. Edinburgh: Chambers Harraps, 2006, 328-383

Morrison, Alan. "Lord of the Rings: The Return of the King" http://www.empireonline.com/reviews/reviewcomplete.asp?DVDID=117407 (25/04/13)

Pound, Ezra. *Make it new. Essays by Ezra Pound*. New Haven, Yale University Press, 1935

Newtown, Isaac. "Letter to Robert Hooke". 15th February 1676

Rilke, Rainer Maria. *Duino Elegies, 1st & 2nd*. Boston, USA: Shambhala Publications, 1992

Scull, Christina, and Wayne G. Hammond. *The J.R.R Tolkien Companion and Guide, Reader's Guide*, New York: Houghton Mifflin, 2006, 8-23

Shippey, Tom. "Peter Jackson's Film Versions". *The Road to Middle-earth. Revised and Expanded edition*. London: HarperCollins, 2005, 409-30

---. "Another Road to Middle-earth". *Understanding the Lord of the Rings: The Best of Tolkien Criticism*. Eds. Rose A Zimbardo & Neil D. Isaacs, New York: Houghton Mifflin, 2004, 233-57

---. "Tolkien" & "Book to Script". Extended version DVDs. Wingnut Films, The Saul Zaentz Company, 2006

Smadja, Isabelle. "Le Seigneur des Anneaux: un film dans la légende". *CinémAction : Contes et légendes à l'écran*. Numéro 116. Ed. Carole Aurouet, Paris: Editions Corlet, 2005, 237-44

---. *Le Seigneur des Anneaux ou la tentation du mal*. Paris: Presses Universitaires de France, 2002, 117-123

Tolkien, John Ronald Reuel. *The Lord of the Rings*. London: Unwin Hyman, 1988

Zusammenfassungen der englischen Aufsätze

Peter Jackson's Adaption von *The Lord of the Rings*: Geld oder Beifall?

Annie Birks

Am 7. Juli 2012 erschien in der französischen Tageszeitung *Le Monde* ein vierseitiger Artikel über Tolkien inklusive eines Interviews mit seinem Sohn Christopher, der seine Meinung zu Peter Jackson's Adaption des *The Lord of the Rings* ausdrücken sollte. Christopher beklagte eindeutig »die Lücke zwischen der Schönheit, der *gravitas* des (Original)Werks und was aus ihm wurde« und fügte hinzu: »Ein solches Ausmaß an Kommerzialisierung reduziert die ästhetische und philosophische Bedeutung dieser Schöpfung zu nichts.«

Auf der Grundlage einer Umfrage unter Tausenden Studierenden in der Stadt Angers (Frankreich), versucht dieser Beitrag mehr Licht auf diese Thematik zu werfen und untersucht den Einfluss der Filme Peter Jacksons auf die Wertschätzung von und das Interesse an J.R.R. Tolkiens geschriebenen Werken seitens der Antwortenden.

Ich komme mir vor, als wäre ich in einem Lied

Musik in J.R.R. Tolkiens Mittelerde und Vertonungen von Liedern und Gedichten aus *Der Herr der Ringe*

Tobias Escher

In nahezu allen von J.R.R. Tolkien beschriebenen Völkern ist Musik ein wichtiger Teil ihrer kulturellen Identität. In *Der Herr der Ringe* zeigt sich dies vor allem durch die hohe Zahl an Liedern und Gedichten, welche in die Handlung eingestreut teils entscheidende Informationen über die jeweilige Kultur enthalten.

Zur Analyse existierender Vertonungen hinsichtlich ihrer Übereinstimmung mit den Beschreibungen des Autors wurden drei Werke herangezogen: Die komplette Vertonung aller Lieder und Gedichte aus *Der Herr der Ringe* durch das Tolkien Ensemble; der Liederzyklus *The Road Goes Ever On* von Donald

Swann mit der einzigen direkten Notenquelle aus der Feder Tolkiens; das *The Lord of the Rings Musical* von A.R. Rahman/Värtinnä.

Die Analyse aller Musik basiert auf dem Grundsatz des Rückläufigen Fortschritts: Die von Göttern gespielte Erste Musik stellte den Höhepunkt jeglicher Musik dar, sodass (im Gegensatz zu dem gängigen Fortschrittsgedanken auch in der Musik) die Musik Mittelerdes sich gegenläufig entwickelt.

Ein besonderer Fokus der Betrachtungen liegt auf der Art, wie sich die Werke auf unterschiedliche Weise denselben Grundsituationen nähern und unterschiedliche Akzente setzen. Während das Tolkien Ensemble alle Lieder und Gedichte im originalen Wortlaut vertonte und nur minimale Änderungen, wie z.B. Textwiederholungen, vornahm, gehen die anderen Werke freier mit der Textbasis um und nutzen teilweise nur einzelne literarische Motive.

Zusammenfassend wird deutlich, dass es allen Werken gelungen ist, die Musik Mittelerdes in die Tonsprache unserer Zeit zu übertragen. Hierzu werden stark verschiedene Stilistiken genutzt, mit Ausnahme der Behandlung der Hobbit-Musik, welche in allen Fällen als orientiert am Irish Folk dargestellt wird. Alle Werke nutzen die Erwartungshaltung des Hörers, um kulturelle Eigenheiten der Zielkultur darzustellen, auch wenn die hierdurch resultierenden Stilelemente und Instrumentierungen teils den aus den Beschreibungen des Autors resultierenden Erkenntnissen über die Musik Mittelerdes widersprechen.

Der Herr der Ringe in Rollen- und Brettspielen. Eine narratologische Analyse

Natalia González de la Llana

Charakteristisch für moderne phantastische Sagen ist ihre Permeabilität: sie fließen ständig in verschiedene neue Medien ein. Es handelt sich nicht mehr nur um ein rein literarisches Werk, sondern um andere nicht rein verbale Diskurse wie Film, Comic, usw., die ein narratives Universum teilen.

Tolkiens *Der Herr der Ringe* ist keine Ausnahme. Diese Trilogie ist der Ursprung einer Reihe von Transfiktionen, in deren Zentrum die Welt von Mittelerde steht. Dies gilt auch für die Spiele: *Der Herr der Ringe Rollenspiel* (Decipher, 2002) und *Der Herr der Ringe Brettspiel* von Rainer Knizia und John Howe.

Im Mittelpunkt steht die Untersuchung, wie Tolkiens Welt sich in zwei verschiedenen Arten von Spielen umgesetzt hat. Dabei werden sie einer narratologischen Analyse unterzogen und folgende Aspekte berücksichtigt: Geschichte, Erzähler, Charaktere, Zeit und Raum.

Eine phantastische Geschichte zu erzählen, ist Ziel des Rollenspiels, und dabei ist das Gewinnen nicht das Wichtigste. Beim Brettspiel dagegen müssen die Spieler, um den Ring zu zerstören, die Reise der Gefährten auf einem Brett reproduzieren.

Der Erzähler ist selbstverständlich eine wesentliche Figur im Rollenspiel. Er erfindet das Abenteuer, das alle »erleben« müssen, jedoch können die Mitspieler seine Pläne und Handlungen mit ihren Entscheidungen auch verändern. Im Brettspiel hingegen ist die Präsenz des Erzählers weniger evident. Doch auch hier gibt es einen, da jede Geschichte eine Instanz hat, die das gesamte narrative Material organisiert.

Die Charaktere werden beim Rollenspiel von den Spielern sehr genau definiert durch Aussehen, Persönlichkeit, Rasse, usw., während im Brettspiel die Spieler die flache Rolle der Gefährten (hier nur durch Hobbits repräsentiert) als Gruppe im Kampf gegen Sauron übernehmen.

Die externe Zeit differiert in beiden Fällen sehr. Im Brettspiel sind es lediglich ein oder zwei Stunden, aber das Rollenspiel kann so lange dauern, wie die Spieler es wollen. Die interne Zeit im Brettspiel ist im Prinzip die gleiche wie in den Romanen (der Krieg um den Ring), wird aber nur durch einige Orte/Schlachten repräsentiert. Beim Rollenspiel ist sie abhängig von der Geschichte des Erzählers.

In Bezug auf den Raum ist Mittelerde in beiden Spielen das Szenario. Die verschiedenen Orte werden von allen Spielern mit ihrer Vorstellungskraft (und manchmal mithilfe von Landkarten und Bildern) gleichzeitig visualisiert. Knizias Spiel bietet auch mehrere illustrierte Bretter, wo die wichtigsten Orte der Reise der Hobbits, sowie ihr Korruptionsniveau, gezeigt werden.

Splatter in Middle-earth?
Krieg und Gewalt zwischen Buch und Leinwand – ein Vergleich
Tobias Hock & Frank Weinreich

Der Artikel berichtet die Ergebnisse einer vergleichenden Inhaltsanalyse von *Der Herr der Ringe* in der originalen Buchversion und der Filmadaption von Regisseur Peter Jackson. Nach einer kurzen Diskussion der medientheoretischen Unterschiede der Erzählmöglichkeiten von Literatur und Kino werden die Ergebnisse einer quantitativen Analyse der Gewaltanteile von Original und Adaption ausgeführt. Es zeigt sich, dass etwa 20 Prozent des Roman-Textkorpus gewalttätigen Inhalts sind, während die Filmversion bezüglich der verschiedenen Arten der Gewaltdarstellung in der Regel die doppelte Menge liefert. Nach einem kursorischen Überblick über die Gesamtkomposition beider Erzählformen wendet sich die Untersuchung qualitativen Aspekten der Gewaltdarstellung zu. Und hier wird der Eindruck der quantitativen Analyse – dass Gewalt bei Jackson eine größere Rolle als in der Buchvorlage spielt, ohne dass deshalb gewalttätige Inhalte die filmische Erzählung dominieren, und dass beide Erzähler sich in ihrer Haltung gegenüber den Konsequenzen von Gewalteinsatz nicht signifikant unterscheiden – zu größten Teilen unterstützt.

Zu Tisch mit Tolkien

Blending und konzeptuelle Metapher in den Brettspiel-Adaptionen *Der Herr der Ringe* und *Der Hobbit*

Timo Lothmann & Nicole Hützen

Nicht zuletzt aufgrund des Kassenerfolgs der Filmtrilogie hat sich *Der Herr der Ringe* zu einem popkulturellen Phänomen entwickelt. Die Filme wiederum hatten einen Multiplikatoreffekt auf diverse andere Adaptionen der Vorlage, die seither auf den Markt strömen. In diesem Hinblick zeigt sich *Der Hobbit* in einem ähnlichen Maße als verwertbare Quelle. In unserem Artikel betrachten wir ausgewählte Brettspieladaptionen der *Herr der Ringe-* und *Hobbit*-Stoffe. Wir gehen von der Annahme aus, dass die Brettspielerfahrung (als Gruppe) in sich die Konstruktion mentaler Repräsentationen des Inhalts birgt. Dies umfasst vor allem die in der Spielhandlung agierenden Charaktere und deren Identität.

Mittels einer interdiziplinär-kognitiven Perspektive zeigen wir, dass konzeptuelle Metaphern (gemäß Lakoff/Johnson) und das damit einhergehende Mapping der beteiligten Domänen effektiv zur Schaffung eines abstrakten, dynamischen mentalen Raums führen können. In diesem ›mental space‹ werden vorherrschende Schemata mit dem Ziel der Konstruktion einer Mischidentität verhandelt. Diesen Blending-Prozess (gemäß Fauconnier/ Turner) vollzieht jeder einzelne Spieler während des Spielens. Mit anderen Worten: Metaphern (in gemeinschaftlichem, intrakulturellem Gebrauch) liegen dem Konstrukt der Spielcharaktere zugrunde. Und ohne Blending entwickelt sich kein Spielfluss.

Wir erproben den theoretischen Überbau insbesondere anhand zweier Brettspieladaptionen für den deutschsprachigen Markt aus dem KOSMOS-Verlag: *Der Herr der Ringe* und *Der Hobbit*. Auf dieser Basis arbeiten wir Gruppen konzeptueller Metaphern heraus, die elementare und unabdingbare strategische Werkzeuge für die Konstruktion des (adaptierten) Spiel-Selbst darstellen. Im Zuge dessen schlagen wir ein Modell vor, das in angemessener Weise die konstitutive Beschaffenheit von Metaphern im Spiel berücksichtigt.

Darüber hinaus geben uns selbsterhobene empirische Daten einen Einblick, was ›Spielqualität‹ jenseits subjektiver Erwägungen auszumachen vermag. Wir zeigen, dass (im Sinne einer Buchadaption) erfolgreiches Spieldesign vor allem von der Integrität des Blends abhängt, d.h. desjenigen mentalen Mischraums, in dem die Charakteridentität kreiert wird. Die o.g. Brettspiele weisen einen unterschiedlichen Grad jener Blendintegrität auf, mit Folgen für die Immersion und Motivation des einzelnen Spielers innerhalb der Gruppe. Im Ganzen betrachtet ist die Möglichkeit von Blending der Motor für die gesamte Spielaktivität.

Die Erzählfunktion der Musik in *Der Herr der Ringe*-Hörspielen
Heidi Steimel

Tolkiens geschriebene Worte sind besonders geeignet für die mündliche Erzählung. Diese wurde von Radiosendern genutzt: Sie produzierten Hörspiele, die heute immer wieder gerne gehört werden. Dabei wurde die Geschichte durch verschiedene Sprecher und durch Musik belebt. Zwei Hörspiele, die deutsche SWF/WDR-Produktion und die englische der BBC, haben trotz ähnlicher Funktionen einen unterschiedlichen Musikstil.

Die erzählende Funktion von Musik in einem Hörspiel ist vergleichbar mit ihrer Rolle in Filmen oder Bühnenstücken. Es gibt »diegetische« Musik, die ihre Quelle innerhalb der Geschichte hat, also von Protagonisten gesungen, gespielt oder gehört wird. Da Tolkiens *Der Herr der Ringe* viele Lieder enthält, ist diese Kategorie wichtig für eine Bearbeitung des Buches. Dann gibt es nicht-diegetische Musik, die von außerhalb hinzugefügt wird. Dazu gehören: Einleitungsmusik als Anfangsthema; Zwischen- oder Brückenmusik, die Änderungen des Ortes oder der Zeit ankündigt; Hintergrundmusik, die dem gesprochenen Wort eine emotionale Komponente hinzufügt. Dabei kann die Musik Menschen oder Orte charakterisieren, indem bei ihrem Auftreten immer das gleiche Instrument oder ein Thema als *Leitmotiv* zu hören ist.

Die Musik zum deutschen Hörspiel wurde von Peter Zwetkoff komponiert, der eine sparsame Instrumentierung und einen minimalistischen Klang benutzte. Die ersten Noten des Liedes *Die Straße gleitet fort* werden als Einleitung und Thema mehrmals wiederholt. Man hört charakterisierende Instrumente: ein Glockenklang für den Einen Ring, Flöten für die weiblichen Hauptpersonen, tiefe Instrumente bei Gefahr, Hörner bei den Rohirrim. Hintergrundmusik unterlegt zum Teil die gesprochenen Worte. Die vertonten Lieder werden von den Darstellern ohne Begleitung gesungen. Dabei sind die Melodien selten so bemerkenswert, dass sie in Erinnerung bleiben.

Im Gegensatz dazu ist die Musik zum BBC-Hörspiel, komponiert von Stephen Oliver, sehr orchestral im Klang und bewusst in der englischen (›pastoralen‹) Tradition gehalten. Auch hier hat die Musik in der Erzählung ähnliche Funktionen sowie einen besonderen Klang für den Ring, Hörner für die Rohirrim usw. Der größte Unterschied findet sich bei den Liedern – sie gehören mit zu den besten Kompositionen für Tolkiens Texte, die ich kenne. Die Melodien sind einprägsam und anrührend. Sie werden zum Teil von den Darstellern, zum Teil von professionellen Musikern, u.a. einem Countertenor und einem Knabensopran, gesungen.

Beide Arten der Musik erfüllen ihre Rolle in der Erzählung und geben dem Hörspiel einen unverwechselbaren Charakter. Ich ziehe die englische Version vor, denn ich halte sie für passender zu Tolkiens Idee, eine englische Mythologie zu erschaffen. Ich finde sie auch musikalisch interessanter, und was ganz besonders ist, empfinde ich sie als kreative Ergänzung. Es gibt einige Augenblicke der musikalischen *eucatastrophe*, die mich beim Hören tief bewegen und dafür sorgen, dass ich mich immer wieder gern von der Musik nach Mittelerde entführen lasse.

Fanfiction als Kritik
Renée Vink

Obwohl der Begriff *Fanfiction* nicht älter als etwa fünfzig Jahre ist, ist die Praxis, sie zu schreiben, alt und respektabel. Große Werke der Literatur basieren auf existierenden Geschichten und wurden durch sie inspiriert – viele arthurianische Romanzen und eine Anzahl der Stücke Shakespeares sind im Wesen Fanfiction – und wenn diese die besten von Fans geschriebenen Geschichten, die im Internet zu finden sind, übertreffen, ist dies nicht per definitionem der Fall. Es liegt eher an internationalen Urheberrechten als an Qualität, wenn erstere kommerziell publiziert werden und letztere nicht, auch wenn die große Mehrheit dieser Texte schweigend übergangen werden kann. Nicht alle publizierten Autoren sind mit auf ihren Werken basierender Fanfiction einverstanden und manche versuchen, sie zu verbieten, aber meist hält das die Fans nicht ab.

Tolkiens Beziehung zum Genre ist ambivalent. Gelegentlich schrieb er etwas, was leicht als Fanfiction angesehen werden kann (z.B. *Sigurd und Gudrún* und *The Fall of Arthur*). Zusätzlich haben seine Schriften über Mittelerde ihrerseits Tausende von Autoren inspiriert – unabhängig von seiner Einstellung gegenüber Fanfiction, die weniger positiv war, als es auf den ersten Blick scheint. Wie dem auch sei, auf seinen Werken basierende Geschichten können interessante Studienobjekte sein. Viele der guten, manchmal von Fans geschrieben, die selbst auch Tolkienforschung betreiben und neben ihren Geschichten wissenschaftliche Artikel publizieren, tauchen so tief in seine zweitgeschaffene Welt ein und betrachten sie so scharf wie wissenschaftliche Artikel und Bücher.

Solche Forschung von Fan-Schriftstellern kann – und tut dies manchmal – zu neuen und originellen Interpretationen führen oder zu kritischen Sichten dessen, was sie vorfinden – von ungenauer Geographie bis hin zu Problemen in sozio-religiösen Strukturen.

Dieser Artikel untersucht Geschichten von acht Autoren tolkieninspirierter Fanfiction, von klaren Interpretationen durch Extrapolationen, Versuchen, gestellte Fragen zu beantworten oder neue zu stellen, über kritische Nuancen und alternative Möglichkeiten bis hin zu Subversionen der Quelltexte oder sogar mehr oder weniger verborgenen Angriffen auf Aspekte der Werke Tolkiens, die diese Fanautoren als unvollständig oder unbefriedigend ansehen.

Alle diese Geschichten haben eine kreative Auseinandersetzung mit den Originalen gemein, die eng verzahnt ist mit neueren Literaturtheorien wie Intertextualität und vor allem Rezeptionsästhetik. Wenn Inspiration eine fruchtbare Einheit mit kritischer Anerkennung eingeht, kann dies zu Resultaten führen, die nicht bloß von Interesse für die Leser von Fanfiction sind, sondern für eine weitere Gemeinschaft von Tolkienfans und Tolkienforschern.

Summaries of the German Essays

Living in Middle-earth – Adaptations of Tolkien in Live Action Roleplay
Stephanie Bauer

Live Action Roleplay for adults, probably the most immediate way to experience fantastic worlds, was up until now mainly a topic for the social sciences, where it was analysed against the phenomenon of children's role plays. After a short introduction on how roleplay games work in principle, this article tries a different approach in applying the ideas Tolkien set in his influential essay *On Fairy-Stories* to the context of roleplay. Parallels can be drawn to the genre of fantasy literature, which also had to emancipate itself from the reputation of a genre for children. By looking into the general clichés cultivated in the portrayal of roleplay characters it can also be shown that the mechanics of adaptation used are similar to those applied in fantasy literature. Of course literary theory cannot be applied as it is, due to the special circumstances of a medium which depends on the material properties of our own world while depicting another one. Both media-specific differences as well as similarities are pointed out, while also showing the specific impact of Tolkien's works. It turns out that Tolkien is the author most frequently named as an inspiration, though his influence can be both factual and merely imagined. Referring to him is, in any case, usually used as a sign of quality.

Narrative Structure in J.R.R. Tolkien's *The Lord of the Rings* and Peter Jackson's Film Adaptation
Julian Tim Morton Eilmann (Aachen)

While most interpretations of Peter Jackson's films are limited to content-related and thematic aspects of the adaptation (especially focusing on additions, omissions and characterisations), this article takes a close look at the structural differences between the book and film version of Tolkien's novel. By comparing how author and filmmaker arrange the story in different ways it becomes clear that Jackson markedly shifts and blends the narrative blocks of Tolkien's novel and thus organises things contrary to Tolkien's strict composition of six separate 'books' that from book three onwards follow the paths of different characters. Jackson instead is keen to create the well-known linear structure that most mainstream movies are based on. This does not mean that Jackson does not heavily incorporate flashbacks, visions and other scenes that break the predominating linearity. Nonetheless, the use of cinematic cross-cutting and an 'economical' narrative approach help to achieve what can be seen as the main structural intentions of the film adaptation: Maximisation of the audience's emotional effect, a fast narrative pace and resulting from that a sense of tension and dread.

To set Jackson's films in context Julian Eilmann refers to professional script writer handbooks and points out that most of the typical principles of Hollywood film making can be found in the Lord of the Rings movie trilogy. With knowledge of this film theoretic background the framework and the intended emotional effects of the films can be understood better. Furthermore, due to the comparison with Jackson's adaptation, we can get a better understanding of Tolkien as an author and his traditional storytelling approach. As the fast-paced style of action cinema is increasingly influencing the writers of thriller or fantasy literature (e.g. best-selling authors like Dan Brown or George R.R. Martin) we can furthermore conclude that Tolkien's narrative structure is in some way out of date. On the other hand, stylistically old-fashioned novel like *The Lord of the Rings* being still a best-seller after more than 60 years shows that Tolkien's block-centred narrative does not deter people to immerse themselves in Middle-earth.

Adaptation:
Poor Copy or Creative Interpretation?
Thomas Fornet-Ponse

Although adaptations are often understood as (poor) copies of an original work and are thus judged according to their faithfulness to the original, it is necessary to regard them as works of art in their own right. 'Adaptation' has a twofold meaning since it signifies the creative and receptive process as well as the formal and definable product of adapting something. Based on Linda Hutcheon's approach, who analyses adaptations as "deliberate, announced, and extended revisitations of prior works" (Hutcheon xiv), this article tries to present them as creative interpretations with many intertextual allusions and references. It is however not sufficient to regard them merely as interpretations, since they are not discursive-theoretical works but independent works of art which are in themselves open for interpretation. Adaptations can be understood as dialogues with other texts (including the adapted works), which are in a dialogue with the adaptations in turn.

An analysis of adaptations as product and process regarding the three fundamental modes of representation (telling, showing and interacting) needs to combine several aspects: the form of an adaptation and how it is influenced by the modes of the adapted work and of the adaptation, the process and motives of adapting, the adaptators, but also the audience—especially concerning its intertextuality and its contribution to interpret the adaptation—and the (cultural, social and historical) context of an adaptation.

Since adaptations tell a story and not only copy it, some scholars propose an analogy to biology insofar as adaptations are the way by which stories evolve and through cultural selection adapt to new times and places. Regarding the history of human imagination, adapting stories is not an exception, but the normal case—as expressed by Tolkien with his "Cauldron of Story".

Anglo-saxon Rohan?
Tolkien's anti-norman Reflex supported by Peter Jackson's Movie Adaptation
Annika Röttinger

Looking at the Rohirrim in J.R.R.Tolkiens *The Lord of the Rings*, one may find many similarities to the anglo-saxons of 10th and 11th century Britain, such as kingship, warfare, ethos, and language. The most significant aspect of rohirric culture though, the importance of horses, suggests a norman model, as anglo-saxon army does not feature cavalry at that time. It is Tolkien's anti-norman attitude that prevents the Rohirrim to resemble anything else than anglo-saxons.

Peter Jackson's movie trilogy (2001-2003) emphasizes the anglo-saxon aspects of rohirric culture, as in the books there are not many visual descriptions. The movies give a visual interpretation of the Rohirrim, which is lacking in the books. Though, when it comes down to more complex subjects, such as ethos and language, the books provide a far deeper insight to the anglo-saxon aspects of rohirric culture.

No Child's Game: Board Games as Adaptations of *The Lord of the Rings*
Christian Weichmann

Board games are not the first thing that comes to mind when thinking about adaptations of a book. But in fact, there are a few board games which use a *Lord of the Rings* theme, definitely more than films or theatrical productions.

There are several reasons why these are not seen as serious adaptations of the book: first, board games are often not seen as an independent work (and a few really are not) but rather as some kind of children's toy. Then, the adaptation in the games sometimes is very superficial and mainly done for commercial reasons. Additionally, some of the adapted games are existing games, like *Chess* or *Monopoly*, which are only designed in LotR fashion. This also shows that the adaptation often is not of the book directly but of an adaptation of it, mainly films.

So what are the reasons to adapt the LotR as a board game? One is of course the idea that if you like board games and LotR, a board game of LotR would be even better—which is often the reason behind fan adaptations. But there is of course also the possibility to use a board game as merchandise to cash in on the film hype, which is often at the root of LotR-ification of existing games. Finally, only a few, mainly traditional, games are really abstract ones. All of the others have a theme, even if it only influences the design, and to attract attention it is advantageous to have a popular theme like LotR for the game.

Why were there so many LotR games published over the last years? Of course, a main reason is the Peter Jackson films, and many games are in fact adaptations of these and not of the book. But an additional reason is the emancipation of board games from the nursery to become a leisure activity for adults which began in the eighties. This led to more complex games which better matched the complexity of the book and also brought the need for adult themes for games. Finally, the LotR games boom was also promoted by some game publishers specialised on such games.

The article takes a deeper look into how one can adapt a book in a game and looks at it as double adaptation: on the one side the adaptation of certain elements (protagonists, places, events etc.) of the book in the game, and on the other the adaptation of elements of an abstract game (game board, pieces, rules etc.) to a given theme. There are some elements from the book which are taken into most of the existing games and mostly in a similar way.

Middle-earth as a Trading Card Game. Is this possible?

Thorsten Werner

In the 1990s, collectible card games emerged, which are games based on up to thousands of collectible and tradable cards. This article focuses on the Middle-earth Collectible Card Game (ME:CCG) which was released in 1995 by Iron Crown Enterprises (I.C.E.), and is based on *The Lord of the Rings* and *The Hobbit*. As I.C.E. went bankrupt in 1998, only seven editions were released.

In the game, the player takes the role of an avatar (one of five wizards) who summons characters to explore Middle-earth. The characters can influence mighty factions and allies, e.g. the Rohirrim or Tom Bombadil, find legendary items, e.g. Glamdring or play out certain events, e.g. the Return of the King, to get marshalling points. These marshalling points represent the ability of the wizard to lead the army of the free people. Alternatively, it is possible to destroy the One Ring at Mount Doom. During a movement phase, characters can encounter hazards played by an opponent, which can be attacking creatures, events (e.g. impassable river) or corruption—a system to reflect the lure of power. Some game mechanics, e.g. combat, are resolved by two six-sided dice.

The ME:CCG is not limited to wizards: In later editions the options to play a ringwraith (The Lidless Eye), a fallen-wizard such as Saruman (White Hand) or the Balrog of Moria (The Balrog) as avatar were added to the game. One feature of the game is the game-play of minions, which is comparable to the game-play of heroes. The destruction / recovery / mastery of the One Ring is however only possible (based on chance) for heroes, as in LotR.

The article concludes that the adaption is a successful one. The whole setting has undergone only lesser changes to fit into game-play in comparison with the novels. The idea of a competition between the avatars of one alignment can also be extracted from the references. One major difference is the time frame, as Bard may for example be in the same group as Pippin even though they never met in the novels. As the description of Sauron's minions in the novels is very limited, only the first edition cards can be referenced to the novels. In later editions, the amount of freely invented cards increases while the amount of cards based on the original decreases. Despite that, the game is one of the most complex trading card games extant and even though the publication of new cards ceased in 1998, it still has a large fan base and new players experience the world of ME:CCG.

Reviews/Rezensionen

Arnulf Krause:
Die wirkliche Mittelerde. Tolkiens Mythologie und ihre Wurzeln im Mittelalter
Darmstadt: Konrad Theiss, 2012, 232 S.

Nein, es handelt sich bei diesem Buch nicht um die deutsche Übersetzung von Brian Bates' 2002 erschienener Studie *The Real Middle-earth* (London: Pan Books) – obwohl es in Aufbau, Inhalt und Zielpublikum seinem englischen Vorgänger sehr nahe kommt. Dies ist vielleicht auch nicht weiter verwunderlich, da auch Arnulf Krause ein Fachgelehrter ist, der sich mit der mittelalterlichen Geschichte und Kultur Europas gut auskennt und Tolkien mit einem Blick auf die Parallelen zur europäischen Kulturgeschichte liest.

Der Autor strukturiert sein Buch nach Themen wie Elben, Riesen, Zwerge, Götter, Religion, Grabdenkmäler, Drachen, Schätze, Schwerter, Magie etc. Er gibt jeweils im ersten Teil eines Kapitels die für das Thema relevanten Passagen aus dem *Herrn der Ringe*, dem *Hobbit* oder dem *Silmarillion* und führt dann relativ ausführlich die mittelalterlichen realweltlichen Parallelen aus. Dabei berücksichtigt er in etwa gleichwertig die nordischen, westgermanischen und keltischen Traditionen.

Da Arnulf Krause bereits einige (eher populärwissenschaftliche) Bücher über die Germanen und Kelten verfasst hat, dürften sich diese Kapitelteile wohl ›im Autopilot‹ geschrieben haben. Sie sind dann zwar gut und informativ zu lesen, aber die Rückbindung an und vertiefte Auseinandersetzung mit Tolkiens Texten fehlt weitestgehend – Tom Shippey zeigt, wie man das besser machen kann.

Mein Fazit:
Krauses ›wirkliche Mittelerde‹ ist ein Buch, das sich für Anfänger als Einstiegslektüre durchaus eignet – mit der Empfehlung, danach gleich mit Shippeys *Der Weg nach Mittelerde* weiterzumachen.

Thomas Honegger

Tolkien Studies. An Annual Scholarly Review. Volume IX. 2012
Morgantown: West Virginia University Press, 154 S.

Die Krise, die Douglas Andersons Weggang aus dem Herausgebergremium auslöste (siehe sein Blog), steht zwar nicht direkt in kausalem Zusammenhang mit dem etwas schwindsüchtig wirkenden Band 9, aber auch so scheinen sich die Schwierigkeiten in der Produktion bemerkbar gemacht zu haben. Der Band erschien mit großer Verspätung, weshalb er auch erst in diesem *Hither Shore* besprochen wird. Die gute Nachricht ist, dass *Tolkien Studies* mit Band 10 (2013) das Formtief überwunden hat und sich wieder in gewohnter Stärke präsentiert.

Doch zurück zu *Tolkien Studies* 9. Neben den Besprechungen, der Übersicht zu den Tolkien-relevanten Studien für 2009 und den Bibliographien der Neuerscheinungen findet der Leser ganze vier (relativ kurze) Essays. Drei davon gehören in die Kategorie ›Arda Studien‹, während der erste Aufsatz von Peter Grybauskas literaturwissenschaftlicher Natur ist. Er untersucht das Motiv der ›untold tales‹ in Tolkiens Werk – eine narrative Technik, die u.a. den Eindruck ›literarisch-kultureller Tiefe‹ vermittelt, wie Tolkien sie aus Gedichten wie *Beowulf* kannte. Grybauskas zeigt anhand zweier Beispiele aus dem *Herrn der Ringe* auf, welche Funktionen dieses Motiv haben kann, und versucht, eine Kategorisierung zu entwerfen, die auf der Dichotomie ›explicitly vs. implicitly untold tales‹ beruht. Die als Appendix beigefügte Liste mit Textstellen zeigt, dass das Thema eine weiterführende Behandlung verdient (evt. im weiter gesteckten Rahmen von Tolkiens Paratextualität) und die vorliegende Studie als ein erster wertvoller Impuls in dieser Richtung verstanden werden kann.

Die übrigen Aufsätze behandeln Themen der ›Arda Studien‹. So zeigt Gerard Hynes in seinem sehr lesbaren Essay auf, wie die zeitgenössische Diskussion um Wegeners Theorie des Kontinentaldrifts sich auch in Tolkiens Sekundärweltschöpfung widerspiegelt. Douglas C. Kane und Amelia Rutledge hingegen beschäftigen sich beide mit ›legalistischen‹ Themen. Während Kane einen relativ umfassenden Überblick über Tolkiens Verwendung rechtlicher Konzepte (und deren Entwicklung) innerhalb seines Werkes gibt, konzentriert sich Rutledge auf den Fall ›Finwë und Míriel‹. Dieser ist von Interesse, da sich anhand der Frage nach der ›Rechtmäßigkeit‹ einer Wiederverheiratung Finwës nicht nur Probleme juristischer, sondern auch ontologischer und theologischer Natur erörtern lassen.

Fazit: *Tolkien Studies* 9 ist von der thematischen Breite wie auch von der geringen Anzahl der wissenschaftlichen Aufsätze (trotz des inhaltlich hohen Niveaus) her der bisher ›schwächste‹ Band – was zeigt, dass auch das beste Herausgeberteam auf gute und zahlreiche Beiträge angewiesen ist, um einen guten Band zu produzieren.

Thomas Honegger

Fastitocalon. Studies in Fantasticism Ancient to Modern. Vol. 3-1 & 2 (2013). Humour and the Fantastic.

Trier: WVT, 2013, 127 pp.

Mit diesem Band wird die erfolgreich gestartete von Thomas Honegger und Fanfan Chen herausgegebene Zeitschrift zur phantastischen Literatur *Fastitocalon* fortgesetzt. Nach den bisherigen Ausgaben *Immortals and the Undead* sowie *The European Tradition of the Fantastic* geht es nun um *Humour and the Fantastic*. Dies mag zwar – wie die Herausgeber in ihrer Einführung einräumen – manche überraschen, insofern Humor nicht zu den Hauptcharakteristika der Phantastik zählt oder direkt mit ihr assoziiert würde. Gleichwohl ist die zwischenzeitliche Abwesenheit des Humors (bis zur Wiedereinführung durch Terry Pratchett?) aber nicht repräsentativ, wie diverse der acht vorliegenden und allesamt lesenswerten Beiträge belegen. Die weite Ausrichtung der Zeitschrift zeigt sich in den behandelten Autoren: Neben zwei französischen Schriftstellern aus dem 19. Jahrhundert (Théophile Gautier und Villiers de l'Isle-Adam) werden u.a. H.G. Wells, aber auch Terry Pratchett oder Jonathan Safran Foer besprochen.

Den Beginn macht indes eine qualitative, nicht-repräsentative Untersuchung zum Umgang kleiner Kinder mit Humor und fantastischen Geschichten (anhand der beiden Kinder der Autorin Virginia Lowe): Lowe zeigt den Kontrast zwischen wahrgenommener Realität und Behauptungen des »phantastischen« Textes und kommt zu dem Schluss, dass Humor Kinder zu meta-fiktionalem Denken zwingt.

Anschließend bespricht Rosalie Sinopoulou anhand von Werken Cazottes, Walpoles, Kafkas sowie Borges die Beziehung von Humor und Furcht und arbeitet die Funktion des Humors als unsere hauptsächliche Beziehung zum menschlichen Element im Übernatürlichen heraus, der trösten kann und daran erinnert, dass selbst im Unbekannten Lachen existiert.

Einer ähnlichen Thematik widmet sich Françoise Dupeyron-Lafay, wenn sie H.G. Wells' Erzählung *The Invisible Man* auf die verschiedenen narrativen Strategien untersucht, mit denen eigentlich furchterregende Dinge zu komischen oder lustigen werden und somit der Eindruck des Grotesken erzeugt wird.

Valery Rion untersucht auf der Basis der Freud'schen Definition von Humor den Humor in den phantastischen Geschichten Théophile Gautiers, betont dabei die Inkongruenz als Quelle sowohl der Phantastik als auch des Humors, geht ausführlich auf die linguistische Ebene (Wortspiele, Bedeutungsebenen etc.) ein und stellt ferner *Omphale* als eine Parodie eines Textes von Vivant Denon vor.

Die kritische Funktion des Humors und die Durchbrechung von Spannung und Illusion durch Lachen werden von Isabelle Percebois anhand von *Claire Lenoir* von Villiers de l'Isle-Adam aufgezeigt, indem sie vor allem die Destabilisierung des Textes durch Ironie und Duplizität (ein doppelter Text, Personen mit doppelter Persönlichkeit etc.) darstellt.

Die eigenwillige Verbindung von Komik, (magischem) Realismus und Phantastik in Jonathan Safran Foers *Everything Is Illuminated* nimmt Mail Marques de Azevedo in den Blick und unterstreicht – neben der fragmentarischen und verschachtelten Struktur dieses Romans, seinem postmodernen Umgang mit literarischen Genres und dem meta-fiktionalen Charakter – die angedeutete Möglichkeit der Wiederherstellung.

Mit Alma Haltofs Beitrag zu den unterschiedlichen Strategien der polnischen und tschechischen Übersetzungen von Pratchetts *Reaper Man* wird auch die komplexe Frage der Übersetzung humoristischer Elemente behandelt, wobei die domestizierende Strategie des tschechischen Übersetzers zwar den Lesern einen leichteren Zugang ermöglicht, aber auch viele Elemente vernachlässigt, während die polnische Übersetzung spezifische Situationen betont und damit an Kohärenz verliert.

Schließlich untersucht Ewlina Nowacka Rick Riordans *Percy Jackson and the Olympians* unter starkem Rückgriff auf Durkheim und Eliade auf die komplexe Wechselwirkung des Profanen und des Heiligen, der die Schilderung der griechischen Götter als zeitgenössische Personen (die Mobiltelefone benutzen oder eine Eheberatung aufsuchen) gerecht werde, da sie zwar anfänglich als lächerliche Charaktere erscheinen, ihr andersweltlicher Charakter aber immer zu spüren und ihre stabilisierende Funktion für die Gesellschaft präsent sei.

Wenngleich im Rahmen dieses Bandes nur eine kleine Auswahl von Autoren und Themen bezüglich Humor und Phantastik untersucht werden kann, zeigt sie doch, wie lohnend solche Analysen sein können und wie weit verbreitet – geographisch wie chronologisch – Humor in der Phantastik ist.

Thomas Fornet-Ponse

Barbara Kowalik (ed.): O What a Tangled Web: Tolkien and Medieval Literature. A View from Poland.

Zurich/Jena: Walking Tree Publishers, 2013, 196 pp.

Early on in her introduction, the editor of this collection quotes Thomas Honegger's opinion that previous studies of the medieval influences on Tolkien "have left little of importance to discover in this field", and there is little amongst these articles to persuade me of the contrary. This is not to say that many of them are not interesting in themselves, but overall they fill in a few blank spaces rather than offering any particularly new insights.

"The Lord of the Rings and the Interlacement Technique"[1] by Joanna Kokot builds on work done by Tom Shippey and others. Kokot contends that, whereas medieval interlacement leaves a sense of vague geography and causation, the different paths taken by the members of the Fellowship display a very precise plotting of time and place, with numerous cross-references. The article explores some of the situations where riddles are set both for the characters and for the reader, such as Pippin's brooch discarded in the grasslands of Rohan, where it is important to remember exactly who knows what.

In "Orality and Literacy in Middle-earth", Bartłomiej Błaszkiewicz applies research in Primary World oral cultures to Tolkien's world. The Elves have both primary orality (a concept that he does not define) and literacy, so they represent culture at a high point. Tolkien's human societies lack the benefit of longevity and long memory, so they need the support of writing with its attendant dangers of physical loss. The Hobbits are the most literate in their everyday activities, as reflected by Bilbo's song of Eärendil in Rivendell, which is clearly composed on paper, even if the delivery and reception are oral. Unfortunately Błaszkiewicz simply records these observations as facts and does not pursue the question of what literary effect is achieved by this distinction in a book which contains so much metafictional commentary.

The third article, "Rohan and the Social Codes of Historic Epic and Chivalric Romance" by Justyna Brzezińska, sets out to demonstrate that Rohan is not just a depiction of a variety of early English society but also has features of the later medieval feudal and chivalric culture, as instanced in the ceremony of appointing Éowyn regent, which the author claims shows similarities to early forms of dubbing a knight. Unfortunately the article then tails off into a rather speculative exegesis of Éowyn's conception of her own role. The amount of paraphrase of events in the story tends to make the argument unfocused, and the author seems to think that Éowyn's broken arm was sustained from her blow that killed the Nazgûl, allowing her to claim that she was not wounded by the enemy.

Two articles deal with the revered queen figures in Tolkien's works: "Elbereth the Star-Queen Seen in the Light of Medieval Marian Devotion" by Barbara Kowalik and "Tolkien's Queen-Women in LotR" by Maria Błaszkiewicz. The first of these contends that, although Galadriel has often been compared to the Virgin Mary, Elbereth from the Silmarillion fits the role more accurately. Kowalik makes a convincing argument by means of some perceptive textual analysis of the scenes where characters invoke Elbereth for aid, but she falls for the temptation to over-egg the pudding by comparing the elvish love of dawn and dusk with the offices of compline and matins, while by the end of the article we are led by association to suspect religious significance in practically every mention of stars, which rather detracts from the entirely valid main argument.

---

[1] Many of the titles in this volume are long, so occasionally, as here, I have shortened them.

Maria Błaszkiewicz claims that the female figures in LotR, in contrast to the more individual, active men, gain importance through representing symbolic, static guardians of sanctuaries. Galadriel is an obvious example, but even Mrs Maggot looking after her guests and Ioreth (consistently mis-spelled throughout) as the guardian of the memories of her people fit into the pattern. This is a brave attempt to counter the usual criticisms of Tolkien's women by claiming that the contrast of roles is deliberate, though some female critics might consider it no worse to be virtually ignored than to be turned into purely symbolic figures, however, awe-inspiring.

Katarzyna Blacharska's "The Fallen: Milton's Satan and Tolkien's Melkor" traces a number of similarities between the two fallen angels, summarised in a table at the end. However, I feel that the writer's contention of consistent and detailed influence on Tolkien from Milton's poem rather than from other versions of a non-scriptural tradition is not convincingly proved. It might have been useful to consider what similarities are inevitable between two characters holding a similar position within differing mythological schemes. It need hardly be added that Tolkien would certainly not have considered *Paradise Lost* as medieval literature!

"The Influence of Selected Medieval Icelandic Sagas on Tolkien's Works for Children" by Renata Leśniakiewicz-Drzymała has the virtue of going straight to the point of a clearly delineated topic. It fills in some of the details of motifs from Old Norse literature which can be traced in *The Hobbit*, *Farmer Giles of Ham* and *The Adventures of Tom Bombadil*. Beorn can be seen as an equivalent to the Old Norse berserker, while Bilbo's riddling conversation with Smaug echoes the exchanges between Sigurd and Fáfnir in the *Fáfnismál*.

For most of his article "Tolkien's Critique of the Northern Courage", Łukasz Neubauer does little more than summarise *The Homecoming of Beorhtnoth* and subsequent commentaries on it. Finally, in the last page and a half, he traces Tolkien's increasing concern with the nature of courage in his fiction: Thorin and Boromir, representing the old concept of personal (vain)glory, are contrasted with Gandalf on the Bridge of Khazad-dûm and Aragorn at the Black Gate, who risk combat in an apparently sacrificial situation not for the sake of their own reputation but for a higher purpose. Neubauer imagines in this something resembling a *post mortem* debate with scholars who had clearly been impressed by the Old Norse theory of courage, including his old colleague E.V. Gordon. The idea is tempting and needs to be put at the centre of the article, rather than being relegated to the conclusion.

"What Exactly Does Tolkien Argue for in '*Beowulf*: The Monsters and the Critics'? An Attempt at a Metacriticism" by Andrzej Wicher is perhaps the most original contribution to the collection. In his opinion, Tolkien concedes that there are manifest weaknesses in *Beowulf* but attempts to pass them off as strengths. He points out similarities between Tolkien's rhetoric and that of the American New Critic J.C. Ransom, before going on to view *Beowulf* as essentially a poem about the human condition, which he links with the main argument of *On Fairy-Stories*. This article is not always easy to follow or summarise, since the argument is not linear but wanders off into a whole slur of subsidiary issues. Its two major weaknesses are that Wicher speculates on what Tolkien saw as the relationship between literature and linguistic research without referring to the Valedictory Lecture which appears in the same volume as the *Beowulf* lecture, and he makes guesses as to what Tolkien thought of as "magic" without considering what he wrote in *Letters*, e.g. no. 155.

As far as I know, this is the first collection of articles all by Polish literary critics to be published in a language other than Polish. The time must be ripe for it, since Tolkien has been known in Poland for many years; in fact the Polish translation of LotR pre-dates both the German and the French versions. This volume is in itself a mixed bag but it is a welcome milestone in the progressive internationalisation of Tolkien criticism. Allan Turner

Julian Eilmann & Allan Turner: Tolkien's Poetry
Zurich/Jena: Walking Tree Publishers, 2013, 221 pp.

This work is indispensable in that it finally fills a lacunae in Tolkien studies. As Michael Drout observes in the introduction, Tolkien's poetry has often been neglected as a subject of study. Nevertheless Julian Eilmann and Allan Turner have compiled a work that illustrates how *The Hobbit* and *The Lord of the Rings* are greatly enriched by the poetry interspaced in the narrative prose. Poetry and poetics can be intimidating to casual readers who have not a background in its theory. Perhaps this is also a reason Tolkien's poetry seems to be overlooked by fans and students. But it is exactly this theory which clarifies the general principles of poetry and enriches the reading experience. On the other hand, Tolkien's poetry, as this book makes clear, has also been overlooked by those with a background in literary theory and poetics.

Tolkien's Poetry, however, is not written only for academia. It does not start with assumptions that the reader is familiar with terms, meter, rhythm, and forms. Indeed, what is nice about this volume is that the contributors make their scholarship accessible to the casual reader of Tolkien's work while at the same time bringing into focus subjects which need further scholarly attention. Many of the contributors remark Tolkien's poetry being the most widely read poetry of the 20th century. It only goes to follow that a volume about that poetry be equally accessible and this book strives to do just that.

In the first essay, Tom Shippey takes the time to summarise and explain the alliterative types of the Siever's system, using Tolkien's own examples, so that we have a basic idea of what alliteration is and what Tolkien was doing with it. While Shippey tells us that "[T]hese principles, however, are not easy..." somehow he makes them easier to understand and his explanations not only help us to appreciate Tolkien as a writer of alliterative poetry but also help us through the essays which follow.

Focusing not simply on Middle-earth, *Tolkien's Poetry* explores poems Tolkien wrote to W.H. Auden, his experiments in tempo and meter, poetical function in his prose, his poetic expressions of 'Faery' as well as the subtle spirituality embedded in his work, his scrutiny of Old English and other vocabularies, the effect of his poetry on the screen, and Tolkien's possible poetical influences. Naturally, such a short volume cannot go into great detail of all the aspects of Tolkien as a poet and of his poems. Nevertheless, what this work does and succeeds in, is introducing us to the various aspects of language, forms, genres, and modes of composition that are relevant to Tolkien the poet and his works. The book points scholars interested in poetics and Tolkien in the direction of further research and it enriches the reading experience of the casual reader by its accessibility and enlightening explanations of the relationship and importance of poetry to Tolkien's works.

Finally, by illustrating the importance of Tolkien's poetry through the essays of the contributing scholars, *Tolkien's Poetry* also makes the argument for a future publication of Tolkien's collected poems, an updated edition of *The Trumpets of Faërie*, which Allan Turner tells us in his conclusion was "promptly rejected" in 1916.   Richard Gallant

Adam Roberts: The Riddles of the *Hobbit*.
Houndmills, Basingstoke: Palgrave Macmillan, 2013,186 S.

Was ist von einem Professor zu erwarten, der an der Royal Holloway Universität in London die Literatur des 19. Jahrhunderts unterrichtet und sich gleichzeitig als preisgekrönter SF&Fantasy-Autor sowie als Verfasser der 2003 erschienenen *Hobbit*-Parodie *The Soddit* hervorgetan hat? Viel – aber anscheinend nicht unbedingt auf einem ihm fachfremden Gebiet. Und das ist das große Problem dieses Buches.

Roberts ist zu sehr Literat, als dass es ihm gelingt, die mediävistischen und philologischen Aspekte seines Themas strukturiert und kompetent zu behandeln (wobei hier ›Literat‹ im Tolkien'schen Sinne von ›Lit.‹ vs. ›Lang.‹ zu verstehen ist). Dies wäre vielleicht nicht so schlimm, wenn er das Hauptaugenmerk des ganzen Buches auf der Verortung des *Hobbits* und des *Herrn der Ringe* innerhalb des Fantasy-Genres gelegt hätte – denn in diesem Gebiet ist Roberts sowohl als Autor wie auch als Kritiker kompetent und bestens qualifiziert. Stattdessen nimmt er den Leser auf eine Achterbahnfahrt mit, die zwar ein paar unterhaltsame Höhepunkte aufweist, jedoch mindestens ebenso viele Tiefpunkte. Dem Buch fehlt dementsprechend jegliche stringente Struktur und argumentative Ausgewogenheit, und die Kapitel variieren sowohl in der Länge (von sechs bis fünfundzwanzig Seiten) als auch in der Qualität.

Nicht dass die 186 Seiten ohne jegliche Einsichten wären! So sind Roberts Überlegungen zur SF & Fantasy als ›ironische bzw. metaphorische Literatur‹ durchaus bedenkenswert und anregend. Für Roberts stehen SF & Fantasy in einem Gegensatz zum ›Realismus‹ des mimetischen Modus und können so die primär- bzw. realweltlichen Ereignisse aus einem unabhängigen Blickwinkel kommentieren. Rätsel funktionieren ähnlich, indem sie dem Leser mit Hilfe metaphorischer Ausdrucksweise bzw. durch Verfremdung mittels Kategorienwechsel eine neue Sicht auf altbekannte Dinge eröffnen.

Leider entwickelt Roberts dieses Konzept nicht weiter, und die angerissenen Ideen spielen auch in den nachfolgenden Kapiteln kaum eine Rolle. Dabei wäre der Ansatz ideal mit Tolkiens *mooreeffoc*-Konzept und der ›Verzauberung‹ (enchantment), wie sie in seinem *On Fairy-Stories* vorgestellt werden, zu kombinieren gewesen. Auch die Idee, dass *Der Hobbit* als ganzes Buch selbst eine Art Rätsel darstellt, kommt nicht wirklich zum Tragen. Stattdessen präsentiert uns Roberts ein Sammelsurium von Ideen, die oftmals nur sehr lose miteinander verbunden sind. Dies beginnt mit dem (Nicht-)Versuch, den zentralen Gegenstand seines Buches, das Rätsel, zu definieren. Allzu schnell bricht Roberts die Fachdiskussion ab und lässt den Leser mit dem Allgemeinplatz allein, dass auch das Lesen eines Textes eine ‚Enträtselung' darstelle (S. 6).

Dass Roberts durchaus kompetent, unterhaltsam und für den Durchschnittsleser verständlich mit der literaturwissenschaftlichen Fachterminologie umgehen kann, beweist er in seinem brillanten Dialog zwischen Ödipus und der Sphinx (S. 53f). Darin besiegt Ödipus die Sphinx nicht durch die Beantwortung des Rätsels, sondern durch die subversive Hinterfragung der verwendeten Begriffe. Mehr davon wäre höchst willkommen gewesen. Roberts versucht sich auch an einem kurzen Überblick zur germanischen Rätseltradition, wobei er nicht immer zwischen der früheren, stark von der lateinischen Antike beeinflussten angelsächsischen Tradition und der späteren, eher noch heidnisch geprägten altnordischen Tradition unterscheidet.

Im langen Kapitel »Riddles in the Dark« werden die Rätsel aus *Der Hobbit* genauer untersucht und mit anderen ›rätselähnlichen‹ Texten wie z.B. dem Goblin-Lied »Fifteen birds in five firtrees« verglichen. Manche der vorgeschlagenen Lösungen sind durchaus überzeugend, andere eher spekulativ und andere wiederum rein assoziativ – wie seine These, dass die zehn Rätsel die Struktur des ganzen Buches widerspiegeln.

Im Kapitel »The Riddles of All-Wise« geht er noch einen Schritt weiter und nimmt die Kategorie der akrostischen Rätsel (Rätsel, deren Gesamtlösung sich aus den Anfangsbuchstaben der gesuchten Begriffe zusammensetzt) als Anlass, die Hobbit-Rätsel als Akrostichon für den Begriff »Alvissmæl« zu interpretieren. Das »Alvissmæl« selbst ist ein altnordischer Rätselwettkampf zwischen dem Gott Thor und dem Zwerg Alwis (›Allweis‹), und ein versteckter Hinweis auf diesen Text würde durchaus zu Tolkien passen. Die Beweisführung ist jedoch mehr als zweifelhaft. So schreibt Roberts, dass der erste Buchstabe des Akrostichon, der Buchstabe A, sich aus dem ersten Berg-Rätsel ergibt, denn »we can see the visual pun between the letter A and a mountainous peak – in Tolkien's own invented script, the Tehtar vowel sign for A is the shape Λ« (S. 84, wobei er seine Information zum Tehtar aus Noels The Languages of Tolkien's Middle-earth, S. 50, 1974 bezieht). Dabei berücksichtigt Roberts jedoch nicht, dass die Tehtar Vokale beim Schreiben nur als kleine Akzente oberhalb der Tehtar Primärlaute erscheinen – vergleichbar mit dem Zirkumflex z.B. im î ... was beim besten Willen nicht sehr ›bergisch‹ anmutet.

Auch die übrigen Kapitel lassen den Leser mit gemischten Gefühlen zurück. Oftmals hatte ich den Eindruck, dass Roberts das Potenzial seiner Ideen nicht entwickeln kann und es eines Co-Autors mit einer philologischen Ausbildung der alten Schule (Tom Shippey wäre der ideale Kandidat) bedurft hätte, um Roberts' Ideen stringent zu entwickeln und ihn vor den gröbsten Schnitzern (und den typischen Tippfehlern in den mittelalterlichen Namen) zu bewahren. So finden wir Tippfehler wie »Aldheim« anstelle von »Aldhelm« (S. 80ff), »Grendl« (S. 103) anstelle von »Grendel« oder »Heotot« (S. 103) anstelle von »Heoreot«. Bei den inhaltlichen Fehlern sind zu nennen: Die altnordische Göttin Hel ist weiblich und somit kein Gott (S. 40), Beowulf ist ein Gaute aus Südschweden und kein Däne (S. 111), das in der *Legend of Sigurd and Gudrún* verwendete Versmaß ist kein »imitated pastiche of Anglo-Saxon alliterative verse« (S. 139), und Snorri Sturluson war ganz sicher kein König (S. 58).

Überdies fehlen einige zentrale Studien zu den Rätseln. Mein Aufsatz »My Most Precious Riddle: Eggs and Rings Revisited« in *Tolkien Studies* 10:89-103 erschien zu spät (September 2013), um vom Autor rezipiert zu werden. Jedoch Verlyn Fliegers »Bilbo's Neck Riddle« in ihrem kürzlich veröffentlichten Buch *Green Suns and Faërie* (2012) wie auch Nigel Barleys »Structural Aspects of the Anglo-Saxon Riddle« in *Semiotica* 10.2:143-175 aus dem Jahr 1974 und Tom Shippeys *Poems of Wisdom and Learning in Old English* (Cambridge: D.S. Brewer 1976) waren leicht zugänglich und hätten substanziell zum Thema beigetragen.

In den besagten Punkten möchte ich auch den Verlag (bzw. die Verlage) mit in die Pflicht nehmen. Leider ist es heutzutage Usus, dass kaum einer der großen Verlage mehr ein Lektorat anbietet. Allerhöchstens gibt es eine Hilfestellung mit dem Layout, aber eine inhaltlich-fachliche Betreuung fehlt zumeist. Es darf dann auch nicht verwundern, dass immer öfter ›unfertige‹, strukturell unausgewogene und in manchen Aspekten fehlerhafte Studien das Licht der Publikation erblicken (ich möchte an Arne Zetterstens *J.R.R. Tolkien's Double Worlds and Creative Process* von 2011 im gleichen Verlag erinnern).

Roberts' Buch ist zwar kein völliger Reinfall und der Leser wird darin manche amüsante oder interessante Anregung finden, aber – und dies kommt in meiner Besprechung deutlich zum Ausdruck – es ärgert mich sehr, dass es anscheinend nicht mehr für notwendig erachtet wird, mehr Sorgfalt, Fleiß und ehrliche Arbeit in das Produkt ›Buch‹ zu investieren. Als Blogeinträge wären Roberts Kapitel ideal (wenn auch manchmal etwas zu lang), aber zwischen zwei Buchdeckeln erwarte ich mehr!   Thomas Honegger

Christopher Scarf: The Ideal of Kingship in the Writings of Charles Williams, C.S. Lewis and J.R.R. Tolkien. Divine Kingship is Reflected in Middle-earth.

Cambridge: James Clarke & Co., 2013, 202 pp.

This book is a welcome addition to Inklings studies, a discipline with a rich potential for comparative literary studies. Scarf's monograph focusses on an analysis of one topic (the theme of kingship) in the works of three of the Inklings: Charles Williams, C.S. Lewis and J.R.R. Tolkien. He bases his book on his much longer PhD (396 pp, University of Sussex, 2007), which has been available as PDF on the net. The study's 'academic roots' are clearly visible in form of a clear thesis, a balanced chapter-structure (something too often missing in other books …) and an approachable scholarly style.

While the main argument is straightforward, namely that all three writers saw the king as the vice-regent of God on earth, it is almost impossible to summarize Scarf's detailed and knowledgeable chapter-by-chapter analysis of the individual representations of kingship in each of the three Inklings. He presents an in-depth, primary-text based analysis that is supported by the writers' statements on the topic in letters or essays and sets those into the wider context of their political and religious convictions. This bio-bibliographical approach has the advantage of privileging the primary texts and avoids imposing a (›partialising‹) reading by subordinating the texts to theoretical concepts. These are not missing, but subordinate to the textual analysis and in the service of an elucidation of the works under discussion. It is therefore a rather minor sin of omission that Scarf, in his discussion of Williams' "distinction between the monarch *qua* monarch and as a private person" (p. 23), does indeed describe but not refer to Kantorowicz' concept of the King's Two Bodies, which would have provided the ideal larger theoretical framework for his analysis of this aspect.[2]

Formally, the study consists of four parts, of which the first three are dedicated to a discussion of the individual conceptions of kingship in each of the three Inklings respectively. Applying the same structure for each author, Scarf first discusses the historical notions of kingship relevant, which he then follows by an analysis of the central themes and concludes with an exploration of the ideal of kingship. This division also allows readers interested in only one of the three authors discussed to go directly to the relevant chapters of the book. The fourth part brings together once more the findings of his study and presents a final comparison of Williams, Lewis and Tolkien.

It is a strength of this book that it engages with the texts in detail, making fine distinctions and arguing within a clearly delineated framework. In order to follow the argument fully, a very good knowledge of the primary texts is required—and anyone who has tried to read Williams' Arthurian poems will know that this is sometimes very hard to achieve. Scarf's book, like his original PhD thesis, is not an 'easy read' but indispensable reading for all those who want to engage on an academic level with the topic of kingship in Tolkien or his two fellow Inklings.

Thomas Honegger

Tolkien Studies. An Annual Scholarly Review. Volume X. 2013
Morgantown: West Virginia University Press, 311 pp.

The tenth volume of *Tolkien Studies* is thinner than some of the recent numbers, but nevertheless it offers eight articles plus one shorter note containing a little-known poem by Tolkien. These contributions will be examined in three groups: those dealing with specific textual features and

---

2   See Ernst H. Kantorowicz. *The King's Two Bodies. A Study in Mediaeval Political Theology.* Princeton, 1957. While it is a minor sin of omission for a PhD student not to include all the relevant secondary literature, I would have expected his PhD supervisors to catch this one.

possible influences on them, those of a theoretical nature, whether literary or theological, and those which relate Tolkien's writing to political or social questions in the primary world.

Among the articles of a textual nature, Nils Ivar Agøy's "Vague or Vivid? Descriptions in *The Lord of the Rings*" examines the contention that descriptions in that novel are deliberately left vague so that the reader is forced to supply the details based on his or her own experience, and so take a more active role in the reading process. On the basis of an informal analysis he concludes that persons are described not so that we can see them but so that we can react to what we take to be their personality; this is true particularly of the main characters, with whom readers may identify. There is more detail in the description of places, particularly refuges such as Bombadil's house, Wellinghall, or even Helm's Deep, although mountains tend to march vaguely in the distance. This is a result of the close hobbit perspective, which contributes in this way to keeping the reader submerged in the text.

In "My Most Precious Riddle: Eggs and Rings Revisited", Thomas Honegger takes a speculative, even playful look at whether Tolkien really needed to re-write the Gollum episode of *The Hobbit* when the nature of the One Ring was established. It is usually agreed that its addictive nature would have made it impossible for Gollum to offer it as a present. However, Honegger argues that re-reading the earlier book in the light of LotR would incline the careful reader to interpret it as an early symptom of Gollum's love-hate relationship with his Precious, with the Ring also exerting its own will. This might give new significance to the "box without hinges, key or lid" as a prefiguration of Bilbo's non-riddle, "What have I got in my pocket?", and as a parallel to certain ambiguous Old English riddles Tolkien must have known.

"Tom Bombadil's Last Song: Tolkien's *Once Upon A Time*" by Kris Swank gives a useful presentation of a little-known poem that is not easily available elsewhere. She suggests that these three stanzas are a late addition to the Bombadil story, written after the publication of *The Adventures of Tom Bombadil* and *The Road Goes Ever On*. This wistful little poem is not in the usual Bombadil metre, and introduces the mysterious "lintips", which have a mousy smell and are the only things that will not talk to Tom, undermining his otherwise undisputed position as the Master.

Michael Organ's article "Tolkien's Japonisme: Prints, Dragons, and a Great Wave" is chiefly concerned with Tolkien's artwork, although it ties this in with motifs in the text. He attributes greater importance to Tolkien's early collection of Japanese prints than do other critics such as Hammond and Scull, and also traces the Japanese influence through the work of Walter Crane. Asian visualisations of dragons may have played a part in Tolkien's conception of the creature, while views of Mount Fuji could have suggested the isolated mountain structures seen in Erebor and Amon Ereb. *The Great Wave Off Shore of*

Reviews / Rezensionen   *Hither Shore 10 (2013)*   243

Kanagawa by Hokusai, reproduced on the cover of the volume, is reminiscent of Tolkien's recurrent dream which he incorporated into the fall of Númenor.

There are three articles of a more theoretical or philosophical nature. One of these, "'The Web of Story': Structuralism in Tolkien's *On Fairy-Stories*" by Derek Shank, works well enough if the reader is prepared to accept a loose definition of structuralism, as the author suggests. This attempt to find a consistent line of argument in what can appear to be an erudite but diffuse essay is to be welcomed in that it recognises the extent to which Tolkien resorts to metaphor to circumscribe the inexpressible nature of Faërie. Although Tolkien specifically rejects the taxonomic approach of comparative studies such as that of Propp, nevertheless he accepts that there are some shared structures which establish the nature of the fairy-story. This article is useful as an analysis of Tolkien's somewhat involved argument, particularly of the last section which introduces the idea of *evangelium*. As a pedantic observation, the name Bettelheim is consistently misspelt in the footnotes.

Benjamin Saxton's "Tolkien and Bakhtin on Authorship, Literary Freedom and Alterity" is thought-provoking in its reading of Tolkien's narratives in the light of the Russian critic's analysis of Dostoevsky. What Saxton has to say about Tolkien is clear enough, particularly his discussion of the sub-creative freedom given to the Ainur by Ilúvatar, which has frequently been analysed in a theological context, in contrast to the total control exercised by Sauron and his Ring over the Ringwraiths, and the illustration of the different possibilities of choice through opposed pairs such as Théoden and Denethor or Gandalf and Saruman. However, for someone as literal-minded as the present reviewer, it is difficult to relate this to Bakhtin's conception, at least as formulated by Saxton, of an equal creative relationship between the *author* and the characters, since all the examples here seem to be taken from *within* the story. If the reference is to the creative process, then it might be relevant that Tolkien wrote of Faramir as someone who as of his own accord "came walking into the woods of Ithilien" (L 79), but Saxton does not mention this aspect. On the other hand, if "the fate of Gollum was not predetermined or scripted in advance" (178) and he might have repented, then this simply shows that Tolkien gave very careful consideration to the logic of the characterisation as he was in the process of creating it. The article would benefit from a more explicit formulation which avoids contradictions of this kind.

The one article of a theological nature in this volume is "Tolkien's Work: Is it Christian or Pagan?" by Claudio Testi. After a critique of critics who claim that it must be either one or the other, Testi first defines his terms and then concludes that internally (i.e. within the secondary world) the characters act only through their natural, innate powers and reason, but externally the reader can see that the events of the story are in harmony with the supernatural plane of Revelation. *The Lord of the Rings* is specifically Catholic because it accepts the idea of virtuous pagans, as did the *Beowulf* poet, a concept that was traditionally rejected by Protestants. The division into the text-internal and text-external positions appears to be a neat solution, but it leaves out of account the motif of pity and mercy in Bilbo's (and Frodo's and Sam's) sparing of Gollum, where Gandalf seems to appeal to some sense higher than mere reason. Also, although Testi admits that an author may be wrong about his own work, he tends to use Tolkien's comments on his fiction as a form of shorthand, which sometimes makes his arguments appear less based on his own principles than they really are.

The last two articles to be discussed here are in many ways the most difficult, since however objective the argumentation may be, the topic inevitably rests upon value judgements. Hope Rogers' "No Triumph without Loss: Problems of Intercultural Marriage in Tolkien's Works" attempts to rebut critical claims either that Tolkien's world presents stereotypical racial oppositions, or else (ironically enough) that it represents a plea for multicultural understanding. Rogers takes a middle line, that Tolkien problematizes intercultural marriage without labelling it as either desirable or undesirable but simply showing the benefits and losses that occur through it. Her point is an effective one, even if she does not explicitly draw the moral that an author is under no obligation to endorse the political orthodoxy of a critic, especially when that critic is writing a good half century later in a world that has necessarily changed. However, the article underestimates the complexity of the question; after all, every marriage in a sense involves different family backgrounds and is a potential source of conflict, as the tellers of tales have known for centuries. Also Rogers tends to forget that Tolkien uses this conflict for literary ends rather than as a moral sermon. In the case of Eöl, Aredhel and their son Maeglin, the (forced) marriage is just one detail in a much greater web of causation. To say that the marriage of Drogo Baggins of Hobbiton and Primula Brandybuck from the Buckland makes Frodo an outsider is simplistic, and to present this episode, which falls on the borderline of the low mimetic and ironical modes, on the same level as Beren and Lúthien (a fairy tale with mythological ramifications) or Tuor and Idril (high romance overlapping with mythology) can only be misleading. In applying her thesis to the story of Túrin—why didn't he marry Finduilas, which would have avoided incest by embracing alterity? —Hope also commits the methodological inconsistency of quoting from widely differing versions, from *The Book of Lost Tales* to *The Children of Húrin*.

"Jewish Dwarves: Tolkien and Anti-Semitic Stereotyping" by Renée Vink is another attempt to dismantle (rather than demolish) excessively sweeping criticisms of social outlooks imputed to Tolkien which have somehow become established without being considered clearly. This article sets out to show how claims by Rebecca Brackmann, that Tolkien originally painted a racist picture of Dwarves with stereotypical Jewish characteristics which he then revised when he became aware of Nazi outrages, are not supported by the demonstrable developments through time in Tolkien's depiction of his Dwarves. Vink's painstaking work in countering ill-considered myths and prejudices should already be well known from her recent study of Tolkien and Wagner. However, hers is an uphill road, since it is far easier to make a greasy smear than it is to clean it completely away to the satisfaction of all onlookers.

The volume concludes with 53 pages of reviews, "The Year's Work in Tolkien Studies 2010" by Merlin DeTardo (including comments on articles in *Hither Shore 7*), and a bibliography for 2011. Allan Turner

Unsere Autorinnen und Autoren

Stephanie Bauer ist Archäologin und arbeitet momentan an ihrer Doktorarbeit an der Goethe Universität Frankfurt. Sie hat sich auf den Fachbereich der provinzial-römischen Archäologie spezialisiert. Ihr langjähriges privates Interesse sowohl an Tolkiens Werk als auch am Live-Rollenspiel hat diesen Artikel inspiriert.
http://www.value-and-equivalence.de/mitglieder/assoziierte-promotionsprojekte/stefanie-bauer/projekt/#c213

Annie Birks, PhD, lehrt Englische Sprache und Literatur an der Katholischen Universität des Westens in Angers (Frankreich). Sie erwarb kürzlich ihr Doktorat an der Sorbonne über Vergeltung in den Werken J.R.R. Tolkiens. Ihre gegenwärtigen Forschungsinteressen fokussieren sich wesentlich auf die theologischen Perspektiven der Schriften Tolkiens. Annie.birks@neuf.fr

Julian T.M. Eilmann studierte in Aachen und Nottingham Geschichte, Germanistik und Kunstgeschichte und ist gegenwärtig Gymnasiallehrer. Neben seinen akademischen Arbeiten ist er seit mehreren Jahren bei einer Film- und TV-Produktion als Autor von Reportagen und historischen Dokumentation tätig und darüber hinaus Inhaber einer Kunstgalerie und Kurator einer Künstlerstiftung. Schwerpunkte seiner Tolkien-Forschungen sind Tolkiens Lieder und Gedichte sowie die Filmadaption durch Peter Jackson. julianeilmann@aol.com

Tobias Escher, M.A., studierte Musikwissenschaft und Anglistik an der Johannes-Gutenberg-Universität Mainz und arbeitet als Komponist und Consultant im Bereich der Medienmusik. Derzeit arbeitet er an seiner Dissertation über Musik in J.R.R. Tolkiens Werken. www.middle-earth-music.info

Thomas Fornet-Ponse, Prof. Dr. theol. Dr. phil., studierte Katholische Theologie, Philosophie und Alte Geschichte in Bonn und Jerusalem und promovierte in Fundamentaltheologie und Ökumene sowie in Philosophie. Gegenwärtig ist er Inhaber des Laurentius-Klein-Lehrstuhls für Biblische und Ökumenische Theologie und Leiter des Theologischen Studienjahres Jerusalem. Er veröffentlichte zahlreiche Aufsätze zu Tolkien, Pratchett und Lewis, war bis 2009 Beisitzer im DTG-Vorstand und ist inhaltlicher Koordinator des Tolkien Seminars wie von Hither Shore. thomas.fornet-ponse@tolkiengesellschaft.de

Richard Gallant schreibt seine Dissertation *The Role and Poetical Function of the Drachenkampf in Medieval Germanic Literature and Contemporary Interpretation: from Beowulf, Sigurð and Wolfdietrich, to Bard and Túrin Turambar* an der Friedrich-Schiller-Universität Jena unter der Leitung von Prof. Thomas Honegger. Derzeit wird der Artikel *Original Sin in Heorot und Valinor* von Kollegen der Fachzeitung Tolkien Studies wissenschaftlich begutachtet. Er kann Abschlüsse in den Fachbereichen Germanistik und Literaturwissenschaften von der Universität Virginia (M.A.) sowie einen B.A. in Creative Writing als auch Russische und Osteuropastudien von der Universität Michigan vorweisen. richard.gallant@uni-jena.de

David Goldie war in Italien und Großbritannien als Berater im Bildungs- und Wirtschaftsbereich tätig und promoviert gegenwärtig in English and Media Studies an der Universität Aix-Marseille, wo er seit 2001 Englisch unterrichtet. Seine Forschungsinteressen umfassen Filmadaptionen von Literatur im Bezug auf die Werke von J.R.R. Tolkien, C.S. Lewis und J.K. Rowling. david.goldie@orange.fr

Natalia González de la Llana, Dr. phil., studierte Literaturtheorie und Komparatistik an der Universität Complutense in Madrid und promovierte dort nach Aufenthalten an der Universität La Sapienza in Rom und der Humboldt-Universität in Berlin mit der Arbeit *Adam and Eve, Faust and Dorian Gray: Three Myths of Transgression*. Gegenwärtig ist sie Wissenschaftliche Mitarbeiterin an der RWTH Aachen und arbeitet an einer Habilitation zum Thema multimedialer narrativer Formen in »High Fantasy«.   natalia.llana@romanistik.rwth-aachen.de

Tobias Hock hat Englisch und Mathematik auf Lehramt an der RWTH Aachen studiert. Seine Staatsexamensarbeit trug den Titel *Violence in Fantasy Literature: A Comparison between J.R.R. Tolkien's* The Lord of the Rings *and Robert E. Howard's* Conan-Stories. Derzeit arbeitet er als Wissenschaftlicher Mitarbeiter im Bereich Didaktik der Mathematik an der RWTH. http://www.didaktik.matha.rwth-aachen.de/de/mitarbeiter/hock/index.html

Thomas Honegger, Prof. Dr. phil, hat in Zürich promoviert und zahlreiche Bände zu Tolkien, mittelalterlicher Sprache und Literatur herausgegeben und verschiedene Beiträge zu Chaucer, Shakespeare und mittelalterlichen Romanzen publiziert. Seit 2002 lehrt er als Professor für Mediävistik an der Friedrich-Schiller-Universität Jena.
www2.uni-jena.de/fsu/anglistik/homepage/Honegger3.htm

Nicole Hützen lehrt und forscht als wissenschaftliche Mitarbeiterin am Lehrstuhl für Anglistische Sprachwissenschaft der RWTH Aachen. Zurzeit schreibt sie ihre Dissertation über Nomen in wissenschaftlichen Artikeln. Zu ihren Forschungsinteressen zählen Registeranalyse, Korpuslinguistik, akademischer

Diskurs mit einem Fokus auf kognitiven und gebrauchsbasierten Ansätzen, kontrastive Übersetzungsforschung und Psycholinguistik.
huetzen@anglistik.rwth-aachen.de

Timo Lothmann, Dr. phil., lehrt und forscht am Lehrstuhl für Anglistische Sprachwissenschaft der RWTH Aachen, wo er 2006 über die Tok-Pisin-Bibelübersetzung promovierte. Er lehrte außerdem an den Universitäten Münster und Paderborn. Seine Forschungsinteressen umfassen Pidgin- und Kreolsprachen, Übersetzungstheorie und -praxis sowie Postkolonialismus. Er legt Gewicht auf eine interdisziplinäre Perspektive. Unter anderem hat er Beiträge in mehreren Auflagen des akademischen Standardwerks *Descriptive English Linguistics* von P.G. Meyer veröffentlicht. Sein Schwerpunkt zurzeit sind Anwendungsfelder von konzeptueller Metapher und Blending-Theorie.
lothmann@anglistik.rwth-aachen.de

Annika Röttinger, B.A., studiert in Hannover Geschichtswissenschaft und ist aktives Mitglied der DTG. Thema ihrer Bachelor-Arbeit war Tolkiens anglozentrisches Kulturbild und die daraus resultierende Ähnlichkeit zwischen Angelsachsen und Rohirrim. Für die bevorstehende Master-Arbeit beschäftigt sie sich derzeit mit Tolkiens Erfahrungen im Ersten Weltkrieg.
annika.roettinger@tolkiengesellschaft.de

Heidi Steimel stammt aus den USA und hat dort Musik studiert (Grace University, Omaha, Nebraska). Sie lebt jetzt in Deutschland, wo sie als Kirchenmusikerin, Klavierlehrerin, Übersetzerin und Dolmetscherin gearbeitet hat. Ihr Interesse an Musik und Tolkien führte zur Publikation *Music in Middle-earth*, die sie initiiert und mit herausgegeben hat, sowie zu verschiedenen Vorträgen und Artikeln zum Thema. heidisteimel@web.de

Renée Vink hat skandinavische Sprachen (u.a. Altnordisch) studiert und arbeitet(e) als Übersetzerin aus dem Schwedischen, Norwegischen, Dänischen, Deutschen und Englischen – u.a. ist sie die niederländiche Übersetzerin der Dichtung in *The Legend of Sigurd and Gudrún*. rvink7@hotmail.com

Christian Weichmann, Dr. rer. nat, hat in Bonn promoviert und verschiedene Beiträge zu Tolkien publiziert. Er war bis 2012 im Vorstand der DTG und ist außerdem Mitglied von Unquendor, Tolkien Society und ÖTG. Er arbeitet als technischer Softwareentwickler in Braunschweig.
christian.weichmann@tolkiengesellschaft.de

Frank Weinreich, Dr. phil., studierte Kommunikationswissenschaften, Politik und Philosophie und promovierte in Philosophie. Seine wissenschaftlichen Arbeitsschwerpunkte mit zahlreichen Publikationen sind Ethik, Ontologie,

Medien, Technikfolgenabschätzung, Wissenschaftstheorie und Phantastik. Gegenwärtig arbeitet er als freier Lektor, Redakteur und Literaturscout für verschiedene Verlage.   fw@polyoinos.com

Thorsten Werner, Dr. rer. nat., hat Chemie in Hamburg studiert und arbeitet derzeit als IT-Berater im Umfeld der chemischen Industrie. Er war von 2006 bis 2011 Mitglied des DTG-Vorstands und beschäftigt sich mit Rollenspiel und Kartenspiel in Mittelerde.   thorsten.werner@tolkiengesellschaft.de

Our Authors

Stephanie Bauer is an archaeologist who currently works on her Ph.D. thesis at Goethe University Frankfurt. She is specialized in the field of Roman archaeology. Her longtime private interest in the works of Tolkien as well as live action roleplaying inspired this article.
http://www.value-and-equivalence.de/mitglieder/assoziierte-promotionsprojekte/stefanie-bauer/projekt/#c213

Annie Birks teaches English Language and Literature at the Université Catholique de l'Ouest, in Angers, France. She has recently received a doctorate from the Sorbonne on *Reward and Punishment in the Works of J.R.R. Tolkien*. Her current research interests focus essentially on the theological perspectives of Tolkien's writings. annie.birks@neuf.fr

Julian T.M. Eilmann studied History, German Philology and History of Arts in Aachen and Nottingham and is currently working as student teacher. Furthermore, since three years he is working as a journalist and author of films and TV productions, and as a developer of historical TV documentation. In addition, he is fulfilling the functions of gallery owner and conservator for an artists' foundation. His work on Tolkien focuses on Tolkien's songs and poems and the adaptation by Peter Jackson. julianeilmann@aol.com

Tobias Escher, M.A. studied Musicology and Anglophone Languages at Johannes Gutenberg University Mainz and works as a composer and consultant in music for media. At present time, he is working on his dissertation about music in J.R.R. Tolkien's works. www.middle-earth-music.info

Thomas Fornet-Ponse, Prof. Dr. theol. Dr. phil., studied Catholic Theology, Philosophy and Ancient History in Bonn and Jerusalem. He received his Ph.D. in Fundamental theology and Ecumenics from the University of Salzburg and his Ph.D. in Philosophy from the University of Bonn. He was a committee member of the German Tolkien Society and has been charged with conceptually coordinating the Tolkien Seminars as well as *Hither Shore*. thomas.fornet-ponse@tolkiengesellschaft.de

Richard Gallant is writing his dissertation *The Role and Poetical Function of the Drachenkampf in Medieval Germanic Literature and Contemporary Interpretation: from Beowulf, Sigurð and Wolfdietrich, to Bard and Túrin Turambar* at Friedrich Schiller University Jena (Germany) under the guidance of Thomas Honegger. Currently, he has an article *Original Sin in Heorot and Valinor* under peer-review. He holds a MA in Germanic Languages and Literatures from the

University of Virginia and a BA in both Creative Writing and Russian and Eastern European Studies from the University of Michigan.
richard.gallant@uni-jena.de

David Goldie has worked in Italy and the UK as a consultant in the educational and business sectors. He is currently a Ph.D. candidate in English and Media Studies at Aix-Marseille University, where he has taught English in the SATIS Department (Sciences, Arts et Techniques de l'Image et du Son) since 2001. His research interests include cinematic adaptation of literature in relation to the works of J.R.R. Tolkien, C.S. Lewis and J.K. Rowling.
david.goldie@orange.fr

Natalia González de la Llana has studied Literary Theory and Comparative Literature at Complutense University Madrid. After winning research scholarships for stays at La Sapienza University in Rome and Humboldt University Berlin, she received her PhD at the Complutense with her thesis *Adam and Eve, Faust and Dorian Gray: Three Myths of Transgression*. She has taught at the Romance Language Departments of the University of Münster and Aachen University where she is now preparing her habilitation *Multimedia narrative forms in 'high fantasy': a model of analysis*.
natalia.llana@romanistik.rwth-aachen.de

Tobias Hock has studied English and Mathematics as a teacher trainee at RWTH Aachen University. His final exam paper had the title *Violence in Fantasy Literature: A Comparison between J.R.R. Tolkien's* The Lord of the Rings *and Robert E. Howard's* Conan-*Stories*. He currently works as a research assistant in mathematics education at RWTH.
www.didaktik.matha.rwth-aachen.de/de/mitarbeiter/hock/index.html

Thomas Honegger holds a Ph.D. from the University of Zurich. He edited several volumes on Tolkien, medieval language and literature, and published papers on Chaucer, Shakespeare, and mediaeval romance. He teaches, since 2002, as Professor for Mediaeval Studies at Friedrich Schiller University Jena (Germany).
www2.uni-jena.de/fsu/anglistik/homepage/Honegger3.htm

Nicole Hützen is a research assistant and lecturer of English Linguistics at RWTH Aachen University and is currently working on her PhD thesis on nouns in the register of academic research articles. Her research interests include register analysis, corpus linguistics and academic discourse with a focus on cognitive and usage-based approaches, contrastive translation studies and psycholinguistics.
huetzen@anglistik.rwth-aachen.de

Timo Lothmann is a researcher and lecturer of English Linguistics at RWTH Aachen University where he completed his PhD on the *Tok Pisin Bible* translation in 2006. He has also taught at the universities of Münster and Paderborn. His research interests include pidgins and creoles, psycholinguistic approaches, and postcolonialism. He lays particular stress on interdisciplinary perspectives. Among other publications, he contributed to several editions of the academic standard volume *Descriptive English Linguistics* by P. G. Meyer et al. Currently, he focuses on fields of application of conceptual metaphor and blending theory. lothmann@anglistik.rwth-aachen.de

Annika Röttinger, B.A., studies History in Hannover and is an active member of the German Tolkien Society. For the topic of her Bachelor of Arts thesis, she worked on the similarities between the Anglo-Saxons and the Rohirrim, resulting from Tolkien's Anglocentric cultural views. At the moment she is doing research on Tolkien's experiences during the First World War for her Master's thesis. anika.roettinger@tolkiengesellschaft.de

Heidi Steimel was born in the USA and studied Music at Grace University, Omaha, Nebraska. She now lives in Germany, where she has served as a church musician, piano teacher, translator and interpreter. Her interest in music and Tolkien led to the publication of *Music in Middle-earth*, which she initiated and co-edited, as well as lectures and articles on related topics. heidisteimel@web.de

Allan Turner, Ph.D., studied German Philology, Mediaeval Studies and General Linguistics. His PhD thesis in Translation Studies examines the problems inherent in translating the philological elements in *The Lord of the Rings*. His main focus of interest is currently on the stylistics of Tolkien's works. He teaches English language skills and British Cultural Studies at the University of Jena. allangturner@aol.com

Renée Vink has a university degree in Scandinavian languages, including Old Norse, and worked as a translator from Swedish, Norwegian, Danish, German and English. Among other things, she is the Dutch translator of the poetry in *The Legend of Sigurd and Gudrún*.   rvink7@hotmail.com

Christian Weichmann holds a Ph.D. in Physics from the University of Bonn. He published diverse papers on Tolkien. He was till 2012 a member of the board of the German Tolkien Society an is also a member of Unquendor, the Tolkien Society and the Austrian Tolkien Society. He works as a technical software developer in Braunschweig.   christian.weichmann@tolkiengesellschaft.de

Frank Weinreich, Dr. phil., studied Communication Science, Political Studies and Philosophy and wrote his dissertation thesis in Philosophy. His primary research interests with numerous publications are ethics, ontology, media, engineering results assessment, philosophy of science and phantastics. He is currently working as free-lance editor and literary scout for several publishers. fw@polyoinos.com

Thorsten Werner, Dr. rer. nat., studied Chemistry in Hamburg and is currently working as an IT-consultant for chemical companies. He was treasurer of the German Tolkien Society from 2006 until 2011 and is specialized in roleplaying and card games in Middle-earth.   thorsten.werner@tolkiengesellschaft.de

Siglenverzeichnis

Die Schriften von J.R.R. Tolkien werden im Text jeweils ohne Angabe des Verfassernamens mit den folgenden Siglen zitiert. Die jeweils benutzte Ausgabe findet sich im Literaturverzeichnis.

AI:	The Lay of Aotrou and Itroun
ATB:	The Adventures of Tom Bombadil and other Verses from the Red Book / Die Abenteuer des Tom Bombadil und andere Gedichte aus dem Roten Buch
AW:	Ancrene Wisse and Hali Meiðhad
B:	Die Briefe von J.R.R. Tolkien
BA:	Bilbos Abschiedslied
BB:	Baum und Blatt
BGH:	Bauer Giles von Ham
BLS:	Bilbo's Last Song
BMC:	Beowulf: The Monster and the Critics
BT:	Blatt von Tüftler
BUK:	Beowulf: Die Ungeheuer und ihre Kritiker
BW:	Die Briefe vom Weihnachtsmann
CH:	The Children of Húrin
CP:	Chaucer as a Philologist
EA:	The End of the Third Age (History of Middle-earth 9). Auszug
EW:	English and Welsh / Englisch und Walisisch
FC:	Letters from Father Christmas
FGH:	Farmer Giles of Ham
FH:	Finn and Hengest
FS:	On Fairy-Stories
GD:	Gute Drachen sind rar
GN:	Guide to the Names in the Lord of the Rings
GPO:	Sir Gawain and the Green Knight, Pearl, and Sir Orfeo
H:	The Hobbit / Der Hobbit / Der kleine Hobbit
HB:	The Homecoming of Beorhtnoth Beorhthelm's Son
HdR:	Der Herr der Ringe
HdR I:	Der Herr der Ringe. Bd. 1. Die Gefährten
HdR II:	Der Herr der Ringe. Bd. 2. Die Zwei Türme
HdR III:	Der Herr der Ringe. Bd. 3. Die Rückkehr des Königs / Die Wiederkehr des Königs
HdR A:	Der Herr der Ringe. Anhänge
HG:	Herr Glück
HH I/II:	The History of the Hobbit
HL:	Ein heimliches Laster
KH:	Die Kinder Húrins
L:	The Letters of J.R.R. Tolkien
LB:	The Lays of Beleriand (History of Middle-earth 3)
LN:	Leaf by Niggle

Siglenverzeichnis

LotR:	The Lord of the Rings
LotR I:	The Fellowship of the Ring. Being the first part of The Lord of the Rings
LotR II:	The Two Towers. Being the second part of The Lord of the Rings
LotR III:	The Return of the King. Being the third part of The Lord of the Rings
LotR A:	The Lord of the Rings. Appendices
LR:	The Lost Road and other Writings (History of Middle-earth 5)
LSG:	The Legend of Sigurd and Gudrún
LT 1:	The Book of Lost Tales 1 (History of Middle-earth 1)
LT 2:	The Book of Lost Tales 2 (History of Middle-earth 2)
MB:	Mr. Bliss
MC:	The Monsters and the Critics and Other Essays
ME:	A Middle English Vocabulary
MR:	Morgoth's Ring (History of Middle-earth 10)
My:	Mythopoeia
NM:	Nachrichten aus Mittelerde
OE:	The Old English Exodus
OK:	Ósanwe-Kenta
P:	Pictures by J.R.R. Tolkien
PM:	The Peoples of Middle-earth (History of Middle-earth 12)
R:	Roverandom
RBG:	The Rivers and Beacon-hills of Gondor
RGEO:	The Road Goes Ever On (with Donald Swann)
RS:	The Return of the Shadow (History of Middle-earth 6)
S:	Silmarillion
SD:	The Sauron Defeated (History of Middle-earth 9)
SG:	Der Schmied von Großholzingen
SGG:	Sir Gawain and the Green Knight / Sir Gawain und der Grüne Ritter (Essay)
SM:	The Shaping of Middle-earth (History of Middle-earth 4)
SP:	Songs for the Philologists
SV:	A Secret Vice
SWM:	Smith of Wootton Major
SWME:	Smith of Wootton Major Essay
TB:	On Translating Beowulf
TI:	The Treason of Isengard (History of Middle-earth 7)
TL:	Tree and Leaf
ÜB:	Zur Übersetzung des Beowulf
ÜM:	Über Märchen
UK:	Die Ungeheuer und ihre Kritiker. Gesammelte Aufsätze
UT:	Unfinished Tales
VA:	Valedictory Address
VG 1:	Das Buch der Verschollenen Geschichten 1
VG 2:	Das Buch der Verschollenen Geschichten 2
WJ:	The War of the Jewels (History of Middle-earth 11)
WR:	The War of the Ring (History of Middle-earth 8)

Index

Aragorn	33, 37, 45, 52f, 55, 59, 65, 69-74, 79, 92, 110, 135, 139, 179, 184, 211ff, 235
Arwen	33, 37, 73f, 89, 207, 209, 211ff
Bakshi, Ralph	67f, 71, 74
Bilbo	54, 89, 92ff, 101-105, 112, 116, 126, 129, 148, 151ff, 234f, 239, 242, 244
[Tom] Bombadil	32f, 37, 57, 90, 97, 184, 229, 235, 242
Boromir	59, 92, 235
Boyens, Philippa	27, 211
Brettspiel	19, 160-175
Bruchtal/Imladris/Rivendell	52, 73f, 90, 99, 102ff, 112, 126, 135, 142, 209, 212, 234
Carpenter, Humphrey	31, 82, 208
Cirith Ungol	52, 66, 209, 214
Decipher	134f, 179
Dickerson, Matthew	51, 54
Elben	74, 126-129, 191
Elrond	52, 71, 73, 112, 185, 193ff, 210, 212
Éowyn	53, 57, 78ff, 84, 89, 213f, 234
Faramir	32f, 46, 53f, 56f, 59, 92, 192, 213, 243
Fidelity	27, 204ff, 215
Film	14ff, 20ff, 26-42, 45-60, 62-74, 77, 80, 84, 87, 128, 131, 146, 157, 161, 167, 174, 189, 205-215
Frodo	32, 37, 39, 52, 54, 57, 59, 65-69, 73, 92, 101f, 112, 135, 139, 143, 149, 162f, 173f, 192, 207-214, 244
Galadriel	89, 93, 99f, 114ff, 173, 194f, 213, 234f
Gandalf	49, 59, 65f, 71, 89, 108, 135, 139, 173f, 182, 193f, 208, 212, 235, 243f
Gimli	37, 55, 71, 90, 92, 98, 106ff, 110, 127, 194
Gollum	59, 69, 72f, 90, 161, 170, 173, 184, 196, 207, 210, 242ff
Gondor	21, 54, 56, 112f, 130, 162, 209, 212f
Hammond, Wayne	27, 205, 242
Honegger, Thomas	26, 232, 233, 242
Hutcheon, Linda	11-23
Imladris	siehe Bruchtal
Isengard	51-55, 209
Isengart	65, 70, 72, 172, 182
Jackson, Peter	10, 17, 19-22, 26-29, 32ff, 36, 38-53, 58ff, 62-74, 76, 79, 84, 126-130, 163, 166ff, 174, 204, 206-215
Karten-/Sammelkartenspiel	178-181, 185
Knizia, Rainer	134, 144, 146, 149, 151, 162, 169-173, 219f
Legolas	33, 37, 39, 55, 70f, 110, 127, 139, 173
Liverollenspiel	118, 122ff, 130f
Lothlórien	52, 115, 135, 142
Menschen	76, 78f. 123, 125, 130

Index

Mercia	82, 109f
Merry	53f, 57, 65, 69, 93, 139, 149, 193, 209, 214
Middle-earth	26ff, 32, 35, 37, 39-42, 50, 53, 55, 86f, 91, 93f, 96-99, 101f, 113f, 116, 127, 134-145, 191-196, 199, 204, 207, 209, 211f, 214f
Minas Tirith	49, 54, 56, 65, 112f, 150
Mittelerde	63, 70, 118f, 122-125, 127, 130, 164, 178-185, 230
Mordor	27, 66, 89, 135, 141ff, 150, 171, 173, 182, 196f, 209
Moria	48, 52, 59, 106, 108, 135, 142, 149f, 171, 173, 181f, 208, 229
Movie	26f, 32, 34-39, 41f, 44, 46, 48, 51ff, 86f, 90, 135f, 138, 188
On Fairy-Stories	40, 45, 83, 121f, 236, 238, 243
Orks	65, 69f, 128f, 131, 164, 170, 179, 181, 183
Osgiliath	51, 54, 59, 72, 183, 209
Pippin	53f, 57, 65, 69, 139, 193, 209
Reiff, Caspar	96, 98, 101, 103, 108, 115
Rivendell	siehe Bruchtal
Rohirrim	46, 51, 54, 56, 71, 76-84, 89, 109f, 130, 164, 170
Rollenspiel	118, 120-124, 127, 129f, 178, 180, 219f
Sam	32, 37, 39, 54, 65f, 69, 89f, 92, 106f, 112, 139, 162f, 196, 209, 214, 244
Saruman	33, 55, 59, 65, 70ff, 89, 180ff, 193, 209, 213, 229, 243
Sauron	54f, 57, 92, 113f, 131, 135-144, 149f, 162, 169f, 173, 179, 192, 196-200
Scull, Christina	27, 205, 242
Shire	32f, 38, 57, 89, 101f, 141f, 148, 208ff
Silmarillion	41, 81, 111, 122, 157, 188, 195, 230, 234
Shippey, Thomas A.	27, 41, 79, 82, 92, 129, 207, 211, 213, 230, 234, 237, 239
Spielwelt	119f, 122f, 128
Stam, Robert	12-13, 16, 19
Théoden	50, 55f, 71, 78f, 93, 110, 213, 243
Tolkien, Christopher	26, 28, 33, 40, 199
Tolkien, J.R.R.	23, 26, 32, 36f, 40, 44f, 50, 53-57, 60, 62-74, 76-84, 86, 90ff, 96f, 103, 115, 121-131, 134f, 138, 141, 146, 156f, 183, 188f, 193f, 197f, 201, 204, 207-210, 213, 215, 230, 233, 236, 240
Tolkien Ensemble	96, 98, 100-103, 107, 110-115, 218f
Walsh, Fran	27, 211
Weinreich, Frank	46, 122, 131
(Werk-)Treue	12-17
Zwerge	125, 129f, 230

www.ingramcontent.com/pod-product-compliance
Lightning Source LLC
Chambersburg PA
CBHW051634230426
43669CB00013B/2296